English Literature in History

1350–1400
Medieval Readers and Writers

Series Editor

Raymond Williams

English Literature in History

1350–1400
Medieval Readers and Writers

Janet Coleman

Hutchinson

London Melbourne Sydney Auckland Johannesburg

Hutchinson & Co. (Publishers) Ltd
An imprint of the Hutchinson Publishing Group
24 Highbury Crescent, London N5 1RX

Hutchinson Group (Australia) Pty Ltd
30–32 Cremorne Street, Richmond South, Victoria 3121
PO Box 151, Broadway, New South Wales 2007

Hutchinson Group (NZ) Ltd
32–34 View Road, PO Box 40–086, Glenfield, Auckland 10

Hutchinson Group (SA) (Pty) Ltd
PO Box 337, Bergvlei 2012, South Africa

First published 1981

© Janet Coleman 1981

Set in VIP Times Roman by Preface Ltd, Salisbury, Wilts.

Printed in Great Britain by The Anchor Press Ltd
and bound by Wm Brendon & Son Ltd
both of Tiptree, Essex

British Library Cataloguing in Publication Data

Coleman, Janet
  English literature in history 1350–1400.
  (English literature in history; 1)
  1. English literature – Middle English,
  1100–1500
  I. Title   II. Series
  820.9 001   PR 69

ISBN 0 09 144100 5 cased
     0 09 144101 3 paper

To Keith and Mo, Elsa and Brigitte

Contents

Editor's introduction

'Literature' and 'history' are common names for two obviously related but apparently distinct bodies of human activity. By 'literature' we commonly mean certain kinds of writing, though at different times, and on different occasions, we often use the term variably, over a range from all printed writing, through printed writing of a certain quality, to the important specialized sense of a body of 'imaginative' writing. Further, because of this last sense, we often extend the term 'literature' to include 'imaginative' composition which was not primarily written to be printed but to be spoken or in some other immediate way performed. Thus 'literature' in the important but narrow sense of printed imaginative writing of a certain quality belongs, in fact, to a specific historical period, after the invention of printing, after further specializations, and before the invention of modern media of delivery and performance (especially radio and sound recording). At the same time, however, our thinking about literature, from the experience of that specific period, is commonly extended before and after it, to other related forms of composition.

These shifting meanings of 'literature' bear closely on the question of its actual and presumed relations with 'history'. Moreover, 'history' itself has a significant range of reference. At its broadest it indicates the sum and detail of all human actions. When this is so it must be held that it already includes the making of literature. In practice, however, 'history' is most commonly used to indicate general and specific accounts of such actions, grouped by period and by place. That is 'history' as an account, a narrative, and the writing of history, in this sense, is often reasonably seen as a form of 'literature'. Regularly, however, this element of account or narrative is overridden by the sense that the actions really occurred, at a level independent from their narration. Historical inquiry is often a continuous and detailed comparison of the received accounts or narratives and what can be shown, from other forms of evidence and record, to have actually taken place. Literature, in some respects, seems different from this process of historical inquiry, in that its works appear to have a relatively fixed form.

Any inquiry into the relations between 'literature' and 'history' has at some point, if it is to be adequate, to recognize these variable and shifting senses of the primary indicative terms. In recent years there has been widespread recognition of the inherent complexities of reference and evidence which these considerations emphasize. This is why there has been a move away from previous methods of inquiry, even when many of their results have been noted and respected. What is now felt as most difficult is the simple assumption that there is, on the one hand, a relatively unproblematic body of 'literature', with its own inherent and autonomous qualities, and on the other hand, a body of general and summary knowledge which is, correspondingly, 'history'. For if these two bodies existed, in simple ways, the study of 'literature and history' would be a matter of tracing and illustrating evident connections between them, in ways that illuminated both but altered neither. That assumption produced a good deal of interesting work, of two kinds. The possessors of 'history' illustrated aspects of their material from the literature of the time, going naturally to those works in which the connections were evident, and feeling no need to deal with those works in which such connections seemed to be absent. Meanwhile the possessors of 'literature' looked to history as a 'background', against which, in a foregrounded emphasis, works of literature occurred. It was then mainly when 'background' and 'foreground' evidently connected, in discoverable and explicable ways, that history – parts of the history – became relevant.

Each of these methods was fundamentally selective and partial, and was at its best when this was recognized to be so. Yet paradoxically the confidence of the initial assumptions – the assumed possession of the bodies of 'literature' and 'history' – tended in practice to produce effects of completeness. The 'background' showed all the history that was relevant. The illustrative literature was all the writing of historical significance. Confident accounts of whole periods, extending in secondary work to fully reasoned catalogues of 'a period and its literature' or 'the literature of a period', had an intended and often achieved effect of completeness.

It is of course easier to criticize these conventional methods than to find better practical ways. Yet one result of this new sense of inherent difficulty has been a widespread retreat from the problems. This has been notably assisted by theoretical developments in which the significance of 'history' has been widely questioned and even denied. In some formalist and structuralist tendencies in literary studies the whole effort at correlation has been declared to be *a priori* irrelevant, and much has been made of the undoubted errors of externality and reduction which could be found in previous studies. Yet these errors cannot reasonably be used to justify the much more fundamental error of declaring an arbitrary distance between the acts of writing and other kinds of human action. It has been useful to define actual and variable distances, but to expand and stabilize them as an *a priori* refusal of relationships is merely evasive. However, it is in this more qualified and sceptical environment that new inquiries into such relationships have in practice to be undertaken.

The aim of the present series is to provide a place for essays of an open investigative kind, which do not have from the outset to be committed, or to pretend to be committed, to explanatory completeness. Its emphasis is on literature *in* history: the study of actual works, practices and conditions, in a particular place and period: some 'literary', some 'historical', but never assumed to belong, by definition, to pre-formed bodies of 'literature' and 'history'. Its authors were invited to choose a period of English life, typically but not exclusively of some fifty years, and then within that period (though looking before and after if it was necessary to clarify or complete an argument) to select two or three themes, in which the relations between actual writing and actual historical events and conditions seemed interesting and important. No author was asked to represent these themes as a whole account of the chosen period, though it is obvious that in choosing their themes authors have taken what they believe to be significant elements of that time. The method of inquiry and presentation then adopted has been the author's own choice of a method appropriate to the actual theme or themes.

It is hoped that as the series develops there will be a broad range of such themes and essays, over the whole run of English writing. It is possible that in particular periods there will be more than one book, representing different selections of themes. Moreover, several authors will have seen each other's work, and there will be cross-reference and discussion. A definite area and style of work may in these ways be expected to develop, but it is intended to be distinct from the pre-planned 'coverage' which is the more expected form of such a series. It follows further from this emphasis that the authors are not writing to any brief or line, and that disagreements and reservations may be expected within the series. I believe this to be a condition of serious work of this kind in present circumstances. It may also in any case be its own form of acknowledgement of the genuine diversities of literature in history.

Raymond Williams

Jesus College
Cambridge
1981

1 Introduction

The English are men of a haughty disposition, hot-tempered and quickly moved to anger, slow to be brought to gentleness and difficult to pacify; they take comfort in battle and slaughter. Covetous and envious of the possessions of others, they are incapable by nature of joining in friendship or alliance with a foreign nation. They are underhand and proud. There is no more untrustworthy people under the sun than the men of middling rank (*hommes mestis*) as they are in England.

There is in England too great a difference in nature and condition between the nobles on the one hand and the men of 'middle class' and the villeins, for the gentlemen are noble and loyal of temperament and the common people are cruel, perfidious, proud and disloyal. And when the people wish to show their villainy and power the nobles offer no resistance to them. For a long time they have been in complete agreement with one another for the nobles only ask that the people be reasonable; but the people will not suffer the nobles to have anything without paying for it – be it an egg or a chicken. The gildsman (*homme de mestier*) and the labourer live in England by the work of their hands, and the gentlemen live from their rents and revenues; but if the king requires their services, they must be paid, for the king cannot tax his people, no, they would not suffer taxation. There are certain ordinances for taxation on the wool trade, and these are an additional revenue for the king above that of his rents from lands. When they make war these taxes are doubled.

England is the best protected country in the world; otherwise its people could not continue to exist. Any man who is their king must conform to the will of the people, bowing to their wishes. If he fails to do this he will be overthrown as happened to this King Edward [II] of whom I have been speaking, the son of that other Edward who was so full of prowess and who overcame the Scots. . . .[1]*

The chronicler Jean Froissart wrote this sometime after 1400 when Richard II had abdicated and been killed. Froissart had gradually grown hostile to the English cause during the protracted Hundred

---

* Superior figures refer to the Notes on pages 281–328.

Years War between France and England, but he had begun his career not as a Frenchman but as a man from Hainault, a region allied in the 1360s with England. Edward III's Queen Philippa came from Hainault and she had taken Froissart into her service as a chronicler. By the latter part of the fourteenth century, that period of the great flowering of literature in English, numerous commentators, speaking hyperbolically for or against the English, noted how the country seemed dominated politically and economically by that part of the population below the nobility, by money and by the professions that required their practitioners to possess the skills of literacy that, in effect, made them England's legislators: in Parliament, in the market place, in the law courts. This book is about some of the consequences of social mobility and about the literature of politics and entertainment, religious didacticism and private piety that recorded and reinforced the role of the expanding 'middle classes'.

There is a long historical tradition which calls the Middle Ages the 'Age of Faith', implying a single orthodoxy. Such a classification does not appear to take into account the numerous heresies, the outspoken scepticism and the secular doubt with which the period from the downfall of Rome to the Protestant Reformation was rife. What it does recognize is a will to orthodoxy, a desire for a single, transcendent truth which was presumed to be attainable through a fixed system of belief whose worldly face is a system of ethics. The thirteenth and fourteenth centuries in Europe witnessed the creation of an elaborate theology in the university theology faculties, and the growth of an elite of educated and powerful men who helped to create, comment upon and disseminate the language and faith of Christian orthodoxy. During the thirteenth century, theology as a complex metaphysics, hedged round by professional jargon. remained the provenance of scholastic centres of learning. The parallel development of church and civil law studies and their practical application in society helped to open up school theology and bridge the results of conceptual theology with a practical work-a-day ethics. As the unity and centralized power of the church located at Rome became a reality for the geographical area bounded by the Atlantic, the Adriatic, the Baltic and the Mediterranean, the scholasticism of the schools penetrated beyond the academic walls to affect the teachings of the myriad of local churches and, consequently, reached to the bottom of the social hierarchy, the unlettered populace.

It is a curious fact that this single Christian orthodoxy and a fairly fixed liturgical church ritual that was applicable to all of Christian

Europe developed precisely at a time when the beginnings of national feelings and local customary law were also being fixed. What has frequently been called the 'golden age of scholasticism' – the second half of the thirteenth century – was, in fact, a momentary hiatus in the more protracted historical tension between local cultures and a universal religious teaching. This book deals with the century after this brief golden era, when the literary consciousness of Englishmen was awakened to the richness of its past – its history, its institutions, its vernacular language – to 'things English', and the literary attempts that reconciled a local culture with a received, universal ethics taught by the universal institution, the Church.

As the fourteenth century progressed, the scholasticism of a university elite changed its focus somewhat and fixed its attention on personal morality in the world and its relation to heavenly reward. As a result, the topics of scholarly controversy were opened up to individuals of a wider, increasingly literate public concerned with their personal salvation. And with the increasing opportunities to acquire literate skills in the fourteenth century on the part of laymen, their own interest in matters of salvation affected the topics of discussion in the schools and in sermons as well. As educational opportunities opened to an increasingly numerous 'middle class', there was a meeting of personal interest with scholarly dispute. This is most evident in the Middle English literature that survives for the latter half of the fourteenth century, that period of England's literary golden age which boasts Chaucer, Langland, Gower and the Gawain poet. At this time we can distinguish a genre of didactic literature whose aim seems to have been the education of its audience in matters of current theological, political and ethical interest. Its means of doing so was to employ mixed and transitional styles: an older method, that of the courtly literary conventions of thirteenth- and early fourteenth-century French poetry, and a newer method, which extended English alliterative prose and poetry and explored the possibilities of journalistic reportage in verse and prose. French and Latin literary conventions and subjects merged with regional interests and poetic traditions to serve as 'frames' for poems whose messages dealt invariably with a Christian ethic as it was simultaneously defined and debated behind contemporary monastic and university doors. The growth in participation of Parliament and particularly the Commons in matters of national interest modified attitudes to secular rule and, by extension, to ethical positions maintained by those custodians of the Christian commonwealth of England.

In the alliterative revival in general, and in the Middle English poetry of Chaucer, Gower, the Gawain poet and Langland in particular, there is a specific technique that is used to tell their stories. This is the technique that, more or less, 'historicizes' its characters so that, while they remain 'types' of virtues or vices, 'types' of Christian or pagan, 'types' of 'people' who so define themselves by their function in society that they become these functions (like Langland's Theology, Dame Study), they are also real men acting in 'realistic' fourteenth-century situations. They become the incarnations of aspects of the living contemporary ethic. What can we say of fourteenth-century English history to provide a setting for such figures? For what we can supply from non-poetic sources will be only what a fourteenth-century audience for the poetry would already know, having lived it themselves. Furthermore, what we can say about the factual history of the period after 1350 (which concerns the war with France, the financial problems resulting from this war and the ravage of the plague on the English landscape, the practices and ideals of Edward III's and Richard II's courts, the 'peasants' revolt' of 1381) arises again as subjects of the contemporary poetry. Not only may we examine the vernacular poetry as an art form of increasing brilliance, but we may also interpret much of its message as the poetic reformulation of contemporary social and religious concerns of authors and audience alike; for this was a period in which the perception of such 'realities' was determined less by men's memories than by the written word. As Froissart commented *c*. 1388:

Each night when we arrived at our inn, I would write down all that he told me, either then or in the morning, so that I might have it fixed in my mind for future use, for there is no memory so exact as the written word.[2]

This book looks primarily at fourteenth-century literature, verse and prose, in Anglo-Norman, Latin and Middle English, which best indicates the function of written literature in a society where an increasing number of men and women could read it. It argues that relatively few works were meant merely to entertain but were intended rather to instruct, exhort and, ultimately, to inspire readers to criticize and eventually to reform social practice, by which was meant the behaviour of church officials and the politically and economically powerful. Much of this literature focuses on individual responsibility regarding salvation and institutional reform. The increasing emphasis on private responsibility to bring the practice of Christian ethics more in line with ideals is also reflected in the increasing emphasis placed on authorial responsibility. I will argue that this concern reflected the development of a public voice of a larger part of the population – what I have called, despite the difficulty of defining the term precisely in this period, the 'middle class'. I see the second half of the fourteenth century as a period of greater transition, in the spheres of literary form and message and in the social and economic sphere of effective political power, than the immediately earlier and subsequent periods. It is true that any demarcated historical period can be described as transitional, just as the 'middle class' can be said to be always on the rise. It is in the nature of both to admit of change. My aim is to signal the importance of the growth in lay literacy and social mobility as it was expressed in fourteenth-century literature, a literature that did not merely passively reflect its time and context but was written as an encouragement to critique and change. There were political and socioeconomic implications in its message, and any reading of this literature without an awareness of these implications gives us a partial if not false impression of its purpose. We can never become a fourteenth-century audience, but we can read fourteenth-century literature with an eye and ear better able to recognize the subtleties of stylistic experiments and to realize the significance of its subject matter. Our journey begins with the vexed question of literacy and lay education, proceeds to an exploration of the growth in the literature of social unrest, attempts to draw some conclusions about the nature of preaching and the gradual decline of the memory in favour of the written text and, lastly, focuses on the way in which school theology filtered down into what I call non-scholastic literature, to enlighten an enlarged readership in the issues that confronted them as private, individual Christians and as servants and citizens devoted to the public weal.

2 Vernacular literacy and lay education

French texts, English texts and their audience

In 1388 the most valuable secular article in a great man's house was judged to be his bed. Simon de Burley, once King Richard's tutor and a court favourite, was forced by the Merciless Parliament to forfeit all his possessions, having been charged with treason by a faction of lords known as the Appellants. His bed of green tartarine, embroidered with ships and birds, was so greatly prized that it came into the hands of the Bishop of Salisbury and in 1392 the King bought it from him for £13 6s 8d. This was considered relatively inexpensive when compared with that of Robert de Vere, Duke of Ireland, also charged by the Appellants and one of Richard's favourites, whose bed was of blue *camoca*, embroidered with gold owls and fleurs-de-lis and valued at £68 13s 4d, excluding the mattresses, blankets, sheets and pillows.[1] But the book of Forfeitures and attendant lists of possessions from which we know about the importance of beds in noble homes also tell us something about the somewhat less important place of books in these homes, and it is clear that French remained the language of literary entertainment in many households that were bilingual.

Simon de Burley possessed nine French romances and only one (now unknown) English book, described as the *Romance of the Forester and the Wild Boar*. He had a *Chronicle of the Brut*, the *Prophecies of Merlin* (both in French), several works including one on the government of kings and princes which was, most likely, the French translation of Giles of Rome's *De Regimine Principum*, a battered unnamed book of philosophy, a French translation by the twelfth-century Peter Comestor – the *Biblia Scholastica* – and one volume in Latin covered in black.[2]

Other fourteenth-century inventories of noble laymen's libraries tell a similar story. Guy de Beauchamp, the grandson of Earl Guy of Warwick who was himself described by a chronicler as *bene literatus*, died in 1360 and left forty-two books to the Cistercian Bordesley Abbey in Worcestershire.[3] Nineteen of these books were romances and the remainder were devotional works. The collection comprised works in French and Latin. Eleanor Bohun, Duchess of Gloucester, left in her will (1399) four French books, a French *Golden Legend*, a psalter, primer and other devotional works, a glossed psalter, *Lives of the Fathers*, St Gregory's *Pastorals*, decretals, a history book and a Bible in two volumes, all in French.[4] Thomas, Duke of Gloucester, one of the Appellants, had an extensive library of eighty-three books at his home at Pleshey in Essex,[5] and these were seized when he in turn was suspected of treason in the twenty-first year of Richard's reign (1397–8), revealing nineteen romances, numerous devotional works, law books including the two civil law texts in Latin (the *Digest* and the *Codex*), six philosophy volumes and nine chronicles. But the Appellant Gloucester's library shows a new trend. As an Appellant, he was presumably as anti-Lollard as his colleagues, but the debate on Bible translations was not yet decided against unauthorized versions, and it is not surprising that he possessed two English Gospels and a magnificent English Bible in two volumes. Before he died, he wrote in English a confession of his treason against Richard which the King then read out to Parliament, in English (1397).[6]

The aristocracy were clearly devout, read books for pleasure and edification, and at times composed them, most often in the language of Richard's court, which was French.[7] And yet, the nobility's attitude to French was, while respectful, rather humble if we can judge from the apologia offered by Henry of Grosmont, the first Duke of Lancaster, who wrote a devotional treatise, *Le Livre de Seyntz Medicines*, in 1354.[8] Henry was a great fighter and a knight of the older tradition who had participated in the victories of Edward III and the Black Prince over the French in the early stages of the Hundred Years War. The book he wrote, possibly a task set him by his confessor, for he was no scholar, was an allegory in which he takes stock of himself, and reveals to the Divine Physician and the Douce Dame his assistant, the 'wounds' of his soul, the misdeeds of his five senses. He confesses that he is a poor writer, having learned late and by himself, but none the less writes in French although he knows he is English, and therefore has, as he puts it, too little acquaintance with the French language.[9] His disclaimer is too modest for his achievement, which combines medieval medical folklore with a personal knowledge of military campaigns and the hunt, expressed in fluent but dialect French – that is, in the French of England: Anglo-Norman. The didactic works and sermons of the period seem to have left an impression on him; he says a good confession is like the smoking out of foxes – the sins of the penitent – by the confessor.[10]

If Anglo-Norman was the language of the court, of chivalry, entertainment and legal transaction, it was making way for English in noble circles. Archbishop Thomas Arundel is reported to have noted in his sermon at Anne of Bohemia's funeral (1394) how happy Richard's Queen was to have the four gospels in English 'with the docturis [glosses] upon hem'.[11] And Lady Alice West (d. 1395) bequeathed in her will to her daughter Johanna 'alle the bokes that I have of Latyn, *Englisch* and Frensch'.[12] If in 1384 Richard II's inventory for his own private chamber showed mainly French works – a French Bible, the *Roman de la Rose* and the romances of *Percival* and *Gawain*, of *Garin de Lorrain* and of *Aimeri de Narbonne* – we have seen that Gloucester was reading his Bible in English. One of Richard's chamber knights, Sir John Clanvowe, wrote his *Book of Cupid* in English, and Gower and Chaucer entertained their patrons in English. If, as is commonly believed, Chaucer wrote for the court circle whose literary tastes were French, why did he write in English?[13]

It is clear that by the latter half of the fourteenth century, authors in England were contributing to a rapidly expanding corpus that was becoming one of the most substantial of vernacular literatures in Europe. It came into existence largely through the demands of a new public: a court that was widely expanded by an urban merchant patriciate of London. Although Edward III, as early as 1337, had ordered the gentry and bourgeoisie to teach their children French 'to be better able and qualified for their wars', he is said to have met with little success.[14] English was becoming the dominant status language.

The continuing war with France and the ever-increasing demands for luxuries directly linked Richard's court with this new, expanding and rich merchant class of London who could afford to make financial loans. The urban 'middle classes' had increasingly direct and personal contact with the King's person as with the fashion and tastes of the nobility. And in 1388, when the Merciless Parliament tried, convicted and subsequently hanged many of Richard's favourites, charging them with treason and requiring them, as we have seen, to forfeit their possessions, they did not stop at an intimate noble faction but included far lesser men like Thomas Usk, the secretary to the mayor of London and later under-sheriff of the city. Usk, like his younger contemporary Thomas Hoccleve, who was no more than a clerk in the Privy Seal Office, wrote verse in English. His *Testament of Love*, and Hoccleve's autobiographical verse, place these men in what has been called 'the new literary movement of the international court culture'.[15] But where the customs of the English court were influenced by the courts of Bohemia, France, Germany and the Netherlands, the language used to express such customs became increasingly the English vernacular, and this corresponded to the narrowing of the conception of nationalism with more defined cultural and geographical boundaries that was also evident in contemporary legal and political tracts. A government that was increasingly dependent on financial considerations, not least to enforce its nationalism by financing wars abroad, depended in part on a wealthy rural gentry but also on the cities that were the centres of international financial transactions. These, in turn, exerted their own influence on court custom, drawing both foreign craftsmen and country-born poets to the centres of reward. Take, for example, the poet John Lydgate. He began as a novice at the Benedictine Abbey of Bury St Edmunds; the Countess of Stafford was his patroness; but he spent most of his life in London, became a court poet, writing in English, and was a favourite of the Lancastrians.[16] It was all too true, as the West Country author of *Wynnere and Wastoure* complained, that country fathers should hold fast to their sons or they would go 'southward' and never return to the provinces.

Dare neuer no westren wy, while this werlde lasteth,
Send his sone south-warde to see ne to here,
That he ne schall holden by-hynde when he hare [for] eld es.

(So long as the world lasts, no western man dares
Send his son southward, neither to see nor hear,
If he wishes to have him near when he grows white with age.)

Wynnere and Wastoure, ll. 8–10

Chaucer's poetry, his own creations and his translations, were intended for a wider audience than that of the nobility at Richard's court, and he shared this public with Gower. He dedicated his *Troilus and Cryseyde* to Gower and Strode rather than to a noble patron. Although his *Canterbury Tales* were read at court, doubtless they survive in so large a number of manuscripts because their appeal was not limited to a noble court audience. It has reasonably been suggested that the first public for the *Tales* was really the *haute bourgeoisie* as well as the court,[17] for surely the Man of Laws and the Merchant were meant to recognize their fellows by the parodies of their vices. While Gower's *Mirour de l'Omme* reflects a short-lived revival, if not a continuation, of Anglo-Norman,[18] even his language is that of a fluent 'foreigner' who felt obliged to excuse it on the grounds of being an Englishman. He includes forty-eight lines on the glory of wool, and the *Mirour* may well have been addressed to a devout group of merchants connected with the Wool Staple.[19] Gower's audience was even wider than this implies because it must have included those learned in Latin, like the hundred-odd Chancery clerks, who would be edified by his *Vox Clamantis*.

The variable nature of literacy

Where did his readership obtain its literacy? The *Vox Clamantis* in its final version was dedicated to the politically active Archbishop of Canterbury, Thomas Arundel, *c*. 1399, and as an allegory of contemporary history its appeal was to those living outside the cloister and familiar with the ways of the world. Its first book, a vision of the 'peasants' revolt', treated unfavourably what Langland treated with greater sympathy. Gower's works in English, French and Latin were written, then, for a varied, rather rich public that was literate in at least one or more of these languages. Langland's *Piers Plowman* addressed an even wider literate audience in the sense that they were prepared to read English interspersed with biblical and patristic lines in Latin, sometimes untranslated.[20] The extent of corruption of the text in the surviving numerous manuscripts of *Piers Plowman* suggests that Langland was favoured not with a court patron but with the patronage of a devout 'middle class', many of whom knew the London of Cornhill, of the merchant and craft gilds, the street cries and the lawyers, the luxury cheek by jowl with the poverty. Langland's use of grammatical analogies and philosophical personages named frequently in Latin (like Anima, Activa Vita), and his use of didactic characters (Dame Study, Theology) who lead his Dreamer Will on to a knowledge of what is necessary for Christian salvation, show a scholastic concern for Christian morality that was shared by those who preserved and copied his text in over fifty manuscripts.[21]

That devout burgesses and rural landowners were literate and displayed a zest for edifying English texts is clear from books they left in their wills and from their desire to beautify their local churches with scenes from this literature which also reflected their daily lives. On the walls of country churches were depicted scenes of Piers the Plowman as Christ and the Christ of the Craftsmen, frequently, as at Ampney St Mary near Cirencester or as once was the case at Stedham in Sussex, in humble colours and executed by local workshops.[22] At least one manuscript illumination showed the boy Jesus as an apprentice dyer.[23] Didactic wall paintings and book illuminations were the pictorial equivalents of medieval sermons, of edifying tracts and of the didactic poetry like Langland's which drew on sermon techniques to illustrate pious, often socially conscious, moral themes.

The poet's material was in part found in or paralleled by preachers' hand-books, like the sermon notes and outlines of Bishop Sheppey of Rochester,[24] which explicitly use English verses to punctuate strategically placed doctrinal points made in Latin. William of Shoreham (*c.* 1320), an Austin canon, also wrote for the private edification of the more educated of his West Kent parishioners, expounding doctrinal essentials through poems and didactic expositions. As we shall see later, the Franciscans were especially active in producing such manuals, arranged alphabetically for reference. John of Gaunt's confessor, Richard Maydenstone (*c.* 1345), a Carmelite friar, produced Latin verses, sermons and tracts, intended for the private use of educated laymen to prepare them for confession. By the later fourteenth century the use of English verses in sermons became habitual.[25] Furthermore, popular prayerbooks, *Prymers*, based on the Office, the Hours of the Blessed Virgin Mary, the seven penitential psalms and the Office for the Dead, included translations and commentaries on the psalm verses. In fact, the most popular of all Middle English poems to survive in more than 114 manuscripts, more than either *Piers Plowman* or Chaucer's *Canterbury Tales*, is *The Pricke of Conscience*, once but no longer attributed to the Yorkshire mystical hermit Richard Rolle. It is a didactic verse treatise in Middle English, an exemplar of the continued production throughout the century of a large number of didactic and homiletic works in verse which indicated a shift towards an increase in private lay devotional reading in the vernacular and continued the tradition of using poetry as a medium of religious instruction. From the *North English Legen-*

dary[26] we may read an expression of a tendency that was to become something of a norm by the end of the century:

Here men may luke, who likes to <u>lere</u>	learn
Of lives and <u>dedis</u> of saintes <u>sere</u>,	deeds; several
And in olde <u>times</u> how it bifell	
As men in inglis tung mai tell.	
Out of Latyn þus er þai draune	
Omong land men forto be knaune.	

What we mean, then, when we speak of the vexed question of lay literacy at the *end* of the fourteenth century, includes an ability to read and write in English and perhaps in either French or Latin. As McFarlane once pointed out,[27] the word 'literatus' in the fourteenth century had more than one meaning: when it applied to an ecclesiastic it meant he was a university graduate with letters after his name; when it applied to a layman it could mean that he was grounded in Latin grammar. It is certain that the governing class could read, and as we shall see, the governing class was ever-expanding; they probably used secretarial help to write as most busy administrators still do. When we add to this the ability to read in French and increasingly in English, then we have a situation in which the word 'literatus', the term 'literate', takes on a multiplicity of meanings. The blossoming of English poetry and prose in the fourteenth century is most easily intelligible, in fact, as the reflection of a changing social structure and its changing ideals: a broadening of the middle range of society, its greater participation in government and its increasing demand for a literature read for information, for pleasure and for spiritual edification.

One of the most significant institutional developments of the century was the development of grammar schools to teach the humbler members of society, who would never get within miles of the royal court, to read and write. An ability to read and write could bring a man to the notice of a local magnate who depended for his wealth and power on the skilful management of his extensive estates, scattered across the country. When he was present on his estates, his manorial household became the centre of winter entertainment, to say nothing of the daily legal affairs which required a group of resident literate men learned in customary law and in the drawing up of documents and manorial court decisions on local matters. The magnate's household provided patronage to reward those who wrote the fashionable household romances associated with particular dynastic founders, like *Guy of Warwick* and *William of Palerne*. The latter was adapted from the French romance for Humphrey de Bohun, Earl of Hereford (d. 1361), but it was not intended for the earl himself, who read French, but 'for hem þat knowe no frensche, ne neuer vunderston' (l. 5533). Hence it was probably meant for those living at his two manors of Wheatenhurst (Whitminster) and Harsfield, south of Gloucester. It has been suggested, therefore, that the alliterative *William of Palerne* was addressed wholly to a non-aristocratic, humble audience rather than to Humphrey and the higher nobility, and that the poem's detailed, romanticized picture of court life was meant as an instructive guide to the courtly virtues for Humphrey's Gloucestershire dependants, who read it in regional dialect.[28] Indeed, the English alliterative revival may reflect the growing literacy of the West Midlands inhabitants who were not aristocratic and whose tastes were not, therefore, as conservative as the French-reading nobility.

With estates scattered across the country the magnate's house can also be considered a roving court, and with the lord went a retinue of the literate. But we must distinguish several kinds of literacy lest we mistake men like Chaucer's Somonour for those who 'wel koude endite [compose poetry]'. For Chaucer's Somonour, only when drunk 'wolde he speke no word but Latyn':

A fewe termes hadde he, two or thre
That he hade lerned out of some decree –
No wonder is, he herde it al the day;
And <u>eek</u> ye knowen wel how that a jay   also
Kan <u>clepen</u> 'Watte' as wel as kan the pope.   call out
But whoso koude in oother thyng hym <u>grope</u>,   grasp
Thanne hadde he spent al his philosophie;
Ay '<u>questio quid juris</u>' wolde he crie.   'what law applies?'

General Prologue, *Canterbury Tales*, ll. 638–46

The Somonour was what might be called a pragmatic reader in that if he could write or read at all it was only in the course of his 'business' transactions. Most of what he wrote and read consisted of formulae which recurred so frequently that he had them memorized, and this may imply that he did not necessarily know the meaning of the individual elements of the sentence.

Then there was the cultivated man or woman who read for private entertainment and had begun to collect books when he or she could afford this luxury. By the latter half of the fourteenth century such a group of cultivated readers included a large number of the urban 'middle class', and manuscripts were written specially for them. Lastly, there was the clerk, who was a professional reader and had a future in the church or in the civil service and law courts, usually after a university sojourn.[29]

As we shall see, there was a significant overlap in the categories of cultivated and professional readers; combined, they constituted the growing class of general readers for whom English vernacular entertainment was becoming at least as significant as the older French romance tradition of the more specifically noble class. The stocks of two London grocers who became bankrupt in the 1390s, for instance, contained four books of romance and two books in English along with a primer.[30] The very low valuation of the books implies not only a cheap form of production, but also a literacy that was used for private entertainment. Without having had recourse to the cheapest form of all of acquiring a book – copying it themselves – they were able to buy them from a local stationer. And the rise in the demands for all sorts of books in the fourteenth century allowed the stationer's craft to assume real commercial significance. One specialized branch of professional writers, the scriveners, 'writers of court and text letter', were recognized as a professional class *c*. 1357 and by 1373 they were taking steps to establish a monopoly of their profession in London.[31] They wrote in French and Latin.

The reading of English, on the other hand, appears to have become an assumed skill. It has even been suggested that when the term 'unlettered' is used of someone in the later fourteenth century, it refers to his inability to read Latin and possibly French, without reference to English.[32] But if English literacy was assumed, it is not always easy today to find documents that testify to its being taught. And if we can say that English literacy was not confined to the nobility, who were, for the most part, still reading French, then what can we learn of the nature of grammar school education available to the wider range of Edward III's and Richard II's subjects?

Schools and education: what was studied, where and by whom

At the grammar schools that had been established throughout England by the fourteenth century, a student learned the rules of Latin grammar and some Latin literature.[33] Most often the fundamentals of Latin had already been learned in an elementary school along with singing. Throughout the Middle Ages grammar was taught from two standard texts written by two late Roman grammar masters, Donatus and Priscian. The former's *De arte grammatica* was nothing more than an analysis of the elements of language: the letter, the syllable, parts of speech, a more thorough study of the noun and its adjectives. Much of this material would have been taught by the local vicar, like the one in Kingston-upon-Thames who, in 1377, was licensed to keep a school for boys learning reading, song and Latin up to Donatus.[34] There are beginning to be earlier examples of private chantries endowed for the continual prayers of a deceased benefactor by his family, which later expanded their charity by establishing an exhibition fund to include several young boys to sing and learn Latin. Such was the case in 1347 when a chantry was endowed in the chapel of St Katherine's at Lincoln for five priests to pray for the father and brother of Sir Bartholomew Burghersh.[35] In 1349 six boys aged eight were added to the chantry who were able to sing and who already knew their Donatus. They were to receive their further education at the Lincoln city grammar school and to proceed to the priesthood when sixteen. In 1388 the Bishop of Lincoln instituted a similar scheme.

In Exeter, the schools for song, grammar and higher studies of theology and canon law were the concern of the clergy, particularly of the Cathedral chapter. The grammar school was supervised by the archdeacon of Exeter, and the Cathedral maintained and educated the boys in its choir. By 1384 the grammar master had a monopoly of teaching in the city and seven miles into the countryside; he received no stipend but lived wholly from his pupils' fees. Grammar scholarships, a new schoolroom and a dwelling for the schoolmaster had been completed by 1344 through the generosity of Richard Brayleigh, dean of Exeter and a protégé of Walter Stapledon, the bishop. Known for his generous patronage of education, Stapledon had originally planned the foundation of grammar scholarships in the Exeter Hospital of St John to follow his foundation, in 1314, of Exeter College, Oxford, to educate West Country scholars. Stapledon's successor as bishop of Exeter, John Grandisson, completed this project and then went on to found, at Ottery St Mary, a secular college with a school for eight canons, eight vicars, eight secondaries (older boys whose voices had broken) and eight choristers, three chaplains and four other clerks.[36] The 1338 statutes provide for the eight choristers to be taught song, organ playing and grammar – the latter by a master appointed by the canons, who also taught the public. The school was open to the public but students had to pay. But as Lady Katherine Berkeley later remarked, 'Many who wished to be taught grammar, the foundation of all the liberal arts, were hindered by poverty and lack of means. The schoolmaster of Wotton [John Stone] and his successors were, therefore, to receive with kindness all who came to them and give teaching without taking fees.'[37]

It is thought by some that even the mendicant order of the Crutched Friars, who rarely seem to have been involved in secular grammar education, acquired property and a licence in 1349 for the maintenance of a free school in Wotton-under-Edge, Gloucestershire. On another view, the licence may have been obtained by the order of the Holy Cross, one of the numerous communities that wore the cross as a badge and lived according to the Augustinian Rule.[38] The significance is that a school was established. In general, more than 120 colleges were founded and many of them maintained grammar schools. The most famous was the College of St Mary at Winchester, founded in 1382 by William of Wykeham. His foundation book inventory listed 240 volumes covering theology, philosophy, canon and civil law. The purpose of the college was only in part educational, in that the warden and ten fellows were all priests, there to celebrate the divine office, and, presumably, to make use of the library when preparing sermons. But the educational function of the college was primarily to teach grammar to seventy scholars aged eight to twelve. A student was admitted when judged already competent in reading, song and Donatus.[39]

In other parts of the country a priest was installed as the grammar master to teach local scholars and anyone else who desired to learn. Sometimes this was free of charge, as at the school in Wotton-under-Edge, established by Lady Katherine Berkeley in 1384. This trend of increasingly open education had already been attempted at the grammar school in Carlisle, which had no conditions of admission and was to give Latin instruction to 'boys, adults and any others who wish to inform themselves in *scientia grammaticali*'.[40] In the earlier fourteenth century this was usually for a fee paid to the master, but gradually the master was endowed and taught any members of the public free of charge. In all, according to one estimate,[41] no fewer than seventy-seven lower, pre-university schools of the fourteenth century have left records of their curricula.

These examples of grammar schools established to teach Latin primarily to young men, only some of whom would become priests or continue their studies in the arts faculties of Cambridge or

Oxford Universities, give us some idea of the level of Latin literacy we should expect from clerks and the laity who were fortunate enough to avail themselves of it; their future careers may never have taken them out of the village in which they were born. We are, therefore, able to define a distinct category of *literati* for the later fourteenth century whose knowledge of Latin and grammar established them as literate, at least to the extent of calling them 'pragmatic' readers if not 'cultivated' to some degree. Who these men were remains something of a mystery to us unless we are able to follow their careers beyond the town schools either to cathedral schools of higher study, dotted around the country, or to university. For this largely anonymous group the town school taught reading, song and grammar; the cathedral schools developed important schools of theology and law. Salisbury, Exeter, St Paul's London and Lincoln Cathedrals had grammar schools, and taught more widely in the liberal arts, while York seems to have had a school of civil law.[42] In addition to providing Latin grammar and reading instruction along with logic and other liberal arts, the cathedrals also arranged for theological lectures to be delivered. In addition to the chancellor's lectures, former fellows of Oxford colleges, now high-ranking ecclesiastics, were known to come and lecture.[43] In this way, current university attitudes to moral issues and events filtered down to the non-professional laity.[44]

At university

Grammar was taught on a more sophisticated level at the universities but not always as part of a university degree.[45] Rather, grammar masters, controlled by university statute, taught not only grammar but *dictamen*, the art of letter writing, and were responsible for instructing students in business methods. It appears that a large number of students came to Oxford only to learn the techniques of writing formal letters and for drawing up documents pertaining to the business of agriculture. They were taught in Latin, and only when this proved insufficient were they instructed in French. Such clerks of meagre attainments, whose stay in the university was relatively brief, are an anonymous force to be reckoned with in the spread of current ideas and controversies raging at Oxford.[46] Should a student wish to master *dictamen* and business methods it was clear that he had to master to some extent the rules of Latin grammar; should he wish to study common law he had to learn Latin first. But what gives us one of our first glimpses of the growth of English as the language of daily professional discourse comes in the *Speculum Grammaticale* of the Oxford grammar master John of Cornwall, for he established in mid-century the precedent of instructing in English. The translator Trevisa, who was himself a fellow of an Oxford college, testified in 1385 that all grammar schools throughout England were using English as the language of instruction, although we must not forget that it was Latin grammar and composition that was being taught. Trevisa sadly noted that this emphasis on English to the detriment of French was something of a disadvantage for it ill prepared grammar school students for travel abroad.[47]

When grammar was studied as part of the university arts course it assumed a knowledge of a whole range of grammatical theory gained from an earlier education, and students were required to hear lectures on parts of Priscian's *Institutes* for at least one term. How dull, we may think. But such knowledge was assumed by writers addressing a wider audience. When we come across the technical grammatical terms 'ex vi transicionis' in one of the passages of notorious difficulty in *Piers Plowman*, B XIII, ll. 150–6,[48] we are witnessing the use made of late medieval commentaries on Priscian by a poet writing in the vernacular for a moral purpose. That Langland used such grammatical analogy in the first place, rather than whether it was successful in clarifying his argument, is what is of real significance when we consider the nature of the degree of literacy of his audience. He must have expected his audience to consist, at least in part, of university arts students who would recognize the specific reference to Priscian's *Institutes*.

Nor does Langland restrict his use of Latin grammatical analogy to these seven lines. In the C text of the poem, its last version, there is a ninety-one-line expansion of the B text to explain the relation of 'reward', characterized as Lady Mede, to God and His commandments. Reward is described in terms of direct and indirect relation. A direct relation between the individual Christian and God, between one's deeds and their just reward, is paralleled with the role of the adjective and the noun, as each is related to the other in the sentence and then in relation to the thing signified by noun and adjective in reality. This analogy reflects a knowledge of fairly simple grammatical elements studied in the university arts course if not earlier. To explain a theological subtlety, namely 'just reward', by means of grammatical analogy indicates that Langland believed a larger number of people would have been more immediately familiar with grammatical terminology than with the terms of theological argument of the schools. But at the same time Langland is concerned to teach his audience current theology through the grammar they already know.[49] When we go on to examine this poem for its use of Latin quotations, sometimes untranslated,[50] it seems reasonable to assume that some of its readers at least had attained a degree of English literacy combined with sufficient Latin, by the end of the century, to enable them to understand the poem in its entirety.

One effect of the proliferation of grammar schools was the turning out of a relatively large number of literate men for whom more opportunities had been created at Oxford and Cambridge to study logic and philosophy and then proceed to the higher faculties of theology and law. They were assured of lucrative posts if they entered the expanding civil service or if they received benefices in the church after they obtained their degrees.[51] At university they were considered ecclesiastics in minor orders, 'clerks', even when only doing the arts course of logic and philosophy; and unless they entered the Church upon leaving the schools they reverted to lay status. What happened to such men? The composition of the Exchequer in 1370, for instance, showed a large number of fairly adequate administrators of humbler status, the majority of whom were perhaps still clerks, but an increasingly large number of whom were also university-educated laymen.[52]

There is a considerable quantity of information available that tells us about the provisions made for further education in theology and law at the universities.[53] A modern reader of *Piers Plowman* or of Chaucer's *Boece* and *Troilus* wants to know what kind of philosophical problem an educated fourteenth-century public would recognize as familiar; was Chaucer's Clerk of Oxenford a well-known type? Was fourteenth-century society riddled with lawyers as the Visio portion of *Piers Plowman* says? Is Gower justified when he complains of the low birth and greed of lawyers in his *Mirour de l'Omme*? Were there university Bachelors of Arts who eked out a living hearing confessions and singing in private chantries in London? In other words, is the English poetry written in the reign of Richard II a realistic 'mirror of man' and the vices and virtues of his world, or is it meant to represent a fictional world of fixed types and homiletic *exempla*?

We know that private and royal efforts were made to expand university education for more men, as in 1337, when Edward III formally established the King's Hall in Cambridge. He stressed the importance of university graduates as a regular source of literate and capable men flowing into ecclesiastical and secular government.[54] The late thirteenth and fourteenth centuries saw the founding of Oxford and Cambridge colleges, in part to answer the need for lodging and financing secular scholars who were prepared to continue their studies beyond the first degree. By offering a relatively large number of postgraduate fellowships, the King's Hall, Cambridge, came to be known as the preserve of lawyers. Its graduate fellows, who were largely recruited from the upper strata in society, were frequently non-resident civil lawyers, employed by the Church and by the king throughout the country and abroad. With the plague of 1349 cutting short the lives of a generation of scholars and administrators, these colleges were increasingly seen as the primary source for administrative and legal personnel. In the second half of the fourteenth century there was a marked increase in the number of fellows who acquired second degrees in civil and canon law; in fact, 58 per cent of all second degrees taken in this period were law degrees and the majority were in civil law. This is clear evidence for the direction English society was taking, and is specially significant when we try to understand why the legal language concerning covenants and justice, as well as, of course, the complaints against the legal profession, in poems like *Piers Plowman* and Gower's *Mirour de l'Omme* would be neither unfamiliar nor unrealistic for the poems' public.

There were two categories of men who went into the Church from university; one group we might call the *sublimes et literati*, for they held prize benefices and were frequently non-resident pluralists; that is, they might live in London but receive payment from more than one parish elsewhere for which they should have been the resident priest. Instead, they paid others to maintain their 'cures of souls'. The other category consisted of the pastoral clergy, and here we may place a man like Chaucer's poor Clerk of Oxenford, who had not as yet gone further than the university arts course, had not as yet received a benefice, nor was he worldly enough to have an important secular office. He was supported by friends or family at home and spent his meagre funds on books. Aristotle was the mainstay of his university arts course.

A Clerk there was of Oxenford also,
That unto logyk hadde longe ygo,
As leene was his hors as is a rake,
And he nas nat right fat, I undertake,

But looked holwe, and therto sobrely.
Ful thredbare was his overeste courtepy;   cloak
For he hadde geten hym yet no benefice,
Ne was so worldly for to have office,
For him was levere have at his beddes heed   he preferred to
Twenty bookes, clad in blak or reed,
Of Aristotle and his philosophie
Than robes riche, or fithele, or gat sautrie.   fiddle; psaltery
But al be that he was a philosophre
Yet hadde he but litel gold in cofre;
But al that he myghte of his freendes hente,   obtain
On bookes and on lernynge he it spente,
And bisily gan for the soules preye
Of hem that yaf hym wherwith to scoleye.   attend school
Of studie took he moost cure and moost heede.
Noght o word spak he moore than was neede,
And that was seyd in forme and reverence,
And short and quyk and ful of hy sentence;
Sownynge in moral vertu was his speche,
And gladly wolde he lerne and gladly teche.

General Prologue, *Canterbury Tales*, ll. 285–308

His career was just beginning. He may well have found himself,
after being made a Bachelor or Master of Arts, among the graduate
academic proletariat, living like the Langland of the C text in
Cornhill, London (the area inhabited mostly by drapers), with a
wife and child, saying his paternoster and teaching with the aid of a
primer, earning a meagre wage singing in the city chantries.

Thus ich a-waked, god wot . whanne ich wonede on Cornehulle,   lived
Kytte and ich in a cote . clothed as a lollere . . .
'Whanne ich ʒonge was' quath ich . 'meny ʒer hennes,
My fader and my frendes . founden me to scole,
Tyl ich wiste wyterliche . what holy wryt menede,   assuredly
And what is best for the body . as the bok telleth,
And sykerest for the soule . by so ich wolle continue.   safest
And ʒut fond ich neuere in faith . sytthen my frendes deyden,   died
Lyf that me lyked . bote in thes longe clothes.   except
Yf ich by laboure scholde lyue . and lyflode deseruen,   livelihood
That labour that ich lerned best . ther-with lyue ich sholde;
    In eadem uocatione in qua uocati estis, manete.
And ich lyue in Londone . and on Londone bothe,   both
The lomes that ich laboure with . and lyflode deserue   tools
Ys *pater-noster* and my prymer . *placebo* and *dirige*,
And my sauter som tyme . and my seuene psalmes.   psalter

Thus ich synge for hure soules . of suche as me helpen,
And tho that fynden me my fode . vouchen safe, ich trowe,
To be welcome whanne ich come . other-while in a monthe,
Now with hym and now with hure . and thus-gate ich begge
With-oute bagge other botel . bote my <u>wombe</u> one,   stomach
And al-so more-ouer . me thynketh, syre Reson,
Men sholde constreyne no clerke . to knauene werkes;
For by laws of *Leuitici* . that oure lorde ordeynede,
Clerkes that aren crouned . of kynde vnderstondyng
Sholde nother <u>swynke</u> ne swete . ne swere at enquestes . . .   work
    [Instead]
Some to synge masses . other sitten and wryte,
Rede and receyue . that reson ouhte spende;

                          Piers Plowman, C VI, ll. 1–69

But the parish priest was not always so sincere and studious, and numerous contemporary scandals implied that some of them were scarcely literate, able, as Langland said, neither to sing nor read saints' lives. A hare is easier to find in a field than Latin case-endings, 'Ac in canoun ne in the decretales [collection of papal decrees]. I can nouȝte rede a lyne' (B V, l. 428), an inability to read linked, no doubt, with a disinclination to do so, when the text was Latin or Church law.

Langland was familiar with the London of the poor priest but he must have been trained at university for he knew the intricacies of the arts course and the required texts. His style is hedged round by the scholastic dispute formulae of the *quaestio*, the *distinctio*, the *sed contra*. He knew enough school logic to be able to use it for a didactic purpose. Quotations from the Church fathers were used to intensify the lesson he taught in English, and he let Dame Study show how she sent Clergy, her cousin, to school and that Clergy's wife, Scripture, was related to the seven liberal arts.

'For thi mekenesse man' quod she [Dame Study] . 'and for thi mylde
    speche,
I shal kenne the to my cosyn . that Clergye is <u>hoten</u>.   called
He hath wedded a wyf . with-inne this syx monethes,
Is <u>sybbe</u> to the seuene artz . Scripture is hir name.   relative
Thei two, as I hope . after my techyng,
Shullen <u>wissen</u> the to Dowel . I dar it vndertake' . . .   instruct, direct
And thus shaltow come to Clergye . that can many thinges.
Saye hym this signe . I sette hym to scole,
And that I grete wel his wyf . for I wrote hir many bokes,

And sette hir to Sapience . and to the sauter glose.　　　*Wisdom* books
　Logyke I lerned hir . and many other lawes,
And all the musouns in musike . I made hir to knowe.
Plato the poete . I put hym fyrste to boke,
Aristotle and other moo . to argue I tauʒte.
Grammer for gerles . I garte first wryte,　　　　　children; caused
And bette hem with a baleis, but if thei wolde lerne . . .　　　　rod
Ac Theologie hath tened me . ten score tymes,　　　　　vexed
The more I muse there-inne . the mistier it semeth,
And the depper I deuyne, the derker me it thinketh; . . .

Piers Plowman, B X, ll. 147–82

The oft-complained-of clerical illiteracy, at least at university level, takes on a new guise when Langland later has Anima tell how the arts course has become debased and useless for spiritual truths. The fundamental study of grammar has become so intricate, theoretical and abstract in the arts course that new clerks, Anima complains, can no longer versify nor write correctly. There is, 'nouʒt on amonge an hundreth [of these new clerks] that an auctor can construe,/ Ne rede a lettre in any langage . but [except] in Latyn or in Englissh' (B XV, 368ff.), implying that it is a knowledge of classical Latin and of French that has waned, rather than that clerks suffered from an ignorance of scholastic Latin and English.

The careers of the *'sublimes et literati'*

As we might expect, the documents give us more information about the lives of the ambitious and successful than about the poor priests. Most of the *sublimes et literati* pursued the Oxford arts course as the initial step along the road to ecclesiastical or administrative preferment. And most of those who held prize benefices and pluralities on the authority of the crown appear to have done so because of personal merit rather than through noble lineage.[55] Consequently, many bishoprics came to be held by sons of franklins, yeomen and merchants in the fourteenth century, and they comprised a new university-educated class.[56] The professional scholars gradually ceased to hold the key episcopal positions: the scholars and theologians remained at the university.[57] But at the same time, more bishops had attended the university to the level of the Bachelor of Divinity than previously, and such men could not have failed to have been taught by the new breed of university lecturer in arts and in theology, the *moderni*, as they were called by contemporaries, whose theology was tempered by two current university interests: logic, and the personal if not private ethics of the Christian pilgrim.[58] It is clear then, that fourteenth-century civil servant bishops had a fairly extensive academic training, and just behind them ran the lawyers, the physicians, the sons of the urban 'middle class' and those with more modest ecclesiastical preferment in the provinces.

Not all university graduates received posts in London, for which Archbishop Courtenay, during his visitation of Exeter in 1384, was no doubt grateful. For the Archbishop fell ill and 'was unable to ride, travel, work or scarcely move himself about in bed without the aid of assistants'. He was visited by the Bishop of Exeter, but also by three canons of the Church at Exeter, all university masters, including one who was a physician – *in arte phisica eruditos.* . . . [59]

Courtenay came from an important landed family, and we shall hear more of him when we follow his dealings with Wyclif and the Lollards. But Richard de Bury was an outstanding example of a civil servant bishop from humbler origins, and appears to have been something of an ideal literate and literary man. He was perhaps the greatest patron of scholarship outside the university in this period. He was also a renowned bibliophile, rivalling Charles V of France. He is a good example of a university-educated man, who, after years of royal service, became a civil servant bishop.[60] His father had been a knight from Leicestershire (Sir Richard de Aungerville), but Richard was orphaned early and educated by an uncle, John de Willoughby, who was rector of a parish grammar school. He proceeded to Oxford, residing there from *c.* 1302 to 1312. He received the degrees of Master of Arts and Bachelor of Divinity. After starting his career as a clerk he became Lord Privy Seal (1329–33) and Lord Chancellor of the Exchequer at Chester (1333) and was made a canon and dean of Wells Cathedral. After representing the crown numerous times on commissions and in ambassadorial capacities abroad, he expressed a desire to renew his scholarly life. Instead he was made Bishop of Durham (1333), and, almost as consolation for not being able to continue his own theological studies, he gathered around him distinguished scholars, like the Mertonian Thomas Bradwardine, later Archbishop of Canterbury; Robert Holcot, the well-known Dominican biblical commentator; Richard FitzRalph, future Archbishop of Armagh; Walter Burley, the influential logician and theologian; John Maudit; Richard Kilmington, Dean of St Paul's – all doctors in theology – along with Richard Byntworth, a civil lawyer who later became Bishop of

London; Walter Seagrave, later Bishop of Chichester; and John Aston, the canonist. John Bale said that it was customary for de Bury's group to have after-dinner disputations.

Richard de Bury was only one among several patron bishops: Ralph Shrewsbury at Wells (1329–63); John Dalderby at Lincoln (1300–20); Roger Martival and Simon of Ghent early in the century at Salisbury; Walter Stapledon and John Grandisson at Exeter (1308–26; 1327–63). But we know surprisingly little about the secular cathedral communities where such patron bishops presided, particularly from the standpoint of the training of the men who may have contributed to the literary entertainments at episcopal visitations. Some of the episcopal registers bring to light the great expenses incurred by these entertainments, which were held at the episcopal manor houses and to which the local clergy and parochial laity were summoned. What does emerge is the miscellaneous character of the men who were drawn to the secular cathedrals, including those clerks who had risen in the royal service or at the universities.

It is also clear that whenever we find complaints about clerical illiteracy, and these become more frequent as the century continues, we are also facing the fact of more widespread literacy of more men, and not only ecclesiastics. Here is the irony, which Alexander Murray has so well illuminated.[61] In a period when more writing was being done, and cheaper paper replaced parchment and vellum, reformers cried out about clerks being unable to read, while, in fact, positive evidence points the other way: 'products, standards and even the equipment of reading and writing were more, or better at the end of the fourteenth century than at the beginning', in the words of Murray.[62] In fact, the evil criticized got less while the criticism intensified.

How do we explain this phenomenon? It has been shown that, at universities like Oxford and Paris throughout the fourteenth century, the numbers of students increased considerably.[63] Furthermore, many more university halls were established during this century. While it is true that the plague of 1349 and thereafter reduced the numbers, there was a new build-up of the population in the 1370s. New College, Oxford, founded in 1379, was able to fill its rooms. At the same time, however, we may observe that no new bishoprics were created, not only in England but also in northern France and western Germany, between the early twelfth century and the Reformation. This is of importance when we consider the increase in the numbers of university graduates who sought jobs in the ecclesiastical hierarchy. Membership in cathedral chapters also appears to have remained constant. At the same time, the parish was relatively stagnant geographically, despite population fluctuations. What happened to all the graduates, we may ask? Within what Murray calls 'the nodes of authority', responsibility ramified and the numbers of administrative staff increased dramatically.[64] And mendicant churches, private foundations and confraternity foundations also increased, which meant that the multiplication of churches and altars actually became an abuse, especially in some cities. The clergy who filled such posts were in dire straits because they shared out the fixed income that was relegated to the largely unramified upper echelons of the ecclesiastical system. The proliferation of parish churches, and the growth of bureaucratic administrative positions, illustrated the principles that governed the job structure for graduates in the latter part of the fourteenth century. With the increased numbers of graduates demanding a still limited number of jobs, it is to be expected that the swell in complaints of incompetency and illiteracy in the Church's posts should reach a crescendo in the last years of the century. It is not surprising, therefore, to find the swell of such complaints in the circles of university-educated men themselves, for they were anxious for a living. When urban churches began to be rationalized (the livings of two or more being offered to one man because he could not live on what was provided for one as in former days),[65] the posts seemed to be shrinking. Aware of this problem into the fifteenth century, authorities tried to create vested interests in lucrative ecclesiastical benefices for the increasing numbers of graduates. The complaints about the inadequacy of graduates and the lesser priesthood were common enough, based on an economic, demographic and social dilemma; de Bury himself entered the debate with hyperbolic criticisms of his own which illuminate current attitudes to what was taught in the schools, and how ill prepared graduates were considered to be for their subsequent positions.

His *Philobiblon* tells us something about the quality of education and literacy one might expect from university graduates in his day, and he paints a pessimistic picture, coloured by contrast, with able Latin rhetorical flourishes of his own.[66] He complains that mere boys are made Masters at the university before they are 'seasoned by the course of nature or ripeness of learning. Today's clerks, afflicted with ambition, prematurely snatch the Master's cap, and mere boys become unworthy professors of the several faculties'. 'They are assisted by papal provisions obtained by the cupidity of relatives who are able to secure ecclesiastical dignities for their nephews and pupils before they can possibly be ready for such offices.'[67] This must have been intended irony, for de Bury had been able to secure just such privileges for his nephew! However, de Bury attacks not the content of the course of study, but rather an inadequate grounding in the prescribed texts. Langland has made Dame Study complain similarly:

for now is iche boy bolde . and he be riche
To tellen of the trinite . to be holden a sire.

Piers Plowman, A XI, ll. 61–2

But Langland also gives us a forthright defence of the arts course, as we have seen, when Dame Study leads Will to her cousin Clergy for further instruction in 'naturally knowing what is Do Wel' (B X, l. 151). De Bury's *Philobiblon* also supports Langland's contention that the liberal arts are studies necessary to scriptural studies, and so to clergy, when he comments how 'the books of the liberal arts are so useful to the divine writings that without their aid, the intellect would vainly aspire to understand them. . . . It follows that because of our ignorance of poetry we do not understand Jerome, Augustine, Boethius, Lactantius, Sidonius. . . .'[68] The university arts course, with its emphasis on logic, metaphysical philosophy, natural philosophy and dialectical debate, was not spending sufficient time on the ancient poets to suit de Bury, or for that matter Langland's Anima (*Piers Plowman*, B XV, ll. 368ff.).

It is true that Richard de Bury was a remarkable, even unusual, product of his time. His humanism most likely did not express the common attitudes of his generation. But it represents the ideals of a period: the humanist emerging from the university arts course aware that what he has learned shall serve him well in the study of texts, scriptural or otherwise. The fact that he was recognized and honoured in the civil service, and that he was a generous and influential patron, are worth considering when we examine his life and his *Philobiblon* in relation to the times in which he lived. For these stand out as epitomes of the attainments achieved by some of the *sublimes et literati*. And the educational institutions, from the grammar schools to the postgraduate colleges of the universities, were established to permit more men to achieve such ends.

On a less exalted plane, the number of people who were not

professional clerks, but who read for pleasure and edification, was also increasing. Literature that was previously read by a scholarly elite, in Latin or French, was being translated into English. When Chaucer translated Boethius's *Consolation of Philosophy* (*c*. 1377–81), he seemed aware that his efforts were intended for a wider public than the court. He wrote for people concerned with serious philosophical problems, like the role of providence and fate in history, and one's personal reconciliation with the vagaries of fortune. In his verse to his scrivener, Adam, he stated that one of the latter's duties was to make copies of his translation of Boethius, an author who treated the issues of fate and fortune in relation to the role of philosophy. Likewise, the vicar of Berkeley, John Trevisa, was asked by Thomas Lord Berkeley to translate numerous works from Latin into English. MS Harley 1900 closes with a note that it was completed 18 April 1387 for Lord Berkeley, and included translations of the French political theorist Pierre Dubois's *Dialogue Between a Knight and a Clerk*, and the famous sermon preached by FitzRalph against the mendicant orders in 1357, the *Defensio Curatorum*. Trevisa also was the translator of Ranulph Higden's *Polychronicon* and of Bartholomew (Glanvill) of Exeter's *De Proprietatibus Rerum*, from which comes the episode of the bees that appears as an *exemplum* in the second part of *Mum and the Sothsegger*. Some believe he translated Giles of Rome's *De Regimine Principum*, which was known to the nobility of late medieval England.

Trevisa's own story is an interesting one in the light of our concern for the whereabouts of educated men in fourteenth-century society, for he came from a Cornish family of gentlemen, and several of his relatives sat in Parliament in the 1350s and 1360s.[69] He entered as a student of Exeter College, Oxford, and later was made a fellow of Queen's. He seems to have been expelled with several others, after a disputed election of the provost of Queen's, for refusing in 1379 to account for money received when the Archbishop of York held a visitation at Oxford, and thereafter, 'took divers charters, books, jewels, money and goods belonging to the college', as the Close Rolls for the third year of the reign of Richard II show. Like Wyclif after him, who held a non-residentiary papal prebend, Trevisa held a non-resident canonry at the same collegiate church of Westbury-on-Trym in Gloucestershire. According to Caxton, writing in the fifteenth century, Trevisa found time to translate the Bible as did Wyclif's Oxford followers, some of whom were also originally at Queen's College, like Nicholas Hereford and William Middleworth. Trevisa then appears to have returned to Oxford in 1386–7 and again in 1395–9, where he was present at the aftermath of Wyclif's disgrace and silencing. He clearly was familiar with the current of thought in Oxford and was in a position as vicar of Berkeley to pass this on in the provinces.

Translations into English

We shall have occasion to look more closely at the influence of Wyclif and Oxford Wyclifites on lay piety and the production of English Bibles in Chapters 4 and 5. But more generally, the increasing frequency of translations of Latin and French texts meant that new attitudes to the availability of Scripture for a wider public came to exist side by side with an interest in the older forms of chivalric and courtly literature. Many of the romances written for earlier French-speaking and -reading generations were translated out of their original Anglo-Norman into English and helped to mould morals and ideals of love and marriage based on an earlier ethic. But even here the chivalric idealism of the French works was replaced in the fourteenth-century English productions with heroes who expressed, in the words of Derek Pearsall, 'a kind of pragmatic piety'[70] not to be found in the French originals; none the less, the English romances maintained the stock incidents of the French romances with the addition of a few local allusions. What is most significant in English romances is the nature of the adaptation of the older French chivalric, aristocratic romances for a lower social class: although they are derivative, the English romances are distinct in their strategic borrowing of older material, meant for another social milieu but modified by the increasing favour in which the religious piety of the heroes and heroines is viewed. Together with the new interest in a specifically English lay piety persisted the older attitudes of chivalry and courtly romance. The Auchinleck MS, comprising romances and other items (*c.* 1340), is a good example of a production prepared by what has been thought to have been a commercial scriptorium for sale to the growing London bourgeoisie.[71] They wanted English romances on the model of the French. The Auchinleck English romances mark the rising social status of the urban 'middle class' and of the English language, and they indicate a simultaneous interest in religious and didactic material.[72] Likewise, the kinds of works Trevisa translated into English were symptomatic of a more widespread interest in current political and ecclesiastical problems; more readers appear to have been concerned with whether the state should be governed by churchmen or by administrators, and they queried the role of the parish priest in contrast to the wandering mendicant friar.

The increasing number of English translations of French and Latin works paralleled similar trends in France. Charles V had a library of French translations of Latin works made for him.[73] The Benedictine Petrus Berchorius (Bersuire) had been asked to translate all the known books of Livy. Nicole Oresme translated Aristotle. The Bible and its glosses, St Augustine's *City of God* and his *Soliloquies*, Boethius's *Consolation of Philosophy*, John of Salisbury's *Policraticus*, were all rendered into French, as were Petrarch's *Dialogues* and a host of astrological and medical works. Somewhat later, the library of Charles of Orleans (1391–1465), housed at the Château of Blois, was almost entirely of French translations.[74] The vernacular was increasingly becoming the means to ancient scholarship and contemporary entertainment for the literate, aristocratic Frenchman who was not an ecclesiastic. Some of these French translations crossed the Channel because the English court was bilingual, but English translations remained localized in English collections and came to reflect the local interests of that part of society that was only just beginning to record its own voice.

The nature of English writing

Hence, two categories of specifically English works emerged in the fourteenth century: there were those texts written for spiritual edification and social reform, and those written for entertainment. The former group included numerous guides to godliness and spiritual perfection, translations of Latin mystical writings, private revelations of pious folk, complaints about the social, political and religious immorality of the times, and a range of encyclopedic works on natural history, political history and folk medical recipes. The vocabulary employed in these works was often local dialect, testifying to a localized audience or readership. The literature of entertainment and delight, on the other hand, included romances which were often highly derivative from French models, saints' biographies and chivalric or military treatises. The vocabulary employed by the latter, in particular, owed much to a highly technical chivalric French, as does some of the poetry of the alliterative revival, particularly when it delights in the technical details of battle borrowed from the

French.[75] The category of entertainment literature, therefore, had stronger links with an older French literature and a thirteenth-century social ethic. The category of edifying literature, however, frequently set up contemporary spiritual and social ideals and compared these with current spirituality to find the present state of affairs wanting. Chaucer's works displayed a genius in uniting these two traditions. The contemporary sermon literature was an important influence on edifying literature in general, and on Chaucer in particular, and it is in this area that much recent research has shed important light.[76] From thence emerged a vernacular literature of social unrest which began with an analysis of the spiritual ills of a troubled, divided and corrupt international Church as well as a denial of spiritual duties in favour of secular reward on the local level.

One particularly good and highly developed example of such literature is, of course, *Piers Plowman*. By the time Langland wrote it he was able to reject the specialized vocabulary of the West Midlands alliterative poetry but could have been influenced by alliterative prose. He appealed consciously to a wider audience that was not localized by dialect peculiarities. Writing in a less formal style, Langland developed a vocabulary that could cope with contemporary theological and social issues, and he thereby influenced later writers of the southern half of the country who were themselves to deal with religious and social reform, like the authors of *Pierce the Ploughman's Crede*, *Richard the Redeless* and *Mum and the Sothsegger*.

By 1400, then, the principal difference between courtly readers and 'middle-class' readers may be said to have been largely one of taste rather than literacy. Where the romance literature spoke more in terms of static ideals pertaining to a former golden age, drawing heavily on gallicisms, the literature of edification spoke of current spiritual and social reform, developing a specifically English vocabulary to suit its polemical purposes. Both categories reflected a piety and concern for social order that was characteristic of the interests of a rising urban 'middle class' and rural gentry.

London and the changing social structure

The picture of London and other urban centres growing in wealth and national importance that is drawn from the documents, shows crowded scenes of buying and selling, legal procedures to regulate trade and the emergence of an urban nationalism that won cities like

Bristol, York, Newcastle, Norwich and Lincoln not only a corporate identity by law, but also a practical independence from the rural counties in which they were located. Royal officials not to the liking of the burgesses or not of their choice were gradually excluded from urban self-government. Replacing royal appointments were local men: Bristol, for instance, was to have its own sheriff, and by 1373 was effectively recognized as a borough incorporate, a prosperous port city, now exempt from external interference 'both by land and sea'. Confidence in self-government, and in a knowledge of the law and custom of the land, marked the wealthy 'middle class' of these cities.[77] A number of English poems written in notable regional dialects originated in the north and south of the West Midlands – Gloucestershire, Lancashire, Bristol – frequently moulding a new, socially conscious message within an older, traditional, but modified alliterative style. Some, like *Sir Gawain and the Green Knight*, were consciously courtly and probably written for a local magnate with a family and manor in south-west Lancashire. Others, like *Piers Plowman* and *Richard the Redeless/Mum and the Sothsegger*, claimed a wider public, among whom were the 'middle classes' of the cities, devout and politically active.

This may be illustrated in the following way. Shortly after Richard's deposition in 1399, a Bristol man wrote in the dialect of the south-west Midlands an alliterative poem in which he tells how he longed to write a treatise to inform and advise the king about the misrule in his kingdom.[78] This poem would teach patience and would counsel the king and the lords to 'be war of wylffulnesse lest wondris arise'. The author has a grievance regarding the law and the current interferences with settled customary procedure. 'How difficult it was for the poor to bring suits against the rich, and how complicated the civil law procedure proved in contrast to the older customary law.'[79] The author of this poem, which is generally called *Mum and the Sothsegger* (the first part of which was originally printed under the appropriate title *Richard the Redeless*, now believed to be an earlier, separate poem (*c.* 1399)),[80] claimed his devotion and pity for the young Richard in troubled times, and he wrote, at least in the poem's first part, to aid him or any king in governing, 'if he were lerned on the langage'.

And every Cristen kyng that ony (croune) bereth
So he were lerned on the langage my lyff durst I <u>wedde</u>　　　　　wager
ȝif he waite well and the wordis and so werche therafter,　　　　　if
(There <u>nys</u> no governour on the grounde ne sholde gye him the better)　　is no

For all is tresour of the trinite that turneth men to gode
And as my body and my beste oute to be my liegis
So rithffully be reson my <u>rede</u> shuld also,   counsel
For to conceill, and I cou3the my kyng and the lordis;   if I could
And ther-fore I [fondyd] with all my fyue wyttis
To traveile on this tretis to teche men therafter
To be war of wylffulnesse lest wondris arise.

Richard the Redeless (*Mum*), ll. 43–52

Conscious of his body and horse belonging to his king, according to feudal law, so, he argues, his advice and counsel ought to belong to the king as well. This is no small presumption on the part of a subject, be he countryman or urban dweller, writing openly in English rather than presenting a case in Parliament; he was not ostensibly a clergyman, from whom moralizing advice would be customary if not excusable. The background to his desire to advise royalty (more of which we shall see in the next chapter, on the literature of social unrest) was, at least in part, the increasing independence of provincial cities which became some of Richard's strongest opponents. Bristol burgesses proved so hostile to royal financial exactions that Bristol castle was surrendered without battle to Henry Bolingbroke, making the latter's victory and Richard's downfall inevitable.[81] Doubtless, urban officials as well as country landowners felt they were the appropriately informed citizens to counsel the king, at least in conjunction with the customary counsel of the nobility. London history also shows this to be the case, as do the events of the Good Parliament of 1376, when the knight from Herefordshire, Peter de la Mare, spoke for the Commons to advise the king of their antagonism towards his counsellors.[82]

The desire of the author(s) of *Richard the Redeless/Mum and the Sothsegger* to advise the king and council recalls the story told in Walsingham's *Chronicon Angliae* of a dream of Sir Thomas Hoo, member of the Commons for Bedfordshire.[83] He fell asleep one evening during the early days of the Good Parliament while thinking 'how or by what means the king could be restored to a more correct life and to employ sounder counsel, and how the abuses hitherto current in the kingdom might be utterly rooted out'. He dreamt he was in discussion with other knights in the Westminster Abbey Chapter House, when he saw seven gold coins on the pavement. A monk explained these as the seven gifts of the Holy Spirit, given to the knights 'for the utility and reformation of the state of the kingdom'. The *Chronicon Angliae*, whose monastic author was hostile to the third estate, assumes that it was neither the lords nor the burgesses but the knights who took the lead in this parliamentary reformation. But seen more dispassionately, it was the resistance to taxation and a group interest in urban freedoms that united the representatives of the merchants and burgesses; and it has been argued that the knights, without a parliamentary policy of their own, merely adopted the grievances of this 'middle class', and presented them.[84]

Our understanding of the changing social structure of this period of the late Middle Ages comes, as we have already seen, from two types of contemporary sources: the records left behind by administrative or judicial action at the local, manorial or central government level, and the imaginative literature of the period. Those who were literate in English, if not also in either French or Latin, contributed to both types of sources in different ways, either as writers or readers. On the one hand, some were authors of the literature, writing for moral and spiritual purposes or for entertainment, and some merely wrote to record deeds of contemporaries for legal or business reasons. On the other hand, there was an extended public for both kinds of writing. Somehow we must achieve a happy medium between reading the imaginative literature as mere sources of social history, assuming what amounts only to a half truth – that Chaucer and Langland were drawing almost entirely on contemporary social life – and reading the imaginative literature according to standards of literary judgement, preferably citing those standards we can discern from the admittedly infrequent contemporary comment. Chaucer and Langland were not, after all, writing manorial court records. But the scrivener Thomas Usk, when writing the accounts of mayoral meetings in London, was not, we assume, writing imaginative literature, except after hours. When we observe both genres together it is clear that more local documents and more vernacular literature were being written, meaning that more people were trained to write and that a larger public was, for professional or private reasons, able to read them. By the end of the fourteenth century, English society had passed beyond the cultural stage where an oral literature and unwritten custom dominated men's lives. Literacy, penetrating beneath the noble ruling class and helping to expand the class of governors, had altered the social structure, as did the reliance on an economy based more on money than on customary feudal dues. In many significant ways serfdom, by which is meant the enforced transfer of surplus labour or the product of surplus labour, was, in fact, dead. Its last but increasingly weak stronghold was among the rural population.[85] But even the small towns shared with the larger cities a sharp functional differentiation from the agricultural hinterland, in that their inhabitants were overwhelmingly concerned with commerce and craft and the concomitant writing down of business and legal transactions, which focused on the weekly market. Literacy was becoming something of a survival skill.

In this light it is not amiss if we recall an insight of early Chaucer scholarship. Some time ago it was shown that Chaucer's Prologue to the *Canterbury Tales* would be more fruitfully read against the backdrop of relevant contemporary social life.[86] The world of fixed ideals and fictional human types culled from old books, an older satiric tradition and horoscopes,[87] was only a part of Chaucer's inspiration, and these influenced him more in the style and form of his portraits than in content. For *what* Chaucer tells us about his pilgrims, rather than *how* he tells us, contemporary society was his model more consistently than literary genres. A venerable tradition of estates literature and satire helped him to characterize his pilgrims according to contemporary social stereotypes of the threefold hierarchy: those who pray, those who govern and those who labour. When he idealized the portraits of the three functional estates of medieval society, the Parson, the Knight and the Ploughman, he held to an older literary tradition and to a cliché social ethic. But by weighting his humanizing descriptions in favour of the very fully represented second and third estates, rounding them out with virtues and vices that were both typical of certain professions and particular to certain individuals, be they fictional or based on real-life models, he created a mobile society, rejecting the static ideal of fixed estates.

The theoretical social idyll of organically related and fixed groups was no longer true, if ever it was, of English society. The village and the urban economy was one of transition. Social mobility was also in transition.[88] Chaucer's success in his own time seems due to his ability to draw on past, highly stylized social images and to reflect them against aspects of his contemporary world. Although fourteenth-century society was a culture permeated by traditional imagery, different elements of the tradition were repeated with a shift in emphasis, corresponding to the shift in the social structure. The overlapping second and third estates were achieving political prominence. There is a direct correlation here with the growth in literacy of the third estate as this class moved upward into the lower echelons of the 'middle class'. The later fourteenth and fifteenth centuries produced literature depicting varied aspects of rural society, treating the two invariable social types, the ploughman and the labourer, as worthy of literary characterization. Much of this poetry developed into an organ of political criticism from below. And when the traditional anti-clerical bias appeared in poems like *The Complaint of the Ploughman* (*The Ploughman's Tale*) or *Pierce the Ploughman's Crede*, it not only complained of the stereotyped laxity and greed of ecclesiastics, but reminded clerks that, although they have the corn and the labourers and ploughmen have only the chaff, the clerks come often from the same class as the labourers and ought to be returned to their original ranking, to 'dig and delve' and 'hang upon the plough' as did their social equals.[89]

Simultaneous with a hardening of legal theory in this period, we can trace a process of rapid social integration among the free and unfree, through intermarriage and the growth of educational opportunities. Social mobility was, it appears, much freer than the law that described and fixed men's status.[90] As we shall see when we look at the literature of social unrest, unfreedom and villeinage had become an outrage because it was an anachronism by the end of the fourteenth century. That the concept of fixed status and especially unfreedom survived at all was due to the growth of the common law, and the antagonism towards lawyers in the literature takes on a new perspective when we observe that society was moving against the restraints set by a legal anachronism. The freeman–serf dichotomy was, indeed, moving into the background of the social structure, and as such is seldom mentioned in literary and other sources.[91] Both in imaginative literature and in the statute law, society was coming to be classified functionally and economically rather than in terms of legal status.[92] Parliamentary terminology divided the population into taxation brackets. Unfreedom and villeinage were simply no longer economically profitable.[93] Nor was it profitable to cultivate lands by customary feudal labour. A magnate did hold his lands from the crown by feudal tenure, but he no longer depended on vassals. His lands were cultivated by rent-paying tenants and he derived his support from his personal retinue and those tenants or landowners who were bound by temporary contracts. However important lordship was in general, many villages functioned without its presence, and a franklin took over the leadership of village society, farming the demesne, collecting taxes.[94] Such examples of the country gentry like Chaucer's Franklin, 'an householdere, and that a greet [great man], was he', took over the responsibilities of local governing:

At sessiouns there was he lord and sire;
Ful ofte tyme he was knyght of the shire.

General Prologue, *Canterbury Tales*, ll. 355-6

Previously he had been a sheriff and an accountant or pleader in court sessions; a pragmatic reader if not a cultivated one, familiar with French and Latin, but to what extent we cannot say.

   Another aspect of the changing social structure is represented by the new problem posed for historians treating mainly political and social documents in the fourteenth century: the official sources themselves are now trilingual.[95] The Latin sources, frequently chronicles written or compiled by monks, are considered the best for political history because their authors were the most highly educated and in close touch with the policies of the ruling class. But for this reason they are the worst sources for dealing with the growing voice of popular discontent, whether municipal or rural, because their authors expressed a uniform attitude of contempt and fear of the lower orders. When Thomas of Walsingham, the monk of St Albans, tells about the 'peasants' revolt' of 1381, he refers to the rioters not only as villeins but as villains, and those who aided them are 'ministers of Satan'. Naturally enough, he was hostile to the rural serfs and the 'free' townsmen of St Albans who revolted against his own abbey. But historians can turn to other narratives for the history of the reigns of Edward III and Richard II; in fact, monastic chronicles seem to have been expiring until the very last years of the century when Walsingham began writing and reviving the tradition. The historian can now turn to the works of secular clerks and laymen. The *Anonimale Chronicle*,[96] possibly written by William Pakington, clerk and treasurer for the Black Prince, and Chancellor of the Exchequer in 1381, certainly shares some of the prejudices of the upper classes, but it is also realistic. It is written in French, by someone thinking in English, by a man of the world, probably an eye witness to London events, and is concerned to tell a story to a general audience rather than to the Establishment. Hoccleve was once thought to have been its author. He tries to present the aspirations of the rioters and provides the fullest accounts we have – names and policies – of the Good Parliament and the 'peasants' ' rising. He traces events to their final climax and writes without comment. The anachronism of the law in contrast with current social attitudes can be safely inferred from *Anonimale*, and the author gives us a view of the lower classes – the third order – that reflects the ferment and violence and the political astuteness of a group that was becoming increasingly vocal.

Such chronicles were no longer restricted to monastic authors or foundations: seculars read them and possessed them – Thomas, Duke of Gloucester's library inventory listed nine of them. But the monastic world was itself changing from outside pressures. Monastic contact with the secular world was much greater than their Ordinals would suggest. The foundation of Gloucester College, Oxford, brought some of the monks to university. St Mary's Abbey, York, housed the royal chancery for long periods. And monastic pensioners, *corrodars*, most of whom had formerly held posts in the royal household, spent their last years there. The *Calendar of Close Rolls* has the rather surprising entry that in 1381 Pierrekin Gyles, the king's minstrel, was sent to St Mary's, York, to be maintained by the Abbey; and in 1389 Adam atte Wode, a sergeant of the king's chamber, was sent. According to Denholm-Young, 'it was these corrodars who in the thirteenth and fourteenth centuries did much to maintain the tradition of literary activity among retired civil servants. . .'.[97]

In what language did the monks and their visitors speak? Were we discussing a century earlier there would be no doubt that French would have been the prescribed language of social intercourse within the monasteries. The Customary of St Augustine's, Canterbury, and for St Peter's, Westminster, forbade both English and Latin in the cloister and chapter house. But the Ordinal for St Mary's, York, of 1390 indicates that a monk would now be trilingual. At confession he would say 'Ma Culpe' and the confessor would respond 'Esteez susez'. Then his confession would be in English. At other times, when no choice of language was offered, he would speak in French.[98] When the monastic compiler copied his sources for the *Anonimale Chronicle* he wrote in French, but the large number of English words and phrases in certain episodes, suggests the scribe was translating from an English original, if not thinking in *lingua materna*.

Chronicles usually comprised transcripts of documents formed into a narrative. The chronicler rarely interpreted material himself unless he wrote of events in his own monastery or was possessed of a particular grievance. Behind almost every entry lies another text, a document, a letter. And letters were coming to be used as news dispatches, circulated widely throughout the country to tell of events in France during the Hundred Years War.[99] Such letters, written in French, were incorporated into chronicle narratives, like the letter from the Black Prince written to his wife Joan after the battle of Najera (1367), which lists all the casualties. Monastic cartularies and bishops' registers indicate how numerous were the documents circulating in this way. The open letter, in particular, had grown into a document of historical importance. It suggests that the close resemblance of chronicles and historical accounts written in different parts of the country was due to the copying of the same independently circulating source, by different compilers. On a wider plane, it also suggests that the skills of copyists were used to broadcast, in written form, national and local news, and the letter was an additional organ for such widespread communication. When, in the late fourteenth and fifteenth centuries, private individuals had taken to writing private letters, as in the case of the Stonor and Paston families, it is evident that a conscious written style had emerged with literary formulae that were quite different from what we can tell of contemporary spoken usage.[100] It is a sign of how sophisticated the literacy of an increasing number of laymen was when the letter had become a means of personal as well as business communication.[101]

The private letter is the logical end of literacy in society. Literacy, when studied in various societies, seems to encourage an emphasis on the expression of individual experiences rather than on those experienced collectively by the group or culture.[102] Literacy also fixes old myths and an historical past, requiring social movements to alter the old social structure which, in a widely illiterate society, would have evolved along with custom to suit the exigencies of the time. In addition to the few private letters of the Stonors, which were in Latin and French, it is significant that English became the vehicle for personal expression. Hoccleve's verses were autobiographical. Chaucer's portraiture in the Prologue to the *Canterbury Tales* is quasi-biographical, and the Eagle addresses the narrator as Geffrey in the *House of Fame*: 'Geffrey, thou wost ryght wel thys. . .' (l. 729). In these instances, as with the standards used by social anthropologists to judge the effects of literacy on a variety of cultures, the sign of widespread literacy was the literary expression of the private, the individual experience, and English was increasingly becoming the medium.

The increasing currency of English used to express political and social matters as well is shown as early as 1327, when Andrew Horn, the Chamberlain of London, expounded the city's new charter in

English at a mass meeting at the Guildhall. The earliest petition that survives in English dates from 1344. FitzRalph delivered sermons at Paul's Cross and elsewhere in English. In 1362 Parliament agreed that pleadings in the King's courts should be made in English.[103] The earliest surviving will in English is that of Robert Corn, dated 1387. When Sir John Knyvet, the Chancellor, met the Convocation of ecclesiastics at St Paul's in 1373 to get them to agree to a relief to help the war effort, he spoke in English, presenting the King's case for financial aid. The Archbishop then preached in Latin, followed by the Bishop of London, Simon Sudbury, expounding 'more clearly in the vernacular' the need for a subsidy.[104] Perhaps the most interesting note was struck in the opening speech of the Hilary Parliament of January 1377, when the Chancellor, Robert Ashton, reminded members that the French were once again preparing for war. With the Spaniards, Scots and other enemies, the French 'make us surrounded on all sides so that [they] can destroy our lord the king and his realm of England, and *drive out the English language*'. This repeats Edward III's speech to the Commons, where he claimed that the French King Philip was resolved to destroy the English language and to occupy England. And this threat was also revived at the Merciless Parliament of 1388.[105]

Perhaps one last source to which we can turn for evidence of the changing structure of fourteenth-century society comprises the documents that illustrate the development of the London gilds.[106] For it is the history of the crafts that shows how early sheriffs and city chamberlains first dealt in skins for the royal wardrobe; how mercers became mayors, vintners, woolmongers and grocers became aldermen. Here is the 'haute bourgeoisie' that came to expand the governing class and on whom royalty had come to depend as its life blood. Across fourteenth-century Europe, the increasing organized power of the craft gilds frequently placed in their hands the whole power of municipal government. By the mid-fourteenth century in London, it was already customary to select the lord mayor from one of the major craft gilds, just as, earlier in the century, the crafts were made the main avenue to citizenship. Chaucer describes such a group of gild members aspiring to the position of aldermen:

An Haberdasher and a Carpenter
A Webbe, a Dyere and a Tapycer –   weaver; tapestry weaver
And they were clothed alle in o lyveree
Of a solempne and a greet fraternitee . . .

Well semed ech of hem a fair burgeys
To sitten in a yeldhall on a deys.
Everich, for the wisdom that he kan
Was shaply for to ben an alderman.
For catel hadde they y-nogh and rente
And eek hir wyves wolde it wel assente;
And elles certeyn were they to blame.
It is ful fair to been <u>ycleped</u> 'madame'   called
And goon to vigilies al bifore
And have a mantel roialliche <u>ybore</u>.   carried

General Prologue, *Canterbury Tales*, ll. 361–78

The typical member of a fourteenth-century gild was a freeman of the city, not a day labourer. He was most often a well-to-do shop-keeper or tradesman. Although he was required to go through an apprenticeship of several years, when he was made a master crafts-man he rose in the social scale, particularly as trade increased. As early as 1312, the mayor and aldermen noted that London ought to be governed by men engaged in trades and handicrafts. The wealth-ier tradesmen, originally drawn from the more successful crafts-men, attempted to procure charters that gave them monopolies over wholesale trade. By levying gild entrance fees beyond the reach of smaller craftsmen, they were able to gain control over civic life. In 1319, London obtained a new charter that confirmed its existing liberties but also ensured that no man of English birth, and no English merchant of any 'mistery' or craft gild, was to be admit-ted to the city without the security of six reputable men of that gild. This new 'middle class', while attacking the privileged few, yet sought to entrench its own status. On the continent, in particular in northern Italy, the governing power passed into the hands of the wealthiest traders and manufacturers, creating from an originally democratic form of government in the gilds themselves an openly plutocratic system, frequently in alliance with the nobility. In Lon-don, the wholesale traders and the wealthy craftsmen accounted for only a relatively small minority of the city's work force. Their charters aimed at destroying the free street markets and indepen-dent hawkers who served the needs of the poorer population. But the members of the gilds themselves ranged widely in wealth, as is evident from tax assessments. With financial matters becoming more significant than birth, the upper level of the new merchant aristocracy was not entirely a closed circle, and those with the funds could buy their way in.

The development of the gilds began in most cases with the establishment of fraternities, coming into existence independently of civic or royal authority, exercising control of their trades at their own discretion and operating, at first, as religious societies, quite secretly. When their records emerge in the fourteenth century, they appear to be sanctioned either by the Church or by civic authorities. Many registered their ordinances in the court of the Commissary of London to secure their enforcement by the spiritual arm of the law. They operated ostensibly as friendly societies, relieving the poor and ill among their members and supporting chantries for deceased members. In early cases of royal or civic incorporation, the grant of liberties was addressed to men of the particular craft, but the body endowed with the legal personality was the fraternity with prominence given to its religious or benevolent motives. One of the means to wealth and power was for successful craftsmen or traders to buy up tenements or to deal with the king's business, either farming taxes or dealing directly with the purchase of the king's wines on behalf of the king's butler. By the mid fourteenth century at least twelve great gilds, with special liveries, were ultimately responsible for the election of the mayor from their midst. By the middle of Edward III's reign, they were replacing foreigners as money lenders and traders, developing a positive hostility to alien merchants not under their control.

During Richard's reign there were great conflicts between the victuallers' gilds and those of the manufacturers. The Calendar Books, letters G and H, tell the story of widescale corruption and price fixing,[107] also recalled in *Piers Plowman*.[108] And when the Good Parliament revealed that certain London merchants were lending money to the crown with exorbitant profits to themselves, men like Richard Lyons were fined and imprisoned, and the call was out for aldermanic reform.[109] The battle for gild control of the city government continued to the end of the century with the manufacturers achieving a revolution in city government under the draper mayor John of Northampton. Northampton had his warehouse and dwelling on the south side of the Thames, and he owned vast properties in the area, had a brew-house, a dye-house and shops throughout the city. His followers were the mercers, drapers, tailors, goldsmiths and the lesser crafts – in fact, the little group of 'haberdasher, carpenter, webbe, dyer and tapycer' mentioned by Chaucer. The reformers appointed a committee to alter the city ordinances especially regarding the sale of food, particularly fish.

Thomas Usk, as scrivener, was present at their meetings in the tavern of John Willingham in the Bowe. The tide turned several years later and the Grocers and Fishmongers seized power, and John of Northampton's Jubilee Book, which aimed at ensuring free trade in food, was eventually burned. The counter-revolution led by the grocer Nicholas Brembre was successful only until the Merciless Parliament tried and hanged him for involving himself and his party in financial loans to the crown in return for charters granting mono-polies, and for throwing in his lot with Richard's increasingly 'absolutist' policies. Northampton, his political career ended, was still a hero, although forbidden to come within eighty miles of London; he died peacefully in 1398.

Enough has been said to gain some idea of the power and wealth of the 'middle class' of London and their relations with a financially dependent nobility. The Goldsmiths' records of 1380 mention a feast they gave to which were invited Lady Isabel and her daughter, the Countess of Oxford, the Lord Latimer, the Grand Master of St John's, Clerkenwell, and the mayor, along with six other high-ranking citizens. It cost the wardens greatly.[110] Such feasts of city merchants and traders compared favourably with the luxury, style and expense of those given by great magnates, and they were not without their literary interest. The Grand Feste du Pui, a fellowship which seems to have had an international membership of urban merchants, was founded to 'honour God, St Mary and all saints, the king and barons, for safeguarding of loyal friendship so that London may be renowned for all good things, and peace and honour, gentleness and cheerful mirth are maintained'.[111] The yearly feast focused on the election of a prince, and a crown was awarded to the best song, a copy of which was attached to the blazon of the new prince's arms in the hall. The Feste, like other gilds, had a common box, provision for poor members, and paid a special chaplain to sing masses for the deceased. After an elaborate repast, the members of the Feste rode through the city, the poet laureate riding between the old prince and the new.

With merchants as literary patrons a new age had begun in which civic responsibility depended on literacy – pragmatic and cultured. It became suitable that the 'middle class' commission books and that scriveners, from 1373, when making 'wills, charters, and all other things touching the said craft' put their own names to the deeds that they made 'so that it is known who had made the same'.[112] Not only did they identify themselves, but they ensured that scriveners were Englishmen. Foreigners, not members of the gild, were to be prevented from setting up open shops for they were held to be ignorant of the 'science' of the craft and sent to the pillory for their errors, 'to the great slander and shame of all the good men enfranchised of the said craft'.[113] This is not to say that foreign scriveners knew no English, but that they were ignorant of the English use of formulae and the particular method of writing French and Latin wills and charters, according to English usage. By 1392 scriveners were so overworked that their shops remained open on Sunday, to the consternation of the Bishop of London who insisted that they alter their statutes.[114] The composition of legal and business documents in a world of finance, trade and international politics threatened to take precedence over the traditional way of spending Sundays hearing sermons and worshipping.

Other traditions were also changing. The former role of the minstrel, the singer of tales, was gradually being replaced by the private reader or the raconteur, who read what someone else had written. *Wynnere and Wastoure*, probably the oldest poem of the alliterative revival (dated 1352),[115] records the growing differentiation between the poet and minstrel to the detriment of the latter. 'Once there were lords who loved to hear':

Makers of myrthes, that matirs couthe fynde,
Wyse wordes with-inn, that writen were neuer
Ne redde in no romance that ever <u>renke</u> herde.   man

Wynnere and Wastoure, ll. 20–3

We are told that 'now mere children who never wrote three words of their own, but who tell jokes or repeat the poetry of others, are praised far more than the man who "makes" himself'. There is an implication here that the minstrel represented an earlier tradition of illiteracy or oral memory similar to the illiteracy of epic singers; his method of composition was different from that of the literary poet. The result of the replacement of the minstrel by the poet was that the poet now wrote to be read as well as heard, and his audience was not limited to the lords who loved to hear 'makers of mirth'. With the growth of vernacular literacy and the opportunities for lay education, written poetry was being used with increasing frequency as one important means of broadcasting general attitudes to poverty and labour, to the theoretically fixed social hierarchy, to corruption among the ruling classes and the clergy. In other words, what was previously described as the category of spiritual edification and social reform was an ever-expanding one, and English verse and prose increasingly became widespread vehicles of education and incitement to change as well as 'mirrors of contemporary man'.

3 The literature of social unrest

When Lewis de Beaumont was consecrated Bishop of Durham it was reported that he was illiterate, meaning that he knew little or no Latin, and this was widely taken as a joke by contemporaries, because he was a *miles illiteratus*, a knight who could not read. As Denholm-Young commented, 'even in Edward III's reign most knights were expected to put up a better show than that'.[1] The *Lanercost Chronicle* describes Earl Guy of Warwick as *bene literatus* and this, according to McFarlane, meant more than that he was able to read and write.[2] When the nobility was charged with illiteracy, it meant rather that they lacked a university degree. Indeed, by the second half of the fourteenth century roughly one in twenty of the population comprised the class just below the knighthood, the 'country gentry'. Such gentlemen, their numbers swelled by the recent rise of the squirearchy, were also expected to be literate because many of them were sent to the nearest school and then on to Oxford and Cambridge or London to read law or be apprenticed to a merchant. The law of primogeniture forced the less endowed younger sons of the gentry to become merchants or lawyers, or take holy orders. There is little doubt such men could read and write. Along with the gentry, the sons of franklins (what later would be called yeoman farmers) and esquires could be said to be the rulers of the nation, for to them was entrusted the daily administration of the realm.[3] It is not insignificant, therefore, to find that the 'peasants' revolt' of 1381 attacked lawyers[4] and landlords rather than the knightly *per se*. It was not only the older landowning monasteries, but the newer country gentry serving as tax collectors and rent-collecting landlords, as well as the upper reaches of the moneyed urban 'middle class', who were hated by the rural and urban poor. Chaucer, when not living in London as a King's squire, lived the life of just such a country gentleman in Somerset and Kent.[5] Gower was certainly one. Court squires, even from the reign of Edward I and more so thereafter, were administrative, unwarlike

men, and there was an expanding group of professional civil servants who were not clerks. Denholm-Young lists them as feodaries,
cooks, castelans, purveyors to the king's household, masons, sur-
veyors, whose pay was often equal to that of the knight bachelor.[6]
Their work frequently demanded a relatively high level of literacy.
Many of the country gentry, at least from the reign of Edward III,
were experienced administrators, rising lawyers, prosperous
businessmen, and some of these collected in the Commons as MPs.
McFarlane noted that, at this level, they did not feel any great awe in
the presence of the king and lords. 'Though few, they preserved
continuity in the frequent and short-lived parliaments of the fourteenth century.'[7] Indeed, few such country gentry were not in some
way employed in local government, and although not all of these
knights of the shire were the rich, top few, there remained a nucleus
of such men in every Parliament, 'skilled in business and ripe in
counsel'. 'If these men were independent and outspoken in criticism, and swayed their fellow knights and burgesses, it is surely no
matter for surprise. . . . Their existence forbids us to divide that
society into powerful barons on the one hand and humble commons
on the other, into leaders among the peers and led among the
knights,' observed McFarlane.[8] Although there is a lack of accord
between the terminology that defined status at court and that which
defined rank in provincial life, the country gentry who were not
returned to Parliament, and the free tenant farmers – the franklins
of the provinces – were also a literate group. Around the core of a
gentleman's household and estate officials accumulated his 'affinity', an indefinite mass of retainers, counsellors, the 'bastard
feudatories' of which McFarlane wrote.[9] Such men were hired for
their skills and were known to change familial allegiance when it
suited their careers.

As soon as we dig beneath the surface of the records of county
archives, there emerges here and there a local, wilder sort of life led
by a selection of rascals, ploughing furrows of corruption and illegality, misusing their status and the otherwise seemingly centralized
royal justice and procedure. Some such miscreants were country
gentry, like the Folevilles.[10] They took on the responsibilities of
country clergy, local landlords and tax collectors. Many had made
their fortunes as mercenary captains in the war with France and had
returned home, sometimes with large ransoms from French cap-
tives. Some country gentry were out-and-out robbers.[11] They
emerge in three dimensions as the subjects of vernacular poetry and

prose, and help to expand an already venerable literary tradition, known as the Abuses of the Age literature, by serving as real-life examples of stock abusers of social privilege.

Social and spiritual complaints

The Abuses of the Age genre is often seen as falling into two categories in the second half of the century: social and political complaints on one side, and religious complaints on the other. It has become customary to treat social unrest and religious unrest separately and each category has become the preserve of specialists with interests either in political history or in ecclesiastical history. On the one hand, the events leading up to the revolt of 1381 are considered with reference to poll tax returns, the Statute of Labourers, political protest in Parliament, the war with France and the Black Death of 1348–9. On the other hand, the problems in the English Church with the mendicants, particularly the Franciscans, the effects of vernacular preaching, Wyclif and the Lollards, the relationship between England and the papacy come in for treatment by scholars interested in theology and Church history. But the poetry of the second half of the fourteenth century does not depict so clear a separation. Instead, it unites social and religious unrest to indicate how the effects of the changing structure of society influenced religious ideals and attitudes to the Church hierarchy and practices, as well as attitudes to the secular feudal hierarchy and local and national government. This sense of simultaneity and immediacy of dissatisfaction with the theoretical and legal *status quo* in Church *and* State, presented in Latin, French and Middle English but increasingly in Middle English alone, by and to an expanding literate audience, requires that we view the poetry, particularly that of Langland, as documents bristling with contemporary issues. Such poetry emphasizes how religious understanding went hand in hand with evaluations of social evils that were seen as incommensurate with social and religious ideals. It has only recently begun to be fully noticed how *Piers Plowman* is itself a victim of the contemporary social and religious crisis and a record of a confrontation.[12]

For this reason poems on contemporary conditions in French, Latin and English are found in all kinds of manuscripts, and the boundary between political, religious, historical and didactic verse is necessarily vague. Frequently, political pieces survive as unique texts, and some we would consider the most tiresome appear to have had the most extensive circulation.[13] Over three hundred English poems on contemporary issues are known, and these have been described as 'intensely provincial, hometown and nationalistic'.[14] Indeed, their significance lay in their appeal to immediate ends, because this was a public poetry inciting to action through a critical description of events with frequent recourse to parody or sarcasm. Of the Middle English poems dealing with contemporary conditions, fewer than fifty survive for the period before 1400; and included in this public poetry are the works of the best known political poets, Lydgate, Gower and Hoccleve, extending into the early fifteenth century. Such men were clearly employed as craftsmen to promote the special interests of those patron classes with the power and money to support them. The poets were themselves frequently from these classes. But there is also a small but trenchant corpus of poetry written by lesser lights expressing a particular grievance against the practices of just such a rising gentry and bourgeoisie, reminding the *nouveaux riches* of their origins among the poor, as in *Pierce the Ploughman's Crede*. Here too social and religious issues are mingled. Likewise, by the end of the century, men who expressed displeasure in the continuing war with France based their complaints on religious grounds as did one Walter Brut, a Lollard with a considerable knowledge of Latin,[15] who in 1391 described himself as 'a sinner, a layman, a farmer and a Christian' and denounced all war as being against both the spirit and letter of the Gospel commandment to love one's neighbour. He gets a mention in *Pierce the Ploughman's Crede* (ll. 657–61) by Pierce the Ploughman hero, who notes how the friars called Brut a heretic.[16] Another West Countryman, William Swynderby, is mentioned in the *Register* of John Trefnant, Bishop of Hereford (1389–1404) as condemning the war, and his views were refuted not by local politicians, but by two Cambridge theologians who defended Richard II's right to attack France.[17]

Two points must, therefore, be made before we can proceed to examine some of the literature of complaint for this period. First, contemporary grievances united spiritual and social abuses in a general condemnation of the age, and social abuses were argued against from religious standpoints just as religious abuses were condemned from social and political positions. Second, the spread of literacy and the greater involvement of more members of society in local and national governing indicates that the 'middle class', if we are to view it as a distinct social category, included urban merchants and gild members ranging from the rich to the relatively poor, country gentry ranging from those bearing arms to lesser squires and humble free tenant farmers. Not only was this middling group expanding in numbers, but its membership had been altered, particularly from the increasing upward social mobility of the third estate, largely as a result of the war. Fixity in social status was not so much a fact in late medieval society as an ideal, and the principle of a functional separation in the social hierarchy carried no clear opposition to social mobility. This means it is inaccurate to suppose that the 'middle class' as a stable social category had an equally stable membership. Indeed, through the further development of the autonomy of towns, the 'middle class' was coming to include an overlap of the second with the third estate. This is perhaps best illustrated by Schumpeter's remark that it is an illusion to suppose that the people in a hotel are always the same people, even when the numbers remain the same.[18] Thus the author of *Pierce the Ploughman's Crede*, and John Ball the renegade clerk who defended the revolt of 1381, may best be seen as 'proletariat' members of the middle group, educated to write and read the literature of complaint. But their sympathy was with the poor – urban and rural – and John Ball was acutely aware of the gap between privileged and underprivileged after he had observed those men, once valets and squires (that is, servants), rising to become newly heraldic squires. These men, in moving upwards, had thrown in their lot with the masters. Thus his 'rhetorical question': 'when Adam delf and Eve span, who was then the gentleman?' Denholm-Young has connected this statement with the rise of the squirearchy, which was due, among other things, to the change in military tactics and the use of such men as military captains and mercenaries after the battle of Crécy in 1346.[19] By the 1380 poll tax followed by the revolt of 1381, franklins (yeoman farmers) had become that class immediately below the gentry and were worth one-sixth of a knight. As a priest, John Ball too may have moved socially upwards, but apparently without losing his identification with his former estate.

The audience for complaint

It is also probably wrong to assume that the audience of such literature was the 'peasantry'. Although it has been queried whether we are justified in referring to the fourteenth-century small agricultural farmer as a peasant in the first place,[20] it is probably true to say that the immobile rural small freeholder was not a member of our poetry's audience. It is probably truer to say that the audience for complaint comprised the lower echelons of the middle class. This means there is an argument to be made in favour of defining a middle class in terms of literacy – which determines social rank – as well as with some contact with at least a market town, rather than defining them simply as those urban dwellers directly devoted to and in control of urban commerce and industry, as was once implied by Henri Pirenne.[21] Rodney Hilton has noted more recently how by the end of the fourteenth century even small towns were functionally differentiated, like the larger cities, from the purely agricultural backwaters.[22] For our literary purposes, it is the split between the rich and poor of the middle group that seems most significant. Dr Scattergood is probably correct in supposing that, in so far as the lower class – the third estate, particularly if we take this to mean the 'peasantry' – was the least literate, whatever poetry expressed their needs and complaints had only an oral existence.[23] But some of these poems, in origin oral, may in fact be those that have been preserved in odd places, like chronicles, city records, legal records and even sermons. Gower, for instance, in his *Cronica Tripertita*, part II, noted that when Richard II avenged himself on the Appellants, 'A song was cried out by the mob in the city':

The Swan does not keep its wings forever,
Nor the Horse its hide;
Now the Swan is without wings,
The Horse is flayed,
The Bear whom biting chains torment does not bite.

The Swan, Horse and Bear were the symbols on the arms of three of the Lords Appellant. Furthermore, Scattergood has noted: 'Whether these are sufficient to give an overall picture of lower class protest remains doubtful; and one cannot be certain of the intention of these verses or even the date.'[24] The well-known early example, the *Song of the Husbandman* from BM MS Harley 2253, although it expresses the bitter resignation of poor tenant farmers oppressed by local officials and high taxation for Edward I's wars, is none the less a work of sophisticated rhyme and alliteration with stanza-linking, written *c*. 1300 by a South-westerner, highly accomplished in his poetic art. It is very doubtful whether it was written by a 'peasant', and it seems more likely to have been composed by a clerk with 'peasant' farmer sympathies.

The literature of complaint, then, while seeming to express the grievances of the third estate, appears largely to be a literature by and for that most fluctuating estate, the wide-ranging 'middle class', newly literate and newly vocal. This 'middle class' displayed sympathies at either end of the spectrum with a strict morality, law and order, religious piety and with quite specific and rigid expectations of how the idealized orders in Church and State ought to behave 'but now never do'. The literature of complaint does not, therefore, appear to be a literature of the 'peasantry' at all, even when it deals with the poor ploughman. Rather, it appears to be the literature of that generation caught in the social shift off the land and dependent economically on urban life. Its treatment of the poverty of the ploughman and attendant social ills is an index of the gradual dissolution of the feudal economy, of aristocratic domination and of the ideal of fixed social status. The poetry of complaint expresses a consciousness of this breakdown, and it is not uncommon to find a nostalgic glance backwards to 'the good old days' when social mobility was at least *perceived* as more static and when the upper class took care of its retainers and poor.

That poetry was a means of expressing such social discontent is not unusual for our period. Not only was poetry traditionally considered the highest form of literary discourse, but it was also a workaday form which came to mind immediately as the means by which a professional craftsman could tell a story or write a political verse tract. Prose, on the other hand, was a specialized and frequently scholarly medium until its range was extended somewhat by didactic Lollard writings in English which had little regard for style;[25] only in the later fifteenth century in the work of Malory and Caxton did prose become significant and conscious of style. But poetry was traditionally the tool by which an author exposed moral truths, and it was the business of the poet to teach by offering moral *exempla* to inspire appropriate behaviour. As Derek Pearsall has noted in his discussion of Lydgate, numerous pamphleteers and anonymous poets were already expressing platitudes about politics, kingship, government, war and peace when Lydgate came on the scene.[26] Born in the last quarter of the fourteenth century, he was to do more elaborately but often less perceptively what had been done anonymously by an earlier generation. Lydgate's great corpus of poetry is the logical extension of the anonymous corpus of political verse of the fourteenth century. While Lydgate was a boy, mature poets were writing both topical verse, which was a response to singular events, and vast *summae*, which attempted to encompass the spirit of the age, like *Piers Plowman*. Langland and Gower were able to establish, on the basis of an already developed anonymous public poetry, the ideal of the 'common voice' to speak poetically about public matters.[27]

Political and satirical pieces *were* composed from the twelfth and throughout the fourteenth centuries, but a glance at Robbins's chapter on poems on contemporary conditions in the continuation of Wells's *Manual of the Writings of Middle English, 5*[28] shows how few complete Middle English works antedating 1300 survive. Quite early on in the thirteenth century and thereafter, professional minstrels had been commissioned by kings to celebrate prospective victories or eye-witness accounts. Somewhat later, in the Anglo-Norman chronicle of the *History of English Kings* written by Pierre de Langtoft, there occurs what is believed to be the first important group of Middle English political songs, and the whole work was translated by Robert Mannyng of Brunne in 1338. As Robbins remarked, 'the sub-verse of men like Langtoft made possible the political lyrics of the following centuries'.[29] What is significant however is that, while the early political verses were commissioned by kings and the nobility, by the mid fourteenth century, if not earlier, the pressure to write about contemporary events in English was exerted from below, and this produced, by the end of the century, a literary equilibrium between French, Latin and English which was soon to be disrupted in favour of English as the lasting status language. Lydgate, following in Chaucer's footsteps, along with Gower, helped to achieve this.

Seven categories of complaint

In what ways were contemporary social and religious events singled out for description, not only in French and Latin but also in the various regional dialects that Chaucer described as comprising 'so gret diversite/ In Englissh and in writyng of oure tonge' (*Troilus*, V, ll. 1793–4)?

First, there was nationalistic anti-French war propaganda which later turned to complaints about the folly of the continuing war with France and the misuse of English wealth to support it. Related to this is the picture painted of the wickedness of the French and the heroism and divine guidance of the English against their effete opponents. This kind of poetry is related to the complaint against the English crusades and the hypocrisy of English lords who lead them – or, as the case may be, do not volunteer to do so, and instead war with France for private gain.

Second, there are complaints against royal advisers and against a corrupt and immoral knighthood, or against urban officials presuming to be lords or who are actually made lords undeservingly. The Commons complain that the lords destroy law and order and that the upper classes no longer conduct themselves in social and moral matters in a manner befitting their station. We hear of how too many men currently with lordly power come originally from the lower estate and, therefore, do not act in accord with their newly won honours. There is a simultaneous praise of the Commons, leading to a third category: advice to the king and his advisers; and there are prophecies to right the wrongs in the realm which are addressed to the king by some humbler countryman. There are also direct complaints against the failings of the king himself.

Fourth, there are complaints against corrupt lawyers and manorial officials interested solely in financial gain rather than in justice. Combined with this are complaints specifically against taxation burdens borne by those least able to do so and, more generally, against the constellation of conditions that led to the 1381 revolt.

A fifth category appears to show something of a shift in its attack by highlighting the hypocrisy of the mercenary friars and generally attacking mendicancy.

Related to this is a sixth type of attack, on the wealthy, corrupt, overly bureaucratic Church, its administration, its absentee bishops, its 'illiterate' clergy, and other kinds of general anti-clerical abuse, particularly against a French-dominated papacy at Avignon. Theologians are attacked as being uninterested in pastoral care and for wasting their time in sophistic and logical disputes to the detriment of what ought to concern them: the salvation of parishioners. Also, we find complaints against laymen involving themselves inappropriately in theological discussions.

Lastly and most numerous are the complaints against Church and State by Wyclif and the Lollards, and the counter-attack of the anti-Lollard literature. These are a microcosm of the other social and religious complaints.[30] In the early Lollard literature, appeals to right social *and* religious wrongs were often made to the king and his 'rewme', that is, to the secular powers. Only later, after 1412 and Sir John Oldcastle's unsuccessful rising, did Lollards come to realize that their notions of reform were viewed unsympathetically by both religious and secular authorities.[31] The ideas of Wyclif and the early Lollards can be taken as the epitome of the general discontent of the age and are, therefore, of crucial importance to an understanding of the context and content of the literature of social unrest that became so much more widespread at the turn of the fourteenth into the fifteenth century. In verse and prose vernacular, Wyclifite literature widely disseminated a didactic religious message as well as political and popular radical views. This was done in a language that, as Anne Hudson has pointed out, had not systematically been attempted since Aelfric. A major charge against Wyclif and the Lollards was their use of the vernacular to discuss theological and political topics, but from the point of view of the development of English as a medium for literature and education, it was 'their greatest achievement'.[32]

All of these seven categories of complaint, somewhat arbitrarily grouped separately above, are brought together in a variety of combinations in individual poems. It is only to indicate schematically the range of contemporary concerns that we may list them in this fashion and so provide ourselves with something of a general overview of the most popular topics expressing social and religious unrest. It will be obvious enough how these themes range widely and overlap when we look at some examples.

The 'realism' of complaint

One of the first features we observe in general is that there is a startling degree of realism in this late fourteenth-century poetry of complaint, which removes it somewhat from the influences of the traditional literary genre of Latin satire of an earlier period. There is so much realism, in the sense of a naturalistic reportage of events and attitudes, that when one turns to the seemingly dry-as-dust records of medieval courts, ecclesiastical and lay, one finds what can appear to be the source material for much of the poetry. Late medieval society was intensely concerned with law and order, with the righting of wrongs and the punishment of crimes, because it had a legal machinery and a personnel trained to accomplish this continually, making members of society at all levels acutely aware of secular and religious misdemeanours and those who committed them.[33] *Ex officio* cases in ecclesiastical consistory courts dealt with all sorts of crimes. Chaucer's Friar's Tale tells us:

Whilom ther was dwellynge in my contree
An erchedeken, a man of heigh degree.
That boldely dide execucioun
In punysshynge of fornicacioun,
Of wicchecraft and eek of bawderye,
Of diffamaccioun, and avowtrye,   adultery
Of chirche reves, and of testamentz,
Of contractes and of lakke of sacramentz,
Of usure, and of symonye also.
But certes, lecchours dide he grettest wo;[34]

The greatest proportion of these cases dealt with sexual offences, but they also included charging people with not attending church, for illicit Sunday trading, for obstructing ecclesiastical jurisdiction, for perjury and defamation. Clerks were brought up on charges of drunkenness, for brawling with laymen and vice versa; laymen were charged for ill treating wives and children; women were cited for fortune telling and sorcery; priests for practising illegally and unsuccessfully as surgeons; others for asking alms under false pretences. There was a wide range of matrimonial cases, tithe cases and non-payment of customary offerings to the Church, rents, complaints against usury. The range of cases is from the highly complex: proving wills of the wealthy and arranging inheritances, to the petty summoning of butchers who sell meat on the Sabbath or of barbers who shave customers at the time of the divine service. One unfortunate man, a certain Robertson of Thanet, was somewhat later summoned for eating too much bread and butter![35]

John Gower saw the ecclesiastical court practice clearly, its corruptions and the ideals behind the practice which were not often heeded. In his Latin poem the *Vox Clamantis* he complains how

the priests' new-fangled decisions declare that because the body has sinned, the sinner's purse should pay. So in these days repeated lust means profits in the account book. . . . Nowadays a judge rages with anger if there is any downright wantonness and he does not know whom to hold guilty of unchastity. If a reckless layman copulates with a reckless woman, the priest shouts out in church and she trembles with fear. Yet if a cleric sinfully indulges in sexual intercourse, nothing is thought of it, for he himself may be both judge and party to his own case. . . . And in such fashion do they weigh other men down under a heavy burden, but how lightly the burden sits on their own shoulders! . . . The purse is as strong as our court of law. . . . Furthermore, the church's positive law is unnecessary for the betterment of the soul. Christ's precepts were set down in a few words and are a

mild yoke. But the clergy's law represents big business. The endless condemning on the part of our law is aggravating and scarcely has any end; for
under the positive law no mercy is freely given without money. [Book Two,
ch. 3; Book Three, ch. 4]

As poetry was taken to be the public voice, the trumpet of
morality, the accepted means of describing the distinction between
the world as it was then – 'up-side down', according to some – and
the world as it ought to be, it should not surprise us to see its subject
matter a mirror of late medieval society any more than we accept
court cases to have been. Poets need not have been lawyers. What
we observe in social and religious complaint poetry is an interplay
between venerable literary forms, inherited from an earlier, more
stylized literature, and a new immediate realism of subject matter,
forging a relevant public poetry that is meant to express the common voice of poet and reader alike, to deal with current issues. It is a
poetry that aims at pointing out social and religious misdemeanours
and morally chastising their practitioners in order to point the way
to a society whose wrongs may be righted.

But such poems are said to be relatively few in number. It is
customary to point out how, in general, the surviving secular poetry
in Middle English dating from the later fourteenth century, of which
complaint poems are only a part, is numerically subordinated to the
religious lyric. There is a problem here in accepting such neat
categories to distinguish secular from religious poems. This is not
only because most problems that dominated the social scene were
taken to have a religious frame of reference, but also because poetry
that was preserved appears to have been collected in larger quantities by religious foundations with the scribal tradition and physical
means to copy and then conserve the texts. That roughly three-
quarters of Middle English poetry, which survives in part by chance,
was religious and one-quarter was secular is also suggested by what
we know of the circulation of manuscripts. There is, however, a
further, somewhat curious observation to be made: it is the rather
long books of Middle English verse that are found in the largest
number of manuscripts: *The Pricke of Conscience*, *The Canterbury
Tales*, the *Confessio Amantis*, and, comparatively, there is a singular
lack of extant secular entertainment like romances. Besides the few
household romances that have much in common with chronicles,
like *Beues of Hamtoun*, *Guy of Warwick* and *William of Palerne*, the
Chandos Herald wrote (1386) a French historical poem about the
Black Prince, recording and celebrating his three great expeditions

(*c.* 1366), as individual heroic acts. It appears that several fourteenth-century romances, particularly those written in Anglo-Norman, in verse and prose, were the works of heralds. With few victories to celebrate in the 1370s and 1380s, this kind of specialized entertainment must have died out.

That few of *these kinds* of historical romances survive may indicate that few were written in the last quarter of the century; but it is of some importance that nineteen out of forty-two of Guy de Beauchamp's books were romances, that Richard's tutor Simon de Burley left nine French romances and one in English, and that Gloucester had nineteen romances out of a library of eighty-three books at Pleshey. These were listed side by side with other more explicitly devotional works. Dieter Mehl has shown that many specifically English fourteenth-century romances were frequently characterized by their devotional and homiletic bias.[36] At the same time it is important to realize that a reader of romances like Gloucester was of the old guard, an old-fashioned courtier, courageous in the French wars and outspoken about the new court modes; a man who may well have had somewhat old-fashioned tastes in literary matters. But we cannot say what kind of romances he possessed: the devotional and homiletic sort of English romance or the older Anglo-Norman type.

Does the fact that fewer copies of traditional romances remain intact, or at all, mean that they were in much use and merely deteriorated as a result, or was it that religious foundations and a new class of pious patrons chose to conserve works even more religious and didactic in tone? Both of these seem likely conjectures, but there is more to be said. Mehl has noticed how those romances that survived in the largest number of versions, like *Robert of Sicily* and *Sir Ysumbras*, are most nearly related to saints' legends. He points out how many of the Middle English romances are characterized by their glorification of a particular hero and are so closely related to saints' lives and moral *exempla* as to be frequently found in the same manuscript collections as explicitly hagiographical works, and are hardly distinguishable from the latter.[37] It is possible, of course, that some versions of romances recited by minstrels were less pious and moral than those preserved, and that the former roused the opposition of religious writers or pious laymen and were gradually dropped from circulation.[38] But what has emerged from recent studies is that the blanket categorization of English romances as either secular or religious literature is not particularly useful. We will have more to say about this later.

Furthermore, an examination of the nature of some of the long poems that were conserved in large numbers, which we would not call romances, shows that these too cannot be accurately classified primarily as secular or religious works. They clearly combine in a miscellaneous and original fashion, social, political and religious themes of evident current interest; some of these longer poems do this more extensively than others. All of them, to some degree, incorporate an element of complaint about the evils of the times. Even the pious *Pricke of Conscience* incorporates forty-one couplets in one manuscript of a complaint against worldly clerics.[39] *Piers Plowman*, in particular, is a poem that is conceived as a *summa* of such selected current issues. Chaucer and Gower exhibit a similar eclecticism in their long poems.

Poetry meant as didactic, social and religious commentary, rather than merely as entertainment, seems to have caught the prevailing mood of the times. It is significant that Middle English romances were themselves used as illustrations of moral and religious principles, unlike German romances, where one can observe certain concrete religious themes 'invading' a primarily courtly text.[40] Thus, as the basis of literature broadened with the extension of the 'middle class' and its patronage, it appears that the newly literate were far less interested in artificial conventions of love, found in traditional older works, than in what concerned pious men of commerce, eager to establish law and order, principles of morality, and peace.

Nationalistic anti-French war propaganda and the changing attitudes of the English to the war

The war was of interest not only to laymen. Responsibility for the discussion of specific events during the Hundred Years War was placed, in part, in the hands of religious orders. Edward III wrote to the Provincial of the London Dominicans in 1346 to inform the Order of the progress of the war and to explain reasons for his involvement in the campaign against Philip of Valois, 'requesting that you will openly set forth the same cause to the clergy and people in public and private sermons and congregations ... instructing them very clearly with regard to it ... and that you will enjoin the same to be done by the brothers of your obedience'.[41] Thus, the poetry that expressed nationalistic, anti-French propaganda,[42] and which later turned to complaining of the folly of the war and the misuse of English wealth to finance it, was often well founded on Christian moral principles expounded by the clergy, who to a large extent were responsible for bringing these topics into the wider circle of vernacular lay discussion. Hence it is of some interest that the patriotic poem on the Black Prince's Spanish victory at Najera, written in Latin by the monk Walter of Peterborough of Revesby Abbey, Lincolnshire, met with no reward, and he complained of its being a pearl cast before swine.[43] But we cannot say that it was ignored because it was written in Latin. Latin poetry remained an outlet for patriotic sentiment well into the fifteenth century and showed, as did the English poems, an increasing antipathy to the French as well as an audience that wished to hear it expressed in Latin.[44] The earliest anti-French poems indicate little of the explicit Christian morality that was to characterize much of the anti-French and anti-war propaganda later in the century, even though these earlier works were largely written in Latin, presumably by monks or secular clerks. They date from the 1340s and 1350s, when England was continually successful in battle against Philip of Valois, and they focus on Edward's rightful heritage and the cowardice and unrighteousness of Philip and his close associates. They comprise a small group, possibly by a single, most likely monkish author: *Epigram on the Assumption of the Arms of France*, *An Invective Against France*; *On the Battle of Nevile's Cross*, *On Crécy and Nevile's Cross*, *On the Truce of 1347*. *The Vows of the Heron* (1338–40) is in French. Thomas Wright noted, but without further comment, that several of the Latin political poems, often written by monks, became such popular celebrations of English victories over the French and their Spanish allies that they were introduced into the schools as books for reading and glossing.[45] In *An Invective Against France* (1346), found in several manuscripts, France is described as effeminate, with characteristics of the lynx, viper and wolf: she is cruel and cold, proud and bitter. The brunt of the poem's virulence is borne by Philip, 'duke Philip Valois', who is fraudulent, an illegal inheritor, a virgin in battle, a monstrous ruler with empty claims to the French throne; and this is indicated by the vessel that once contained the consecrating oil of Clovis, establishing the tradition of regal inheritance, now being empty. Biblical and legal references are marshalled to point overwhelmingly to Philip's unworthiness and to the appropriateness of Edward's claim and the splendour of the English tradition in peace and war. There is little here that one could call religious in tone or message. Instead, one may see this poetry as the negative of the romance: its theme is largely concerned with the villain who is described as fully as is his heroic and knightly counterpart in the traditional romance.

Soon enough the papacy would be seen to be a further threat to the English cause, and church policy would be brought into the discussion. In the various mid-century poems of Laurence Minot (who appears to have been a camp-following minstrel), which celebrate Edward III's campaigns, this time in Middle English, the emphasis is once again on 'Philip the Valayse' and his cowardice in battle:

Unkind he was and uncurtayse,   unnatural
I praise no thing his purviance;[46]

He [Philip] bad his men tham purvay
Withowten lenger delay
But he ne held it noght.
He broght folk ful grete wone,   in great number
Ay sevyn agains one,
That ful wele wapind were;   armed
Bot sone when he herd ascry
That king Edward was nere tharby,
Than durst he noght cum nere.[47]

Bot, unkind coward, wo was him thare;
When he sailed in the Swin it sowed him sare.   affected; sorely
Sare it tham smerted that ferd out of France;   marched
Thare lered Inglis men them a new daunce.[48]

At the same time that he celebrates Edward's prowess, Minot praises the Flemish burgesses for joining battle with the English against the French:

The burjase of Bruge ne war oght to blame;
I pray Jhesu save tham fro sin and from shame!
For thai war sone at the Sluse all by a name,
Whare many of the Normandes tok mekill grame.[49]   much anger

And he highlights the theme of riches and profit to be won by the victors in battle. The French are blamed not only for wanting to harm the English but for wanting to take their goods:

The Franche men said, 'All es wun,
Now es it tyme that we bigin;
For here es welth inogh to win,
To make us riche for evermore.'
Bot, thurgh thaire armure thick and thin,
Slaine thai war, and wounded sore.[50]

. . . Kend it es how ȝe war kene
Al Inglis men with <u>dole</u> to dere;   sorrow
Thaire gudes <u>toke</u> <u>ȝe</u> al bidene,   you took meanwhile
No man born <u>wald</u> ȝe forbere;   would
ȝe spared noght with swerd ne spere
To stik tham, and thaire gudes to stele.[51]

But a boar, Edward, 'sal now abate ȝoure blis'.[52]

In this latter poem on Edward at the Battle of Calais, Minot
inserts verses on the perfidy of the papal cardinals who have
taken up the French cause. Already in the 1340s, the papacy was
being mentioned in vernacular poetry as one of the three great
threats to England, along with the French and Scots. England is
righteous and isolated. The war with France gave impetus to
xenophobic and anti-papal sentiments alike:

The Franche men er <u>fers</u> and <u>fell</u>,   violent; cruel
And <u>mase</u> grete dray when thair er <u>dight</u>;   confused crowd; prepared
Of tham men herd slike tales tell,
With Edward think thai for to fight,
Him for to hald out of his right,
And do him treson with thaire tales.
That was thaire purpos, day and night,
Bi counsail of the cardinales.
Cardinales, with hattes rede,
War fro Calays wele thre myle;
Thai toke thaire counsail in that <u>stede</u>   place
How thai might sir Edward bigile.
Thai lended thare bot litill while,
Til Franche men to grante thaire grace.
Sir Philip was <u>funden a file</u>   found to be a woman
He fled, and <u>faght noght</u> in that place.[53]

Minot mentions not only Edward's noble knights in battle, but
also the willingness of the defeated burgesses and commons of
Calais to pledge themselves to Edward. What emerges from these
poems is a distinction between the relatively blameless French

and English non-combatant peoples and their unworthy leaders, who are united by the rules of chivalric war governing their class:

The nobill burgase and the best
Come unto him [Edward] to have thaire hire;
The comun puple war ful prest
<u>Rapes</u> to bring about thair <u>swire</u>.   ropes; necks
Thai said all, 'Sir Philip, oure syre,
And his sun, sir John of Fraunce,
Has left us <u>ligand</u> in the mire,   lying
And broght us till this doleful dance.'[54]

Starving and defeated, deserted by the cowardly French nobility, the good burgesses offer Edward the 'kayes of the toun'.[55]

The theme of victory in pursuance of the just war lies just below the surface for Minot, and it is the weakness of the French ruling elite rather than of the second and third estates that is pointed out. Furthermore, it is Philip who is said to have sent the Scots David the Bruce as a French ally, to claim England. But he too was defeated, at Neville's Cross, and in the end, as was to be expected, the French provided their Scottish allies with no help. Once again, the point is that the pursuit of unjust claims to the French throne had caused David and Philip to lose all to Edward in his just war with the cowardly usurper. Not only had Philip wrongly claimed the throne, but he showed himself to be an oath-breaker and no ally in crisis. He had contravened the chivalric code. 'But Christ who died on the cross for men's sins' preserved Edward in his just cause, and the English, particularly Minot's heroes Master John of Doncaster and the shipmaster from Rye, consequently 'taught the French their creed' – 'ken tham thaire crede'.[56]

Pride, falseness, treason, cowardice and lust for booty are all ranged on the side of the defeated French and their allies – the papacy and the Scots. Edward and his 'right' are protected by God, who is petitioned further to teach Edward to lead his life well and thus win heavenly reward. Chivalric conduct in war, with its attendant moral expectations of honourable dealings between knights who were bound by a code in which warfare was an ennobling experience, lay behind these vilifications of the French nobility. They are described as not playing the game according to the accepted rules of conduct.

The short Latin poem Wright calls 'The Dispute between the

Englishman and Frenchman' (anon., *c*. 1340) is a flyting which illustrates the growth in hatred between France and England, by emphasizing the various defects in the national character of the two countries. Throwing a curious light on the manners of the times, it shows the French concerned with their vanity, constantly combing their hair, speaking and walking effeminately and generally acting licentiously. The English, on the other hand, are gluttons; knowing nothing of fine wines but swilling ale, their stomach is their God. Although Philip and his noble allies are not singled out for parody as they were earlier, the French upper classes and their culture are ridiculed, as are the English upper classes, both of whom are said to reserve their national brews for the few.

In general, the poetry that inspired patriotism and anti-French feelings was predicated on a code of chivalric conduct in war that, it has been argued, did not dissociate honour from financial profits.[57] If John Barnie is correct, the development of a crass patriotism and xenophobia were characteristic of the common Englishman, involved in the war and at home, rather than of the English and French aristocracy who, to the contrary, maintained an intense caste solidarity until the 1390s.[58] What we are very likely observing, then, in the Latin, French and English anti-French poems of mid-century, is a propaganda expressing the attitudes of an expanding 'middle class'.

Finally, by the end of the century, when nearly everyone was writing in favour of ending the war, particularly as English fortunes had suffered setbacks in the 1370s and 1380s, only a relatively small, hawkish coterie was in favour of continuing it. By this time, that international aristocratic 'caste solidarity' inspired only a minority of war enthusiasts, like Gloucester, to call Richard 'a francophile and no knight' for desiring peace.[59] Froissart attributed to the mature Richard the conviction, now held by most Englishmen – 'les bourgois', 'le commun' and some of the nobility – that the war had lasted too long.[60] After assuming royal power, Richard had started a series of ambassadorial negotiations to establish a lasting truce. In Philippe de Mézières's *Songe du Vieil Pèlerin* (*c*. 1388–9), the attempts at arranging this lasting peace are allegorized. Although Philippe had never travelled to England, he says he knew Richard indirectly through other members of the royal household. Richard is characterized as a white boar, miraculously begotten of a line of black boars – the King's uncles, his father and grandfather. Richard desires peace; but the older 'careerist' veteran knights – the black boars, who have ravaged France's vineyards in the past – disagree. Only some among the knights, along with all the merchants, the 'bourgois', want an end to the warfare, but fear the 'caste solidarity' of the black boars, particularly the Earl of Arundel.[61]

The poetry that expressed at first an extreme patriotism, then a disappointment at England's losses in war, owing in some measure to the minority of Richard, and finally the desire to wind up the war altogether, can be taken to be the voice of those ranked below the noble magnates of the realm. The gentry and urban burgesses not only bore the tax burdens of war but also were no longer able to reap the spoils from the business side of chivalry, as they had done during the 1340s when England was victorious. The Church was similarly heavily taxed for the war effort. It is their combined attitudes that are reflected in the anti-French, anti-war verse, and this no doubt resulted from the expanding influence of an increasingly literate and politically active 'middle class' with the finances to patronize verse and support or reflect national policy. Their convictions were coming to be shared widely, so that Sir John Clanvowe, an intimate of the King, could write a religious treatise that is a condemnation of the chivalric ideals of the age that had been personified by the Black Prince and the Chandos Herald – and which, no doubt, he once had supported.[62]

In the English poem found in the compilation known as the Vernon MS, dated *c*. 1400,[63] which laments the death of Edward III in 1377 and the earlier death of his son the Black Prince, there is a reminder that England's chivalric valour was supported by the 'good commons'. They are likened to the ship of state's mast, maintaining Edward's vessel afloat and on course by their wealth. And the whole was guided by the winds of prayer, although nowadays 'devotion is cast out':

This god comunes, by the <u>rode</u>,	cross
I likne hem to the schipes mast;	
That with heore catel and with heore goode	
Mayntened the <u>werre</u> both furst and last.	war
The wynd that bleuȝ the schip with blast,	
Hit was gode <u>preȝeres</u>, I sey hit atrete;	prayers
Nou is devoutnes out icast,	
And mony gode dedes ben clen <u>forȝete</u>.	forgotten

Once again the proud French are mentioned with distaste, but now also with fear because England has no firm ruler, only an 'ympe', Richard, who, one hopes, will eventually prove himself to be of Edward's stock when he matures.

The Frensche men cunne bothe boste and blowe,
And with heore scornes us to-threte;
And we beoth bothe unkynde and slowe,
That selden seʒe is sone forʒete.[64]

Although such a poem was written during the early troubled years of Richard's reign, it was included in a collection made at the very end of the century, the Vernon Manuscript Miscellany, which also brought together many earlier fourteenth-century texts like the *Ancrene Riwle*, the *Life of Adam and Eve*, a version of *Piers Plowman* and *Joseph of Arimathea*. A closely related miscellany, the Simeon Manuscript, bears the name 'Awdri Norwood' on the last folio, and it is thought that this woman was a relative of the Cistercian monk John Northwood who compiled a parallel miscellany, Add. MS 37787, sometime around 1400. If we may assume that the Simeon Manuscript belonged to and possibly was compiled for a literate woman, and if we take note of the wide-ranging dates of the material collected therein, then it appears that literate patrons possessed collections of poems that were taken to have contemporary relevance even when some poems were written explicitly about events earlier in the century. It is important to consider this when we try to determine literary antecedents for later fourteenth-century complaints which continue to deal with over-taxation, the war and the French in particular, corrupt officials and merchants, popular unrest and ecclesiastical criticism in general. If, as Elizabeth Salter has suggested, we cast our nets more widely for the literary antecedents of, say, *Piers Plowman*,[65] and observe the numerous stylistic and subject parallels between *Piers* and a poem like *The Simonie* from the Auchinleck Miscellany (comprising French, Latin and English works, dated 1340–50, of which more later), then it is also reasonable to assume that those who wrote and read the complaint poetry of the 1380s knew of and were influenced by similar complaint poems written in the time of Edward III and earlier.

The role of the Commons

In the famous manuscript Harley 2253, which, like other miscellanies, is a commonplace book with no apparent unifying principle of selection beyond the personal whim of the compiler, there is a mixture of Latin, French and English works in verse and prose, the dates of which range widely from the thirteenth century to, it is believed, *c*. 1340. It has been suggested that the manuscript was compiled either for or by a Benedictine at Leominster or, what seems more likely, by or for an important civil servant, Bishop Thomas de Charlton, of Hereford. This manuscript contains the first love lyrics in English, but it also has Latin and French social satires and political pieces which are unique.[66] There is a striking example of complaint poetry, *Against the Kings Taxes*,[67] which unites religious and social sentiments in a macaronic mixture of French and Latin verse, of which there are numerous examples from earlier in the century. Its historical realism is extraordinary, and yet sufficiently general to establish a continuity between conditions when the entire Harley compilation was brought together, *c*. 1340, and the conditions obtaining during Richard's reign of the early 1380s. The king in the poem, presumably the young Edward III, is warned to beware of wicked advisers. God is invoked not to allow the king and his followers to perish in their worthy activities beyond the sea. No king, we are told, ought to carry on war outside his own kingdom without the consent of the Commons, whose counsel is necessary if the destruction of a great number of men is to be avoided. The growing importance of the Commons in Parliament is emphasized – the Commons are presented in their advisory capacity, actively pursued through parliamentary counsel;[68] and the will of the Commons must take into account the views and condition of the poor in the kingdom.

Roy ne doit a feore de gere extra regnum ire
For si la commune de sa terre velint consentire.
Par tresoun voit houme sovent quam plures perire;
A quy en fier seurement nemo potest scire.
  Non est ex regno rex sine consilio.

(A king ought not to go forth from his kingdom in manner of war unless the community of his realm consent to it. Full often does one see treason bring many a man to grief; none can know who is wholly to be trusted. Let not the king leave the land without taking counsel.)

Against the King's Taxes, ll. 6–10

Such counsel of the community of the realm would remind the king how, from year to year, a fifteenth is paid for the war effort, and that this is borne by the Commons, who are least able to do so. Thus, those who once sat as justices can no longer afford to do so,[69] and this fifteenth further forces common men to sell all they have, to the displeasure of all. Miss Aspin noted that several of the poet's traits, like his mention of the fifteenth, 'bespeak a man whose sympathies are with country folk', because this tax was a country rather than a town levy.[70]

Ore court en Engleterre de anno in annum
Le quinzyme dener, pur fere sic commune dampnum;
E fet avaler que soleyent sedere super scannum,
E vendre fet commune gent vaccas, vas et pannum.
  Non placet ad summum quidenum sic dare nummum.

(Now the fifteenth runs in England year after year, thus doing harm to all; by it those who were wont to sit upon the bench have come down in the world; and common folk must sell their cows, their utensils and even clothing. It is ill-pleasing thus to pay the fifteenth to the utmost farthing.)

Against the King's Taxes, ll. 11–15

What is worse, half of what is raised by this tax never reaches the king anyway, and the Commons are even further taxed to compensate (ll. 17, 19):

Que le meyté ne vient al roy in regno quod levatur.
. . . Le peuple doit le plus doner et sic sincopatur.

(. . . not half the tribute raised in the land reaches the king. . . . The people must pay more and thus they are cut short.)

Wool is collected as a levy by middlemen to help pay for the war effort (with reference to 1337–40, presumably), and this not only destroys the poor but is also against God's wishes, against sound law ('the law that makes my wool the king's is no just law'), and ultimately against the desire for peace. This desire for peace rather than victory over the French makes the poem sound like a piece written in the 1380s. Lines 21–5:

Unquore plus greve a simple gent collectio lanarum,
Que vendre fet communement divicias earum.
Ne puet estre que tiel consail constat Deo carum
Issi destrure le poverail pondus per amarum.
Non est lex sana quod regi sit mea lana.

(Still more hard on simple folk is the wool collection; commonly it makes them sell their possessions. It cannot be that such a measure, crushing the poor under a grievous load, is pleasing to God. The law that makes my wool the king's is no just law.)

The king's financial needs ought to be supplied by the rich rather than the needy in the kingdom, but the advice to tax the poor comes from evil counsel, for the king is not yet of age: 'est jeovene bachiler, nec habet etatem', an observation appropriate to the young Edward III as it was later to the young Richard. The counsel he receives causes general harm, for it is nothing for great men of the realm to grant a tribute to the king when it is paid for by the numerous poor and simple (ll. 41–4, 50).

Rien grave les grantz graunter regi sic tributum;
Les simples deyvent tot doner, contra Dei nutum.
Cest consail n'est mye bien sed viciis pollutum.
Ceux que grauntent ne paient ren est male constitutum.
. . .Qui satis es dives, non sic ex paupere vives.

(It does not hurt the great thus to make the king a grant; the lowly have to give all, against the will of God. This measure is in no wise good but tainted with vice. It is wrong to ordain that those who make a grant pay nothing. . . . Thou who art rich enough, live not thus on the poor man!)

Nowadays, the poet observes, people are proud and place great store by other men's goods. But these shall rapidly pass away, for when mankind is judged in the end, men shall perish lest they amend their ways. God says to the unrighteous 'depart' and to the good he says 'come' (ll. 51–5).

Je voy en siecle qu'ore court gentes superbire,
D'autre biens tenir grant court, quod cito vult transire.
Quant vendra le haut juggement, magna dies irae,
S'il ne facent amendement tunc debent perire.
    Rex dicit reprobis 'ite', 'venite' probis.

(I see at the present time men giving themselves airs, living in great state on others' goods, a life that soon will pass away. When the last judgement comes, that great day of wrath, if they do not mend their ways they must surely perish. The King shall say unto the unrighteous: 'depart from me', and to the righteous: 'come'.)

Continuing with a prayer for divine aid, the poet makes a perceptive legal point: that when property, even that which belongs only to the poor, is taken against their will, it is, in fact, stolen (l. 60).

Res inopum capita nisi gratis est quasi rapta.

(To take the goods of the poor against their will is as good as spoliation.)

And, even more significantly, he notes that when people have been reduced to such poverty, possessing nothing further to give even for the defence of the realm, then, were they to find a leader, they would rise up in revolt! If we are not to revise the date of the entire manuscript (*c.* 1340), this cannot refer to the popular revolt of 1381 or to the trouble with labourers after the 1349 plague. It must be taken as an extraordinary prophetic statement in sympathetic explanation of what was yet to come as a result of the poor having no legal recourse against excessive taxation (ll. 63–4).

Gentz sunt a tiel meschief quod nequeunt plus dare.
Je me doute, s'ils ussent chief quod vellent levare.

(The people are in such an ill plight that they have nothing more to give. Had they but a leader, I doubt there might be a rising.)

The loss of their property, he says, often makes men 'fools', a nice play on the word, for the fool's courtly role was traditionally that of truth-teller, and yet he maintained his immunity at the price of being taken as no more than a jester. The poor too are fools, powerless without property; and while foolish in acting illegally by violently reacting against those who imposed and collected the taxes, they ought not to be held responsible for their actions, for these were caused by the loss of their possessions. The poet continues in this remarkable vein by describing the realities of life for the majority of men. The market is empty, people having no money to spend although there is enough cloth, wheat, pork and lamb available.[71] He shrewdly notes that a healthy economy is not dependent solely on products but on money, and this has been taken from the people through excessive taxation. He advises the king to turn his golden and silver vessels into money, for it is better to eat off wooden plates and pay in coin for food than dress one's body with silver and use wood for coins (ll. 66–70).

Yl y a tant escarceté monete inter gentes
Qe houme puet en marché, quam parci sunt ementes,
Tot eyt houme drap ou blee, porcos vel bidentes,
Rien lever en verité, tam multi sunt egentes.
Gens non est leta cum sit tam parca moneta.

(There is a desperate shortage of cash among the people. At market the buyers are so few that in fact a man can do no business, although he may have cloth or corn, pigs or sheep to sell, because so many are destitute. The people are not cheerful when money is so scarce.)

Furthermore, he complains, those who are employed overseas, in France, are paid far too much (l. 76):

Lur commissiouns sunt tro chiers qui sunt ultra mare.

And, mixing the spiritual with the secular, he wonders how those who live off others will ever be able to save their souls in the end. Not only is it illegal to dispossess men of their rightful property, but it is also spiritually vicious to covet the possessions of others. Let God, therefore, confound the errors of those who contemplate treason and who disturb the peace for private gain. The poet concludes (ll. 84–5):

E confermez e grantez inter reges amores.
    Perdat solamen qui pacem destruit. Amen.

(. . . and confirm and grant brotherly love between princes.
May he who destroys the peace lose consolation. Amen.)

Here, then, is a poem that reminds us of the degree to which early to mid fourteenth-century complaint poetry was trilingual. Gower can be seen to be its heir a bit later in the century. The poet repeats the glorification of English valour abroad that one finds in other mid-century Latin, French and English poetry, but instead of dwelling on anti-French sentiment he critically focuses on the situation at home. The poet argues for an end to the war on religious and social grounds, a theme that would be taken up in the 1390s. He is most acute in his analysis of the economic breakdown which can and did lead to the social revolt of the lower orders and the wide-scale withdrawal of support for campaigns abroad. He is antagonistic towards the rich advisers to the crown who develop policies to exploit the poor and the 'middle classes'. He makes legal points to bolster his argument as well as arguing spiritually. Furthermore, he understands how the fourteenth-century economy depends on money rather than produce and trade in kind. This is the sort of analysis and the kind of language we should expect to appeal to the literate civil servant who had become so indispensable to town and country administration. This is the kind of statement we should expect to have been appreciated by someone like Chaucer's Franklin, who in the

1380s would possibly be writing something similar in English, when peace was uppermost in people's minds. It is a popular complaint in a learned form, written for an audience with French and Latin; and, as Miss Aspin suggests, it may well have been the manifesto of a political pressure group and therefore possibly written to order.[72]

The message of the political poems from Harley 2253 maintains a continuity with complaints written later in the century. Their themes would be further elaborated upon in Gower's long works in French, Latin and English, and in the social realism of episodes in *Piers Plowman* (A text, *c*. 1360). If Harley 2253 is, as a collection, correctly dated *c*. 1340 and the Auchinleck Manuscript dates from *c*. 1340+, then a generation of poets writing in the 1360s, after the decimation of the population in the 1349 plague, would very likely have used these political poems of the immediate pre-plague generation as inspiration and as models to describe social and political conditions in Richard's reign that showed strong parallels with Edward III's early years.

Thus far we have observed the variation in sentiment from nationalistic anti-French war propaganda to the complaints against the misuse of English wealth to support the war. The popular poetry of these fifty-odd years reflected attitudes we know of from other, in some sense less colourful, sources. But the poetry is more than a mere documentary of political events and social grievances. The use of Latin, French and English, at times interchangeably in a single poem, helped to create a broader vocabulary for complaint and critical analysis of the historical situation as it was understood at the time. There is little use of archaic forms, and a minimal romance vocabulary. This kind of poetry is not backward-looking but is consciously of the present. When, in the fifteenth century, English alone was to become the status language of the politically conscious 'middle class', it would have already benefited from the trilingual attempts made in the fourteenth century to express the 'now'.

Later fourteenth-century anti-war complaint

From 1369 to 1389 the war with France moved into its most bitter phase. There were constant hostilities, with only brief, intermittent truces. The effects on the overtaxed English population of altered living conditions, trade interruptions and losses, of the continuing mortality abroad, were numerous. The war most clearly affected their political interests, but it also affected their attitudes to the French language and to travel abroad, and it inspired a sense of English geography[73] as French naval activity harried the English coasts and three massive invasions by the French were expected. There was, as Palmer has described it, 'no Crécy or Poitiers [to] shed their lustre on the later period, no captive kings paraded through London, and the Tower was nearly empty of French aristocrats for the entire twenty years'.[74] England was gradually driven out of the greater part of Aquitaine and was without any major allies for most of this period. While the French suffered a long war of attrition on their own soil, the English felt it in their purses. Taxation had never been as high as it was during the first ten years of Richard's reign. Parliament heard the increasing volume of financial complaints, at the same time that the crown was in debt, Richard's jewels pawned, and the army abroad, or those waiting to go abroad, remained unpaid. In the 1381 and 1382 Parliaments all war subsidies were rejected – an unprecedented occurrence.

Financial and political incentives to end the war were further stimulated by moral considerations concerning the state of a now divided Christendom. The war between France and England had served to continue the Schism in the Church begun in 1377, with each nation supporting the legitimacy of rival claimants to the papal throne. The French were Clementists; the English, Urbanists. Not only was Christendom internally divided by the Schism but it was also externally threatened by the Ottoman Turks, who in 1371 were already in the Balkans, then Bulgaria, and finally made Byzantium their tributary.

Richard and his advisers were, by the mid-1380s, ready to accept a French offer of peace, but Gloucester, Arundel and the other Lords Appellant acquired enough power eventually to try Richard's advisers at the Merciless Parliament (1388) for treason. By this they meant, in part, that such men had attempted to arrange a meeting of Richard and France's Charles VI to conclude a five-year truce based on territorial concessions that were not previously approved by Parliament. The war policy of the Appellants found favour in the Commons to such an extent that Richard's prerogatives over his inheritance were severely limited. But this was because it was approved that the war was to continue by Richard's financing it at his personal expense with only minimal parliamentary subsidies. The forfeited estates of Richard's 'treasonous' advisers, Robert de Vere and Michael de la Pole, were to be used by the government largely for the war effort. As we have seen, their beds and their books were sold for the war! The approval of the Commons was, however, short-lived, even though the Appellants had reduced taxation, and it was finally proposed that the King's wars be examined with a view to ending them. Another council was to be appointed to introduce general financial reforms. The Appellants themselves were called to account for monies they had received. The final element in the mass of complex factors that led to the abandoning of a hawkish foreign policy after 1388 was the Scots campaign.

Thereafter, proposals were put forward to unite France and England, including Richard's marriage to Charles VI's little daughter Isabel after the death of Richard's first queen, Anne of Bohemia, in 1394. It was also thought that a crusade to the East would unite Christendom, as of old, against an outside enemy, and this would be accomplished by the chivalric aristocracy of the two countries who would, together, liberate the Holy Land. The expatriate King Leo of Armenia had appeared as early as 1384 at the French court to try to establish the cause of crusade in Asia Minor (and thereby regain his lost kingdom) by actively playing a role in Anglo-French peace negotiations. Furthermore, something had to be done with the English mercenaries in France who ravaged the countryside during the intermittent truces. A similar phenomenon of unemployed soldiers roaming lawlessly had occurred in the north-west of England. Such men could be well employed on a crusade against the infidel.[75] As was the case during the first crusade at the end of the eleventh century, so too at the end of the fourteenth an Anglo-French alliance against the Turks would mean not only a new focus for piety, but an outlet for the unruly elements in society who, according to Walsingham, were still opposed to what they saw to be a dishonourable peace.

To modify the English antagonism to the French, built up over a century and expressed in numerous poems, Richard encouraged great peace tournaments like the one at Smithfield, to which the French and Scots were invited. The French reciprocated with an event of their own, in 1389, at St Ingelvert. But this only fostered the caste solidarity of a jousting aristocracy, which had never seriously been antagonistic to one another to the same extent as were the commercial rivals – the lower and middle classes of France and England. After the tournaments, the French and English knights combined in a crusade to North Africa under the Duke of Bourbon. Likewise, there was a Prussian campaign in which Henry Earl of Derby, later Duke of Lancaster and future monarch, participated. A joint Anglo-French crusade marched to help Sigismund of Hungary against the Turks. That section of the knightly class which inherited the chivalric warfaring traditions of ancestors and who were veterans of Edward III's campaigns were able to muster sufficient idealism in the early 1390s to unite under the banner of Christendom against the infidel. The Earl of Derby's Prussian ventures of 1390 and 1392 are well documented, including the names of those in his retinue. Traffic to Jerusalem increased. Manuscripts survive that record various pilgrimages like that of Sir Thomas Swinburne made in 1392. The deaths of John Lord Roos, Sir John Clanvowe and Thomas Lord Clifford inspired contemporaries to record for posterity their otherwise undistinguished pilgrimages to Palestine.[76] Documents record how Charles VI sent luxurious furnishings to Jerusalem's Holy Sepulchre in 1393. By the end of 1394 enthusiasm reached a high point when John of Gaunt joined Louis of Orleans and Philip Duke of Burgundy in collecting troops in aid of Sigismund of Hungary, for this was a crusade that received the backing of Pope Boniface IX. But when the allied armies met the Turks outside Nicopolis in 1396, it is said that 'the foolhardy bravery of the French and Burgundian knights' disastrously lost them the battle.

The defeat at Nicopolis dashed the hopes of Christian unity and proved the helplessness of an outworn chivalric code confronted with the Ottoman power. Nicopolis was the last great international crusade, and the defeat drove yet another nail into the coffin of Christian internationalism.

The last flame of catholic supra-nationalistic idealism behind such ultimately doomed crusading ventures was fanned largely by one man, a Frenchman from a minor noble family of whom we have already heard. He was the tutor to Charles VI, former chancellor of Cyprus, and guiding spirit behind a new order of crusading chivalric knights: the Military Order of the Passion. This was Philippe de Mézières. As soon as the Turks entered western Europe in 1356 and later captured Adrianople (1361), Philippe began a propaganda campaign in the West for a crusade. In 1388, when Charles VI assumed his majority, Philippe expressed to him his hopes for an Anglo-French peace and a united crusade, and wrote his *Songe du Vieil Pèlerin*. In 1395 he wrote an *Epistre* to Richard II,[77] which was less a letter than a tract, in French, setting forth his views, as an Old Solitary, on the issues of the day: a lasting peace between France and England; an end to the Great Schism in the Church; the creation of a new chivalric Order of the Passion to enable the two kings to regain the Holy Land; a marriage alliance between the two kings as a seal of peace. He proposed, in several other works as well, a permanent Christian settlement in Palestine with an administration organized along the lines of the French royal household mixed with a conventual life of a military organization that was required by the environment. He envisaged a life career for many in his new international order, and the spiritual orderliness of this chivalric life would have its beneficial effects on the whole of western society.

Using the dream convention in the *Epistre*, he portrays a curious blend of supra-nationalism and nationalism when he says that God only allowed English knights to enter other kingdoms to punish iniquity rather than to obtain full lordship; for, as the proverb says, Lombardy will belong to Lombards, Spain to the Spanish, France to the French and England to the English.[78] It appears that such national sovereignty was appropriate only for Christian nations! Because Christian kings of Europe have for so long delayed the recovery of the Holy Land while being occupied in shedding the blood of fellow Christians, they may truly be called *roys malavisez*, which is a great dishonour to the fame of their royal lineage. According to the laws, sons are bound to redress the mistakes of their fathers; that is to say, those that can be redressed.[79] Philippe proposes his cures for the mistakes of the past with familiar and wide-ranging medical prescriptions: he seeks to heal the wound of war between France and England. Instead of arguing from an economic standpoint, Philippe ignores the obvious financial advantages of peace and emphasizes chivalric and pious idealism instead. But he does point out that if the two kings continue to make war on one another they will become serfs of all their subjects, and he means this in economic terms.

You will become a slave to the armour makers and all other tradesmen who are necessary for waging war; to your treasurers, to the commons, to clerics, and right down to the humblest of your valets who will grumble that now, because of the war, they must arise earlier in the mornings than usual. Subjection of the royal majesty to the soldiery whose demands are impossible to satisfy, and subjection to the abuse of your commanders are what is in store. Even if Fortunë turns her wheel and you triumph in battle, you have slain many, who, unshriven, will go to hell because of your faults.[80]

The disadvantages of the Anglo-French war are also described in terms of servitude to pride and greed. He completely reverses the argument for the just war that was used in the poems on Edward III's rights earlier in the century.

Some may say that, according to divine and civil law, to recover a heritage, to mete out justice to evil doers, or for the defence of the public good, war between Christians is justified. To these we may reply that if a man weighs in the balance of truth the main pretext for which the war is to be waged, which to human wisdom seems good, but often in the sight of God, because of man's ignorance and lack of understanding, must be seen to be unjust; and if countless ills and cruelties which occur in war, against and outside the laws of chivalry, are also well weighed in the said scales, it will be found that, before the outbreak of war, it would have been better if one king, out of respect for God and to avoid so much harm, had freely surrendered to the other two-thirds of his claim, so that they remained friends, without future grievances over the surrendered claims.[81]

Phillippe's Christian crusading idealism, crystallized in the platform for his new order, attracted the patronage of the French and English nobility. Although some historians have judged his *Epistre* to be too utopian to have been either genuine or influential, Palmer has convincingly argued for the extent of Philippe's influence, as Charles VI's tutor, on the latter's foreign policy. 'Philippe de Mézières', Palmer asserts, 'was responsible for the pervasive idealism behind the desire for peace.'[82] Between 1390 and 1395 he was able to recruit sixty-one candidates for admission to his new order: twenty-four from France and twenty-two from England. Assistance was offered by yet another twenty-seven, including five from the Church. This was achieved through the preaching of the crusade gospel by members of this new order of knights, represented as his Four Evangelists: Robert the Hermit, Jehan de Blezi, Loys de Gyach (who was the chamberlain of Charles VI and Duke of Burgundy), and Othe de Granson (a Chevalier d'Honneur to Richard II and John of Gaunt, and *persona grata* at the Burgundian court, who went with the Earl of Derby to the Holy Land in 1393. He was also a poet and known to Chaucer). But after Nicopolis (1396) their crusading spirit was of little use, and England seemed to sink back into a phase of what many called moral decline.

Gower, echoing Philippe's complaint that European rulers were more concerned with profitable wars between Christians than with fighting the infidel and liberating the Holy Land, wrote (1399?):

The worldes cause is waited over al	
Ther ben the werres redi to the fulle,	wars
Bot Cristes oghne cause in special,	own
Ther ben the swerdes and the speres dulle;	
And with the sentence of the popes bulle,	
As for to do the folk paien obeie,	
The churche is turned al another weie.	

Address of John Gower to Henry IV[83]

Instead, he advises that rulers should fight the infidel:

So mai the knight his dede of armes righte.

And in a Latin poem, *On the Vices of the Different Orders of Society,*[84] he complains of the lack of chivalry and of crusading enthusiasm among the current knightly generation. Playing on the notion of light, he says: the nobility have no light, trusting only in their own power which has led them to ruin. The kingdom's chivalry has lost its light because proud men have been concerned with splendour and luxury. Likewise, light was foreign to the council of kings. Indeed, God has become secondary, a remote light.

Teste paganorum bello furiente deorum,
Raro fides crescit, ubi regia lux tenebrescit.
(ll. 33–4)

. . . Si bellatorum lucem scrutabor, eorum
Lucernae lator tenebrosus adest gladiator.
Sunt ibi doctrina, luxus, jactura, rapina,
Quae non splendorem quaerunt, sed habere cruorem.
Et sic armatus lucem prae labe reatus
Non videt, unde status suus errat in orbe gravatus.
(ll. 49–54)

Sic prior est mundus, et si Deus esse secundus
Posset, adhuc talis foret in spe lux aliqualis.
Sed quasi nunc totus Deus est a luce remotus;
Sic absente duce perit orbis iter sine luce.
(ll. 85–8)

On the Vices of the Different Orders of Society/De lucis scrutinio

And yet in Gower's *Confessio Amantis*, a poem specially written in English for Richard II – for, as he hyperbolically says in the Prologue, 'fewe men endite/ In oure englissch'[85] – Gower is as unconvinced of the chivalric stance of his lover as were his French immediate predecessors and contemporaries, Froissart, Machaut and Deschamps, in their verse. As Burrow noted, Gower's narrator speaks of love service by war and knightly adventure as something alien.[86] He is a private, polite kind of person, 'but definitely not chivalrous'.[87] The *Confessio*, like the long poems of Machaut and Froissart, is quasi-autobiographical and singularly uneventful, adopting a kind of realism that gives the impression of being true even if it is not in fact, and therefore singularly unheroic. It describes its main character in terms which do not accord with the canons of chivalric conduct. Burrow also points out that in the *Confessio* Gower never places much emphasis on fighting and expresses a love of peace rather than of war.[88] This is taken to absurd and comic lengths in Chaucer's *Sir Thopas*, 'where a fight rather conspicuously fails to occur'.[89]

The theme of the lost light of chivalry and crusading zeal continued into the fifteenth century, when Hoccleve was to make similar observations in his *Regement* (l. 5436). Although he too would argue, somewhat anachronistically, for a 'merritorye werrying', not between Christians but against the 'Sarazins', his complaint against the times was to no avail.[90]

But does this disappointment in England's chivalry reflect only a late fourteenth-century attitude? The seeds, I believe, were already sown at least a century earlier. If one looks at the development of Middle English romances even of the thirteenth and early fourteenth century, one finds the social ethic they propound to be a striking anachronism; for in the same period that saw the emergence of the romances there was a simultaneous decline of the knight. The romances, very much like Edward III's revival of tournaments, kept chivalry alive artificially, in an archaic, nostalgic atmosphere for what had been. Most of the English romances were, in their chivalric elements, far from depicting a confrontation with any specific element of the present reality. They were, instead, generally homiletic in intention, exemplifying moral truths by depicting events of a timeless past, in the guise of fairy tales.[91] It has been noted how they came increasingly to show numerous parallels both with Saints' Lives and Legends, and with selected aspects of historical chronicles. Where the change in literary taste appears to have taken place is in the gradual highlighting of the anti-hero in the later fourteenth century, who is pious, moral, not particularly heroic or self-assured but more often simple, questioning, a *viator* in matters of love, warfare and spiritual salvation. It appears that a psychological realism was of greater interest to author and audience alike towards the end of the century, and the romance genre in its older form died out for some time.

The relationship of romance to complaint

In the earlier fourteenth century political verse that was contemporaneous with some of the romances, we can perhaps see characteristics that are similar to the narrative techniques used by the Middle English romance; and these techniques survived to be used in an eclectic manner by poets at the end of the century, in what Burrow wants to distinguish as Ricardian verse. Both romances and complaint verse owe something to the minstrel's tags and biddings for silence of an oral literature that would also be used by Chaucer and the *Gawain* poet, who were decidedly not minstrels. Comparing the romance narrative technique with that of the political poetry, the difference is primarily one of *degree* when we consider what we have called the greater 'realism' of the socially and politically critical verse. The miraculous of the romance is entirely dropped in favour of natural prowess and God's grace. But as often happens in the romances, the poet intrudes: Minot works his name into a line of poetry and speaks of his own evaluation of Edward and Philip: 'I praise no thing his purviance', he says of Philip of Valois, and then he narrates the great moments of battle, telling the listener–reader the plans and the outcomes of the combatants: 'than durst he [Philip] noght cum nere'; 'the unkynd coward'. He moralizes: the English taught the French 'a new dance', 'they taught them their crede'. He prays to Jesus that He may join grace to the natural prowess of the righteous English. He attempts to get his audience on his side by reminding them of how the French, with the aid of the cardinals, spoke treasonous lies about Edward: 'and do him treson with thaire tales'. He quotes the 'noble burgesses' of Calais, as if to say, 'look, this is how they saw Philip's cowardice and treachery: he left his own people "in the mire" '. There is a general abundance of the direct address, an inheritance of the minstrel tradition, shared by romances, where the audience was asked to listen and judge.

In the largely anonymous Latin, French and English complaint poetry, minute attention is paid to national or personal characteristics, but this is mainly ornamental when compared with the fundamental narrative line which weaves a story round the face-to-face relationship of narrator and audience. The general impression is of a greater concern with the content, with the events the poet wants to relate, rather than with how he does so. Likewise, the striking characteristic of romances is 'the good story', told episodically with a predominant emphasis on plot and action. The political poet contrasts the expected heroic acts of both protagonists – the English and French – with the failure of the French to achieve their own and an audience's ideals. The French are simply neither chivalrous nor noble. The French, the nobility, later as we shall see the clergy, the king, his advisers and even the fictionalized narrator or dreamer in some of the longer and more ambitious complaints, are all presented as less than what they believe themselves to be. The satire in the poems that present them thus is a normalized satire. What will be exploited to the full in the long poems of Langland, Gower and Chaucer, but which we can trace to the largely anonymous war and tax complaints, is a satirical sense, a scornful comparison of what *is* the case with what ought to be.[92] Using the metaphor in a severely limited and subordinate position, the poems of social unrest and protest are meant to be taken literally. As poems, they play only an ancillary role to the moral message, something I believe we can also say of many of the homiletic Middle English romances. The romances focus on the exemplary hero; the complaints contrast the heroic, the morally right, with those who fail to live up to the ideal. Both genres rarely leave behind in one's memory a striking phrase or an aesthetically memorable juxtaposition of image and sound.

Nor ought we to look either to romances or to these political poems for an account of historical events not elsewhere recorded – in chronicles, or in administrative documents. But the political poems, in particular, distinguish themselves from chronicles in expressing the personal reaction of an anonymous ordinary man to selected public events of the time. And, far more than the romances, political poetry acts as a kind of partisan journalism: ephemeral incentives to action and reform. Where the romance often leaves the hearer or reader in suspense as to the outcome of events, the political poet gives all away at the beginning, reserving any dramatic tension for accounts of the battles whose victories are assumed from the start. His message is more immediate.

It is inappropriate to ask of the poets if what they are describing is true. The politically and socially critical verse is opinion disguised as reality, and in this sense these poems have met Matthieu de Vendôme's criterion that 'descriptive skill constitutes the poetic faculty . . . so that either what is real or what gives the appearance of reality may be described'.[93] Because the romances and the complaint poetry were meant to be exemplary, didactic, and also entertaining, the poet as truth-teller, as the commentator on the particular, often by means of the general statement, was fulfilling an expected role. He was to be a 'réalisateur', a realizer of past exemplary 'real' events, and thereby was to initiate *at least* a passive reflection on this reality (as in the romances), but *at best* his poem inspired action to alter the thus-described 'real situation'. And the 'real' was largely verisimilitude rather than historical truth, a personal choice of events but also a convincing *fiction*, limited only by the poetic form and style of the medium.

From the standpoint of our modern investigation into the veracity of this apparent realism in complaint poetry, it is important for us to find the personal attitudes of the narrator corroborated in non-poetic sources. In the fourteenth century this kind of complaint poetry seems to have forfeited the satisfying but passive response to, say, a satirized situation that was elicited by the minstrel's fable or the romance. It sacrificed the more drawn-out poetic neatness of the general moral platitude of a minstrel's imaginary tale or romance, to the comparatively precise presentation of a life-like situation which was immediately recognized as true by an audience. It is interesting that the shorter English romances, based on stories that are treated at far greater length in French or Anglo-Norman, also abridged their originals by swiftness of narration and lack of lengthy description. Political verse took this further. By sacrificing the length as well as the style and form of what we may consider a more highly wrought and traditional art form – the romance – it had turned itself into political journalism and confronted the present 'reality'. Langland, Gower and Chaucer were to reintegrate such anonymous political journalism into an episodic art poetry that was recognizably written by them, to produce part of a larger picture of the age and its values.

Complaints against royal advisers and the contemporary knightly class

An interesting example which demonstrates the relation of complaint to romance is the poem *Mede and Muche Thank*, dated *c.* 1400 from Digby 102.[94] Using a romance setting, just as the alliterative debate poems, *The Parlement of Three Ages*, *Wynnere and Wastoure* and *The Ploughman's Tale*, do, the flowery wood is the setting for a similar flyting, here between Thanks and Worldly Reward (mede):

In blossemed buske I bode boote	wood; went out
In riche array, with ryches rank,	
ffaire floures under foote,	
Savour to myn herte sank.	
I sawe two buyrnes on a bank.	
To here talkyng I tok hede	
that on preysede moche thank	praised
that other held al with mede.	
(ll. 1–8)	

Although the Middle English romances created a new literary type for a partly non-aristocratic audience – Mehl notes how English romances frequently addressed themselves to 'lewed men'[95] – the hero was always noble and a knight. The protagonist of *Mede and Muche Thank* who is to be favoured is 'a travaylyng man . . . in mene array'. But this does not mean he is a labourer; rather, he is an old-fashioned knight who earns his fame and honour through the hard labour of chivalrous warfare. He debates with a court fop dressed in 'gawdy gren, blasande briȝt, embrowdid gay'. The latter is questioned about how he receives his wealth – did he earn it through good deeds or by lounging at home, and flattering his lords? There is here a pervasive sense of the satirical: who ever asked a nobleman how he obtained his wealth in *Richard Coeur de Lion*, or *Kyng Alisaunder* or *Guy of Warwick*? Here we see emphasized 'the trewe travayle of a trewe servant [who] is worthy hys mede'. The implication is that the poor knight follows the true standards of noble behaviour that belongs to an older, aristocratic and knightly epoch, but the new class of courtiers operate otherwise. Contrasting an older, nobler chivalry with the new form of earning 'worship through glosyng, flateryng, play and daunce', the author has the courtier defend himself as follows:

'Say, felowe, what doth the greue
My glosyng, flateryng, play and daunce?
Shulde my souerayn aske the leve,
Whom hym list to avaunce?
Tho getest the <u>thonke</u> with spere and launce   thanks
Ther-with thou might the clothe and fede;
I gloser wil stonde to my chaunce,
And mayntene my men al with mede.

My flateryng, glosyng, not me harmes.
I gete love, and moche richesse,
When wel-faryng men of armes
In fight, in <u>presoun</u> and distresse.   prison
When thou art old and feble, y gesse,
Who wole the fynd fode or <u>wede</u>?'   clothes
(ll. 41–54)

It is apparent that sixty years of warfare had created a cynical attitude to the 'glories' of war and its rewards. The ideals of honour and fair play were lost to the realities of fighting, prison and hardship; and, as we have met with elsewhere, those who wished to continue the war with France ostensibly did so not out of a sense of honour, but for profit. Warfare, 'the real thing', taught some men to be cynical: to be victorious one need not abide by chivalrous rules. The 'travaylyng man' responds:

Thou woldest evere more were <u>werre</u>,   war
(ffor profyt and pilage thou myght glene,)
Cristen blod destroyed clene,
And townes <u>brent</u> on a <u>glede</u>.   burned; glowing coal
Thy conscience is ful lene;
Thou noldest not come there but for mede.
(ll. 67–72)

This critical realism has taken the romance ethic beyond itself. Not only is it now a disgrace for a true knight to kill fellow Christians and destroy their civilization, but it is indicative of a 'lene conscience' to fight for no other reason than booty: and it is the poorer but nobler and more pious man who relates these moral truths. The 'travaylyng man's' attitude is also very similar to the Lollard condemnation of war. In the heroic romance the pious separation of booty from the purpose of warfare, as well as any mention of the horrors of war, would be unthinkable.[96] The criticism of the new kind of courtier brings out an indirect contrast with a general characteristic of the earlier heroic romance poetry. The earlier poetry steered clear of describing the true horrors of war by distancing the audience from them with a rhetoric of heroism that is not unlike the rhetoric used to retell heroic exploits of the two world wars in this century. If the teller dehumanizes the opposition sufficiently and elevates the protagonists on the 'right' side to the superhuman, there is no place left to relate the countless horrors of war for both sides. The unchivalric experiences of the 1370s onwards apparently taught at least some Englishmen the consequences of this kind of destruction, and this poetry represents their voice. The true hero was hard to find. This useless warring is likened to the kind of wastage and destruction inspired by flattering counsellors who are the drones of the bee hive, reminding us of the argument against Waster in *Wynnere and Wastoure*. The Digby poet has the 'travaylyng man' say:

I likne a gloser, in eche weder	flatterer; weather
To folwe the wynd, as doth the fane.	(weather) vane
3e begeten hony togedere;	honey
To stroy3e that cometh the drane.	drone
Me thenketh there wit is wane	
To stroi3e the hony, and foule hit shede;	shed
Gloser hath brought faytour lane	hypocrite lean
To halle and chambre, to lordes, for mede.	reward
(ll. 57–64)	

The complaint verse, then, strikes out in a new direction from the romance, precisely in its confrontation with current moral dilemmas constituting the 'real' and the 'now'. It is also a personal condemnation as opposed to a cultural glorification of events. These poetic critiques are the satiric underbelly of the romance's ideal of heroism, contrasting with the political virtuousness of the romance's perfect rulers and loyal subjects.

By providing a more rapid entrée into the highlighted events of an episode than the romance was able or willing to do, these complaints frequently show characteristics one tends to associate with prose. What, we may ask, makes some of the anonymous reportage poetry at all? If, as in some cases, the texts are arranged in the manuscripts as though they were prose (Digby 102), what distinguishes them from chronicle accounts of the same or similar events? There are several characteristics that enable us to find the classification 'political verse' or 'complaint verse' a consistent and useful one, and which separate these poems from the wide assortment of Middle English verse. The most obvious common denominator is their collective, socially critical subject matter. The next obvious characteristic is their poetic form, because they are concerned to preserve rhymed narrative reportage which mingles allusions to specific events with homiletic truths and a general moralizing about conduct in the world. The statements are necessarily more epigrammatic if not cliché in verse than would perhaps be the case in an unmetrical line.

Digby 102

The Digby 102 collection, dated *c.* 1400 or shortly thereafter, gives us a clear picture of the unity of such a largely undistinguished, frequently occasional body of complaint verse. Preceding twenty-four political poems in this manuscript is Langland's *Vision Concerning Piers Plowman*, imperfect at the beginning, but then starting in the middle of Passus III, C text. There is also a metrical paraphrase of the seven penitential psalms, and a *Debate Between Body and Soul*, thereby illustrating the religious–political miscellany in which complaint poetry is often to be found. (We can compare the Vernon, Simeon, Harley and Auchinleck manuscripts.) The dialect is Western or South-West Midlands according to the editor, J. Kail. Digby 102 also permits us to examine more closely our somewhat arbitrary categories (2, 3 and 4 on pages 65–6 above) of complaint poetry aimed more specifically at chastising royal advisers, the king himself, corrupt or immoral knighthood, and government officials who distort the law and the truth. At the same time, advice is often proffered in the sort of exhortatory generalities that are common to the 'mirror for princes' prose genre that goes back to the twelfth-century *Policraticus* of John of Salisbury and thence to Cicero, where the sovereign is advised how best to behave and be educated to maintain a just and peaceful realm. But in these poems, representative members of the Commons are seen as the reforming life blood of the peaceful realm instead of the solitary sovereign. The apparent intention of such poetry is a general statement, first in support of the Commons who make the kingdom by bolstering the lords and the Church morally, politically and financially, and then a reminder that the goods and possessions that distinguish the social orders from each other, rather than one's birth, belong in the final analysis to God alone. The Commons are taken to be the mainstay of moral rectitude, and on to them devolves crucial political power.

In a long-winded homiletic narrative that Kail entitles *Love God and Drede*, we read a general warning to men 'that bereth a state' to beware of unjust encroachments on the property of the poor, for the people belong to God and officers of the realm have been ordained to govern according to right and reason. The theme is one that a Langland would have condensed into much smaller compass, drawing the moral from an exemplary episode rather than by means of exhorting imperatives. But here there are twenty-one eight-line stanzas with a homiletic refrain – 'Man, knowe thy self, love God and drede'[97] – to make the point that each man of each estate should be recognized to have his due, and that the rich and powerful should support the poor and virtuous. England is seen as governed by a host of administrators rather than by a single omnipotent sovereign, reflecting what was indeed the situation throughout Richard's reign, and, more generally, describing the transformation that monarchical rule had undergone in the later Middle Ages. The emphasis is on the just administration of law in an extensively legislated kingdom where positive legal enactments were viewed as the secular manifestation of God's law and will.

Eche mannys gouernours
Of hous or lordshipe or cite,
The puple is godes, and not ȝoures,
Thow they be soget to ȝoure degre.   subject
Governe the puple in unyte,
In the comaundements that god bede,
And ȝe wole lyue in charite.

Knowe they self, love god, and drede.
    (ll. 17–24)
. . . Lete no falshed <u>blome ne sede</u>.   bloom nor go to seed
And lawe be kept, <u>no folk wyl ryse</u>. . . .
    (ll. 62–3)
. . . Whanne a fool stereth a barge,
Hymself and al the folke is <u>shent</u>.   destroyed
There as conscience is large,
By wrath or mede the doom is went.
The bowe of goddis wrath is bent
On hem that doth not that god bede.
War wordes of double entendement,
Knowe they self, love god and drede.
    (ll. 65–72)
. . . Why pore men don riche reverence,
To skylles y fynde therfore:
To tyrauntes don hem grevaunce,
To <u>rewe</u> and aȝen restore.   repent
Goode men for love they worshipe more,
That don hem good and help at nede;
ffor god seeth thurgh every bore.
Man, knowe theyself. . . .
    (ll. 89–96)
. . . In love and drede worshipe the wyse.
Be suget to resoun in lengthe and brede,
ffor god seeth thurgh eche mysse.
    (ll. 101–3)
. . . Who that taketh fro pore to eke with his,
ffor that wrong is worthy wo;
A-nother, richer than he is,
Of the same shal serve hym so.
That <u>ȝeveth</u> to that <u>liȝe</u> or go,   give; body
Mete or drynke, <u>herborwe</u> or wede,   lodging
God sendes y-now to tho
That loven god, and hym wolen drede.
    (ll. 145–52)
. . . Let not lawe be favoured ne sold.
Suche maken fals men be bold,
And fals men myghte stroye a <u>thede</u>.   people
Er charite in hert wexe cold,
Man knowe theyself. . . .
    (ll. 156–60)

Love God and Drede

In *Lerne to say wele, say litel or say no3t*,[98] the opinion of the people is the final arbiter in matters of right and wrong; nothing may be hidden from the common voice:

Man may not staunche a comoun noys	satisfy; outcry
Nother for love ne for awe.	
After men lyue is comoun voys,	
In wrongwys dede, or ry3t lawe.	
Who doth hem pyne, who doth hem pawe,	grieve; caress
Eche on telle other, child and may.	kinsman
(ll. 17–22)	

Lords are described as fools, not knowing themselves because they have no way of distinguishing their flattering enemies from their friends, although the poor have such wisdom.

A lord of hym-self hath no wyt,	
He knowth wele, but no wo;	woe
Of pore men he mot have hit,	
Knowelechyng of frend and fo.	
(ll. 65–8)	

Although some will call the bidding of one's conscience merely an excuse to pursue the desires of the flesh, the truth, says the poet, is that the rational soul is a spiritual possession and the judgements of conscience can save a man from 'ffleschely wille' which is the 'fendes knaue' (devil or fiend's knave). While the Church should enable men to mend their evil ways and fleshly wills, some men believe they are forgiven by bribery, or some so defend their faults 'with maystri3e' (mastery, power) that Holy Church fears them and from cowardice refuses to separate the corn from the chaff. Flatterers convince lords that they are beloved of those who, in fact, despise them. Every estate shall be judged as it has lived, for nothing is hidden from God's sight, and

The comoun voys nyl not hele	conceal
But love, or hate, as werk is wrou3t;	
. . . Of al degre, of eche astate,	
After desert the name hath prys.	
(ll. 155–6, 161–2)	

In the 'mirror for princes' tradition the poet notes how a good man is a blessing to a lord, for he is a 'trewe officere', not step- ping beyond the powers of his office, neither stealing nor gossip-

ing about the lord's private business. Likewise, the poet wishes
that there were a statute to make a sovereign swear to what he
was told by his subjects in council, preventing the king from
denying or concealing what he in turn told his subjects.[99] But
flatterers encourage lords to 'passe the bounds of here play'. As
in chivalric conduct, so too in just governance, there are specific
moral rules of the game which structure man's behaviour in a
potentially disorganized world; the game-like quality of so many
aspects of medieval society, depicted in the elaborate rules for
hunting and acting courteously, is extended here to government.
The poet moves on to a moral platitude: that nothing in and of
this world is either fair or valuable, for the world is 'a fals lem-
man that chaunge lest'. After observing the false deeds of the
world, all men are ultimately confronted with the retrospective
disappointment that is encapsulated in the phrase 'had-I-known',
'had-y-wist'. And all that the executors of a man's will shall say,
after his death, is that he may be missed for a little while.

His laste ende is had-y-wist,   had-I-known
When deth hath thy lyues kay.   life's key
'Litel while he mon by myst',   'He may be missed for a little while'
So the executours wol say.
   (ll. 229–32)

The poet concludes with the biblical admonition that there is
one law for all the estates, rich and poor: 'do no wrong ne [no]
debate/ But as thou woulde men ded by the.'

   In *Wyt and Wille*[100] we are once again reminded that what
troubles a kingdom is bad, inexperienced counsel and private
interest, where wisdom is rejected in favour of will.

In kyngdom, what maketh debate,
Riche and pore both anoy3ed?
3ong counseil, and prevey hate.
And syngulare profit ys aspi3ed,
Hi3e and lowe men aby3ed;
Echon wayte other for to kille.
That kyngdom mot nede be stri3ed   destroyed
That leveth wit, and worcheth by wille.
   (ll. 25–32)

The last line, a refrain throughout, recalls the line in *Wynnere
and Wastoure*'s prologue: 'for nowe all es witt and wy[l]le that
we with delyn [deal]'. We are reminded that the poor ought not

to be scorned, as in *To Lyf Bodyly is Perylous* (no. 6), where the poet presents a satirical list of vices in the imperative such as 'to reve [steal] fro pore take no hede'; and 'cause your good servant to be imprisoned'; if these are followed, the poet sarcastically says, 'then wole they drede the bodylye'.

In *A Good Makynge of Iour Delaye* (Digby 102, no. 8) those in power are once again advised of their duties; uniting worldly power with spiritual aid.

That overe puple have astate,
Colege or eny other degre,
Mayntene no debate
ffor synguler profyt of temperalte.
ȝoure rule is grounded in charyte
Aȝ liȝte of lanterne to lede the way.
To gouerne the puple in unyte,
God bad hem make no iour delay.   no day's delay
   (ll. 57–64)

It is better to win a little with righteousness in dealing among the poor than to acquire wealth by sinful deeds and thereby 'helpe not the soule to hele'. Those who are guardians of the law 'holde no pore men in awe/ To storble [injure] here ryȝt or lette here nede'. And those who hold inquests and assizes and receive payment 'lette not lawe fro riȝt gyse [custom]/ Ne mayntene wrongis as master and sire'. This kind of exhortation – that those with worldly power, the masters and sires, are to keep the law – is followed by a similar catechetical list of do's and don't's to be heeded by the clergy and parishioners; each 'commandment' is to be kept in mind if every member of every estate is not to forfeit his heritage among the saints in heaven.

The poem Robbins has called *What Profits a Kingdom* (c. 1400)[101] is entitled in the Kail edition of Digby 102 *Treuth, Reste and Pes*[102] and may serve as a last and superior model of the relatively undistinguished late fourteenth-century type of admonitory poetry on the nature of good governance by kings and advisers, and the duties required of citizens in a just and peaceful realm. The poet begins by pointing out how false reports often conceal the truth, but Charity charges him to speak.[103] Truth, he says, is worshipped everywhere in a righteous kingdom, for justice is to be identified with God. He exhorts all men to be equitable to others, applying the law equally to the foolish as to the wise, and thereby preventing revolution.

Set mesure in evene assise,
The ri3te weye as lawe ges.
And lawe be kept, folk nyl not ryse.
That kyngdom shal have reste and pes.
   (ll. 13–16)

The king, as arbiter, should hear both sides of any story and punish those who are false for their defamations, because falsehood slays both the body and the soul.

Trouthe is messager to ry3t,
An ry3t is counseille to Iustice;
Iustice in goddis stede is dy3t.   appointed
Do evene lawe to fool and wyse.
   (ll. 9–12)
. . . The kyng shulde bothe partyes here,
And punysshe the fals for defame.
Than fals men wolde ases for blame;
For falshed, body and soule it sles.   slays
   (ll. 18–22)

When law is misused and judges conduct their affairs according to the principle of 'mede' or bribery, then 'ffor fawte of lawe 3if [if] comouns rise/ Than is a kyngdom most in drede'. The effect of private illegality has public ramifications: not only is the citizenry harmed, but the misuse of the elaborate legal system inspires active rebellion, particularly in an urban setting, recalling that subjects have been known to judge the social consequences of maladministration and actively reject them. There seems to be an implicit understanding that the 'peasants' revolt' was precipitated by legitimate causes. But when the Commons are led to avenge wrongs, 'thei do gret harm er they asses'. The only guarantee of 'rest and peace' in the commonwealth is for all men in positions of power to act righteously. Otherwise, and with an indirect reference to the revolt of 1381 and the disturbances in London in the 1380s and 1390s concerning Northampton and Nicholas Brembre, mayors,

Whan craft riseth a3ens craft,
In burgh, toun or citee,
They go to lordes whan lawe is laft,
Whoche party may strengere be.

But wyse men the sonere se
By witles wille they <u>gedre pres</u>,   gather in a crowd
Or lordis medle in <u>foly degre</u>,
Let lawe have cours in reste and pes.
  (ll. 33–40)

There is little confidence here in the power of the common men
to right social wrongs. Rather, the poet stresses the influence of
mob psychology, men being led by their wills rather than by
reason to support the stronger party when there is internal
strife. The burden of good governance in a realm where all
estates are aware of the personal consequences of injustice lies
with the governors rather than with the governed. Reform may
issue only from above. However, there is yet another factor to
be considered if reform is to come from within the governing
estate, and this is that a 'change of governance' frequently
upsets the balanced system. There is no guarantee that a new
king will be any the better apprised of the true situation than
was the former sovereign, for he will be surrounded by the usual
collection of true-speakers and dissemblers. The burden to
maintain social stability lies with the governing administrators,
the MPs, the justices, the lawyers, the clergy, and their perception of moral duty.

ʒit there is the <u>thridde</u> distaunce   third
Bryngeth a kyngdom in moche <u>noyʒe</u>:   injury
Ofte chaunge of governaunce
Of all degre, lowe and hyʒe.
A kyng may not al aspie,
Summe telle hym <u>soth</u>, summe telle hym <u>les</u>.   truth; lies
The whete fro the chaf ʒe tryʒe,
So mowe ʒe leve in reste and pes.
  (ll. 41–8)

And to emphasize that his point is a general one for all realms
that desire peace and harmony, the poet indicates the applicabil-
ity of the biblical principle of selling what you have to ensure
peace rather than war.

I speke not in specyale
Of oo kyngdom the lawe to telle;
I speke <u>hool</u> in generale   wholly
In eche kyngdom the lawe to telle.
Also is writen in the gospelle
A word that god hym-selven <u>ches</u>:   chose

Rathere than fiȝte, a man go selle
On of his clothes, and biȝe hym pes.
  (ll. 49–56)

Thereafter, he analyses the requirements of worthy living for the
various social categories: a knight is worthy who will not yield
to threats but will courageously quench malice and dissension
through lawful behaviour. The kingdom's treasure lies not only
in 'bestayle' (cattle) and 'corn stuffed in store' but more generally in 'riche comouns and wyse clergy', in 'marchaundes,
squyers, chivalry/ That wol be redy at a res [an attack];/ And
chevalrous kyng in wittes hyȝe,/ To lede in were and governe in
pes'. Ultimately, the responsibility for a peaceful realm is with
'the good lyuere [who] hath god in mynde'. This sort of man
will give wise counsel in the public arena and his wit will not
desert him when faced with issues that concern the common
profit. This praise is largely meant for those who are more
directly concerned with what profits the entire realm in times of
war and peace.

To <u>wete</u> ȝif parlement be wys,	know
The comoun profit wel it <u>preues.</u>	proves
A kyngdom in comoun lys,	
Alle profytes, and alle myscheues.	
Lordis <u>wet</u> neuere what comouns <u>greues</u>	know; grieves
Til here rentis bigynne to <u>ses.</u>	cease
Therre lordis ere pore, comons releues.	
And mayntene hem in werre and pes.	
(ll. 97–104)	

And if God is one's friend then following his moral code
ensures private and public victory and peace, and prevents
internecine warfare.

God is chief lord of toun and pyle.	
God maketh mony heire in a whyle,	
ffor god ressayveth eche reles;	
God kan breke <u>hegge</u> and style,	hedge
And make an hey wey to pes.	
(ll. 124–8)	

It is God who makes lords to be governors to govern the people
in unity. Thus, those in positions of power are reminded that the
people and the nation's wealth is not theirs but God's.

Al is goddis and so be ȝe.
  (l. 132)

The entire political order is a reflection of a higher divine order.

Eche kyng is sworn to governaunce
To governe goddes puple in riȝt.
Iche kyng bereth swerd of goddis vengeaunce
To felle goddis foon in fiȝt.
And so doth everons honest knyȝt
That bereth the ordre as it wes;
The plough, the chirche to mayntene riȝt,
Are goddis champyons, to kepe the pes.
  (ll. 137–44)

The Augustinian interpretation of worldly government as the maintenance of the peace of Babylon until death takes all, is the implicit political ideology at work here.

The world is like a chery fayre
Ofte chaungeth all his thynges.
Riche, pore, foul and fayre,
Popes, prelates and lordynges,
Alle are dedly and so ben kynges;
<u>Or</u> deth lede ȝow in his les,   before
Arraye by-tyme ȝoure rekinynges
And trete with god to gete ȝow pes.
  (ll. 145–52)

Warfare is justified only when its aims are a just peace which comprises 'wys counseil', 'good governaunce', love between lords who 'rul wel labourers sustynaunce'. The decisions of politics are made on the basis of a private, godly morality. Consequently:

Good lyf is cause of good name;
Good name is worthi to have reveraunce.
. . . Eche kyngdom hongeth in goddis balaunce;
. . . ȝe have fre wille; chese ȝuore chaunce,
To have with god werre or pes.
  (ll. 161–8)

    The sermon-like quality of the Digby poems is obvious. Kail has speculated that the poems have a single author; possibly a cleric who voted with the Commons in Parliament.[104] Robbins further noted that the Digby poet wrote not for serfs but for the House of Commons and friends who were upper-class supporters of the king, not the 'commons' of peasants, who distrusted Parliament as the vehicle that passed laws subjugating them.[105] The concern for peace and a consequent rejection of internal and external dissension and warring illustrates an attitude that we have already observed was prevalent by the end of the fourteenth century. The *raison d'être* of the knight has been largely transformed from that of the righteous warrior to that of the just administrator, and this is an accurate description of the direction English society had taken. A similar tone is adopted by Gower.

Where the Digby poet is homiletic and prescriptive, setting forth precepts for a new regime to treat with the problems inherited from the late Richard's reign, the poem *On the Times*, presumably of Richard II, ascribed to *c*. 1388, is more of a complaining description of the corrupt practices of the age, and an inspiration to act: 'Englond, awake now/ nunc consurgunt jugiter hostes/ And good heede take thow,/ fac hostia, dirige postes'. From the numbers of copies preserved, it was evidently popular. Written in alternative English and Latin lines, the poet rehearses the by now traditional complaints against flattering royal advisers and against the corrupt upper classes who have no concern for the poor, and satirizes the kind of impious preaching of the day and the prevalence of simony. Money decides all, especially in courts of law, and it overcomes right. The King is surrounded by people who conceal from him the true state of the realm. With a specific reference to 'Jake and his fellow Jake noble', Richard's favourites, identified by Wright as Robert de Vere, Duke of Ireland and Michael de la Pole, Earl of Suffolk, who have escaped abroad, the poet warns that still others remain to take their place and lead the King and the nation into further decline.[106] The extravagant fashions of Richard's court exemplify the widespread hypocrisy and general impiety of the times. Drinking and swearing is on the increase; simony rules in the Church as among the corrupt laity; the law, as practised unscrupulously, has corrupted the meaning of justice; and the estates are no longer differentiated, all being involved in conspicuous consumption. There are some especially nice touches, like the image of courtiers unwilling to bend in pious prayer for fear of ruining their hose.

A strayth bende hath here hose
laqueant ad corpora crura;
They may noght I suppose
curvare genu sine cura;
Qwen oder men knelys

pia Christo vota ferentes,
thei stond at here helys,
sua non curvare valentes.
For hortyng of here hosyn
non inclinare laborant;

The pepul ys weri
quia fermo depopulatur.
The chyrche is grevyd
quia spiritualia cedunt;
Englond goth to noght
et plus hoc facit ut vitiosus;
. . . Gentyl, gromys and boyys
socii sunt atque gulosi.
<u>Soget</u> and sovereynys   subject
uno quasi fine trahuntur.
. . . At Westmynster halle
legis sunt valde scientes;
Never the lesse for hem alle,
ibi vincuntur jura potentes.
In that he never herd the cause
juramento moderavit.
The mater wyl he have
et justum damnificabit;
And an obligacion
ac de jure valitura;
thorgh a fals cavelacion
erit affectum caritura.
his own cause many a man
nunc judicat et moderatur
Law helpeth noght than
ergo lex evacuator . . .
. . . Gret hurt to this lond
est usurpata potestas . . .
The kyng knoweth not alle
non sunt qui vera loquuntur.
. . . The cattys nec to the belle[107]
Hic et ille ligare veretur
Qwat is the cause of this?
vere violatio legis.

                                      On the Times in Wright,
             Political Poems and Songs (vol. I, pp. 270ff.)

Using a similar image to Gower's, he says: 'the lanterne of lyght-
te/ non fulget luce serena'; and the poet ends with a statement
that is reminiscent of the goliard's admonitory verses to the king

in *Piers Plowman*: 'O rex, si rex es, rege te, vel eris sine re rex,/ Nomen habens sine re, nisi te recteque regas rex.'

In its description of the more specific political illegalities of the times, this poem directly parallels some of the charges presented at the Merciless Parliament's appeal of treason (1388) against Richard's favourites. They had wrongly used their influence with the King to procure 'diverses manoirs, terres, tenements, rentes, offices' for their own affinities.[108] Royal patronage had become a politically contentious issue by 1388 and Richard's method of government was attacked through his ministers, who, it was argued, took advantage of his youth to control the government, the patronage system and the courts of law, and accrue to themselves immoderate wealth and power. The Appellants had objected, as Tuck has shown, not to the traditional patronage system as such but to its successful use by a group of courtiers who prevented the King from paying attention to his true advisers, namely themselves and Parliament.[109] As the poem *On the Times* (1388) succinctly puts it:

Gret hurt to this lond
est usurpata potestas.
. . . The kyng knoweth not alle
non sunt qui vera loquuntur.
O rex, si rex es, rege te, vel eris sine re rex,
Nomen habes sine re, nisi te recteque regas rex.

> Wright, *Political Poems and Songs* (pp. 270–8)

The poem presents indirectly a good reason for the Appellants' opposition to Richard and the court party, and may well have been composed as propaganda for the opposition.

The aesthete who is Shakespeare's Richard II does not appear to have had much in common with the historical Richard, who tried to model himself on the continental imperial tradition, claiming in 1397 to be 'entier emperour de son roialme',[110] and granting annual pensions to two German electors. His foreign policy was extensive, and many aspects of his rule at home verged on the absolutist, and therefore appeared somewhat outmoded to men who saw government along the lines of the Digby poet – less an affair of noble patronage than the affair of the gentry, the upper echelons of the urban mercantile bourgeoisie, the educated but not necessarily noble by birth.

Between Richard's deposition and the minority of Henry VI

came the real break in the sense of an obvious change in the
English court culture concerning the arts and the poetry, a break
that not only established the hegemony of the English language,
but also determined the more 'middle-class' themes of composition that were already being developed during Richard's reign.
Likewise, the provincial art of the late fourteenth century is due
less and less to noble patronage and more to the lesser gentry,
some village church wall paintings even giving the appearance of
peasant art.[111] As we have seen, during Richard's reign an
already strong rural 'middle class'[112] emerged with an increasing
interest in didactic, edifying narrative – in their literature and on
their church walls. And it was such politically astute and pious
men who would find the complaint poetry like *On the Times* a
mirror of their own views.

Mum and the Sothsegger as complaint

Mum and the Sothsegger is one of the best examples of complaints against the king, royal advisers and government officials,
harnessing a number of traditional medieval genres in the kind of
uneasy combination that makes it comparable with *Piers Plowman*: debate, sermon, encyclopedic satire, quest and dream vision.[113] The complaint about social mobility, and the ideal of
truth-telling, make *Mum and the Sothsegger* an archetypal
description of the age and its attitudes. It advocates the development of the individual's social conscience and the need for a
voice to express it, rather than keeping silent and uninvolved, as
a previous generation was implicitly advised. That Sothsegger and
not Mum is the hero is of crucial significance. To 'do well' is to
air arguments and grievances over current social abuses, and to
do so publicly. This may be compared with some of the Digby
poems, where truth-telling to the king, to his advisers, to the
people and to God is of primary importance, and on this truth-
telling hinges both private and national salvation. It is comparable to the attitude adopted in the C text of *Piers Plowman* (C
XXII, ll. 303f.) where we are advised:

... spareth nat to spille
Hem that beoth gulty and for to corecte
The kyng, and the kyng falle in eny thynge gulty.

Furthermore, like *Piers Plowman* (as we shall see in greater detail in Chapter 5), *Mum and the Sothsegger* makes use of the apparatus of scholastic learning in the service of good governance. As Blamires has pointed out,

the seven sciences consulted about the problem of whether or not to remain silent about social grievances, respond like a collection of cartoon characters; 'Sir Grumbald þe grammier' is unable to 'knytte togedre' such opposites as Mum and Sothsegger; Physic defies both, Astronomy is useless – is unable to focus on the problem at all; Rhetoric is incoherent; Logic, 'that subtile sophister jabbers away but does not oppose Mum, and Geometry casts his compass irrelevantly, with the upshot that the narrator who seeks the truth is "not þe wiser by a Walsh note" '.[114]

The poet is hostile to the friars and monks, to the priesthood in general. His final dream is the climax of the poem, and although the work is incomplete, the didactic message is beyond doubt. When the narrator–dreamer meets the ancient man in the garden, the political focus of the poem returns to the forefront. The gardener and garden, an allegory of the king and state, point to the necessity of keeping society just by punishing the wasters – or drones – in the body politic.[115] The allegory of the bees illustrates how the gardener must be able to recognize the drones who sap society, and he must do this 'kindely', naturally.[116] The ancient gardener attacks those who keep mum, and he rebukes all the cowardly members of Parliament who do not speak out; they thereby cause society to harbour grievances which will erupt into rebellions.[117] Mum, he says, is in the service of Lucifer, conniving to destroy both the individual and the state.[118] The dreamer asks for directions to that court where Sothsegger lives and he is told, as in the Digby poems, that the direction is inward: 'Yn man-is herte his housing is'.[119] The old man advises the poet to continue 'þy boke-making',[120] to speak out on the page. And what remains of the poem is a seemingly random series of complaints, or truth-telling, focused on all sections of society. This is the logical extension of less distinguished complaint poetry's realistic reportage. Like the Digby poems, the poet is not in favour of ignorant scandal-mongering by the common folk who complain ignorantly about taxes and affairs of state. It is the role of the common subjects to serve the king so that he can rule efficiently in harmony with the more politically aware Commons in Parliament. It is clear that the poet wants to show the gentry, who are aware of the needs of the poor, to be the true support of the realm.[121] The poet is defending, as the Digby poet and the C version of *Piers Plowman* defend, the role of the 'middle class' in positions of political power. They, in conjunction with the king and his council, ought to rule the country without the meddling of 'þe comun' and we may compare this with *Piers Plowman*, C IX, ll. 85–91:

Consaile nat the comune the kyng to displese,
Ne hem that han lawes to loke lacke hem not, ich hote. . .
Maistres, as the mayres ben and grete men senatours
What their comaunde as by the kyng <u>contrepleide</u> hit neuere. . .
contradict

Mum, like Digby and *Piers Plowman*, reflects government of the times where the bourgeoisie, the administrators and the university-trained, and not the hereditary nobility alone, have the political responsibilities, finance, education and power. Like other complaint poetry, *Mum* is essentially a political pamphlet in verse, accurately describing the responsibilities of the knightly class and expanded gentry whose role was the administration of just government.

Anticlerical complaint and social unrest: *The Simonie*

If we return once again to the Auchinleck Manuscript, assuming the collection to be no later than *c.* 1340+, then we may see how there was already an extremely deft Middle English poetic voice of complaint concerning social evils during the reign of Edward II, similar to those described in *On the Times* of Richard II. *The Simonie*,[122] a poem that has been seen as a forerunner of the type of alliterative social critique found in *Piers Plowman*, is remarkable for its skilful attempt, possibly thirty or more years before Langland, to understand

Whii werre and wrake in londe and manslaught is i-come,
Whii hungger and derthe on eorthe the pore hath
     <u>undernome</u>,   experienced
Whii <u>bestes ben</u> thus storve, whii corn hath ben so dere,
ʒe that wolen abide, listneth and ʒe muwen here the <u>skile</u>.   reason

Auchinleck MS fo. 328a; Wright, ll. 1–4

This poem, assumed to have been written early in Edward III's reign about the troubles during the times of Edward II, is found somewhat modified in a Peterhouse, Cambridge, MS 104, f.210a, written in a later fourteenth-century hand than the Auchinleck Manuscript, and is also incompletely included in Bodley MS 48. Not only are there numerous parallel alliterative couplets with *Piers Plowman*, as Elizabeth Salter has demonstrated,[123] but there is also a similarity with later political complaint verse (which we have already examined), in its concern for immediate and striking communication rather than elegance or richness of language. As Professor Salter has said:

It would not be an exaggeration to say that its bitter review of the secular and spiritual ill-health of the earlier fourteenth century comes nearer in subject and tone to some parts of *Piers Plowman* than any other single extant work. The range of its material is similar to that outlined by Langland in the Prologue and the first few passus of *Piers Plowman*: anti-papal denunciation, examination of a corrupt church at home, the arraignment of worldly priests, cynical bishops, avaricious friars. Lawyers, sheriffs, knights and squires are stringently dealt with, but the church is held primarily responsible for temporal suffering.[124]

There is a pervasive sympathy with the poor and an antipathy towards the simoniacal clergy at all levels and of all orders, at home and abroad, who are responsible for the fact that 'holi churche is muchel i-brought ther doune'. The Church is rotten from within, but those secular estates bound to serve and protect the Church do no better. Earls, barons and knights that are pledged to fight for holy church are now the first to assail her. They brew dissension where there should be peace; they should be off to the Holy Land, fighting for the cross, but they remain at home, dressed like fops and minstrels, glorifying pride, whilst boys of low birth are knighted.

Thus is the ordre of kniht turned up-so doun.
... Knihtshipe is <u>acloied</u> and <u>deolfulliche i-diht</u>;   debased; lamentably arrayed
Kunne a boy nu breke a spere, he shal be mad a kniht.
And thus ben knihtes gadered of unkinde blod,
And <u>envenimeth</u> that ordre that sholde be so god and hende;   poisoned
(ll. 259, 265–9)

Nor are there any worthy squires, but

A <u>newe taille</u> of squierie is nu in everi toun;   new cut
The <u>raye</u> is turned <u>overthuert</u> that sholde stonde adoun;   garment; crosswise

... Gentille men that sholde ben, ne beth hii none i-liche.   there be
none such
  (ll. 283–4, 288)

Justices, sheriffs, mayors and bailiffs act illegally; they

... maken the mot-halle at hom in her chaumbre wid wouh;
court; wrong
  (l. 292)

Instead of good soldiers being sent to fight for the king, the rich pay for 'a wrecche' to go in their place 'that may noht helpe himselve at nede' and thus is the king deceived and the poor destroyed out of the covetousness of others. When the king decrees a national tax, the money collected is squandered before it reaches him. 'The pore is thus i-piled [robbed], and the riche forborn.' As in the later fourteenth-century poems and in the Digby verse, where the rich and the noble are blamed for keeping the king in the dark about the estate of his realm, so too *The Simonie* poet supports the king while complaining of his administrators:

Ac if the king hit wiste, I trowe he wolde be wroth,
Hou the pore beth i-piled, and hu the silver goth;
Hit is so deskatered bothe hider and thidere,
That halvendel shal ben stole ar hit come togidere and acounted;
An if a pore man speke a word, he shal be foule afrounted.
Ac were the king wel avised, and wolde worche bi skile,   work by
reason
Litel nede sholde he have swiche pore to pile;   such
Thurfte him noht seke tresor so fer, he mihte finde ner,
At justices, at shirreves, cheiturs and chaunceler, and at les;
escheators
Swiche mihte finde him i-nouh, and late pore men have pes.
For who so is in swich ofice, come he neuere so pore,
He fareth in a while as thouh he hadde silver ore;
... Whan everi man hath his part, the king hath the leste.
Everi man is aboute to fille his owen purs;
And the king hath the leste part, and he hath al the curs, wid wronge.
God sende treuthe into this lond, for tricherie dureth to longe.
  (ll. 313–26, 332–6)

Lesser officials are described as spending their time finding ways to grieve the poor: summoning them to assizes while the rich stay at home. Those at the bench and country attorneys charge exorbitantly for minimal services,

And have he turned the bak, he makketh the a <u>mouwe</u>!   contemp-
                                                              tuous gesture
    (l. 348)

Merchants who once were honest now are false, and the widespread 'game' of back-biting among the learned and illiterate
that has lasted for so long is now unstoppable. God, who once
had provided so well for the world, had sent a famine out of
anger over men's ways, but it was the poor who suffered most,
crying:

'Allas! for hungger I die up rihte!'
    (l. 400)

When plenty was restored to the land, men 'were also muchele
shrewes' as they were previously, forgetting God's commandments and man's former wretchedness. Thus God sent another,
even worse famine, so that the rich, who were so concerned
with saving their possessions and their own lives, were prepared
to sacrifice even their own kin. The great lords were undone,
the prelates of the Church slept and awakened too late, and
feared losing their own lands more than losing Christ's love.

For hadde the clergie harde holden to-gidere,
And noht flecced aboute nother hider ne thidere,
But loked where the treuthe was, and there had bileved,
Thanne were the <u>barnage</u> hol, that nu is al <u>to-dreved</u> so wide;
                                              baronage; separated
    (ll. 451–5)

According to the poet, the structure of society could have been
preserved intact by a pious, uncovetous clergy. 'But pride has
caught both high and low in his pantry.'

Alle wite we wel it is oure gilt, the wo that we beth inne;
But no man knoweth that hit is for his owen sinne.
Uch man put on other the wreche of the wouh;
    (ll. 463–5)

No one blames himself but blames others for the wretched state
of affairs.[125]

Ac so is al this world ablent, that no man <u>douteth</u> sinne.   fears
But bi seint Jame of Galice, that many man hath souht!
The pilory and the cucking-stol beth i-mad for noht. . . .

[here the poem ends, incomplete in all the MSS]
    (ll. 475–7)

Although the most heavy vilifications are borne by the various orders in the Church, the latter part of the poem runs through the expected duties of members of the first and second estates, constructing a theory of what ought to be the case contrasted with how men in fact behave in the secular world, and the dire consequences of their wilful disruption of the fixed social hierarchy. It is interesting that the poor have no duties, but are described as passively exploited, 'foule a-frounted' should they speak out against the financial exactions demanded of them. The poor are described not in feudal terms but rather as victims of financial exploitation by the possessionate and powerful higher orders who are ruled by simony rather than Christian morality. A Christian morality based on principles of action that may be decided on only by the responsible *individual* is fundamental to the poet's complaint. This is clear when he notes how the salvation of England rests not on a righteous sovereign alone, but on individuals who, in these evil times, blame others rather than themselves. Although he takes justices, sheriffs, knights and squires as representing functionally differentiated groups with characteristic vices, his ultimate concern is for the responsibility of the individual member of every class, without which there shall be no final and lasting reform. The responsibility of the individual Christian for his own deeds and decisions was, as we shall see later, a constant theme in poetry and prose of the fourteenth century, in the schools and among the laity. In the political and social complaint verse it assumes an interesting form.

The condemnation of individuals; 'Richard the Redeless'

At the end of the century the tendency to blame individuals rather than groups is clarified by poets in one of two ways. Either, as often but not always with Langland, the characteristic vices and virtues of a class or group are typified by a single representative who is given a personality that includes *but extends beyond* the habits of his group or profession – as with Hawkyn, Will and Lady Mede; consequently they are more than mere allegorical types and possess ambiguous personalities (their ambiguity has caused considerable distress among modern critics); or, as in *On King Richard's Ministers* (1399), specific culprits are named, albeit indirectly through plays on their names or by symbolic representation using aspects of subjects' coats of arms (should they have them). If we look at *On King Richard's Ministers* we shall see how an extreme example of a complaint against the times is made specific with reference to responsible, here historical, royal advisers and officials.

Ther is a *busch* [Sir John Bushey] that is forgrowe;
Crop hit welle, and hold hit lowe,
    or elles hit wolle be wilde.
The long gras that is so *grene* [Sir Henry Greene]
Hit most be mowe, and raked clene;
    forgrowen hit hath the fellde.
The grete *bagge* [Sir William Bagot] that is so <u>mykille</u>,   tall
Hit schal be kettord, and maked litelle;
    the bothom is ny ouȝt.
Hit is so roton on ych a side
Ther nul no stych with odur abyde,
    to set theron a clout.

Thorw the *busch* a *swan* [Gloucester] was <u>sclayn</u>;   slain
Of that sclawtur fewe were fayne;
    alas! that hit betydde!
Hit was a <u>eyrer</u> good and able   heir
To his lord <u>ryȝt</u> profitable;
    hit was a gentel <u>bryde</u>.   bird

          Wright, *Political Poems and Songs* (vol. I, p. 363)

This esoteric means of identifying individuals, telling of the events that brought them low, is an extreme example of a tendency in the complaint verse to move from class caricature to individual responsibility. There was something of this desire to attribute specific blame in Minot's poems as well, but this was the more easily and openly achieved since the villains were individual members of the French (Spanish and Scottish) nobility. When the political situation at home made it unsafe to name names, poets adopted a device that was extensively used in prophetic verse: speaking obliquely, in riddles, employing animal symbols, the cryptic utterance. The most popular and explicit instance of this was the Latin verse prophecies attacking Edward III and his government, ascribed (wrongly) to John Bridlington (otherwise attributed to John Erghome, a Yorkshire Austin friar). These later appeared in a parallel English form in *The Cock in the North* and *When Rome is Removed*, printed by Robbins.[126] Bridlington/Erghome, thus, sounds as follows:

Capitulum tertium docet mores Edwardi de Wyndesore, et accidentia
regni Angliae tempore juventutis suae, unde versus sequuntur.

Taurus erit fortis, metuens nil tristia mortis;
Sobrius et castus, justus, sine crimine fastus;
Ab bona non tardus, audax veluti leopardus.[127]

The English verse prophecies of Thomas of Ersseldoune may
also have served directly as models for those complaint poems
that attempted an indirect identification of blameworthy individuals.

This technique is used in an elaborate way in *Richard the
Redeless*, the first part (and according to Embrée a different
poem altogether) of *Mum and the Sothsegger*, to which it has
traditionally been affixed. In *Richard the Redeless* the poet
puns on the names Bushey (Speaker for the Commons,
1394), Greene (son of the former Justice of the King's Bench),
Bagot (Sheriff of Leicester) and Scrope (Treasurer) and, ostensibly addressing King Richard, describes in a covert way, using
animal and bird types, the ill-doings of his favourites. To anyone
familiar with current events in the political world, this mode of
identifying important persons would be sufficiently explicit. The
author, who says he is connected in some way with Bristol,
speaks of having long meditated on writing a treatise on good
government for princes and their advisers. He sounds like one
of the lesser landed gentry who was acquainted with the Parliaments of the late 1390s, and is largely concerned with the
events that surrounded Richard's deposition. He makes clear in
the Prologue that his poem is meant to discuss the misrule of
Richard and his advisers, counselling the King to repent of his
errors and endure his imprisonment with patience while reading
the poet's treatise. Then he expounds on the nature of Richard's
misrule – over-taxation, oppressive treatment of the Commons,
legal abuses – and implies that his verse tract is meant as a mirror for those princes who come afterwards; Richard is beyond
hope. He ends with the proceedings of what may have been the
January 1398 Parliament where Richard was deposed, and
refers to Bushey, Greene, Bagot and Scrope as directly as he
may:[128]

Now, Richard the redeless . reweth on ȝou-self,   unadvised
That lawlesse leddyn ȝoure lyf . and ȝoure peple bothe;
ffor thoru the wyles and wronge . and wast in ȝoure tyme   through

ʒe were lyghtlich y-lyfte . ffrom that ʒou leef thouʒte,   carried away
And ffrom ʒoure willffull werkis . ʒoure will was chaungid,
And rafte was ʒoure riott . and rest, ffor ʒoure daiez   taken away
Weren wikkid thoru ʒoure cursid counceill . ʒoure karis weren
  newed,   renewed
And coueitise hath crasid . ʒoure croune ffor euere!   covetousness;
  broken

Richard the Redeless, *Passus primus*, ll. 1–8

Richard, he says, had come to the throne young, but the crown was virtuous then. Soon enough he was ignorantly in the clutches of his favourites and no one had the courage to complain against them.

But where this croune bicome . a clerk were that wuste;
But so as I can . declare it I thenke,
And nempne no name; . but tho that nest were,   mention
ffull preuyly they pluckud . thy power awey,
And reden with realte . ʒoure rewme thoru-oute,
And as tyrauntis, of tiliers . taken what hem liste,   husbandmen;
  they desire
And paide hem on her pannes . whan her penyes lacked.   heads
ffor non of ʒoure peple . durste pleyne of here wrongis,
ffor drede of ʒoure dukys . and of here double harmes.   dukes

Passus primus, ll. 49–57

The ruling elite of favourites was united in the 'ffelawschepe' of the patronage system and Richard's counsellors are described as 'to ʒonge of ʒeris to yeme [govern] swyche a rewme', for they were mainly concerned with acquiring more for themselves.[129] The poet then puns on Bushey's name:

And ffor curinge of hem-self . cried on ʒou euere,
ffor to hente hele . of her owen greues,   obtain recovery; grievances
More than ffor wurschepe. that they to ʒou owed,
They made ʒou to leue . that regne ʒe ne myʒte,
Without busshinge adoune . of all ʒoure best ffrendis,   striking
Be a ffals colour [Green] . her caris to wayve
And to holde hem in hele . if it happe myʒte. . . .   prosperity
  They bare hem the bolder . ffor her gay broches,
And *busshid* with her brestis, and bare adoune the pouere,
Lieges that loved ʒou the lesse . ffor her (lither) dedis.

Passus primus, ll. 95–101; *passus secundus*, ll. 38–40

But the Duke of Lancaster saves the day by catching the scoundrels and finally beheading them.

Thus baterid this bred . on *busshes* aboute,
And gaderid gomes on *grene* . ther as they walkyd,
That all the schroff and *schroup* . sondrid ffrom other.

Passus secundus, ll. 152–4

'Thus this bird [Lancaster] battered the Bushes around, and gathered up men as they walked on the Greene, until all the "scruff" and Scrope parted asunder.' Lancaster, as the Eagle, 'euere houed on hie on the skyes', excellently perceiving the tiniest pie crumbs, the various misdemeanours of these 'kytes'.

In this way the poet refers obliquely to Richard's favourites, allegorically outlining the precise activities 'aʒeins kynde' in which they were involved. Using analogies from natural history turned into fable, he describes how Richard's liveried men, bearing the sign of the white hart, should have been keen to catch and destroy adders 'that harmen alle hende bestis'. He repeats the story of the hart that is found in contemporary Bestiaries, which tells how, when the hart grows old, it is natural for him to seek out the poisonous adder, swallow him and then drink water to render the venom harmless. In this way he renews his strength. Instead, Richard's harts attacked colts, horses, swans and bears, the emblems taken from the badges of the many magnates of the Appellant faction, whom Richard had destroyed: Arundel (horse), his son Thomas FitzAlan (colt), Gloucester (swan) and Warwick (bear).

This (is) aʒeins kynde . as clerkis me tolde:
Propter ingratitudinem liber homo revocatur in
    servitutem, ut in stimulo compunccionis, et in lege civili.
. . . Now constrew ho so kunne . I can saie no more.

Passus tertius, ll. 32, 35

He continues with another bestiary parable to illustrate how, although a partridge's nest may be usurped by a 'congioun', another partridge will come to deliver the young ones out of bondage. Likewise, Henry Duke of Lancaster restored whom he could to his proper estate and punished the wrongdoers:

ffor he was heed of hem all . and <u>hieste</u> of kynde,   highest
To kepe the croune . as cronecle tellith.
He <u>blythid</u> the Beere . and his bond braste,   gladdened
And lete him go at large . to lepe where he wolde.

Passus tertius, ll. 92–5

Like the author of *The Simonie*, the poet blames the excessive
concern for riches and fashion on an ineffectual clergy, who do
nothing to reprove robbers, flatterers or knights who are ignorant of their duties. He proceeds to outline, in the manner of a
mirror for princes, the prerequisites of a well-governed realm:
governance ought to be by those tried in age and experience.

That iche rewme vndir <u>roff</u> . of the reyne-bowe	covering
Sholde stable and stonde. be these thre degres:	
By gouernaunce of grete . and of good age;	
By styffnesse and strengthe . of <u>steeris</u> well <u>y-yokyd</u>,	oxen; yoked
That beth myȝthffull men . of the mydill age;	
And be laboreris of lond . that lyfflode ne ffayle	
Thanne wolde [right dome] reule . if reson were amongis us,	
That iche <u>leode</u> lokide . what longid to his age,	man
And neuere ffor to passe more . oo poynt fforther,	
To vsurpe the service . that to sages bilongeth,	
To be-come conselleris . er they kunne rede,	
In <u>schenshepe</u> of souereynes. and shame al the last.	disgracing
ffor it ffallith as well to <u>ffodis</u> . of four and twenty ȝeris,	persons
Or yonge men of yistirday . to <u>ȝeue</u> good <u>redis</u>,	give; advice
As be-cometh a kow . to hoppe in a cage!	

Passus tertius, ll. 248–62

Governments are founded on and preserved by the law, just as
'lewed men' depend on the plough. Thus 'myssedoers', even if
they be 'peeres', should be put in prison. But when the law is
hardly considered and the well-being of the people even less so,
and when men are only concerned with honour and their ease,
then the state may not endure for long. Those in power 'prien
affter presentis' and they 'meyneteyne myssdoers . more than
other peple' (ll. 306–11);

They leid on thi leigis, Richard . lasshis y-now,	
And drede neuere a dele . the <u>dome</u> of the lawe.	judgement

Passus tertius, ll. 338–9

Speaking directly of all the different taxes, the rents, the wool
and cloth customs, that impoverished the Commons in order to
pay for the debts incurred by Richard and his affinity, the poet
describes the assemblage at Parliament where yet more money
was requested. He describes how an attempt was made to blame
the master of the ship of state who was sailing a course that was

ever more treacherous. Others were more concerned with getting their money back from the King than for the 'comfort' of the commonwealth. And the poem ends abruptly in the midst of this parliamentary confusion as to what might be done to rebalance the financial and legal state of the kingdom.

Richard the Redeless is an excellent example of the fully developed complaint poetry that was achieved at the end of the fourteenth century. Using the alliterative line, and mixing the journalist's direct reportage of parliamentary proceedings with bestiary parables and indirect references to specific individuals who were seen to be responsible for the corruptions of the age, the poet has selected events and intruded his opinion and advice, scolded, threatened, despaired and rejoiced. The poem is a personalized commentary of a Bristol man on what we might otherwise read in a less emotional chronicle of the last years of Richard. But it is precisely his interest in alliteration and in a colourful analysis and allegorization of the bald facts as he saw them that makes the poem a surprisingly complex and personal art form.

Richard the Redeless has been made out of contemporary disturbances, a factor that is important to recall in any discussion of *Piers Plowman*, *Wynnere and Wastoure*, *Mum and the Sothsegger*, and Gower's works as well. A pictorial parallel to this verbal art issuing from dissension occurs in the violence portrayed in the French Rohan master's illuminations, and, generally, in the rather morbid cast of the art produced after the Black Death of 1349.[130] So many of the literary products of the fourteenth century, verse and prose, may be considered to be records of some confrontation and of social disorientation. The wide range of Middle English literary genres, particularly from the second half of the fourteenth century, had, despite different experiments in form and style, broken out of the traditional bonds of the Abuses of the Age category to enable our retrospective analysis to erect the classification 'political and social complaint poetry' and apply it at once to the Digby 102 poems as well as to *Piers Plowman*, *Richard the Redeless*, and even to the descriptions of some of Chaucer's pilgrims. Collectively, we have before us a body of literature that extends beyond the chronological limitations of the Ricardian period, which was written in large part for a blossoming, keen-witted, politically astute audience in town and country.

Reflections on the new consciousness

As Spearing has said in his *Medieval Dream-Poetry*,[131] a new consciousness of and interest in the nature and status of literature began to develop to replace the earlier attitude of minstrel story-tellers, who made little claim to an artistic identity beyond the anonymity of entertainer and purveyor of traditional fare. *Wynnere and Wastoure* is quite clear about the distinction between minstrel performers and creative poets who write their own works *c.* 1350. There developed an increasing concern to write didactically and to be personally instructive and exhorting. The dream poetry, like the political complaints that proliferated in the later fourteenth century, was intensely self-conscious poetry. Inevitably it brought the poet into the poem as the person who experiences his own fictional 'facts' and becomes part of them, rather than as someone who merely retells them. The political complaint poetry from the Harley 2253 to the Digby 102 collections, written over a time span of nearly 100 years, shows, as do the dream poems like *Piers Plowman*, *Pearl*, *Wynnere and Wastoure* and so on, the gradual development of technical devices to make room for the poet's consciousness of himself as a poet, as an eclectic eye witness to 'events', as a 'complainer', a biased reporter, a prophetic reformer. One can observe that provincial school of poetry which produced dream poems like *Wynnere and Wastoure* and *The Parlement of the Three Ages*, which are, as Elizabeth Kirk has called them, '*in*conclusive social debates',[132] developing into *conclusive* didactic social debates like *Richard the Redeless*, *Piers Plowman* and even the *Pearl* poet's writings (regarding the proper religious attitudes to adopt) and the poetry of Digby 102. In other words, the earlier poems of this genre present, in a rather scholastic, aporetic manner, the two sides of an argument, as in the thirteenth-century *Owl and the Nightingale*. But the later poems adopt a stance and are decidedly didactic – the poet is seen as a moral guide to the making of political, social and religious choices.

Thus, the realism of socially critical verse became a technique used to highlight the position of the poet. The growth in realism and naturalism was also typical of other late medieval arts in general, where there was a movement from the abstract principle to the concrete specific, most clearly exemplified in the portrayal of the individual personality and social standing of characters and subjects in their particular milieu. Such portraits provided insight into some distinct aspect of contemporary life, either through the individual characterization of an abstraction like Hunger, Anima, Justice, even Wynnere and Wastoure, or through an oblique but obvious reference to the 'players' in the contemporary historical drama, as in *Richard the Redeless*.

The realistic self-consciousness of the poet can be seen in the justification of the didactic aspect of the poet's craft set forth in *Piers Plowman*, B XII, ll. 1–30. Here Langland says that the poet is no mere entertainer but a guide to moral discovery, and he emphasizes throughout the dream poem the 'I' of the narrator. His *via* leads us beyond the narrower complaints against corrupt officials and ecclesiastics to a personally constructed panorama of late fourteenth-century social, political and religious concerns, and suggests numerous personal, moral reforms that must be undertaken before the commonwealth may be restored. Although we shall have occasion to consider Langland's poem more fully in a later chapter, it is important to emphasize here once again how social reform had come to be seen as dependent on the active participation of private, morally upright citizens rather than the sole responsibility of an autonomous sovereign.

If, as I believe, we can support the notion of so chronologically limited a category as a Ricardian poetry when we examine the poetry of social unrest, then the complaint literature of the earlier period must be seen as a channelling medium, a tradition that is used but elaborated upon and then transformed by Gower, Langland and Chaucer. It should be clear that it is less the traditional French/Latin satire of the twelfth–thirteenth centuries that stands directly behind the Ricardian success, than the topical verse journalism of the political and social commentary poems – like *The Simonie* – of the early to middle fourteenth century. I cannot agree with Robbins that the sort of social critique lyric like *Against the King's Taxes*, found in the poetry of the Harley miscellany, was unique and did not continue in the later part of the century.[133] Elizabeth Salter has effectively shown the close relationship between *The Simonie* and *Piers Plowman*. Despite the break that occurred in the poetical and scholarly enterprise caused by the decimation of the population in the 1349 plague, which limited by sheer numbers the readers and writers of the 1350s, there can be seen a clear continuity of socially critical verse until the end of the century and beyond into the next. Thus, what Langland, Gower and Chaucer did, each in his own way, depended on an existing and apparently well-known Anglo-Norman, Latin and English verse tradition already reforged in England amidst the circumstances of the war and the changing conditions of social mobility. The models of Ricardian complaint and critique were identifiably English productions rather than the more neutral French/Latin of the school or art poetry tradition of the thirteenth century. Although we may fruitfully approach aspects of Chaucer and Gower's art from the French tradition, it is their topical political and social commentary – what strikes us as their very English view of their fictional society – that rests more on the sixty-odd-year complaint verse tradition created out of the English experience, of war and its consequences on home policy. In the early stages, these productions by an anonymous group of Englishmen used the vehicles of Latin, French and English. Gradually, English prevailed for reasons we have discussed. One might say that the distinctive artistry of Chaucer especially lies in his narrative technique rather than in his subject matter, particularly when he is socially critical or satirical. When he borrows his subject matter from stock contemporary complaint, his content is neither more nor less than his more dreary models, the frequently undistinguished literature of social unrest.

John Gower's complaint

To turn lastly to Gower is to turn to the craftsman who brought the various strands of anonymous socially critical verse to fruition in an art poetry that was patronized and appreciated.[134] Chaucer called him the 'moral Gower'. He was, perhaps, more representative of his age and the second estate's attitudes to warfare, practical government and administration, and a modified chivalric code concerning love and appropriate attitudes in times of peace, than any other poet one can name for the last quarter of the century. More old-fashioned in his sources than Chaucer, he seems almost unaware of what was happening artistically in Italy during his century. His tendency to plagiarize unashamedly from Ovid, from Peter Riga's *Aurora* (*Biblia Versificata*), from what was believed to be Alexander Neckham's *De Vita Monachorum* and Nigel Longchamp's *Speculum Stul-*

torum, prove him to have been a man influenced by a curious combination of thirteenth-century texts and their ideals,[135] along with the practicalities of life in the fourteenth century, when a strictly stratified society with fixed estate expectations was no longer a reality. His bitterness against lawyers; against the whole range of the bribable, administrative bureaucracy; against the bestiality of the peasantry; against the current practices of monks, nuns, indolent university students, secular clergy and friars, the papacy; against Richard's advisers and the blameworthy Richard himself, place Gower in the vanguard of Ricardian critics. He was remarkably quick to support the Appellants and reject Richard for Henry of Lancaster, boldly re-dedicating his *Vox Clamantis* to Henry in 1393 and later to Thomas Arundel, Henry's ally against Richard and the court party.

Some have seen the landowning Gower to have been the very voice of gentry conservatism, although Gower himself believed he was setting down the more general voice of the people.[136] His primary concern in his French and Latin works, and to some extent also in his English *Confessio Amantis*, is to examine society in order to determine at whose door the current evils of the age may be laid. The trilingual chancery clerks who copied in Latin and French, as well as creating a correspondingly official language in English, may well have been his most obvious readership, and Tout estimated that *c.* 1400 chancery consisted of around 120 clerks.[137] Gower names names and describes events with a thoroughness, at times verging on the verbose and tedious, that we have not previously met. The *Mirour de l'Omme*, the *Vox Clamantis* and the *Confessio*, along with his English, French and Latin poems on topical and courtly issues, unite to condemn the avarice of the age in which law has been so corrupted by low-born lawyers and officials that the moral principles of the times may be summed up, strikingly, by his own statement in the *Mirour* (ll. 20149–50): 'The prostitute is more profitable ... than the nun'. The *Vox Clamantis* with its appended *Cronica Tripertita* deals with selected events of the 1370s, then of 1387–8, and then hops to 1397 and thereafter. Book One, on the 'peasants' revolt' of 1381, was added after the *Vox* had been completed in its first version. Above all, it is an extension of the socially critical reportage we have examined in the much briefer compass of anonymous verse. Gower has presented something of a systematic survey of the three estates, much the same as in his French *Mirour de l'Omme*, using the pretence of merely reporting the *vox populi* which was also meant to be the *vox dei*. There is a special poignancy in Gower's stress on the aural nature of the *vox populi*, for as he makes plain in his dedication of the final version of the *Vox Clamantis* to Archbishop Arundel, he had gradually gone blind. The events that are central to his historical narrative are now present only to his mind's eye and to his astute ear.

In Gower's gradual blindness may be the clue to his dependence on certain older sources for his form and style, and his frequently unsuccessful attempts to mix too many genres: was he recalling phrases he had learned by heart from Ovid *et al.* in his youth, so that his models were not current literature but the aural memory of classic lines? Furthermore, is there not something that shocks the modern consciousness when we learn that the highly visual events of the 'peasants' revolt' and the visually striking aspects of London's vices and excessive luxuries are being recounted by one who was losing his sight? I have noted that he wrote Book One on the revolt after the rest of the work was completed. Wickert has suggested a date as late as *c.* 1400,[138] when Gower was already blind. What kind of an attitude to history is implied by a man who was a witness to events recalled during a period of near or complete blindness? His audience or readership must have been content to accept that Gower's history, or the convincing fiction presented by him, was no more than hearsay, the opinion of the poet and the group he represented with only the appearance of a more neutral historical veracity. At the same time, Gower uses the traditional dream frame for his description of 'real' events like the revolt, and some commentators have pointed to his unsuccessful attempt to sustain this dream throughout his work.[139] Is there not a remarkable fictional irony (perhaps intended?) in a man going blind yet attempting to retain his vision, even in a dream, but without success? Although Gower appears to have been an eye-witness to some of the events in London, the horror of those days when the 'peasants' rose up and were likened in their actions to beasts run wild and acting unnaturally were recalled by a man whose sight may already have been failing and whose memory of those events rushed forth in the monstrous images of a nightmare.

Fisher has described Gower as a man of absolute integrity

with a 'coherent grasp of the values and ideals of his age, and [with] his fearless expression of the moral judgments growing out of these ideals'.[140] It is his representation of a certain estate's opinions of events and his own class's fears and biases that, in fact, make him a remarkable spokesman for the emergent gentry and bourgeoisie, fearful of the traditional world being turned upside down by the rising third estate amidst the remnants of a largely fictionalized because anachronistic feudalism. His trilingual works, running to over 80,000 lines, are in their way an encyclopedia of current prejudices and ideals, didactic and rhetorical, the moralistic mode of medieval complaint brought to its end. Gower was a cultivator of complaint. Chaucer, as Fisher has indicated, built his more individualized satire on Gowerian complaint,[141] and by implication on the anonymous complaint genre of the century.

Gower was born *c.* 1330 and lived until 1408. He thus witnessed the reigns of three kings, Edward III, Richard II and Henry IV, and his active life placed him in the heart of the turmoil of those years. It is likely that he was in some way connected with the legal profession, and his knowledge of their carryings-on was an intimate one. With property in Kent and London, he seems to have taken up residence at St Mary's Priory (now Southwark Cathedral) sometime after 1377, apparently in semi-retirement. During this time he devoted himself to writing his three interlocking works in French, Latin and English: the *Mirour de l'Omme*, the *Vox Clamantis* and the *Confessio Amantis*. Whether this literary retirement can be related to the failing eyesight that was to render him blind by the end of the century may only be speculation. At St Mary's he had the leisure and a library of sorts to get on with his project, and a scriptorium was at hand to produce the many sumptuous editions that he required for presentation to wealthy patrons. From the east side of the priory close where a gate opened on to Pepper Lane and the High Street, he would have been able to witness the scene of the peasants' attack on London Bridge in June 1381, their attack on John of Gaunt's Savoy Palace nearby and, in 1392, the grand reconciliation between Richard II and the citizens of London who had previously refused Richard the loan of a huge sum, which had inspired the King to withdraw the city's liberties and remove his administration to York for several months. Chaucer's pilgrims' Tabard Inn, from whence they began their journey to Canterbury, was also close by. His circle of friends included Chaucer and a number of civil servants with clerical and legal training as well as literary interests.

As Fisher has shown, all of Gower's associations for business or friendship clustered around the Inns of Court, the Chancery and Guildhall, the Staple and Customs House. Such a circle of friends was necessarily influenced by the fluctuations of the political scene in this period of civic and national turmoil, so that men like Usk would be killed for associating with a treasonous party in 1388, others like Chaucer would fall out for a time from his position at the Customs House. From the facts known about his life as well as from what his own historical and moral poetry can tell us, Gower was a man involved in politics from the theoretical and practical standpoint. If Fisher is correct in speculating that some of Gower's earliest poems, *The Cinquante Balades*, were written for the merchant Pui of which we spoke earlier,[142] then his alliance with those merchants with literary interests was an early one. The increasing urgency of his complaint against social divisiveness, injustice and fraud in society, heightened by his own association with the legal profession, enabled him to take the clerical tradition of complaint against the immoral behaviour of the three estates away from generalized clichés. Although his complaint was never quite couched in terms of one individual's response to the evils of the times, because he was concerned to speak for all men as they viewed the present situation, Gower nevertheless spoke personally, but with the *vox populi* of the expanded second estate during the 1380s rather than with the generalized 'national' voice of traditional complaint verse. His *Vox Clamantis* made him into a single, individual voice crying in the wilderness, saying: 'To me, the things which were done in the past are not so grievous but that these things which are so well known to me at present are much more grievous. For the calamity which I now saw at hand in my own time brought about horrifying deeds of much greater suffering.'[143]

From an early period Gower's poetry was intensely social and political. His *Vox Clamantis*, written *c.* 1378–80 for, it may be assumed, a clerical, Latin-reading audience along with others who had Latin skills, addressed the young Richard, blamed the King's mistakes on bad counsel, and generally was concerned to speak of the appropriate behaviour of the three estates in a justly ordered realm. The original edition of his English *Confessio*, dating *c.* 1390, was dedicated to Richard; and later, in 1392–4, he altered the dedication, excised certain passages and offered the work to Henry of Lancaster. He seems to have discarded early much of whatever influence was ever exercised on his poetry by the French courtly poetic tradition. Rather, he seems to have extended the native Anglo-Norman tradition, that is, the tradition established in England by writers in French whose debt to early troubadours was perhaps stronger than it was for the French court poetry of mid-century. But most important was his presentation of a mixture of aristocratic and bourgeois sentiments on the state of society, with its elaborate apologia for a theoretical feudalism based on fixed and functionally distinct estates. His hymn to the divinely ordained merchant class in his *Mirour* is a remarkable example of his championing of the 'middle class', much as we have seen it but with a more general message in the anonymous Digby poet's complaints: in translation from Gower's French,[144]

God established rightly
that one country should
have need of another.
Therefore God ordained merchants
who should search in other
lands for what one does not have.
Therefore one who looks to himself
and trades honestly
is blessed by God and man.

> *Mirour de l'Omme*, ll. 25192ff.

It has also been commented upon that Gower speaks in defence of the capitalist who risks his money in hopes of winning profit, and this too he justifies:

The law ordains and it is right
That one who puts himself in
danger of loss should also win
when his good fortune procures it.
Therefore I say to you that
he who ventures to trade
and risks his silver
is not to be blamed if he gains,
if he does so in measure
without fraud.

> *Mirour de l'Omme*, ll. 25201ff.

Fisher says it nicely: 'Gower is an excellent subject for Marxist analysis because on the one hand he subsumes so much that is characteristic of the medieval mind, while on the other hand his understanding of the function of the entrepreneur and his spirited defence of the reward due risk capital read like something out of Adam Smith.'[145] He includes a patriotic praise of the wool trade which has prompted some critics to suggest wool merchants were his patrons:

O leine, dame de noblesse,
Tu es des marchantz la duesse. . . .

You are born in England.
Mirour de l'Omme, ll. 25369ff.

In no way would he excuse the upper classes being intimidated by the peasants; that 'violent nettle', the disruptive force of the common people, ought to be watched and rooted out by those in authority. The mob of common people was like a flood or like wild fire, incited by lawless instigators, and would be stopped by neither reason nor discipline. If we see Gower as one who first moved from the courtly love topics of the *Cinquante Balades* to the more devotional mood of the beginning of the *Mirour*, it is clear that current events inspired him to alter his mood and his theme yet again in order to treat of the causes of social and political unrest. The *Mirour* and the *Vox* most directly address these issues. Mixing allegory with chronicle, Gower sets out unsympathetically the condition of the labourer after the severe population decline which resulted from the deathly plague in 1349. He says:

Little was their labour but great the wages
three times more than their work
that they wanted without deserving.
So goes the world from bad to worse
when they who guard the sheep
or the herdsmen in their places,
demand to be rewarded
more for their labours than
the master bailiff used to be . . .
the labourer is so expensive
that whoever wants anything done
must pay five or six shillings
for what formerly cost two.
Mirour, ll. 26434ff.

At the same time that he wrote of the declining state of the nation in French, that is, prior to 1381 when the peasants revolted, he worked on a Latin version in the *Vox*. 'Nothing I write', he said, 'is my own opinion. Rather I shall try to speak what the voice of the people has reported to me.'[146] As the Digby poet says, 'the voice of the common people is the arbiter of just acts in society'. Gower adopts this universal prophetic voice of the citizenry to contribute to the mode of perception that distinguishes the complaint from the more personal, particularizing, satire that we find both in Chaucer and in classical satire. Gower will later, in the *Cronica Tripertita*, affirm that the common opinion, the *vox populi*, helped to bring 'the hateful Richard' to his downfall.[147] His poetry is a testament to the power of parliamentary sovereignty at the end of the fourteenth century.

But would such men, even those members of the gentry and the merchant elite in Parliament, be content to read Gower's analysis and warnings in Latin? Fisher has, probably accurately, identified the audience of the *Vox* as those members of the clerical estate like Bishop Courtenay of London, William of Wykeham of Winchester, Archbishop Sudbury, Thomas Brinton Bishop of Rochester, along with all parliamentary representatives and high-ranking clerics.[148] To these we would add all those whose educations had taken them through the university system to the Inns of Court and into the legal profession; all those for whom Latin was required in ecclesiastical or administrative duties; all those who had once made their start on the road to administrative or ecclesiastical preferment in the local schools now dotted thickly across the map of England. In numbers they were not large, but they were definitely of the blossoming 'middle class' whose political and financial power had raised them to dominance. It was to them that Arundel referred in 1388 when he said that Parliament could make or break laws against the King's will and have it binding.[149] Thus the *Vox Clamantis*, with all its revisions, is to be seen not only as a unified commentary on the tragic course of Richard's rule from 1381 to 1399, as Macaulay, the editor of the entire Gowerian corpus, saw it, but also as a document testifying to the critical role of the governing 'middle class'. As Gower said in his smaller Latin poems as well as in his monumental works, law and those who maintain the law, rather than fate, govern the health of kingdoms. In *O deus immense* he noted that an astute king 'should see how the cart is running and take care not to fall under its wheels'. Monarchical absolutism, as Richard was inclined to interpret it, or as his subjects believed him to be interpreting it, was both inappropriate to England's social and political condition and lethal to the King himself. The similarities between Gower's requirements for good and just government of the state and the charges brought against Richard during his parliamentary deposition are not fortuitous. They reflect, as did the anonymous poetry of the last quarter of the century, the popular sentiments (largely of those who supported the Lords Appellant) concerning social order, political and judicial governance and a pious, private morality. Gower advised that the clergy could not be looked to for responsible political guidance in a time when the Church was itself split by the Great Schism. Instead, nations must turn to their own positive laws, justly upheld, to obtain internal peace. Unlike some of his anonymous predecessors, Gower does not blame the clergy alone for the corruption of the realm. Men are and must be turned in on themselves and demand of themselves strict adherence to law, guided by reason, if they are to save the commonwealth and thereby themselves in the political arena. (We have already heard this message from the Digby poet, who may well have copied them from Gower.) Thus his great fear of those classes or members of classes who defy reason, disrupt the theoretical order of the fixed estates, and act wildly like beasts, obeying no law but natural urges. He says in his last important poem, *In Praise of Peace*,

If holy cherche after the duete
Of Cristes word be nought al avysed
To make pes, acord and unite
Among the kinges that ben now devised,
Yit natheles the lawe stant assised
Of mannys wit to be so resonable,
Withoute that to stonde hemselve stable.

Fisher has extracted three interconnecting themes in Gower's long works: individual virtue to counter man's sinful nature; legal justice to keep men in check by reason and positive enactment: and the administrative responsibility of the king to keep the whole political machine running smoothly.[150] These themes may be found both implicitly and explicitly in the complaint poetry we have previously considered. Macaulay and Fisher are correct (if we accept these themes as fundamental to the entire message that Gower wished to offer), in not ascribing his three works to the penitential tradition which produced the variations on the *Manuel des péchés/ Handlyng Synne*.[151] Although Gower drew on the penitential, the sermon, the homiletic and hortatory tradition, he did so more with the purpose of ornamenting what was primarily a politically and socially critical theme. Seen in this light, Gower is the century's poet of political and social unrest *par excellence*. It is true that thirteenth-century preachers developed the 'abuses of the age' genre to scrutinize the three estates, producing *sermones ad status*, but as Fisher has said, 'when Gower uses political figures or ideas he is likely to show affiliation with the publicist literature rather than with the sermon'.[152] The *Vox Clamantis* treats the different classes and the abuses of their station and duties, and Gower apparently sees himself as criticizing the estates in the tradition of the *sermones ad status*; but his solution to this problem of divisiveness is moral and political rather than religious. By drawing extensively on Ovid *et al.*, using what we would today call a scissors-and-paste method of borrowing suitable lines from other authors but reuniting them in a new context, he combined aspects of the traditional complaint, political theory, classical expression and penitential rhetoric to create a distinctly Gowerian pattern of fourteenth-century society that was to be regulated by law and love under a king who is aware of the legal interrelationships of his society. Consciously combining the 'mirror for princes' genre with current political theory and the colour of topical social complaint, he is historically accurate about events in his own lifetime up to a point. He was not, however, writing a chronicle but a moral tract in verse, which redefines the king's role in a law-bound society. In the *Vox*, as Fisher has noted, the king's judicial role is so emphasized as to enable Gower to group the monarch with the lawyers rather than with chivalry.[153] The principles Gower wishes to teach, the vices and virtues he illustrates, pertain, even in the *Confessio Amantis*, as much to the governance of a just ruler as to a courtly lover.[154]

Like many of the anonymous complaint poets of the time, Gower also wants an honourable end to the wars with France. Law and love between rulers and between subjects are the only principles that may reconcile social men to peace and harmony. This means for Gower that the fixed estates must remain so and must recognize their respective duties within the bounds of the law of the land. And as was pointed out earlier, the law was far more rigid, and therefore anachronistic, than the actual flexibility of mobility in late fourteenth-century society, and this was realized in the *Anonimale Chronicle*. Gower does not seem aware that his own estate, the second, had emerged, swollen with new recruits, during the fourteenth century, and that they became politically strong with a voice to be heard, precisely as a result of the loosening of the feudal structure during the early phases of the Hundred Years War. Instead, Gower vividly paints the chaos that has ensued from men moving unnaturally out of their divinely ordained and allotted stations. His fear of the unreasoned bestiality of the 'peasants' sounds not unlike the similar fear expressed by the monk Walsingham whose St Alban's Abbey was a primary target of the rioters. It is only the *Anonimale* chronicler who begins to show the peasants' own view during those riotous months.

Rather than see Gower as more progressive than many of his contemporaries, as Fisher wishes to do,[155] largely because of his emphasis on the concept of legal justice and a regal responsibility for all the estates that is defined in terms of the common good, I believe Gower should be seen as a precise mirror of contemporary, legal *theory*, and therefore a conservative voice that spoke anachronistically about affairs in which presumably he played some part, if only as witness. By speaking so often about the place of law in the sense of positive enactment guiding society, and the king's role in seeing that the legal system operates equitably, Gower was merely parroting the ideology of his class and time. The anonymous complaint poetry we have already examined produced a wealth of examples where law and just administrators, backed by their mounting financial strength, were considered the very heart of a just and peaceful realm, and this theme was developed as early as *The Simonie* of the Auchinleck Manuscript. Furthermore, in terms of historical accuracy, Gower was hopelessly behind the times. But this was true of social theorists and the clichés of the general citizenry well into the fifteenth century if not beyond. He and they were simply unconscious that there *were* changes of which they were a part. Yet, ironically, Gower supported and praised the rise of a successful merchant bourgeoisie moving into positions of governing power, as the sustainers of the nation, financially and morally. Gower himself complained about the low-born status of lawyers, although it is clear that the entire, extensively legalized structure that he wished to preserve was erected with them as the cornerstone.

On the theoretical plane, what Gower tried and failed to reconcile, was Augustine's inclusion in his *City of God* of selected portions of Cicero's notion of a *res publica* made up of a three-tiered society, with a static membership that was functionally fixed. Like Cicero, who was himself a political success as a *novus homo* because he had been able to move up from the second order (the equestrians) to the governing class as member of the Senate, many successful fourteenth-century lawyers or civil servants or newly armigerous members of the gentry in Gower's day were the first to cry for an end to social mobility. Their demand was unrealistic. Those members of the second and even third estate who mouthed the commonplaces of fixed estates on which complaint and satire were based, did not, in fact, live according to such principles: franklins or yeoman farmers made themselves lords of the town; drapers made themselves mayors of London. McFarlane's 'bastard feudatories' were the sign of the times. No amount of special pleading for a return to the good old 'feudal' days would either bring them back or reflect the situation as it then stood.

Where Gower was more historically accurate, at least in terms of what was realizable in his own times, was in his view of kingship as a shared, judicial role: the king was a maintainer of a system that could and did operate without him but not always justly; he was also a protector of the Church. Langland, similarly, has his king the arbiter of justice in the Mede episode, and the king is also thus presented in the Digby poems. Parliament, which was also a judicial court, had so evolved by the end of the century as to be financially and politically dependent on the Commons, and no king interested in maintaining his power could choose to neglect his dependence on the 'middle class' for the maintenance of the legal system. One law, as Gower said in the *Confessio*, must govern all estates if the common weal is to be served. Likewise, in Digby and elsewhere such a sentiment was expressed, based on a notion of Christian equity, each man getting his due and all men being equal before the law. Such

principles were inherited from a partially known Cicero, baptized for the Latin Middle Ages by Augustine's commentary,
and 'made life' in the practical governance of an extensively
legislated fourteenth-century England.

To what extent the previous half-century or more of verse
complaint was a mere prolegomenon to Gower's achievement in
the *Vox Clamantis* becomes clear as the reader perseveres
through the thousands of lines of the poem. Although one mis-
ses the sound of Gower's Latin lines in Stockton's able prose
translation,[156] and we must keep in mind that Gower's message
was a poetic one, his analysis of his own times, his frequent
humility and the touching personal elements that show through
his extensive use of the Latin verse of his sources combine to
make the *Vox*, even in English, a compelling and revealing
work. Whatever permitted Gower to name names (although he
also uses the heraldic devices for the Appellants in the 'Tripertita') and be uncompromisingly explicit about the waywardness
of members of the three estates, without losing either his life or
his good name, remains something of a mystery. It bespeaks
patronage in high places and personal courage. Some of what he
has to say about the 'peasant' class in particular, has an
extremely unpleasant ring in the modern ear. But here was a
man who wrote simply of his own biases, making of English and
London history of the 1370s, 1380s and 1390s a record of private experiences and tribulations with only the smallest reliance
on obfuscating and ambiguous allegory. The explicit purpose
and the final achievement of the *Vox Clamantis* show Gower to
have been more in touch with the spirit of his age, its political
expectations, its piety and its ideals, than any other writer of the
times.

It is easy enough to demonstrate this by allowing the *Vox* to speak
for itself. In Book One, he tells how he had a bad night and could not
fall asleep for worry about the future and because he was reflecting
on times past. 'Finally, darkness had closed my eyes. So when the
greater part of my wasted night was spent, sleepiness suddenly
overtook my weary eyes. I took a little rest while Lucifer called forth
its fire at dawn and then I had a dream-vision.' We shall be
reminded only infrequently that the events described in seven
books of the *Vox Clamantis* occur while the poet sleeps. Striving to
present the reality of the political and social injustices of his time, it
appears that Gower simply could not sustain the distancing mechan-

ism of the dream frame. He begins, however, by seeing 'bands of
rabble changed into asses, terrifying monsters, rascally bands of the
common mob wandering destructively through fields in countless
throngs. God's curse had changed them into irrational wild beasts
whose former usefulness as tamed beasts of burden was now lost.
They demanded greater delicacies, refusing to be beasts of burden,
and imitated the style and dress of horses trying to aggrandize
themselves with what nature had denied them' (Book I, ch. 2). They
refused their divinely appointed duties as did subsequent bands of
rabble turned into oxen, swine, birds of prey, all acting unnaturally,
in the manner of a nightmarish presentation of the traditional
animal fable where beasts take on the attributes of men. 'Those
birds who used to stay at home and tread on dung dared to assume
the eagle's prerogatives for themselves, and by this means they
dragged the naturally higher beasts down. Law and order in nature
was banished.' Another band of rabble was turned into the flies and
frogs of the biblical plagues: 'this was a day when everywhere the
weak man terrified the strong, the humblest the noble, and the little
the great. This was the day [obviously the day when the 'peasants'
marched on London in 1381, which, Gower says,] no record had
previously told the likes of, if we confess the truth. A Jackdaw
commonly called Wat [a conflation of Wat Tyler and Jack Straw]
assumed command over the other wild beasts with great rhetorical
skills. Behold, the untutored heart's sense of shame was lost and it
no longer feared the terrors of crime or punishment. Just as the
lioness rages when robbed of her nursing cub and attacks the cattle
near her, so the angry peasantry, bereft of the safeguard of justice,
attacked the nobles with greater ferocity. Misfortune is common to
all men, but nevertheless the same calamity does not confer the
same status upon all' (Book I, chs. 8, 9). Gower here recalls that
those who fall from higher up on fortune's wheel fall the harder. But
he will not ordinarily place much faith in fortune, and by the end of
the *Vox* will blame Richard's misrule as the cause of the rising of the
'peasants'. 'The peasant attacked and the knight in the city did not
resist. Troy was without Hector. I saw that law and order took no
further cognizance of the world and rumour of various calamities
everywhere was on the increase.' Thus he rushes from the city,
wandering in tremendous fear through the countryside, afraid to
speak his mind to anyone. Although the text is riddled with passages
excerpted from Ovid, Gower has astonishingly made the lines,
written in another time and for another context, work well to

describe his own private anguish at the events of 1381.

After the revolt is quashed, Gower extends his dream allegory to the Tower of London, likened to a ship, in which all the nobles have taken refuge. The ship comes near the shore of some island, and Gower asks 'what island is this?' He is answered by a worthy old man:

This once used to be called the island of Brut, an exile, Diana gave it to him out of pity. The people of this land are wild. Their way of life involves far more quarrelling than love. They are fair of form but see, by nature, they have more cruel fierceness than wolves. They do not fear laws, they overthrow right by force, and justice falls in defeat because of their violent warfare. This rough, pernicious people devises more treachery, crime, fighting, uproar and harm than laws. This land which bloodshed and slaughters and wars always control, was born of mixed stock. Yet I do not think there is a worthier people under the sun if there were mutual love among them. [Book 1, ch. 20]

This recurring theme of mutual love and maintenance of lawful justice runs throughout the remaining six books, well after the dream-vision mechanism has receded into the background. For the peasantry, the law is something not understood but feared, unquestioningly.

The peasantry had been bound in chains and lay patiently under our foot, for the peasant always lay in wait to see whether he by chance could bring the noble class to destruction. He has a rough, boorish nature which is not tempered by any affection, but he has bitterness in his hateful heart. In his subjection the lowly plowman did not love, but rather feared and reviled the very man who provided for him. [Book 1, ch. 21]

Gower must therefore exclude the peasantry from the commonwealth since they do not contribute to the maintenance of law and love. Rather, the third estate is held in check by fear of the legal machinery of a just state. If there is any class that is the direct descendant of Adam and his first sin it is the peasantry. As Augustine saw all positive law as punitive and preventive for all men, society being held in check by the public executioner, Gower here sees it as largely playing this role for the lowly agricultural and day-labouring class. There is no doubt that his attitude in the first book of the *Vox* is harsher than what we find in the subsequent but previously composed books, but he will never be a man who sees the third order as other than obediently in its place, held there through fear rather than love. Gower's is the voice of the possessionate class:

he is a compassionate man but with a very clear, rather Platonic understanding of the characteristics of the three estates into which one is fortuitously born but as a result of which one receives, as though from birth, the distinguishing functional potentialities, which tutoring merely develops further.

In Book Two of the *Vox Clamantis* he begins to speak of fortune, in whom he says he does not believe, and it is clear that the entire work is a testament to men's manipulation of their potentials rather than the vagaries of chance. 'Fortune', he says, 'is nothing, and neither destiny nor fate nor chance has anything to do with human affairs. But each man fashions his own destiny and opposes chance as he pleases and creates his own fate. And indeed, a free mind considers what it voluntarily does for its own benefit as done in the name of fate. If your will is good, a good fate follows,' he says optimistically; 'if your will is bad, through the operation of your own mind you cause fate to be bad. It is to your advantage to shun the worst fate, for your soul is free to follow the one as well as the other.'

As we shall see later,[157] there was a wide-ranging free will–determinism controversy in the schools which escaped the walls of the universities to reappear even in the Nun's Priest's Prologue of Chaucer's *Canterbury Tales*. There is, however, something odd in reading this confidence in the human will expressed so soon after the literary hysteria of the first book, where it appeared that so much of Gower's own fortune was not of his own making or willing. Gower then goes on to speak of what he considers to be a divine *fiat*: that there are three estates, not fortuitously so, but divinely and, therefore, rationally ordained. 'Everyone in the world lives under them and serves them,' he affirms. He will blame no estate in its entirety as being at fault for the evils of the times, but when estates or their members transgress against virtues, their fault declares against them and thus they create their own ill fortune. These three estates are the clergy, the knighthood and the peasantry. 'Through their going astray, the misfortunes of the world befall us.' History is thus made by appropriate or inappropriate actions of three given estates. Structured play is the primary feature of secular behaviour, and a game with divinely ordained ethical rules is implied: play accordingly and all goes well; otherwise, misfortunes and personal and public tribulations are humanly caused. History is, for Gower, made by men.

Gower first treats generally of the waywardness of the clergy, especially of prelates, 'because they are more powerful than others', and thus, with greater social effect. He draws extensive parallels between Christ and his faulty followers in the Church. In Book Three Gower continues to speak of the functional differentiation of the three estates, and this sounds like the original beginning of the entire poem. It is interesting that he characterizes the function of the clergy as *teaching* rather than praying; the knight fights and the peasant tills the fields. His is a narrower conception of the more diversified 'field full of folk' found in Langland's prologue to *Piers Plowman*. 'What is wrong with the clergy today', Gower says, 'is that its worth is measured now in terms of its wealth; property confers honours and abject poverty is an object of reproach.' Not only is this a cliché of social complaint literature, but it is corroborated in Archbishop FitzRalph's *Defensio curatorum*,[158] where he definitely affirms that poverty is a sign of divine displeasure and that the poor are to be shunned as suffering exceedingly from their sins. Goods of the world, according to the Archbishop of Armagh, are there to be used if not enjoyed, so that poverty can only be a sign of the reprobate. But Gower opposes this attitude for the clergy and says,

when a rich man speaks, then every ear will pay attention, but the words of a poor man are worth nothing. The intelligence of the wise man is as nothing if he is without property. Without property there are no attainments, there is no true faith, no gracefulness of speech, no originality of wit, no uprightness. Where there is property there is an abundance of good sense. We reject the man whom the world rejects. But we acclaim that man as worthy whom the world's bounty has brought to worldly riches. And so the world is inwardly preferred by prelates. They now cater to their fat snug bodies. Nor are their feasts open to the poor. [Book 3, ch. 1]

It may be argued that nature takes care of itself: the plague had naturally so reduced the population, and war had become so profitable, that those who survived plague and wars were not only the fittest but also were fewer in number and thus the better able to dispense with and increase the wealth of the nation. After years of widespread death, natural and man-made, England did not experience an economic decline, but the contrary.[159] The effect on the clergy was to increase their material expectations, and men devised further, legal means of doing so. Gower complains that

the priests' new-fangled decisions declare that because the body had sinned, the sinner's purse should pay. So in these days repeated lust means profits in the account book. Nowadays a judge rages with anger if there is any downright wantonness and he does not know whom to hold guilty of unchastity. If a reckless layman copulates with a reckless woman, the priest shouts out in church and she trembles with fear. Yet if a cleric sinfully indulges in sexual intercourse, nothing is thought of it, for he himself may be both judge and party to his own case. And in such fashion do they weigh other men down under a heavy burden, but how lightly the burden sits on their own shoulders. The purse is as strong as our court of law. All these positive laws of the clergy are unnecessary for the betterment of the soul but they make a profit out of them. Before such forbidden acts are committed they sell dispensations and then freely allow these acts to be committed for the sake of gold. [Book 3, ch. 4]

Clearly the positive law of the Church had followed the same road as the civil law. It had expanded upon the precepts of inherent moral obligation to create a more structured, social and clerical discipline, and careers in Church and State were created out of this expansion of legislation. But, as Gower reminds the reader, 'Christ's way was straight and a mild yoke; his simple precepts were set down in a few words.' 'But the positive law of the Church', established by a covetous clergy, 'represents big business', and under this expanded legislation, 'no mercy is freely given without money.'

The clergy are not willing to battle with pagans in the cause of their faith nor even spread the gospel according to Holy Scripture. But if one were to oppose them in regard to their worldly kingdoms, they then put up a savage fight. As a result of their positive laws, the church wars even against Christians for worldly goods. They strike with the sword; if anyone strikes back the positive law of some new book damns him for it. Peter preached, of course, but today's pope fights. The clergy must not assume the function of the knight whose role it is to carry on wars of state. It is of no use for those who can bind all things by word of mouth to employ force in any way. [Book 3, chs. 6 and 8]

Gower then speaks of Christians' rights to the Holy Land and admonishes the Church for not wishing to support a war against the 'pagan interloper'. He argues for the legal probity of the Christian claim to Jerusalem:

The lineal descent by right of His mother proclaims Christ as the heir of the land in which He was born. If any of this world ought to be our property it should be Christ's part, which is made over to Him by legal title. But a pagan interloper holds it now, and he pays no tribute into our treasury for it. But we do not carry on war against these men by attacking either their persons or their property. Our law is silent about this. Instead we say – 'Let Christ himself claim whatever things that are His, if He wants them; let Him fight for his own property. We are not interrupting our leisure for wars so far away and not even an envoy is going there on behalf of Christ's portion. Instead we are fighting open battles over worldly possessions with our brothers whom the water of baptism indicates as reborn.' [Book 3, ch. 9]

We can see striking similarities with the arguments advanced by Philippe de Mézières.

When he speaks of the 'unnatural lack of affection of the clergy' he presents a theme that underlies the whole poem: 'if love were more common, then everything would be in common so that one man could clearly help another'. This love, as with the law, is of course limited to the Christian fellowship and does not spill over its boundaries to include pagans. 'But because the clergy mulct the laity without hinderance, so too the laity find in this wrong living an example to follow. In this way the sheep become tainted with the shepherd's stains and each falls into the ditch like a blind man.'

'The voice of the people agrees with the voice of God, so that in critical times it ought to be held in greater awe. Common talk has taught me what I shall say, and my words contain nothing new.' In general, very little that was new or modern (*modernus*) was considered a virtue throughout the Middle Ages, so that the rhetorical platitude that an author's truths have been uttered by the orthodox before is not a surprising occurrence. Gower may then proceed to reaffirm that

nowadays money controls the just men and Venus the holy ones. So justice does not govern affairs, but instead willfulness does, corrupted by evil and lacking in judgement. In plain words, false men determine what is right for you and they do little or nothing for the sake of justice. They take what is rightly mine away from me. [Book 3, ch. 17]

Indeed, Gower is saying nothing new, but the expansive analysis he gives to the nature of current wrongdoing makes his *Vox*, thus far, a *summa* of traditional anticlerical complaint. Furthermore, 'the secular clergy neglect their cures of souls and stay close to the courts in order to dance attendance upon important men'. We have heard this before. Gower assures us that he writes of the faults of the negligent bishop exactly as he had heard them spoken of and his pen has stopped at that point. 'The lesser clergy also degenerates in their splendour like the knight only without the spurs. In fact, the man who seeks to keep his wife chaste nowadays and his chambers clean will wish that the pigeon and the priest stay away from his room: the one spreads dung and the other spreads lewdness.' [Book 3, ch. 20]

It goes for the whole ecclesiastical establishment that 'it is not right that anyone esteem a man who does not hold justice in awe. One who presumes to indulge in practices prohibited by law ought to go without the benefits conferred by law.' How personal his message appears when he concludes: 'for these reasons, which I have carefully considered one by one, I conclude that priests are guiltier than you are.'

Nor are scholars exempt from his complaint.

They go under the name of the clergy whilst they study, but scarcely a one studies for the sake of the necessary subject matter; instead the mere shadow of its outline is enough. A cleric used to go to school with a patient spirit, but now worldly glory is his master. He rambles here and there, a lazy, wandering drunkard, wayward and given to lust. Why, in fact, do scholars wish to become priests? To escape the scourgings of the harsh common law; one does not have to sweat with toil and one can live in idleness; he is provided with food and clothing. This is the reason for going to school which makes one study civil law which skillfully teaches its logic. They find holy orders pleasant, the clerical learning is useful, so long as they can make a fat profit from their studies. [Book 3, ch. 28]

'What an astounding state of affairs,' says Gower. 'The scholar reads and studies about virtue while his own actions become more and more vicious.' He concludes the third book with the familiar light analogy: 'because the clergy without the light of virtues is blind, we errant laymen wander in darkness'.

Book Four treats of the waywardness of monks acting against the sanctity of their orders. He also speaks against wayward friars. He lists the traditional complaints against straying friars and against those who aim at the highest teaching positions for the sake of worldly reputation and in order to become more privileged to hear confession, 'as if they were exempt from the yoke of their order'. When we look at anticlerical and monastic abuse, particularly from the Lollards, we shall see that Wyclif's and the Lollards' fury was traditional and orthodox enough when compared with what Gower and the anonymous complaint literature had to say on the matter. Gower argues that those friars who live in disorderly fashion are not necessary for the guidance of the Church or for the common good. 'Nevertheless, honour is rightfully due those who obey Francis' rightful commands in honest fashion.' He alludes to the traditional complaint against their luring thoughtless and immature boys into their orders, and to the unnecessary travelling and the luxurious buildings of the mendicants. Their buildings have decorated walls,

marble columns, with various pictures on them; they are surrounded with every elegance. They have rich carving in their cells
and carved doorposts. Although their attire may appear simple,
their rich dwellings mark them as insincere.

Gower turns next, in Book Five, to the knighthood, established to
protect the rights of the Church and to foster the common good, not
least by upholding the rights of orphans and widows. 'In the past a
knight did not bear arms for fame but performed his deeds for the
sake of justice.' But today the love of women has betrayed their
ideals. 'What honour shall a conquerer have if a woman's love can
conquer him? I do know he will have no praise from Christ.'
Gower's attitude to knighthood is not only one of strict piety but is a
remarkable rejection of the courtly love relationship which inspired
chivalry of the thirteenth century. His is a return to an earlier ethic,
when knighthood was established for holy warfare and for protec-
tion of the people, as one finds it in the early *chansons de geste* and in
the *Roland*, where women find no place at all. He speaks of 'how the
knight who engages in the use of arms when he is burning with lust
for a woman's affection certainly does not deserve the honour of
praise for it at all'. 'Love', he says,

is an unjust judge; marrying opposites it makes the very nature of things
deteriorate. In love, discord is harmonious, learning is ignorant, anger
makes jests, honour is base, hope is afraid, harms are helpful. . . . Love is
sickly health, pious sin, warlike peace . . . a capricious law without justice
. . . irrational reason, a living death, a dying life. . . . [Book 5, ch. 2]

Assuming a distinctly clerical pose in rejecting worldly love and lust
for higher spiritual love, Gower presents knighthood in the old
guise of warriors for Christ and the people's commonwealth. And
yet he realizes how 'nature grieves because of love and yet is joyless
without it'. He is at pains to show, however, that the knight's goals
must be a higher love than that which the world offers. 'The knight
who engages in feats of arms for a woman's love or for worldly fame'
acts without real purpose, for 'in the end both pass away in vain
without the reward of divine commendation'. Instead, a 'properly
constituted knighthood is responsible for the general establishment
of security for all other classes of society'. Knighthood's role is
social rather than private. His proper knight is married.

If knighthood were worthy then the husband would prepare himself for his
ventures together with his wife, with peace being restored to the realm. If
knighthood were worthy, then the harsh estimate [of it] which is noised

about in the land, would be of no importance [for he would] battle on behalf of Christ's name and defend the common cause with his valour. [Book 5, ch. 7]

Once again, Philippe de Mézières's principles for his Order of the Passion find confirmation in Gower. So important is the knightly estate that if, as a model for proper conduct in society, it fails, then 'what can the cleric and peasant do for themselves when war looms at their doors?'

Feats of arms thrive upon good morals; otherwise good fortune vanishes. Therefore, resist vices, O warrior, and strongly cherish your public duties. Let no man be loved who is unworthy of love and let the man lack love who refuses its responsibility [which is clearly a social one]. But the knight whom the sake of gain moves to enter into battle will have no righteous honour . . . those who want war and who follow the camps and are eager for spoils and thirsting for loot are similar to the vulture who eats men and follows camps of war. . . . But I see the honour is now neglected for gold. . . . The number of knights increases but their activity decreases. Thus their honour is empty, since it is without responsibility. [Book 5, ch. 8]

We have here a *summa* of already examined anonymous complaints against the growing number of men who undeservedly are knighted and given family arms, and yet who achieve fame and respect illicitly or through money. War is fought for booty rather than for moral ends which may lead to peace on the home front. This negative, chastising element in Gower's complaint against contemporary knights is one way of maintaining the purity of the older chivalric, crusading ideal. Chaucer's knight in the *Canterbury Tales* is the positive side, which reinforces the same moral idea. The commitment to a crusading ideal, in theory, was of course well-ingrained in a generation that not only went to Prussia and Bohemia in the 1380s and 1390s, but remembered the feats of arms in the 1360s of members of families like the Lovels, Moreleys, Hastings, Greys, Scropes and Grosvenors. The evidence for such families' involvement in crusades survives in the records of three famous armorial cases.[160] But it seems more accurate to say that the crusading ideal kept an armchair form of chivalry alive, rather than to say the reverse: that chivalry kept the crusade alive. Crusading had become the class philosophy of the knight who, in an earlier period, would have seen his task to be the maintenance of law and morality at home in Christian lands. Gower's knightly class at home were to be legal administrators rather than men of arms. Abroad, and only against the infidel, was the knight to assume the war code of an armed elite.

Having spoken of those of knightly rank who ought to keep the state unharmed, Gower next speaks of those

who are under obligation to enter into the labours of agriculture, which are necessary for obtaining food and drink for the sustenance of the human race. After knighthood there remains only the peasant rank – the rustics in it cultivate the grain and vineyards. They are the men who seek food for us by the sweat of their heavy toil, as God Himself decreed. The guiding principle of our first father Adam, which he received from the mouth of God on high, is rightly theirs. . . . Now, however, scarcely a farmer wishes to do such work, and instead he wickedly loafs everywhere. [Book 5, ch. 9]

'An evil disposition is widespread among the common people and I suspect that the servants of the plow are often responsible for it,' says Gower, writing before the 'peasants' revolt':

For they are sluggish, they are scarce, and they are grasping. For the very little they do they demand the highest pay. Yet a short time ago one man performed more service than three do now. The servant of the plow, contrary to the law of the land, seeks to make a fool of the land. They desire the leisure of great men, but they have nothing to feed themselves with, nor will they be servants. God and nature have ordained that they shall serve, but neither knows how to keep them within bounds. Everyone owning land complains in his turn about these people; each stands in need of them and none has control over them. God imposed servile work upon them so that the peasantry might subdue its proud feelings; and liberty, which remained secure for freemen, ruled over the serfs and subjected them to its law. [Book 5, ch. 9]

The experience of yesterday makes us better informed as to what perfidy the unruly serf possesses . . . yet the principle which the old order of things teaches is not wrong: let the law accordingly cut down the harmful teasels of rabble lest they uproot the nobler grain with their stinging. Unless it is struck down first, the peasant race strikes against freemen, no matter what nobility or worth they possess. Its actions outwardly show that the peasantry is base and it esteems the nobles the less because of their very virtues. The serfs perform none of their servile duties voluntarily and have no respect for the law. Whatever the serf's body suffers patiently under compulsion, inwardly his mind ever turns toward utter wickedness. Miracles happen only contrary to nature; only the divinity of nature can go against its own powers. It is not for man's estate that anyone from the class of serfs should try to set things right. [!] [Book 5, ch. 9]

Here is the most extensive and clearest attitude we may find towards the post-plague third estate, more elaborate than Walsingham's and more personal than anything promulgated in the laws of the land to keep them in their traditional roles. When we consider that Gower wrote this before the 'peasant' uprising, it is not surprising that the eventual revolt was as violent and lawless as it was, particularly against lawyers, the gentry and men with the hostile and traditionally conservative views of Gower's estate. At once denying them participation in the making of the laws, Gower yet demands that they be bound to contribute to the common good. He goes on to speak of the various kinds of workers from the rabble who are employed under the supervision of others.

They ought to be bound over to their diverse tasks for the common good. These day-labourers are associated with the peasants and have even less discipline. They are not willing to serve anyone by the year; one cannot retain them even for a single month. There is scarcely one worker in a thousand of them who wants to remain faithful to his bargain with you. . . . Born of poor man's stock and a poor man himself, he demands things for his belly like a lord. The established law is of no help to one, for there is no ruling such men, nor does anyone make provisions against their misdeeds. This is a race without power of reason, like beasts, for it does not esteem mankind nor does it think God exists. I believe that in a short time the lords will submit to them, unless justice shall have been obtained by means of fear. [Book 5, ch. 10]

Gower follows this outburst with a paeon of praise for the ideal behaviour of city burghers.

Since no single region by itself produces all the various kinds of things necessary for human use, merchants, among others, have been appointed to assist the world's citizens. Through their agency the goods of all regions are mutually shared. The noble city dwellers have an honour and they have an onus. It is an honour that the citizen possess such great wealth; it is an onus that he then seek after ill-gotten gains [implying that he punish the wrong-doers]. It is an honour for a citizen to take the office of mayor; it is the onerous responsibility of his office to uphold the laws. The ordinary city depends upon two groups of people: there are merchants and there are artisans. The one needs to have the assistance of the other so that there is a general esteem between them. As long as firm affection endures between the greater and the lesser, the city is happy and the state is prosperous. As long as unity of the people endures, justice will endure for both parties of the city and everyone will approve conditions.

But

I can testify exactly as I have heard: just rule hardly sits upon the bench now. The man who clings entirely to worldly pomp in order to increase his reputation does not realize that he must hold with God. I do not judge or condemn any men in particular [he hastens to add], but only those who have neglected God for the world. For we are all so bent upon money at all hours that scarcely one festival day remains for God. Tell me what citizen now remains without a share in the defrauding? Even if there were such a man, my city scarcely recognizes him. [Book 5, ch. 11]

Gower tells how Fraud rules among sellers of fish and meat, among bakers, purveyors of beer and roast meat sellers in the market. Fraud the hostess is delighted by pilgrims in her guest lodgings, for she is short in her measure; she cuts her hay short but takes good care of the money. 'Fraud is known as general manager in the city. When she enters upon any business, it always pays. Even though Fraud is ruler, her activity does not further the common profit, but she keeps an eye out for her own gains. Fraud brings in nothing to the honest citizen.'

Becoming even more specific, Gower complains about low-born men in positions of civic responsibility.

Nothing is more troublesome than a lowly person when he has risen to the top, at least when he was born a serf. [Gower seems willing to accept social mobility, however, within the second estate.] His thinking continues along the old way of a serf, let fate confer upon him whatever high rank it will. The rude, untutored man is not transformed by an honour, but will be cruder because of his rusticity. No matter how a false destiny may place a man of no character in charge of a city, Fame will ultimately establish who he is. Everyone can observe these things well enough in the mirror of today. [Book 5, ch. 15]

When Gower begins Book Six, he has reached much of the heart of his argument, for here he treats the ministers of the law, the most obvious perverters of justice. Everyone must be governed by the justice of the law, according to Gower, 'however much these very men confound all justice by their chicaneries, and in various ways debilitate it for the sake of worldly gain' (Book 6, ch. 1). With the increasing numbers of men associated with the maintenance of the law of the land, it has become clear that their purpose is connected with payment rather than with law and order.

A struggle for gold so consumes the law like a fresh ulcer, that stricken justice is no longer safe. I cry out what the voice of the people cries out and I take note of none except those whom wickedness stigmatizes. Under the cloak of law hides cleverness. When lawyers can twist this kind of law, they transmute the justice begotten of their own words. They care not in what way a case is just or unjust, but that it be rich in return for them. Indeed, unless he knows how to mask the laws with his stratagems, then others will say that his work is a failure. I wonder at the fact that the counsellor who ought to defend legally the causes of the poor instead aggravates their need. I grant that law is good in itself, but I now see its wicked masters distorting justice. If the law makes it necessary that I act in opposition to a lawyer and I ask to have my own legal counsel, then they all say they are not willing to oppose a colleague. Thus they strike, but no one can strike them. Law is disturbed by bribery, favour and fear, so that under today's law justice refuses to act in a poor man's case. This changed law is turning into a school of logic. Indeed, there are students of the law without numbers in the world. [Book 6, ch. 3]

Gower describes not only a situation in which money opens the lips of professional lawyers, but one in which the law itself has become a technique of logic chopping, available only to those who are able to play with the Latin, disregarding the moral principles behind the original purpose of the positive law. He reminds the judge who has created a material empire for himself out of his legal skills that he has sold himself for worldly possessions. 'You own everything that is on earth, but you do not possess yourself. O you who know others but not yourself . . . know yourself first and me second.' We are reminded of the Digby poet's admonition to all those 'who beareth estate' and are responsible for the laws, to 'know thyself first'.

You build castles and newly decorated chambers and you cherish whatever is worldly more than divinity. You build huge buildings, you enclose them with a wide, deep ditch, so that when closed, the front gates may shut out the public. But Babylon fell, and even mighty Troy, and world-ruling Rome scarcely retains her prestige. That which is justice or that which is the just kind of judge, is not to be seen at the present day. If there is a justice who acts falsely under such a title, he bears the empty title with no justice. . . . [Book 6, ch. 5]

This statement recalls the goliard's reference to the king in *Piers Plowman*: a king is not one but in name unless he acts according to justice. Passing rapidly over the sinfulness of sheriffs, bailiffs, jurors in assizes who support unjust lawsuits because they have been hired by the money of the rich, Gower complains that they all combine to slander unjustly and oppress the poor, and thereby do injury to the common people. It must be clear by now that Gower means by the common people and the poor those who are free, rather than the irrational and bestial serfs – in other words, the poor with small holdings, the city dwellers at the lower end of the gild associations, the unbeneficed scholars honestly working in chantries in London. The overwhelmingly legal framework of his conceptualized England is most strikingly confirmed when he says 'Just as it is necessarily ordained for men to be on earth, so it is right that laws be instituted for governing them, provided, however, that the guardians of the law discern truth from falsehood and render every man his due with impartial authority.' Yet up to the present, that is, up to the late 1370s, he is willing to absolve from blame the young king for he is 'innocent of the sins and injustices now going on, because of his minor age'.

Laws were established for the transgressor so that each man might receive his due rewards. What is a people without law or what is law without a judge or what is a judge without justice? If anyone looks at the doings in our country he will observe three things which are frightening to me. All misfortunes are burdensome, but none more so than when a just man cannot get justice. Kingdoms divided against themselves cannot stand. Therefore all who govern kingdoms can see that the greatest part of our fate depends on them. The people must atone for whatever errors the great commit, since a weak head makes the members suffer. Peoples have perished because of a king's sin and writings rarely teach anything to the contrary. But royal goodness brings the joys of peace to the people, for God looks with favour on the deeds of a pious king. [Book 6, ch. 7]

Thus Gower has come to the real purpose of his *Vox*, for it is meant as a mirror for a prince to see himself reflected in the just or unjust legislation that maintains his realm.

Finally, in his advisory capacity, he warns that 'wars alone with their triumphs are no ornament to a king's reign; rather, he should obey good laws at all times'. Gower, therefore, sees the king as *sub jura*. What he expects of his people he must demand of himself. The king is model citizen, maintainer of the just realm and of its positive laws. 'Of what use are the people [to the earth] unless a king governs?' he asks.

Of what use is a king unless he has sound counsel? And of what use is counsel unless the king trusts it? But in our land there is such disunion that each man now chooses to go his own way. Discord troubles the fellow-citizens in the city today so that each destroys the right of the other. Nor is the law heeded now by rural leaders; rather he who is most powerful is master. The clergy blame the people and the people blame the clergy [as we have seen in the earlier anonymous complaints], but both persevere in their guilt. Envious of one another, each man blames the other and no group mends its own course. [Book 6, ch. 7]

We may compare the lament of *The Simonie* here.
  Modifying his attitude to Richard, he later adds:

the king, an undisciplined boy, neglects the moral behaviour by which a man might grow up from a boy. Indeed, youthful company so sways the boy that he has a taste for nothing practical unless it be his whim. The young men associated with him want what he wants; he enters upon a course of action and they follow him. Vainglory makes these youthful comrades vain, for which reason they vainly cultivate the royal quarters more and more. They abet the boy king in his childish behaviour whereby he wields the authority of virtue the less. [Book 6, ch. 7]

With further, astonishingly pointed remarks he continues:

there are also the older men of greed who in pursuing their gains tolerate many scandals for the boy's pleasure. Men of good character withdraw, those who are vicious come in, and the king's court contains whatever vice exists. Sin springs up on every side of the boy and he, who is quite easily led, takes to every evil. To boys it is not wrong-doing but joking, not dishonour but glorious spirit, but his destiny does arise out of this wrong-doing. Everywhere the voice of the people cries out about such things. . . . I accordingly grieve even the more than they over the disgusting things which I see, for which reason I offer the following writings for the boy king. [Book 6, ch. 7]

We may pause here to register astonishment at Gower's forthright criticism, and wonder, if it was meant for Richard, how he was able to speak so plainly. In the earlier version it was the king's counsel which was seen as the cause of sorrow. In the earlier version Gower stressed how, if the king were of mature age, 'he would set right the scale which now is without justice. For a king's moderation moderates other men and he is said to be the leader in the promotion of justice'. But when Richard persisted in his wantonness, Gower chastised him directly.

Since all men whatsoever of earthly estate are governed under the justice of royal authority, [the author] consequently intends to write this epistle, set forth for the sake of instruction to our king now reigning at present. With the help of divine grace our king, who is now in his youthful time of life, may be more plainly instructed by this letter in his royal functions when he has afterwards reached more mature years. However much the royal power may be exalted in any way above the laws, it is nevertheless only proper that his royal highness be persevering in good behaviour, zealously govern himself under the laws of justice as if he were a free man, and his people, as if in the presence of the Almighty King. O pious king, hear what your kingdom's rule should be, in harmony with the law and joined with God's justice. When I grasp the reins of the laws, I hold you in check more strongly than a fortress. [!] While you fear no man, be fearful for yourself. It is better for you, O king, to govern yourself according to the law than to subjugate all the kingdoms of the world to yourself. For the sake of the world, the fate of others is subject to you; for the sake of heaven be subject yourself to God. When rendering justice to the people you should likewise render justice to yourself. If you wish to be king, rule yourself and you will be one. By what right could a man who does not even reign over the workings of his own mind say he was a king? [!] The sovereign cannot confer wellbeing upon others as long as he is not ruler over himself as he should be. You are above the laws but live as a just man under them and because of you there will be hope of welfare for us. Firm vows of justice must guide you . . . drive wicked men quickly away from you. . . .

A man who urges war, who advises plundering and who conspires to get your people's taxes – O king, I implore you to shut your ears to such men, lest your renown crumble to pieces, struck down by them. [Book 6, ch. 8]

Gower reminds the young Richard of the prowess and honour of his just father the Black Prince, through whose wars 'the land was quiet'. He advises fighting just wars 'when our tried and tested rights call for war', but a king should not make war without a demonstrably just cause.

O king, if you were to look at yourself well in this mirror you could learn how very helpful it is to you . . . perform your duties to your laws . . . be a lover of justice. Be dutiful and govern your people according to law. Restore our common justice, now lost; bring law back to the realm and banish all crime. Pacify your people towards yourself, not by means of terror but rather through love. [Book 6, chs. 9, 10, 18]

Book Six, then, is the undisputed heart of the *Vox Clamantis*, a poetic treatise on the duties of the three estates under a law-abiding and just king who is at once above but also beneath the law. From these theoretical and hortatory heights Gower descends in the final and seventh book to a recapitulation of the horrors of his disorderly times, the more felt because of his intense patriotism which he allows to be expressed in a final, personal elegy. 'Now the clergy is turned into rabble and now the rabble preaches God's works like the clergy', which may be taken as a reference to John Ball or to the Wyclifites.

The peasant pretends to imitate the ways of the freeman and gives the appearance of him in his clothes. And the gentleman changes himself into this base fellow and wants to enjoy his churlish vice. In the eyes of the king, an immature boy is now wiser than Cicero and more welcome than Cato. All men lack any distinction except that of the tongue which sounds its harmonious words in the king's ears just like Echo. Fawning words now clothe with linen the infant whom a shepherd's cloak once covered. Boldness of tongue thunders strongly in its chambers about wars, but that ridiculous creature does not move a hand toward the battlefield. Taxes oppress us on all sides under the pretext of war and I know that a thousand misfortunes are for the profit of one man. The discipline of old does not serve as an example now; on the contrary, whim now governs our actions, instead of justice. . . . [Book 7, ch. 4]

Man is a microcosm; the world is good or ill in consequence of his acts. It is clear [since man is a miniature copy of God] that man's essential nature is mightier than any art and it plunges into death those whom its course attacks. Therefore, provide for that death which will be your end. As a result of man's sins, famine, pestilence, earthquakes and signs from heaven have led the way and now there is also war. . . . [Book 7, ch. 8]

I love all the kingdoms which the Lord has established for Himself throughout the world and which bear standards in Christ's name. But above all I love my own land, in which my family took its origin. If the native land which bore me as a young child and within whose realms I always remained fixed – if she suffers anything, my innermost feelings suffer with her and she shall not be able to suffer her misfortunes apart from me. I am almost overwhelmed by the weight of her adversities. If she stands firm, I stand firm; if she falls, I fall. [Book 7, ch. 24]

This moving passage is concluded with Gower's last assertion that 'what I have set down is the voice of the people, but you will also see that where the people call out, God is often there. The world', he concludes, 'will be such as a man shall have been during his life.' Thus the analysis of the three estates and their separate obligations has been reduced to an analysis of the responsibilities of each individual member of every estate, and the system of positive justice redounds on the actions of each Christian.

I have quoted at length and refrained from interrupting the flow of Gower's message to allow the most accomplished example of social complaint to have its say in something like its own voice. The Latin is even more stirring, not least because Gower's masters included Ovid, moulded neatly to suit the situation of the late fourteenth century. With all that has been said about the largely anonymous body of relatively undistinguished complaint verse that preceded Gower's work, it is hoped that Gower's own *Vox Claman-*

tis has provided sufficient testimony of the direction such verse had taken in the hands of a sincere and artful 'maker' who exposed his intense biases and his loves in a work that deserves to be read by students of medieval history and Anglo-Latin verse, as well as by students of Middle English literature, using it to reconstruct the context for contemporary vernacular texts.

Gower was to continue the *Vox* with the *Cronica Tripertita* in prose, which was meant as a tribute to Henry of Lancaster and an outright condemnation of Richard, who had become 'a man hardened to a tyrant's ways'. It ranks with other chronicles, biased in favour of the Appellants against Richard's court party, who finally were defeated and, for the most part, killed. Richard had so erred along with his favourites as to be seen as unregenerate to Gower, morally and politically, and therefore in no way suited to the role of kingship as Gower had defined it in the *Vox*. His telling of the events that led to the triumph of the Merciless Parliament and the subsequent vindication of Richard's rights and the King's attempt to destroy the Appellants is largely inaccurate.[161] The work is Appellant and Lancastrian propaganda. Its importance lies primarily in Gower's assertion that Henry Duke of Lancaster was finally made king not only by right, but by the people. Likewise, it was the people who deprived Richard of his rank. What is also clear is that Richard not only acted the part of the absolutist tyrant[162] but also tried to use Parliament to do so; and thus Gower indirectly confirms that no king by the end of the fourteenth century could rule without the Commons' support, even if a Richard could attempt, ultimately unsuccessfully, to 'pack the court' of Parliament in his favour. That he attempted to use Parliament in this fashion was yet another vindication of the growing recognition of the hegemony of the expanded middle estate – the audience, the patrons and the authors of the literature of social unrest.

4 Memory, preaching and the literature of a society in transition

Writing and remembering

It is related in Plato's *Phaedrus* how the Egyptian god Theuth invented writing, and when he brought it to the ruler of all Egypt, the god Thamus, he was told that his invention was calamitous as it would cause those who used it to lose the learning in their minds by neglecting their memories. Through the reliance on letters, which are external to the mind, men will lose the ability to recall things that are within themselves. 'You have invented an elixir not of memory, but of reminding.' Thamus warns him that henceforth his students will be purveyors of false wisdom and that they will appear to know much of what they are, in fact, ignorant. They will become public nuisances, these men who look wise but lack wisdom.[1]

The role that memory has played in a variety of cultures, particularly in those that have had a developed tradition of oral poetry which instructed members of the society in the values that bound generations together, has long been recognized as vital to an understanding of these values and their transmission. The development of English literacy in the fourteenth century, charted in the rapid growth of a written vernacular poetry and prose that expressed social and religious complaint and, more specifically, in the development of handbooks logically and alphabetically arranged to aid preachers in broadcasting theological and ethical orthodoxy, brings us face to face with a society that is losing the art of memory. Literacy was providing the means by which a larger number of men and women could actively participate in reforming their tradition as it was embodied in social, religious and aesthetic standards. It has been argued that the written character of information causes a wider dissemination of knowledge, and that reading promotes the ability to conceive more complicated structures so that men may think more abstractly, particularly about the social world they inhabit and their roles in it.[2] This has recently been questioned,[3] but

Plato's warning that writing would turn men into public nuisances is borne out by the development of a critical public voice for the increasing number of literate laity in the fourteenth century. There are parallels here with the special case of classical Greece, where alphabetic literacy first emerged, and there is a lesson to be learned if we digress for a moment. Early, pre-Socratic Greeks were essentially oral thinkers, 'prophets of the concrete', linked by habits of oral dissemination to traditions of the past and formulaic ways of expressing past experience. Only by Plato's time, when literacy and writing was becoming widespread and the general public could read its own laws and history, did the Greek language change sufficiently to express new ideas, which were for the first time metaphysical and political ideas, abstract ideas; and the shift from what is called the mythical to the logico-empirical mode of thought occurred.[4]

Writing appears to establish a different kind of relationship between the word and its referent which is a more general and abstract one, less closely connected with a particular person, place or time, than obtains in oral communication. This does not mean that the mental attributes or capabilities of literate and non-literate people are different, but that certain mental potentials are activated by communication when it is frozen in the written text, and memory becomes akin to a vestigial organ. Likewise, in England, when most men were illiterate from the Anglo-Saxon period through at least the thirteenth century, most customs were orally transmitted and remembered, despite attempts to codify and fix tradition in theoretical law books like Bracton's, meant to apply to all of England.[5] Differing regional custom in land tenure, for instance, prevailed despite attempts to unify traditions by a strong monarchy and its centralized administration. In fact, oral tradition was so strong that *quo warranto* cases, which tried to establish the requirement of *written* titles to land, were suspended in the 1290s. Nearly all the magnates who held property did so customarily and according to memory, and the king's government was forced to recognize as legitimate tenure that was held 'from time out of mind'.[6] Furthermore, a distinct sense of the past as an objective reality was not articulated: myth was not distinct from history for most men and women. Even when reading and writing was limited to a priestly and/or administrative class who conceived of themselves as guardians of a fixed tradition (but were themselves literate reinterpreters of that tradition, and therefore altered it), the vast majority of people until and throughout the thirteenth century were cast in the passive role of recipients and rememberers of a mixture of local and national custom. Traditions did change in response to economic and social experiences, but the non-literate's own perception of his present would have been continuous with his perception of the past.

Furthermore, in medieval Europe, as in sixth-century Greece, when a widespread alphabetic culture was becoming a reality, the very idea of logic as an unchanging and impersonal mode of discourse could and did develop. Such a new methodology for the learning and analysis of language led to fourteenth-century universities basing their curricula on logic as an abstract methodology that could investigate questions of how the mind perceived, learned and responded to the natural and the supernatural. This had revolutionary consequences in the now separately conceived academic fields of logical discourse, philosophy and theology. We shall have occasion to return to this later.[7] But one of the effects of the growth in literacy on literature and the consequent development of fixed modes of discourse and a fixed logic to analyse discourse was the development of the use of allegory and figural interpretation as an attempt to 'read' and reinterpret aspects of the fixed, cultural tradition, not least the Bible. This had already been developed by the literate minority in monasteries and cathedral schools of the earlier Middle Ages. Allegorization in general seems to develop only in literate ages, when the complex traditions of a society, which are previously expressed in myths and disseminated orally, are now fixed in a text for all to read. Any evolution of the myth previously effected by a minstrel or singer's oral adaptation to the needs of his audience, is replaced by allegorical interpretation of the traditional story, explaining away the inconsistencies that an oral tradition, not based on fixed texts, would have been able to subsume. Thus, what happened in Greece in the sixth century BC, when literacy became more widespread, can be compared with fourteenth-century England.

And not so long after the widespread diffusion of writing throughout the Greek world and the recording of the previously oral cultural tradition, there arose an attitude to the past very different from that common in non-literate societies. Instead of the unobtrusive adaptation of past tradition to present needs, a great many individuals found in the written records, where much of their traditional cultural repertoire had been given permanent form, so many inconsistencies in the beliefs and categories of understanding handed down to them that they were impelled to a much more conscious, comparative and critical attitude to the accepted world picture and notably to the notions of God, the universe and the past. Many individual solutions to these problems were themselves written down, and these versions formed the basis for further investigations.[8]

Instead of evolving new and gradually different social and political structures, as would have been the case in a non-literate society where men's memories would act selectively, recalling aspects of the past that were suitable to present conditions and silently eliminating the inapplicable and archaic, literate men looked at the fixed descriptions of their tradition, concretely defined, for instance, kingship, and rebelled against the incumbents rather than against the social institution itself. Kings were good or bad, but kingship was unquestioned. Thus, in so far as writing provided a fixed world picture, an unchanging source for the accepted traditions of English society, it also inspired men to observe deviations from that tradition and incited complaint against inconsistencies between the ideal and the actual. Men who were literate ceased to exercise their memories, relying on what was written, recalling, as Plato said, 'by external signs'. Literacy, not only in its more functional aspects of recording for administrative and tax purposes, but as a means of transmitting traditions to the next generation, through story-telling, can be said to have caused social change to come about through rebellion and complaint rather than through silent evolution and selective remembering. The growth of the uses of literacy beyond administrative and fiscal documents to include moral edification and an art literature from the twelfth century onwards was, perhaps, the most important factor in the gradual destruction of the freeman–serf distinction that had its effect by the thirteenth and fourteenth centuries, because it encouraged the mobility of men and their ability to conceive of themselves as having a function apart from the land. They came to distinguish themselves either as 'lewed' or 'lered' far more frequently than as free or unfree.

The uses of prose

When Trevisa could ask the question in his *Dialogue between a Knight and a Clerk*[9] whether English history should be written in prose or in verse and decide in favour of prose, 'for it is more clear than rhyme, more easy and more plain to know and understand', he was making a statement that was crucial to our understanding of the transformation and demise of the oral tradition in England. Not only had verse been the traditional means of communicating social and religious values to a non-literate audience, from Anglo-Saxon times into the fourteenth century; but it was verse that had provided the structure for formulaic patterns that built up the repertoire of the minstrel who relied on his memory to construct a story that would gratify his audience, not least because he told them what they expected, told them a story they already knew, in a language they already knew, and which he embellished by adding new episodes and descriptions to a mythic and conventional core.

As the fourteenth century progressed, the tiny proportion of the English prose that survived the Conquest only in private devotional works, written largely for women, broke away from the confines of a religious literature meant for withdrawal from the world and came to be used by citizens of London and Norfolk, in wills, for everyday affairs, in business and private communications. The widespread use of prose by Wyclifites merely confirmed a trend that was already dependent on at least a semi-literacy that was widespread: written prose and verse alike immersed themselves to an ever expanding degree in the realities of everyday life, and prose did this more easily because it was free from the structure and content that linked even the contemporary verse with the oral non-literate tradition of earlier communication, although poetry was now being composed for the page to be read by the eye as well as the ear. The 'pretentious yet inefficient prose'[10] of Thomas Usk's *Testament of Love*; the scientific prose of Chaucer's *Astrolabe*; Trevisa's translation of Bartholomew of England's *De Proprietatibus Rerum* into English prose; William Thorp's dramatic and forceful account of his dispute over Wyclifite principles with Archbishop Arundel;[11] Gloucester's statement of his own treason[12] and his will in English prose; Henry IV's challenge to the throne in English prose; and Chief Justice Thirnyng's two speeches on Richard's deposition and Henry's accession;[13] even the emergence of a standard written chancery prose,[14] Wyclifite sermon cycles in prose,[15] and the Bible translations in prose[16] – collectively serve as an index of the degree to which the use of English and the recently acquired reading and writing skills of the laity helped to alter some of the most fundamental perceptions of society in its public and private aspects and the individual's relation to it. The strikingly brief period of transition from a society that consisted for most people in essentially traditional and oral values to a society where literacy was no longer unique brought about the achievements of a Chaucer on the one hand, and the alliterative revival in prose and verse on the other.

The vast proliferation of preaching handbooks and dictionaries of *exempla*, as well as the demand for the Bible in the vernacular, buttressed by the composition of vernacular expositions of lay preachers (usually Wyclifites, and produced by apparently well-financed and carefully supervised but illicit workshops),[17] combine to give us a picture of an English society coping with an unprecedented degree of disruption and change, and expressing its discomfort. Out of these fifty-odd years of turmoil emerged the variegated cloth of an identifiably English literature in verse and prose, which had forged a new tradition out of the largely non-literate, oral English tradition of old.

The alliterative revival: oral and written composition

The alliterative revival, dated *c*. 1352 with the composition of *Wynnere and Wastoure*, perhaps best illustrates some of the consequences of the emergence, first of all, of a large, written, vernacular body of verse meant to be read. Recently, Turville-Petre has argued that there is no reason to suppose there was a venerable tradition of alliterative verse surviving and continuing on Anglo-Saxon traditions, written for aristocratic patrons.[18] He questions what he describes as Chambers's assumption of a hidden or lost corpus of oral poetry that faithfully preserved the expression and style of Old English poetry and that was inherited by fourteenth-century poets. Instead, Turville-Petre accounts for the development of a *new* creation, the *unrhymed* alliterative line, as being based, if anything, on all sorts of other written models – prose and verse: particularly the unrhymed verse of the Laȝamon type, and the rhymed alliterative poetry of the Harley lyrics.[19] The unrhymed alliterative line was essentially new and, one might emphasize, was written to be read, aloud or silently. The poet of *Wynnere and Wastoure* himself asserts the demise of the minstrel and his patron, for, whatever may have survived into the fourteenth century of an oral poetic tradition 'that writen were neuer', by 1352 it is the repeaters of other men's poetry, presumably read or rehearsed and memorized from a text rather than 'made' with the skills of memory, who were rewarded.[20]

The alliterative revival was a northern phenomenon, which came to centre in the West Midlands. Gloucestershire and adjoining counties were already the homes of the earliest Middle English alliterative works in prose and verse: the Worcester fragments, Laȝamon's *Brut* (Worcestershire), the Katherine Group of homilies, the Harley lyrics (Herefordshire), *Joseph of Arimathie* (Gloucestershire), *William of Palerne* (Gloucester). The two fragments of the *Life of Alexander*, *Alisaunder of Macedoine* and *Alexander and Dindimus* are thought to originate further north (Shropshire).[21] Also from the North-West Midlands (North Shropshire to Lancashire) comes *Wynnere and Wastoure*, which shows linguistically close relations with *The Parlement of Three Ages* and *Death and Life*. And of course, the finest of the alliterative poems of the North-West Midlands, found in the unique MS Cotton Nero A.x, are the foursome, *Pearl*, *Purity*, *Patience* and *Sir Gawain and the Green Knight*. Turville-Petre argues that primarily a self-contained revival of alliterative verse, beginning in the 1340s in the South-West Midlands, where alliteration had previously flourished in both poetry and prose, by the 1350s was being composed in the more northern reaches of the West Midlands. There is little evidence of any contact with urban poetry of the Chaucerian tradition. Indeed, the poetry of the alliterative revival derives from another tradition and Norman Blake has recently argued for several alliterative revivals and for a continuing interaction between alliterative poetry and prose. In addition to the explicit nostalgic reference in *Wynnere and Wastoure* to an earlier, but apparently not much earlier, minstrel mode of composition and delivery, the formulaic character of the episodes and descriptions, what Turville-Petre prefers to call 'collocations' rather than formulae to describe the recurrent use of word pairs and phrases[22] and the frequent use of the dream-vision to frame the episodes, remind us that this verse is a verse in transition. The story-teller is, as yet, moved primarily not by a creative impulse, but by an impulse to recreate, at least in part, within a tradition.

The line between oral and written literature, is, of course, not clear-cut. To refer to a poetic tradition that relied on men's memories rather than on the prompting of written texts, as appears to have been more the case in Anglo-Saxon society, is not to classify the audience and poets who use their ears and memories rather than their eyes as primitive or less civilized, or necessarily more cut off from urban culture than those societies where the text was paramount: it is merely different, and the consequences of a more general literacy created different characteristics in the society thus developed. And whether or not oral poetry is properly defined as poetry composed in oral performances by people who cannot read or write, it is certainly not the case, as demonstrated by recent

intercultural studies, that oral poetry is composed entirely of formulae, while lettered poetry is never formulaic, as Magoun once
quite erroneously stated.[23] Written compositions in Old English,
including those translated from the Latin, have been shown to be as
heavily formulaic as is the oral epic *Beowulf*.[24] Furthermore, if
Goody is correct, then societies where oral literature functions are
evolving societies, where moral and institutional structures change
and are incorporated *as though* they were venerable and traditional
into a poetry that purports to describe and praise tradition.[25] Whatever may have survived in structure and style of the Old English
scop's method of composition and performance, and of his social
function down into the fourteenth century, it seems logical to conclude that, if people cannot read or write, and we are told they have
a poetry in addition to our having surviving examples of it, then we
must assume that they were entertained and instructed orally, either
by those who were literate, or by those who were able to compose *ad
libidem* from memory. This was done within a narrative tradition of
accepted themes and was expressed in stock phrases that are
observable, even to some extent calculable,[26] when the poetry
finally gets written down. But to assume that such repetitious stock
phrases were developed only by poets who could write, that it was a
phenomenon of literacy, is not justified by the evidence, scarce
though it may be. That written poetry continued to be composed
using formulae, stock phrases and themes – 'collocations' – is evident in the newly composed written poetry of the alliterative revival. On the other hand, to assume that a vast corpus of alliterative
revival poetry has been lost merely because it was never written
down also appears doubtful. Rather, the loss of poetry is more likely
a loss or mutilation through excessive use of manuscripts, or the
gradual rejection of what is seen by contemporaries as archaic or no
longer of interest, so that scribes no longer copy it. However one
enters the debate on the classification criteria for oral poetry (a
debate that has its origins in the Parry–Lord hypothesis on the
mechanics of oral epic composition as observed among Yugoslav
minstrels of the twentieth century, who demonstrate remarkable
feats of memory),[27] it is clear that a distinction must be drawn
between the psychological requirements of a kind of orally *composed* poetry, as described wistfully by the poet of *Wynnere and
Wastoure*, and the oral *performance* of a memorized written text.
The distinction is one that relies on an understanding of language
acquisition based entirely on sound, as opposed to learning which

requires at least some help from the eye. When signs substitute for the learning that is achieved purely by memorizing sounds, then another psychological process evolves.

By the fourteenth century, at any rate, there could not have been a pure genre of oral poetry – that is, one entirely composed, transmitted and performed without any contact with a text – if only because even the non-literate lived at least on the margins of a literate tradition, literate in the functional and administrative sense,[28] and literate in the sense that the dominant ruling elite was familiar with French and Latin and the poetry written in these languages. It is, therefore, not surprising to find poetry of the alliterative revival, as well as Chaucer's urban poetry, sharing some of the same preoccupations, the same descriptive techniques, both looking to French for models, themes, motifs, structural devices and the like.[29] The finely wrought poem *Pearl* is a good example of a work that draws on the alliterative constraints common to an earlier, oral, tradition but is clearly intended to have been read and appreciated on vellum because the geometric shape of the poem and its stanza links could not have been adequately appreciated with the ear alone. At the same time, it transforms the dreamlike, 'unconscious' style – which many believe to be particular to oral poetry[30] – into the dream frame. The dream frame, in fact, appears to be a literary device in the poetry of the alliterative revival that probably can be traced back to what is an apparently 'unconscious' method of oral composition, a characteristic that is charted throughout a variety of cultures that possess an oral tradition. Spearing has written in an illuminating way on the development of a new consciousness of an interest in the nature and status of fourteenth-century poets and poetry, particularly among poets of the alliterative revival. This new artistic consciousness (as opposed to the mere entertainer status of the anonymous minstrel) should not be confused with the appearance of dream poetry as though the latter were a new if only quasi-distinct genre.[31] The alliterative revival does indeed appear to illustrate a consciousness of writers working within a distinct literary tradition of dreams and visions, but the 'unconscious' dream tradition itself is a characteristic more likely to be associated with non-literate oral composition. As Ruth Finnegan has explained, 'in practice, the interaction between oral and written forms is extremely common and the idea that the use of writing *automatically* deals a death blow to oral literary *form* has nothing to support it'.[32] The alliterative dream vision is, rather, a

conscious literary device that has hardened into a structural principle from having been a more fluid performing convention used to
transmit moral, religious and socially relevant truths. In fact, if
Spearing is correct in seeing a new self-consciousness on the part of
the poet who is no longer a mere entertainer, it is also true that, at
least in the early years of the alliterative revival, the poet's status
was nowhere near the quasi-prophetic stature of the Old English
scop, despite his Middle English counterpart's claims to be a
speaker of largely orthodox religious truths within a highly wrought
literary structure. To shift Spearing's argument somewhat, we can
see the venerable dream-vision being used in a very shrewd manner
to solve what Spearing recognized must have been a new social
problem: that of the socially inferior poet – the newly literate – who
addresses himself to a rural but sometimes aristocratic audience.[33]
In taking on the traditional role of the seer, the unconscious bearer
of tradition akin to the oral poet, the literate poet could be said to
have hidden himself within the venerable tradition of the prophetic
dream and allowed himself a didactic stance from a position of
traditional impunity. But he does something more. It is possible to
see the situation in *Pearl*, where the Dreamer never appears in the
role of the poet, as an early attempt to come to terms with what was
an evident dichotomy in the real world: on the one hand, the poet as
purveyor of traditional orthodoxy – here demonstrating the correct
attitude to adopt regarding a reconciliation of God's justice and his
reward in relation to the salvation of a baptized child whose life was
too short to have *earned* her the reward of salvation, but who none
the less is saved; on the other hand, the realistic portrayal of his
Dreamer who is a doubting, secular man, 'who does not adequately
respond to the orthodoxy of the visionary experience', as Spearing
so nicely put it.[34]

To place the dream-vision convention of the alliterative revival in
the context of comparative literature is only to take Nora Chad-
wick's insight a step further: that the poet, especially the oral poet, is
frequently cast in the role of seer, or prophet.[35] It is certainly not
uncommon for poems to be dreamed, for instance, in Eskimo and
South Indian poetic traditions where the poet is a channel of communication with the dead, not unlike the situation in *Pearl*. But this
does not necessarily allow us to conclude that the society in which
fourteenth-century alliterative poetry flourished was similar to that
of the Eskimo or the Indian. The theory that relates a particular
type of society with a particular genre of poetry is not always a

promising one.[36] Instead, the maintenance of the dream convention can be taken as further evidence of a society and a literature in transition, just as the realistic portrayal of the doubting Dreamer is a movement away from the idealizing stance of the traditional oral poet. While it may be questionable whether the minstrel gave an accurate picture of the world about him, and the heroic society described by a Homer, for instance, was not necessarily the historical reality of the society in which Homer himself lived and worked,[37] it seems clear that the poet who composed *Pearl* and *Sir Gawain* was developing a genre that combined what was to become an increasingly realistic image of his world as well as a self-conscious attitude to his art, with selected aspects of an idealizing poetic tradition long established. Not only was there a constant interaction between written and oral models, but there was also an interaction between a notion of poetry as a mirror of society and the individual Christian on the one hand, and the notion that poetry ought to depict an ideal society and individual on the other. Elizabeth Salter referred astutely to a situation in which Langland and the *Pearl* poet were asking us 'to accept as historically real what cannot be historically verified'.[38]

A poetic corpus with such a mixed adherence must have reflected the social and aesthetic attitudes of the audience that served it as patrons. In this sense, the poetry of the alliterative revival is at least an eclectic reflection of Midland society in the fourteenth century. But it was no mere epiphenomenon of rural social and religious institutions. It can also be seen in its more active guise as an initiating factor in social attitudes: the difficult moral lesson about pride, chastity and truth-telling in *Sir Gawain* is meant didactically, although what precisely we are to learn from the testing has puzzled present-day readers and critics.[39] We have already seen how so much of the literature of the fourteenth century was a form of preaching. Only with the increasing emphasis on the *written* message of verse does Yeats's description of art as 'the social act of a solitary man' become an apposite description of the position of the self-conscious alliterative poet writing in the vernacular.

Changing characteristics of narrative

The gradual movement away from narratives that are dominated by what has been called 'the mythic impulse' to tell a story with a traditional plot has been charted by Scholes and Kellogg, for the classical languages and for the vernacular. Their analysis is instructive if we apply it more rigorously to the poetry of the alliterative revival. To avoid what they describe as 'the tyranny of the traditional in story-telling',[40] two types of narrative can be seen to have emerged both in Greece and in medieval Europe: the empirical and the fictional. Although they see these genres as strictly antithetical and these distinct genres can help us to see certain kinds of medieval verse and prose as developments away from the requirements of an oral tradition, poems like *Pearl, Sir Gawain, Wynnere and Wastoure, Piers Plowman, Mum and the Sothsegger* and others of the alliterative group occupy an ambiguous position somewhere between the categories of fiction and empiricism as they emerge from the earlier, fixed traditions of oral verse narrative. According to this classification, the empirical mode of narrative replaces the traditional story either with history (biography) or mimesis – slice-of-life realism, adhering more to the truth of sensation than to neutral fact. We can see how the journalistic realism of complaint verse falls here. The fictional mode of narrative replaces the myth with an allegiance to the ideal, be it romantic or didactic. Romances, saints' lives, sermons using *exempla* and fables fall here.

But the art of the alliterative poet hovers between these two neat classes, defying categorization, selecting elements of each of these supposedly distinct, break-away categories of non-traditional narrative. Scholes and Kellogg are aware of how long, didactic and yet socially critical (empirical) poems like *Piers Plowman* fit uneasily between their two extremes of the disintegrating epic: the prose history (empirical) and the metrical romance (fictional). What appears to have happened is that many of the written alliterative narratives adopted the empirical mode only as a method to describe and expound what was in fact an ideal, albeit unachievable, in this life: the hero has become a humbler creature, someone who attempts to find a way to be the perfect Christian dwelling in the perfect Christian society; and the story focuses on the political, moral or religious *via salvationis*.

These alliterative poets frequently adopted the satirical stance that operated through a critical social realism in the service of a theoretical ideal that did not exist in the reality around them. Much of the alliterative poetry like *Mum, Piers Plowman* and *Pierce the Ploughman's Crede* adopted the satirical mode, explicitly rejecting the ideally oriented and archaic moral scheme – as well as the structure and pace – that was imparted by the romance tradition, in favour of a greater degree of empiricism, natural description and social commentary. But these were employed in the service of a new, more relevant ideal image: that of true courtesy, the true Church, the true Christian, the peaceable kingdom. This satirical mode is what we described earlier as the 'realism' of the complaint poetry written by less talented contemporary poets. And as we saw, the romance genre died out in comparison with the flourishing of satire. The morality of the old romance, rather like the message of the poetry of the oral tradition, could not be re-worked and tacitly adapted in a literate society that possessed the older texts because more men could now read them critically. Somehow, the old ideals had to be destroyed and replaced by a new moral scheme in a new form. The growth in vernacular satire was, therefore, one of the most important consequences of the expansion of literacy.

What Scholes and Kellogg describe as a general phenomenon is particularly apt when applied to works like *Piers Plowman*:

The force of this superiority of satire over epic, romance and sacred myth as a representation of the real world is double-edged. It strikes out against a particular society for having fallen away from conformity to an ideal past and against the ideals of the past for having so little relevance to the real world. The values of the satirist himself are, therefore, notoriously difficult to locate.[41]

But that Langland had an ideal cannot be doubted: a peaceful realm, a united Church, and salvation for the individual. Langland seems to have had difficulty in locating his own values only in relation to the *means* of achieving his ideal. Not only does his Dreamer Will never quite resolve the original questions about how to attain the salvation that inspired him on his quest for truth in the first place, and ends by continuing his quest for Piers Plowman, somewhat the wiser but not yet saved; but the three versions A, B and C of the poem follow a variety of roads, which lead – when compared at critical moments – to quite different moral solutions to the wider issue of salvation.[42]

Langland also developed satire in a new direction. He took the alliterative revival's self-conscious narrator and widened the distance between the author and teller of his story until we have glimmerings of an identifiable author in the latest (C) version of the poem – Long Will Langland, as distinct from his simple and questing Dreamer Will. Chaucer, of course, reached this point of self-identification and distinction via the continental route travelled by

Dante and Boccaccio. There is a striking contrast with most of the authors of the earlier works in the alliterative revival who refined themselves out of existence, imitating the traditional teller who recites his traditional story to an audience knowing what to expect. But Langland in his own way, like Chaucer in his, was able to turn his narrative inwards, highlighting the eternal weaknesses of mankind in general as well as revealing something of the individual Christian author in particular. This inward and individual focus on private responsibility was also taken up to a far less sophisticated degree by the didactic complaint poetry of the Digby Manuscript and in the mosaic of borrowings by Gower. And it is this self-conscious awareness of individual responsibility in the world, and for one's private salvation, that marks a literate age off from a more traditional one, which so often expresses its shared values in the third person. Taking the art of alliterative verse beyond its local dialectal and thematic home in the Midlands, Langland's combination of social satire, and inward and personal exploration, was the logical outcome of a localized but new verse tradition that owed much to the traditional poetry of the past and, as we shall see, to the art of preaching. But the poem in its three versions owes most to the development of a *written* alliterative tradition that was a result of the emergence of a newly literate laity.

The Bible and the art of memory

The literary nature of the poetry of the alliterative revival in general reminds us not only that English literacy was growing and the inhabitants of the Midlands were more than on the margins of a literate society, but also that fourteenth-century Christians were becoming more aware of their heritage as people of The Book. By illustrating how rare it was for the laity and the lesser clergy to possess or even read Bibles throughout the thirteenth and fourteenth centuries before Wyclif, Margaret Deanesly pointed to the peculiarly ironic situation most Christians of the Middle Ages were in. Adherents of a religion based on a text, the word as written by God, fourteenth-century English men and women were none the less never confronted directly with The Word. The vast majority heard about the gospels in sermons, and even here the biblical text was not presented but rather was expounded by the preacher in his own paraphrases. Most people's conceptualization of the Bible was almost entirely dependent either on Church art[43] and mystery plays,

or on the sound of re-interpreted sacred texts, rhythmically patterned and rhymed by poets and preachers, the better to impress
holy images on the memories of those forced into scriptural illiteracy even when some of the laity were developing literate skills.

It is particularly in this context that the art of memory remained
most active for the laity,[44] whereas for preachers who worked in
Latin but increasingly in the vernacular, memory of biblical parallels and of the very text itself was falling further into disuse because
of the proliferation of alphabetically arranged preaching handbooks that substituted for memory. These were not new
phenomena, having their origins in monastic centres of reading and
learning even before the twelfth century. But certainly, in the
cathedral and secular schools of the twelfth century, the *ars dictaminis* was taught more generally to students in order to instruct
that tiny minority of the population who were able to avail themselves of such education how to excerpt and adapt the sayings of the
philosophers and Church fathers. They produced handbooks like
the *Rationes Dictandi* to indicate how proverbs or quotations should
be used.[45] Anonymous florilegia of extracts from ancient and patristic letters and orations were compiled to be used in the composition
of letters.

This minority of men knew the past only in fragments taken out of
context. Theirs was a florilegia culture. Gerald of Wales, for example, used the *Florilegium Angelicum*[46] like a mine, inserting extracts
that were previously wrenched out of their original context by the
compiler into already written structures. Such quotations were
Gerald's stock formulae, used more than once in a text, to confirm a
variety of his own views or to bolster his own arguments. Gower's
procedure in writing the *Vox Clamantis*, where he used Peter de
Riga's *Aurora* – another well-known florilegium – was similar. By
appealing to authority and to illustrate his opinions on moral virtue,
vice or the ideal state, Gerald combed florilegia for confirmatory
apophthegms and *exempla*. His contemporaries did likewise, which
is not to say that he and they *never* read the whole of some of
the works that the compiler of the florilegia plundered; but he, like
others, was taught the *ars dictaminis*. Rouse and Goddu have shown
how the literate men of the twelfth century perceived inherited,
written authority not in the form of whole works or structures, but in
the form of *sententiae* or authorities taken out of their original
setting and applied in a variety of new structures, often foreign to
the original intention of the authority. In fact, the main set texts of

the Church, especially from this period onwards, were structurally nothing more than mosaics of such collected authorities: Gratian's *Decretum* for ecclesiastical law; Peter the Lombard's *Book of Sentences* for a summary of orthodox theology; the *Glossa Ordinaria* for commentaries on the Bible. By the fourteenth century a compiler of such florilegia, Thomas of Ireland, was well aware that his extracts were only tit-bits of the original, but this had not prevented him from using the *Flores Paradysi* to compile what became one of the most important medieval handbooks: the *Manipulus Florum*.[47] It is very likely that those who used the *Manipulus Florum*, and there were many more requiring such aids to preaching in the fourteenth century,[48] never were inspired or, in fact, had the time or opportunity to return to the originals.

There are parallels here with the method of composing alliterative verse, which also uses stock formulae repetitiously in a variety of contexts. Much of the art of writing was conceived of as a scissors-and-paste affair; and without any additional information to go by, we can only draw parallels with what we know about the psychological process involved in composing an oral literature, be it non-literate or in some contact with a written exemplar. Stock phrases are a key, a memory device. Aside from the evident concern to adhere to authority and not to say something new (for newness frequently had a pejorative sense for much of the Middle Ages), this method of writing by linking together approved formulae may well have its origins in a non-literate culture from which Europe as a whole had only quite recently emerged.

Memory and the preachers' handbooks

Theologians, philosophers in the arts faculties and letter-writing administrators were not the only ones to use collections of extracts from authorities.[49] Preachers did so as well. Despite the conservative nature of the medieval Church regarding the availability of Bibles, particularly for the laity, and its hostility to the translation of Scripture into the vernacular,[50] there is evidence to show that preachers preached in the vernacular from an early period; they certainly did so in the Anglo-Saxon period. There is sufficient evidence to show that, well after the Norman Conquest and throughout the twelfth century, bishops and abbots, that is, those licensed to preach, did so in English. Jocelin de Brakelond says that Abbot Sampson of Bury St Edmunds (1135–1211) was eloquent in

French and Latin but could also read English books and preached to the people at Bury in English, in his native Norfolk dialect.[51] In France, the eminent prelate Jacques de Vitry, canon of the parish church at Oignies and later Bishop of Acre (1216), preached in French, and not only to the laity: seventy-four of his *sermones vulgares* are extant, and these are addressed to prelates and priests, various orders of hermits, judges and lawyers, theologians and preachers, canons, military orders, pilgrims, crusaders, merchants and moneychangers, husbandmen, vinedressers and other labourers, citizens and burghers, artificers, servants, young men and women, widows and the married.[52] Clearly, ecclesiastics and the laity heard Jacques de Vitry in their native language.[53] In the mid fourteenth century the distinguished ecclesiastic, the Archbishop of Armagh, Richard FitzRalph, delivered many sermons *in vulgari* at Paul's Cross in London and elsewhere. The practice of transcribing such sermons in Latin obscures their vernacular presentation. Even ecclesiastics in convocation were often preached to in English, and this raises the question of whether Latin readers – as such men undoubtedly were at this time – were also equipped to be Latin *hearers*, having learned Latin as a formal text-based language rather than as a spoken one. Owst insisted that 'evidence there is in plenty that knowledge of Latin possessed by even the average priest would hardly enable him to follow the intricacies of a Latin oration with any ease'.[54] This is another issue altogether. Adequate Latin readers may not have been aurally competent, as is proved by twentieth-century experience, where schoolchildren may learn to read Caesar and Virgil but can hardly say a sentence in Latin or understand it when read aloud or spoken. The Yorkshire lawyer William Nassyngton, who translated John Waldby's *Speculum Vitae* into English (*c*. 1375), perhaps best described the linguistic abilities of his contemporaries in the following words (and in 1384 his text was examined for four days in Cambridge for heresy but acquitted):

ffor why that in your kyndly langage
that ȝe hafe here mast of usage
that cane ilk man undirstand,
that is born in ynglande:
ffor that langage is mast shewyd
as wele amange lerede as lewede;
ffor Latyn as I trow cane <u>nane</u>   none
bot thai that hafe it of scole <u>tane</u>.   taken

(And in the fourteenth century, those who studied Latin in school were not necessarily potential ecclesiastics, as we have seen; nor by mid-century were they unique.)

Some cane franche and na latyn,
that used has court, and dwelled therin.
And some cane of latyn a party
that cane franch but feberly.
    And some undirstandye ynglych
that nouther can latyn ne franche.
Bot lerede and lewed, alde and yonge,
all undirstandys ynglych tonge.[55]

Even Benedictine monks were required, when at Gloucester College, Oxford, to be trained in vernacular as well as Latin preaching (1363) – a rule that Barbara Harvey has shown[56] does not necessarily imply that vernacular preaching was meant only for a lay audience; in the fourteenth century the provincial chapter was occasionally regaled by selected preachers in English, and the public were admitted.[57] The Benedictines were particularly conscious of training monks at the university specifically to preach *extra muros*, in the face of mendicant rivalry,[58] and they possessed the standard preaching handbooks to aid them in their efforts to educate the audience that attended sermons given in cathedral monasteries.[59]

But most influential in the art of vernacular preaching were the two mendicant orders, the Franciscans and Dominicans. It was they who totally changed the character of thirteenth- and fourteenth-century preaching. The Dominicans in particular were founded to win heretics back to the orthodox Church by preaching and living the example of the simple Christian life. Dominic himself was described as one who, in no matter what company, be it humble or exalted, was always ready to preach and offer pithy stories about men and women who had lived well or ill.[60] And here is their significance. It was the Dominicans who first began to collect these *exempla* in handbooks for other preachers. Within the period 1250–1350, thirty-four out of forty-six distinct collections dating from 1200 to 1500 were made and twenty-nine of them were compiled by either Dominicans or Franciscans: sixteen by the Dominicans, thirteen by the Franciscans;[61] seven came from the Cistercians and two from the secular clergy. Most of the Dominican collections are attributed to top-ranking and highly educated men in the order: Humbert of the Romans, the Inquisitor Etienne de Bourbon, Martin of Poland, Arnold of Liège, Jean Gobi, Jacques de Cessoles, John Bromyard, Jean Hérolt. The Franciscans seem to have been somewhat humbler when it came to putting their names to their collections, and only two authors are known: John of Wales and Nicholas Bozon. Nor did the separate collections remain exclusively within their respective orders. The collections made by the Dominican Etienne de Bourbon, for instance, greatly influenced those made by the Franciscans. Furthermore, the oldest Franciscan collection extant, the *Liber Exemplorum Ad Usum Praedicantium*, is not, in fact, the oldest known collection. In thirteenth-century England there were collections that now are lost, and the *Liber Exemplorum* is an echo of these. The Franciscan John of Kilkenny's *Liber*, another anonymous Franciscan *Liber*, a collection known as the *Exempla Communia* and the *Exempla Deodati* of an Irish Franciscan were all available to preachers in search of stories to serve as amusing and edifying examples from authorities which would illustrate their chosen biblical theme. One of the greatest collections of all for such purposes was the Franciscan *Gesta Romanorum*.

It is not only the contents of such handbooks that are of interest, but their arrangement to facilitate consultation. The Franciscans were the first to arrange their *exempla* alphabetically, and they were followed soon after by the Dominicans. And the rubrics under which *exempla* are grouped give us some idea of the most frequent themes preached on by the mendicants. In his *Alphabetum Narrationum*, the Dominican Arnold of Liège recognized that different *exempla* could be used to illustrate a variety of sermon themes, and so he introduced the several sequences of each *exemplum*, with 'Hoc valet eciam ad . . .' in order to indicate that a certain section of the *exemplum* could be used in discussing, for example *accidia* or *pigritia*, although the main *exemplum* rubric is listed under *De Abstinentia*. Collections of *exempla* were, therefore, atomized in the extreme by a system of rubrics alphabetically and logically arranged, sending the preacher to other words related to his theme. The most evolved and most useful kind of collection not only has a logical and alphabetical arrangement of *exempla* but also presents cross-references: the logical order of the text and the alphabetical arrangement are listed together in a table of contents. The Milanese doctor Mayno of Mayneri, sometime after 1326, prepared this for his collection, the *Dialogus Creaturarum*.

What this means for the consultant is that the semantic field available to him in preaching is already defined by one word, which is linked to others in what the *compiler* conceives to be 'related' *exempla*. An assiduous use of such a compilation with its Table of Contents could well limit the creative use of the *exempla* arranged therein, and it is not surprising to find a vast number of sermons trotting out the same *exempla* for the same biblical themes. Owst put it well when he described the boringly repetitive sermon collections showing preachers 'plagiarizing wholesale from one another' (that is, from the manuals), 'laying out the same dreary matter throughout the liturgical year – as with one voice from many pulpits came the same *de tempore* sermon'.[62] From the point of view of composition, this means that any alternative knowledge and memory of the Bible and its standard commentators get replaced by the *compiler's* authoritative association of text and example. The use of such preaching handbooks is akin to being enclosed within something far more tyrannizing than an oral tradition; the permissible is now made concrete by its visual availability on the page. Creative preachers must have been at a premium, therefore, since the handbook had assured that they either lost their memory or never acquired one. These handbooks may, in part, be the origin of frequent satirical complaints against a clergy illiterate in the Bible.

An example will suffice. Should a preacher want to discuss abstinence, say for a theme in Lent, he looks under *Abstinentia*, and there he finds: *quere alimentur*; *cibus*; *comedere*; *continentia*; *continens*; *gula*; *iejunium*; *monachus*; *parsimonia*; *religiosus*; *sobrietas*; *temperentia*. This is the scope for his associations, and he then looks up *exempla* that deal with the above list and inserts them into his sermon, which may have as its theme only a single line, out of context, from, say, the Epistles or somewhere in the Gospels.

When the Dominican Hugh of St Cher went further and developed his *distinctiones* for the use of preachers, they were then able to find, behind a list of often abstract words, the summation of orthodox symbolic significations of this vocabulary. Such distinction collections were made and used mainly in the university milieu. The more common *exempla* collections, which kept mainly to concrete words, had a far wider circulation. We need to note, however, that they are primarily in Latin. Owst suggested this was out of a fear of being suspected of heresy, since vernacular theology at whatever level was always eyed with suspicion by the ecclesiastical authorities.[63]

English collections like the Franciscan *Liber Exemplorum* and the *Speculum Laicorum* were used at Oxford, particularly in the Franciscan *studium* there, and these handbooks formed the lectors who would then be sent to outlying convents. Not only were such preachers confronted with alphabetical indices of *exempla*, but they found there an alphabetical index of social conditions: *Ad abbates*; *ad usuarios*; *ad uxoratos*. The familiar order of the same *exempla*, and the same key words associated with them in the indices, must have facilitated the memorization of biblical, theological and even socio-political associations, not unlike the formulae or collocations associated in the minds of poets and audiences with certain conventional events to be described in the alliterative verse tradition. Hence, a limited number of essential theological and moral notions, illustrated in a concrete way by the same conventional recitations, were presented time and again to the laity, and helped to construct their biblical, theological, literary and political vocabulary.

Because the same *exempla* from classical sources – the *Gesta Romanorum*, the *Glossa Ordinaria* from Gregory the Great or the *Vitae Patrum* – were used over and over again in such compilations, some of the manuscripts give only one or two lines of each story to serve as jogs to the memory. Such memoranda were to be expanded on by the preacher. But by the later fourteenth century and certainly by the fifteenth, collections like the well-known *sermones dormi secure* were produced for priests, pastors and chaplains by the obliging German Franciscan Johannes of Werden. Seventy-one sermons, usually for Sunday preaching, with the themes taken from the Gospel were prepared, apposite *exempla* and all. The priest could 'sleep securely' on Saturday night knowing that his sermon was prepared for him, witty stories illustrating his theme included. Other interesting collections like the fourteenth-century BM 11284, *Fabularum anecdotorumque collectio ad usum Praedicantium in seriem alphabeticam digestam*, included 572 stories under ninety-one rubrics. The compiler was, most likely, an Englishman who included anecdotes of a local character.[64] Then there were collections of moralized *exempla*, such as the famous *Liber de moralitatibus* by the Dominican Robert Holcot, each followed by an elaborate exposition and displaying an impressive acquaintance with classical sources: Ovid, Pliny, Valerius Maximus and ancient history. Holcot was one of a growing number of classicizing friars whose influence beyond academic circles was profound;[65] it is his collection of authorities on the significance of dreams to be found in his *Commentary* on the biblical *Wisdom* literature, written either at

Cambridge *c*. 1334–6 or in the Northampton Dominicum *studium*, that has recently been shown to have been Chaucer's source for the 'Nun's Priest's Tale'.[66]

Not everyone was satisfied with the contents of such handbooks, and the friars in particular were attacked for emphasizing fables and drolleries at the expense of the biblical message. Even Dante had complained early in the fourteenth century about fables being shouted from the pulpits, confusing the people, making them laugh, but teaching them nothing of Christ.[67] But criticism notwithstanding, some compilers were sufficiently convinced of the usefulness of such collections that they became literary works in their own right, the *exempla* being linked by a thread of discourse, as in the Dominican Johannes Junior's *Scala Celi*, which he dedicated to the provost of Aix. Etienne de Bourbon's influential *Liber de Septem Donis Spiritus Sancti* presented *exempla* connected by a running commentary, arranged around the seven gifts: fear, piety, knowledge, might, counsel, understanding and wisdom. At the close of the thirteenth century the French Dominican William Peraldus collected a string of sententious extracts on the virtues and vices culled from Christian and pagan classical authors; and Holcot's Commentaries on the *Wisdom Books* were a scholarly series of 213 *lectiones*, which used the biblical text as a jumping-off point to present a vast repertory of *exempla* and historical anecdotes. These were couched in elaborate metaphors and extracted from classical literature, especially from the poets, and even from the rare hermetic corpus which seems to have been known only by that select band of scholars in Richard de Bury's circle.[68]

But perhaps most important among *exempla* collections for fourteenth-century England, because most synthetic and complete, was the scholarly Cambridge Dominican John Bromyard's *Summa Praedicantium*, written in Latin and dated *c*. 1356.[69] Bromyard probably studied in Oxford, and was granted a licence to hear confessions in the diocese of Hereford in 1326. He compiled several handbooks for preachers, the *Opus trivium ex tribus legibus divina, canonica et civili (Distincciones)*, arranging articles in alphabetical order. He too was interested in educating the laity, although along lines established by his order, and he did his best to provide the preacher with an augmented collection of *exempla* that was as complete as possible. He combed every conceivable source for profane and sacred stories, fables and jests, arranging these according to alphabetical topics. His *Summa* was, apparently, widely used:

at least, most *exempla* found in contemporary sermons and literature can also be found in Bromyard. His *Summa* expects the preacher to do his part and expand on the relatively brief and dry summaries provided, but he cites his sources, and this may have inspired some of the more scholarly of his consultants to seek out the originals to refresh their memories.

These collections in Latin, although exceedingly useful, were really quite erudite, and they existed side by side with dry legal compendia for priests like the *Oculi Sacerdotis* and the *Pupilla Oculi*. Furthermore, there was an increasing number of *summae* for confessors, based on the *Raymundina* (of Raymond of Penafort, *c*. 1245, later modified by the theologian John of Freiburg), which represented the hierarchical Church to pastors and their teachers, so that they could deal with the following: (1) sins against God, (2) sins against neighbours, (3) problems relating to holy orders and penance, (4) matrimony. These included opinions of recent theologians and enabled priests to keep abreast of orthodox scholarly opinion concerning current issues in canon law, papal and conciliar legislation and the more general experience of pastoral authorities.[70] These *summae* must have been created for an intellectual elite, despite their optimistic preface: *ad informationem simplicium sacerdotum*. Nevertheless, they were not discussions of complex legal and moral prescriptions on an abstract level but were practical. Tentler is of the opinion that 'their very structure and the order of their presentation and the concreteness of the cases, made it easy for literate people of only average intelligence to use them'.[71] The most popular of these, too, were alphabetically arranged, instructing the confessor in ways to establish his authority, providing guidelines on how to deal with varieties of behaviour and recalcitrance. They were meant to provide the confessor with the 'key to knowledge', enabling him to discern moral from venial sins; but, more importantly, they offered him the 'key to power', making the confessor secure in his authority to hear and absolve men from their sins. Thus, in a more formal and yet still practical way these *summae* for confessors defined behaviour that was forbidden, just as the collections of *exempla* provided perhaps more amusing instruction in the same.

Who read these *summae*? Tentler believes they were meant for future curates and mendicants, providing them with a reliable guide to the theory and practice promoted by the clerical elite. And just as the vast majority of preaching handbooks were written by mendicants, so too all the summists were either Franciscans or Dominicans. As Boyle has argued, the *summae* were meant for priests with the *cura animarum* who did not have access to the great commentaries and specialized writings of the major scholastics. 'These manuals and *summae* [for confessors] contributed in no small way to the spread of the latest theological positions on the sacraments and pastoral practice in general. . . .'[72] Their purpose was akin, although at a more sophisticated level, to the preaching handbooks filled with *exempla*.

But the preachers' handbooks forged a link between practical theology and secular morality that was not explicitly envisaged by the compilers and consultants of the *summae confessorum*. By including vast quantities of pagan *exempla* side by side with excerpts from the church fathers, the preaching handbooks integrated pastoral theology into current attitudes to morality, employing homely stories which were amusing but had some didactic message, and could be shown to be universally and eternally true and relevant to the Christian dilemma. Owst was surely mistaken when he argued that the mendicant involvement in the production of Latin handbooks to aid preachers either caused them to lose touch with the deeper religious life and needs of the masses, or reflected that they had done so, despite their continuous preaching at street-corners.[73] There is, however, something in his idea that mendicant *exempla* handbooks were viewed with hostility by the Wyclifites as being out of touch with the spiritual needs of the laity. Wyclif's followers took up the position that vernacular preaching should be based only on the literal exposition of a vernacular Bible. But Bromyard was seen by many more as having numerous tit-bits that were relevant to all situations a preacher or his flock might encounter, and its encyclopedic nature meant there was something for everyone here. Bromyard, for instance, included the appealing *exemplum*, also found in Jacques de Vitry, which if used in a sermon would surely have struck home with those who preached to the rural laity, warning preachers against a tedious and irrelevant sermon:

A man caught in a crowd in a church is obliged to listen to the sermon against his will. Fearing lest he be enchanted like the serpent, he said: would that by the grace of God I might escape from the sermon as I have already done from a hundred.[74]

The mendicants were not snobbish Latinists, even at a time when more of the laity were learning to read some Latin. Instead, they were famous (in some quarters notorious) not only for preaching in the vernacular, but for including verses in their sermons. A good example of this is the Norfolk Franciscan John of Grimestone, who assembled some preaching notes in 1372.[75] He included Latin quotations and *narraciones bonas* as well as *multas notabilitates in Anglico*, grouped under the familiar headings, *De Abstinentia* to *De Vita Christi*. He selected a wide assortment of the usual authorities, from the Bible and Cicero, Seneca, St Ambrose, Chrysostom, Gregory the Great, St Bernard, Hugh and Richard of St Victor, Isidore and the *Glossa Ordinaria*. Less frequently cited authorities who none the less find a place, as they do in all the other preaching handbooks, include Aristotle, Valerius, Origen, Cyprian, Eusebius, Macrobius, Boethius, Cassiodorus, Bede, Rabanus Maurus, Peter Damian, Peter Comestor, John Beleth, Grosseteste, Aquinas, Durandus, and 'Holkote'. But most interesting is his collection of English lyrics and tags which explain in verse a one-line quote in Latin. His poems are exceedingly simple theologically, philosophically and poetically, even when he has incorporated a Latin line within the verse. In his edition, Wilson notes that Grimestone's Latin is a confessor's Latin. It is also something of a schoolmaster's Latin. See what he has under *De Detraccione*:

To eueri preysing is knit a knot	praising
Þe preysing wer good, ne wer þe 'but'.	
I ne woth neuere wer it may ben founde	know
Þat with sum 'but' it is ibounde.[76]	connected

(On detraction: There is always a 'hitch' in praising; The praising would be good if only there were not included a 'but', a qualification of the praise.)

or, 'Tu quis habes curam animarum tripliciter debes eas pascere et custodire, videlicet' (You who have a cure of souls in a threefold manner must shepherd and guard [your flock] as follows):

Þoru suetnesse of lore in preching	
Þoru fair conuersacioun in leuing,	
Þoru ȝefte of elmesse in fynding.	gift; alms
Per dulcedinem doctrine in predicando.[77]	

(Through the sweetness of doctrine in preaching.)

or *De Gracia*:

Man ne hat nouth grace for God ȝef hit nouth	
But for it is nouth rediliche of man isouth.	readily; sought
Homo non habet graciam non quia hanc non dat Deus.[78]	

(Man has no grace, not because God does not give it, but because man does not readily seek it.)

or *De Lege*:

Lawe is leyd vnder graue,
For þe demeres hand hat idrawe.   judge's
Forþe wich hand-drawing [bribery]
Lawe is withseth in prisuning.
Lex est defuncta, quia judicis est manus vncta,
Ob cuius vnguentem lex est in carcere tentum.[79]

(Law is defunct, because the judge's hand is withdrawn since his bribery has imprisoned the law.)

Luxuria:

Is a robour of rentis and londis;
It is a prisoun of stronge bondis;
It is a front of sorwe and care;   sorrow
And it is a swerd þat wil nout spare.[80]

De multiloquendo:

ʒif þu wilt nouth here, but spekt wordis manie and veyne,
Betre þu were to han on ere and mouþes to haan tweyʒe.   two
For to eres God vus ʒaf, and mouth he ʒaf but on.
[Heren michil] and speken litel becomet wel ich wis man.   To hear
Cum nihil auscultes, set plurima vana loquaris.[81]   much

(If you will hear nothing but speak many vain things.)

And then there are miscellaneous verses which are also translations of Latin tags like:

Man is but a frele þing
Fro þe time of is genning.   beginning
Nou he is an nou (e) nis.
Als þe flour þat springet in gres.
Est homo res fragilis, et durans tempore parvo.[82]

(Man is a fragile thing, and endures for a short time.)

There is, in addition, an interesting long poem of 195 lines that is based on Revelation 5:1, which teaches the significance of Christ's passion. Grimestone instructs by drawing the analogy with a child's experience – apparently any child is meant – when he goes to school to learn to read. This surely must have been no unfamiliar experience for John of Grimestone's audience, but it is not clear if such children were any more sophisticated than Bishop Grosseteste's (thirteenth-century) 'ABC' children, who went to parish schools to learn to read the psalter or primer in preparation for singing treble in church.[83] The proliferation of schools for seculars in the fourteenth century, however, at least argues for a larger number of children able to read in this manner.

Rith as man may se
Wan child to skole set be
A boke him is ibrouth
Nailed on a brede of tre
And is icleped an ABC
Perfeliche iwrouth.

Wrouth is on þe bok withoute
Fiue paraffes grete and stoute,
So red so rose schape.
þan is withinnen saun doute
Ful of lettres al aboute,
Boþen rede an blakc.

Blake letres in þe perchemyn
Maket þe child <u>sone a fyn</u>   at last
Lettres to knowen an se.
Be þis bok men may devyn
Cristes bodi, ful of peyn.
þat deyȝed on <u>rode-tre</u>. . . .   rood tree (cross)

Abouten þis ABC wold I spede,
ȝef I mithte þe lettre rede
Withouten [distaunce].
God þat let his bodi sprede
On þe rode for mannis nede,
In heuene vs all avaunce.[84]

Verse translations of Latin tags like those collected by Grimestone were already being prepared before 1333 by Friar Herebert, and they too are most likely to have been designed primarily for the use of preachers.[85] There are others, and Owst discussed two Franciscan productions from around 1350 which alphabetically arranged preaching material in verse. Such preaching handbooks, filled with unsophisticated English verse, were not rareties throughout the century, and a nice example of the use of verse, in a vernacular sermon that follows the 'school' method, takes as its theme 'Erumpe et Clama' (Galatians 4: 27):

Ryght worshippull frendes, ȝe shall undirstond
þat þese wordes þat I have seide in Latyne, þei
are wrytten in þe <u>pistell</u> of Seynt Poule and arn   Epistle
Þus muche to sey in Engliss tonge un-to youre
undirstondynge: 'Breke out and crye' or els þus:
Breke owte and not <u>blynne</u>   cease, put an end to
And cry God mercy for þy synne.[86]

The Bible in translation

Later on, and by the turn into the fifteenth century, Myrc's *Instructions for Parish Priests* and Graytrik's imperfectly alliterative Sermon, meant for priestly instruction, as Owst pointed out, also used rhyming verse as a medium for doctrinal instruction. Wyclif was not alone in complaining about rhyming sermons, accusing the friars of perpetrating folly on the laity. But by arguing that the Bible should be available in the English tongue for all to read, and this would mean a literal prose translation, he inspired his followers to reject in a revolutionary manner the traditional method of doctrinally instructing the laity – in verse – and they proceeded to translate the whole of the Bible into simple prose. The debate about mendicant preaching methods could have taken place only in a milieu where the possibility of the laity being able to read the Word of God themselves had become a widespread reality. Hence, it could only have meaning in the latter part of the fourteenth century.

The metrical tradition of theological and biblical instruction was, as we may expect, a comparatively venerable one for England. If, as is believed, many of the thirteenth- and fourteenth-century verse translations of books of the Bible, the Psalms and so forth were not meant to be used from the pulpit, then they were meant to be read by readers of English even quite early on in the fourteenth century. By 1357 Archbishop Thoresby of York thought it would be extremely valuable to have a catechism translated with expanded commentary in English, and he commissioned the monk of St Mary's, York, John de Graytrik, to do this in verse, the more easily to be memorized. This text would be expanded further with Lollard interpolations later in the century. An even earlier fourteenth-century preacher may have been instructed to omit certain Latin passages when preaching to the laity, as one finds in the prologue to the *North English Homily Collection*,[87] and this is taken to mean that the laity could understand neither spoken Latin nor written Latin. But this says little about the ability of at least a number of men and women early in the century, and even before the full effect of an expanded school system was felt, to read edifying literature based on the Bible *in English*. While the whole of the Bible was not literally translated into English prose until the Wyclifites did so during the 1380s, there were numerous metrical versions of separate biblical books from the thirteenth century onwards.[88] Genesis and Exodus were translated into a metrical version in rhyming couplets based on Peter Comestor's *Historia Scholastica* and Josephus's *Antiquities of the Jews*. This means that the text was not literally rendered but was summarized and versified; however, the basic narrative of the entire Pentateuch, ending with the death of Moses, was available from around 1250 in a northern Norfolk dialect. At various other times in the fourteenth century, other parts of the Old Testament were translated into Middle English: Job, the Wisdom of Solomon, Adam and Eve and legends of the Holy Cross. An extended metrical paraphrase of the Old Testament, including the Pentateuch (excluding Leviticus), Joshua, Judges, Ruth, the four books of Kings, Job, Tobias, Esther, Judith and parts of Maccabees, was available in a northern dialect from the end of the fourteenth century. These were followed by a brief *sanctorale* or saints' lives collection in prose. None of these was a literal prose rendering in English; as was usual in such paraphrases, they were extensively elaborated, showing quite explicitly the influence of the minstrel tradition as it operated in romances, particularly in the apocryphal additions to the life of Moses. There was a corresponding use of the Bible by minstrels who added narrative material to their repertoire from the biblical stories, as in *Jacob and Joseph* and *Susannah*.

The Psalter, in particular, was translated three times apart from other condensations and extracts: the earliest, *Surtees Psalter* in rhyming couplets; an early fourteenth-century metrical rendering by a Yorkshireman, the Oxford mystic Richard Rolle, which also contained his commentary; and a West Midlands prose Psalter from the middle period of the century. The Lollards interpolated into Rolle's Psalter their own heretical additions, but what was significant in Rolle's method in the first place was the presentation of each verse of Latin text, followed by a literal verse translation and then a commentary in English. This must have been meant for private readers rather than for use from the pulpit, and it offered its readers the views of the authoritative *Glossa Maior* on the psalms along with Rolle's changes and interpretations. There were also numerous legendaries and passion narratives prepared in Middle English, selections from the New Testament, and especially a series of gospel harmonies which presented in simplified format the life and deeds of Christ in a single harmonizing narrative, collected together from the different versions of the four gospels.[89] Christ's life was usually made known, with apocryphal additions, in sermon cycles and private meditations, prayers and spiritual handbooks, to say nothing of pictorial representations in glass and carving which increasingly emphasized the personal sufferings of the human aspect of His nature. A monk of St Werburh's Abbey, Chester, prepared a stanzaic life of Christ. Versions of the Pauline and Catholic Epistles, a translation and commentary on the Apocalypse and numerous translations of the thirteenth-century Anglo-Norman Apocalypse were circulating. Again, none of these was a literal translation of the biblical Latin; instead, they were expanded narratives incorporating for instance the *Golden Legend*, and sections of Higden's *Polychronicon*. Furthermore, a translation of the New Testament, which Anna Paues edited at the beginning of this century,[90] included the Pauline Epistles and parts of Acts with the beginning of Matthew. The Acts and Matthew are in a Midlands dialect, while the Epistles are in what was possibly Kentish.

It is important to realize not only the quantity of material paraphrasing the biblical narrative that was available to English readers throughout the fourteenth century, but also the continuation of the didactic tradition of teaching in verse. Verse was a hangover from a period of oral and customary communication, and it remained an important mode of transmitting the morality of the biblical narrative as reinterpreted by the thirteenth- and fourteenth-century Church during a period when an increasing number of the laity and lesser clergy were also confronting texts. When we ask the question, why was England alone in Western Europe in not having a vernacular Bible,[91] which surely was an odd state of affairs, before the Wyclifite Bible was brought out (illegally) during the 1380s, we must attempt an answer that takes into account the remarkable variety of Middle English texts that *were* available and, at least, presented aspects of the biblical narrative to those who could read. Although they were not confronted with the Word of God, they were acquainted with stories and parables, what might be called the *exempla* of Scripture, and these indicate the popular devout attitudes to the life of Christ and other biblical personages. The personalization of the lives of scriptural characters and the personalization of their situations is a remarkable feature of the Middle English narrative accounts. It is not to these metrical translations and paraphrases that one can turn in order to form an accurate conception of the *theological* or *philosophical* sophistication of some pious laity. Much of this literature is neither distinguished nor profound in the way that a pious work like *Piers Plowman* is both.[92] Instead, the purpose of the metrical versions of biblical stories, like the pagan and ecclesiastical *exempla* in sermons, was to teach a more practical message about the moral standards to be observed by Christians in the world, and the consequences of recalcitrance. Together, they can be taken as a contemporary *Ethica*. The *exempla* and metrical versions of Scripture were, to use a fashionable term, a means of social control, a way of educating men and women into the standards obtaining in their world. The emphasis in such Middle English texts was on the individual and his acts, his or her virtues and vices as these were manifested in public situations that Christians could recognize as parallel with their own, as they worked in the world. Hence it is not surprising to find the re-writing of Middle English romances, not only with local colour, but along the lines of the didactic saint's life, as we have seen.[93]

The sources from which metrical paraphrases, *exempla* and verse renderings of biblical situations sprang were many, but among them were memory and imagination. Especially when a text was meant for private reading and devotion, its purpose was to turn the individual's thought inwards on the consequences of his own acts and attitudes within a moral framework that was considered acceptable by his society. This inward focus, highlighting personal responsibility, was a trend to be found in the current scholastic theology of the schools; and the growth of Middle English texts of all sorts – pious, didactic and entertaining – reflected as well as inspired such personal attitudes, although they were expressed in genres that had been developed in a previous age. Fourteenth-century society maintained a continuity with its past, and contemporary narratives provided a textual formulation of moral continuity as well as change.

Should we wish to see the growth in a questioning and critical attitude towards institutions to a heightened and more explicit degree, as well as a more lofty theological interpretation of the Christian *vita*, we must turn to a related but distinct genre of literature, the non-scholastic but theologically and philosophically informed literature that grew up alongside the more standard didactic and general works we have been discussing. Some of Wyclif's Latin works can be seen as contributions to this genre. The non-scholastic literature was not written explicitly for the schools, in the sense that they were not texts lectured on; but they were school products, and their proliferation reflects an audience that was created by the widening of opportunities for more men to spend some time at Oxford and Cambridge, and at cathedral schools, in preparation for lives that would take them further into the Church hierarchy or into a civil service bureaucracy that was, by the end of the century, extensive.[94]

The *forma praedicandi*, the loss of memory and *Piers Plowman*

Only a few works like *Piers Plowman* were able to draw together the tradition and authority, as it was formulated in the schools, with the secular realities experienced by the less educated in their daily routines, and Langland did this with a confidence in mixing Latin and Middle English, theology and secular *exemplum*, that few were able to master. For the most part, there remained something of a dichotomy between school literature, which was extensively imbued with the logic, philosophy and theology of the trained scholastic, and the literature meant for a laity, whose patterns of thought were still heavily informed by custom, by the slightly archaic morality of the romance, and either by the strictures of rural life or the economic realities of urban existence.

We have already seen something of the development of preaching techniques to be used in sermons meant especially for the laity. But aids to preaching were not limited to compilations of *exempla*; for those interested in the rhetorical skills required by the art of preaching, and this meant those who would be preaching in the university or cathedral school milieu where an audience would be sensitive to the proper *forma praedicandi*, treatises existed which outlined the methods of Paris and Oxford universities. Robert of Basevorn's *Forma Praedicandi*, written c. 1322, was to become the exemplar for this more scholarly method, and well illustrates the 'lered' end of the spectrum of expectation.[95] Indirectly it reinforces the distinction between what educated men established in theory and what the relatively uneducated, in fact, received. Basevorn gives us more of the theory as it flourished in the schools; Grimestone tells us more about the practice in the wider world. There is little doubt that what the Franciscans were doing reached a vaster audience than any follower of Basevorn; as Oberman pointed out in discussing the 'timbre' of fourteenth-century spirituality as it filtered through to the masses, this was, if anything, a Franciscan century.[96] But just as it was instructive to see the theoretical underpinning of confessional attitudes of the elite in the *summae confessorum*, so too it is instructive to see what the formal art of preaching meant to men who were theologically and rhetorically sophisticated. Only in a work like *Piers Plowman* do the two worlds unite, and this must be one of the main reasons both for its having survived as the possession of different classes of men, and for our inability to link it specifically with a well-defined audience.

Robert of Basevorn was probably once at Oxford himself, but during what seems to have been his retirement he dedicated a *forma praedicandi* to the Cistercian abbot of Basingwerk, Lord William. He wrote it because he was bored (!) and hoped that in applying his mind to other things he would lighten his boredom and at the same time comply with requests of his patron, different religious of various orders, and seculars; he had no desire to 'grow stale through leisure'.[97] One would think that this kind of introductory admission did not bode well for his treatise, but he has some interesting things to say about the various methods of finding a theme for a sermon, and dividing or amplifying it for the amusement and edification of an audience. In running through his fifty chapters on ornamentation, theme invention, concordances, techniques of persuading and winning over the audience, it is clear that the university sermon was a highly wrought and structured creation, as impressively complicated to the ear as to the eye, with its subdivisions and amplifications. It was unusual to find this university style sermon in the vernacular, although those Middle English sermons in BM Royal 18 B xxiii, edited by Ross for the Early English Text Society, show evidence of the university style in their structure. But Robert of Basevorn refers not only to a method that should be employed in Latin sermons: he says in his index that chapter 49 is devoted to a method that is similar to that practised by Parisians, and which is 'very effective in every language'. Furthermore, chapter 50 is cited in the index as dealing with a method *used in Latin* which in part is like the Oxford method, and this specific reference to Latin may imply that a modified *forma praedicandi* obtained for vernacular sermons as well.[98]

What distinguishes this kind of treatise from the ordinary preaching handbook filled with *exempla* and *bons mots* is its concern to theorize about oral discourse and to refer the reader to Aristotle or to analogies with the requirements of philosophy: a structured, patterned method, a *forma*, is required as the foundation of good preaching, just as the syllogistic form and its place in the wider discipline of logic as a methodology is the foundation of philosophy.[99] He is concerned to set out precisely who has the authority to preach, and he is particularly hostile to a laity that may wish to attain the pulpit: to prevent them from doing so is one of the aims of an elaborate and impressive *forma praedicandi* which they cannot hope to imitate.

Many uneducated men would usurp the act of preaching except that they see this great finesse to which they cannot attain. And for the same reason, when [English university preachers] preach to lay people they give their theme with its division in Latin, because it is difficult for the ignorant to do this.[100]

Furthermore, no lay person or religious, unless permitted by the bishop or the pope, and no woman, no matter how learned or saintly, ought to preach, he says, and refers to canon law.[101] He is particularly fearful of parish priests preaching without licence because they disseminate error. The average priest has the duty to teach publicly and privately the articles of the faith, the Ten Commandments and other standard things, 'even subtleties, if they know how to do so'.[102] He does not encourage individual preachers to translate biblical passages or phrases themselves, but advises that the preacher put in his theme a quotation from the standard literal translation commonly used by the Church:

[If one used any translation] . . . liars, heretics and ignorant men could make themes as they pleased and devise an unknown translation of which the exemplar could not easily be found and there would be a great occasion for error.[103]

Writing in 1322, what does Basevorn mean? To which translation does he refer which is considered literal and standard for the Church? When he says the sermon method of Oxonians 'is used throughout England', having referred the preacher to Aristotle's *Prior Analytics* and Boethius's *Topics* for material on the syllogism that he may use in the sermon's introduction, it is clear that he means those preaching largely to audiences with a level of competence and expectation that came from a university-type arts course where logic was studied – and this means audiences in the cathedral schools, or certain mendicant *studia*.[104]

The modern university sermon had six parts: theme, protheme and introduction to the theme (using a non-biblical authority, namely philosopher or poet), division, sub-division and discussion. The theme was a quote in Latin from the Bible: if the sermon was to be preached on a saint's day any biblical passage would do; if it was to be preached on Sunday it was best to select a phrase from the gospel or epistle of the mass for that day. The biblical theme should be long enough to have three main topics for discussion. This would allow the preacher to divide the theme, each division being confirmed by a biblical authority, ensuring that those ideas that are suggested to him when he divides his theme are legitimately related to it. This means that the words of a division, associated with the biblical words of his theme, are 'legitimate' associations which explain his theme. This prevents him from distorting the theme and associating the wrong words and explanations: finding real and verbal concords between his division and authorities is the preacher's main job.

This is a fascinating and complicated procedure. The ideal is to find a division of a theme where both the words and the ideas can be found in corroborative authorities. Now the words of the theme are not the same as those in the division. The division is a statement of sub-topics that are derived from the theme and explain the theme's meaning. It is the validity of the division, that is, the preacher's mental associations with the first biblical statement, that is tested. The words of his division are merely associated with the theme, and he structures his sermon by justifying the apposite divisions or amplifications that he uses. A variety of methods was suggested to obtain an appropriate division, which depended to some extent on one's audience. Writing in 1322, Basevorn notes that it is inappropriate in sermons to the laity to use the kind of *amplificatio* that requires a knowledge of multiple meanings of, say, a noun; it is appropriate to divide a word into its various meanings only when one lectures in the arts course 'to solve contrarieties' or in disputations 'to solve paralogisms'. But it is legitimate to divide a word into genus and species, and Basevorn goes on to discuss the word 'just', as it is focused on in the theme: The lord led the just man. 'The just man is defined as he who renders to everyone his due; [dividing] to his superior God; to his equal, say, himself; and to his inferior, say, his neighbour.'[105]

A late fourteenth-century or perhaps early fifteenth-century sermon in the vernacular that Ross prints and which oddly addresses 'Good men and wymmen' but then goes on to speak of 'the philosophers of this worthy university', shows the influence of the divided university sermon in English.[106] It takes as its theme for St Clement's Day a phrase from the introit of the Mass: 'Adest nomen tuum, et munera tua accepta erunt' (Psalm 6) and was perhaps delivered before town and gown in Oxford on this feast day. After saying the Latin text the preacher continues:

wherfore I may sey to hym to wordes of my teme þus moche in English: Lorde, þi name is with us and þi ȝeftes ben take to us.

translating his theme and repeating it further in his introduction, a practice that is common in all the vernacular sermons printed by Ross.

Good men and wymmen, as I seyd afore, þe wordes þatt I have take to sey at þis tyme ben þus muche on Englyssh to youre understondynge: 'Lord, þi name ys with vs and þi ȝeftes ben take to vs.' In þe wiche wordes I vyndyrstond too þinges: a glorious felyshyppe when I sey 'þy name ys with vs'; kyndenesse of lordeshippe when I sey 'þi ȝeftes ben taken to vs'.

His theme is now divided. Then when he gives his biblical authority, here Paul (Phil. 2: 10), he gives the Latin: 'In nomine Ihesu omne genu et cetera' (which he completed) and follows this too with the English: 'in þe name, seys he, of Ihesus every knee of heven, erthe and hell ys bowed'. Then 'name' is further divided and related to 'felyshyppe'. Thus the strict, formal structure is adhered to, and the preacher repeats his theme and provides associations with the use of concordances, finding real and verbal concords between theme and divisions. Virtually all his Latin quotes, which are very short, are translated, preceded with a statement like: 'It is as muche to youre vndyrstondynge. . . .' Further on, after giving the story of St Clement and St Barnabas from the *Legenda Aurea*, which treats of the puzzle about why a little flea has six legs whereas a big camel has only four (!), a puzzle that Clement solved and which inspired Barnabas to become his disciple, but which solution the preacher does not understand, he says: 'þe question þat þe phylosofres asked of Seynt Barnabas I cannot asoil [solve] it; but I preye þe phylosofres of þis worthy universite to assoyle itt whan þatt semeth good'. This preacher is also careful to refer to the sermon sections or parts as he comes to employ them; e.g., 'as I somwhat seid in myn antetheme'.

I have elaborated on the use of division in sermons because it gives us some idea of the underlying structure involved in constructing a sermon into a series of related parts. The structure itself can be remembered by the preacher: he knows where to go next after he has selected a biblical theme. But what he does with the theme, *how* he divides it, does not depend on his having a good memory for biblical phrases that use the same words and have the same meaning as his divisions; rather, he uses a handbook of some sort which allows him to look up the words of his division as they are used elsewhere in the Bible in a like manner. The *Glossa Ordinaria*, comprising brief comments on each verse drawn from the church fathers, was the most frequently used source for the interpretation of a biblical theme. This means that even where the preacher includes complaints about the clergy or avaricious lawyers in his text, he is less likely to be drawing on his own experiences than on standard authoritative sources which speak in clichés about the laxity of the clergy or the avariciousness of the legal profession. The abuses in his society may be real, but the language used to describe them in the sermon comes from set texts. The kind of concordance between life and his handbook complaint can be said to be, in the terminology of the *forma praedicandi*, only a *real* concord: this occurs when the ideas or *sense* of a theme and the division appear in his authorities but the *words* do not match. The authorities are then said to be only in real concord (as opposed to verbal concord) with the theme.[107] So too, the reality of social abuses is related only to the *sense* of his conventional complaint.

This leads to a startling unoriginality in most sermons, because there is no concern to offer experiences from the preacher's own life. The structure of the sermon and its dependence on set text descriptions, which are only clichés when compared with specific historical realities, is paramount. Academic preaching is not an individualizing act, but one judged successful by the skilful manipulation of the rules of composition – the scissors-and-paste method – and this means a use of handbooks and legitimate associations immediately backed up by expected and conventional authorities. Once again, we can see a mode of composition at work which depends on the formulaic, the florilegial extract, a method of communication that has links with the earlier oral formulaic tradition of composition but which now follows a set *ordinatio* that relies on a compilation of conventional *exempla*.

The greatest scope for originality is *amplificatio* by *exemplum*, and Basevorn says this is most appreciated by the laity. Related to the use of *exempla* is the mode of explaining a theme historically, allegorically, morally or anagogically: 'faith is built by allegory, morals are formed by tropology, the contemplatives are raised by anagogy'.[108] But each time one divides a theme according to one or more of these classifications, one consults an authority to corroborate one's associations. This was a mode of thought that was common wherever the literate medieval mind focused.

This highly structured method of composition not only reveals the severe limitations placed on creative preaching; as Alford has shown, it is a key to understanding the restricted *forma* of a poem like *Piers Plowman* as well, and Alford has linked the poem to the art of preaching in a more convincing way than has heretofore been done.[109] The biblical, Latin quotations in *Piers Plowman* comprise a central principle of construction, from which the Middle English 'divisions' fan out and the quotations tell us about the compositional method which Langland used: he frequently began with a Latin quote and, using the aids of a medieval preacher, derived much of the substance of his poem.

The manuscripts show numerous incomplete Latin quotations or tags, but Alford is surely correct when he says this owes more to standard scribal practice than to the author himself.[110] The lengths of the quotations vary from manuscript to manuscript and presume a certain degree of acquaintance with Scripture on the part of the reader, who is required to say the quote completely in order to understand how the following Middle English verses divide or explain the quote.

In the thirteenth century Bonaventure could advise fellow theologians that 'only by constant reading can one fix in one's memory the text of the Bible to the very letter'.[111] Those who could recall the completion of a biblical quote and associate with it verbal concordances from elsewhere in the Bible could be considered 'living concordances' themselves, because from the use of memory they could link appropriate biblical texts spontaneously and effortlessly. While Bonaventure's advice was appropriate to preachers and biblical exegetes alike who possessed personal treasuries of memory, and a similar procedure could be said to operate when constructing a sermon along the lines indicated by Basevorn or by Waleys's *De modo componendi sermones* (*c.* 1340), the increasingly common handbook of biblical concordances came to substitute for personal memory or even acquaintance with the biblical text. The creative role of memory was becoming lost altogether; the easy way to preach, and even to structure a didactic poem, was to use repositories of concording texts with increasingly elaborate but helpful indices. The biblical concordances of, for instance, Hugh of St Cher, where there is a list of concording quotations from the liturgy grouped together for the convenience of the preacher, sometimes as informally as in the margins of the sermon itself, serve as a good example.[112] Memory thus becomes spatial and visual, and helps the reader to locate the place of information in a compilation, but withdraws to second place with regard to recalling the information itself. Hence the usefulness of Bromyard's *Summa*, which provided a vast compilation of articles from *Abiecto* to *Xtus* with *distinctiones*, *exempla* and many concording biblical and patristic quotations. What appears to have been the odd situation described by Deanesly, where the Bible, even in Latin, was not widely available, becomes modified when we take into account the spread of handbooks of extracts and concordances that replaced it. And with the eye replacing the ear and aural memory in the composition of sermons and didactic poetry, one can well expect the verbal concordances in sermons and the like to become increasingly elaborate because the pattern they enabled the writer to create was visual, spatial, arranged on the page and based on the availability of indexed florilegia of *exempla* and paired quotations to hand.

As with sermons, so too with the contemporary *Piers Plowman*, as Alford has shown:

The quotations are primary and the English functions mainly as an amplification of the texts, achieved by straight exposition as in a commentary and – in due consideration of the audience – by more popular means such as exhortation and exempla ... the preacher is not trying merely to gloss Scripture but to dramatize its meaning for his flock, and thus he places his quotations where they will have the greatest rhetorical effect. . . . The quotations are the points towards which as well as from which the preacher is constantly working.[113]

Much of *Piers Plowman* was composed with this method in mind. But the poem is artistically more complex than this, and in its revisions it shows a movement away from its original structure: the divisions or amplifications get reworked. But Alford shows how Langland, like the preacher of academic sermons, began with quotations; we need to complete them when they are not fully given in the manuscript in order to reveal the concordance that is picked up in subsequent Latin quotes, and from here we move with Langland 'outward into the text of the poem'.[114] Alford chooses as a particularly sustained and successful passage Passus XIV in the B recension of *Piers Plowman*. The parable from Luke 14: 15–24 (Douai) provides the theme for B XIV – 'only those who do the will of the Lord will eat bread in the kingdom of God'. Then, finding verbal concordances in other parts of the Bible, Langland, still on his theme, inserts concording Latin texts in the manner of a preacher using a concordance who divides his theme according to the topics in the parable. The Latin texts show verbal similarities with the original theme and are then elaborated on through English dramatization, paraphrase and the use of *exempla*. And because the commentary tradition of glossing a text by means of another led to certain biblical quotes being taken in pairs or families, it is not surprising to find Langland using conventional concords, which are also found in the standard reference books, alphabetically arranged and indexed.

Whenever we find a long stretch of Latin quotations in *Piers Plowman*, then, we can be certain that he is constructing his narrative along the lines of the preacher using a concordance. This is the strongest argument yet advanced to indicate that the enormous complexities of Langland's poem do not result from impulsive associations. In fact, nearly all of Langland's quotations (Alford looks at those concording on 'rich' and 'poor') can be found in Bromyard's *Summa* under the obvious headings (here: *paupertas* and *divitiae*).

Briefly, what this means for our understanding of consciously structured verse and prose in Middle English is that authors *were* operating in a tradition, but in one that was transitional in replacing memory with ordered texts: didactic formulae were written down in compilations and no longer held only in the memory, and yet the creative story-teller was still seeing himself as recreating, at least in part, within a tradition of composition. To compose a didactic poem rather than a sermon was merely to adopt a more universalized stance, relating school attitudes and interests with those of the secular world. Within a pronouncedly Christian world, where even one's secular vocabulary bore a close relation to spiritual and moral attitudes, there was a necessary unity in one's conception of secular life as a *spiritual* journey. To notice that most of the Middle English poetry of the fourteenth century is sermon-like is merely to point out how the secular world was viewed as a manifestation of the spiritual. Thus when Basevorn described, formally, the way to impress on the laity the meaning of the state of perfection or perseverance, and elaborated on the method of Paris and of St Gregory the Great as 'effective and understandable to the ordinary people in any vulgar idiom',[115] he emphasized the method of preaching that chose something evident in nature, in ordinary life, in art, and adduced a biblical authority that contained an example of it. One went further and showed how other authentic narratives, from Augustine, Gregory, Valerius, Seneca, Macrobius and the like pointed to the same truth. Langland and Chaucer did this with consummate skill, but they entertained as well as instructed, and it is their wider ability to use the exegetical tradition to yield *literary* fruit that earned them a place in the homes of literate Englishmen, beyond their own lifetime.

Ordinatio of the literary *compilatio*

Because *Piers Plowman* has such close structural links with the *forma praedicandi*, it also is likely to have been a work that was read aloud, that is, in some sense declaimed like the sermon. This way of hearing a written text – having it read to one – was rather common in the fourteenth century, and was not limited to the hearing of sermons. It is quite clear that people were read to in many situations that were entertaining and didactic. In fact, students who attended the arts faculty in the university did not usually possess texts but were lectured to *viva voce*. The master read out a text, sentence by sentence, and commented upon it. Students were able to write and take notes as was done in the higher faculties but even this does not appear to have been done at arts lectures, for the arts school, at least in Oxford, apparently had only benches and no desks. The law and theology schools, however, had to be furnished with benches and desks,[116] and students of these higher faculties were required by statute either to possess or to have legitimately lent to them a copy of the set books. Furthermore, since all undergraduates could write and most of them were proverbially poor scholars, they frequently hired themselves out as scribes to copy the most urgently demanded school texts from separate quires or *peciae* obtained piece by piece from university stationers. At Paris in particular, not only university texts were copied in this way, but also the works that were useful *extra muros* to preachers. A surprisingly large proportion of manuscripts that are extant today on all subjects, but particularly on theology and law, are in fact the *peciae* copies made by the stationer or by those students either whom he hired as scribes, or who copied a work for their own use.[117]

The declamation of a text, the structure of its composition imposed by its author, the perception of that structure when heard aloud by an audience or read by a reader, and the implicit principle of ordering, indexing and cross-referencing of episodes in a text, be it a sermon or the individual tales of Chaucer's *Canterbury Tales*, are illuminated by the study of scribal methods of reproducing a text and the gradual development of concern for the text's *mise-en-page*. From the thirteenth century onwards, the layout and decoration of a text became more and more important. The way a text is arranged on a page can function like punctuation, and this is important not only regarding how a text is read aloud, and consequently heard and understood. It also guides the private reader, as well as telling us something about the way scribes interpreted the text they were transmitting. Doyle and Parkes have recently pointed out that, 'because we tend to take the layout found in fourteenth-century books for granted, it is possible to overlook the elements of interpretation involved'.[118] A good example of this is the San Marino, Huntingdon Library MS 26 of Chaucer's *Canterbury Tales*, known as the Ellesmere Manuscript. The way the scribe perceived the series of tales sets the *Canterbury Tales*, in a startling manner, into the tradition of ordered and indexed preaching handbooks we have previously discussed, and it tells us something about the way a text's structure, no matter what its content might be, was understood in the wider context of fourteenth- and fifteenth-century thinking about the written word. First of all, the Ellesmere Manuscript is wonderfully illuminated with depictions of Chaucer's pilgrims, and although some drawings are traced from copy-books, the pilgrims themselves are individually depicted with details taken from Chaucer's text. If Frances Yates is correct when she says that the 'pictures' verbally described by Holcot in his *Moralitates* were never meant to be drawn but instead to be held in the memory,[119] then by the end of the fourteenth and early fifteenth centuries men's memories were no longer being thus exercised. Chaucer's pilgrims, furthermore, were not mere types but poetically created individuals, who, as literary individuals (not photographic portraits of real men Chaucer had known), manifested the vices and virtues of conventional social types, and the Ellesmere illuminator was able to realize this in his depictions.

Furthermore, there is a sense in which the editor of the *Canterbury Tales* who commissioned the scribe to prepare an organized series of the tales saw the work in a conventional form not unlike the preacher's handbook of *exempla* which linked the stories with a thread of narrative. The colophon at the end of the Ellesmere Manuscript reads: 'Here is ended the book of the tales of Canterbury *compiled* by Geoffrey Chaucer of whos soule Iesu Crist have mercy, Amen.'[120] What does it mean to see the *Canterbury Tales* as a *compilatio*? The manuscript is set out with marginal headings and gives the names of *auctores* cited in the text as well as indicating what are regarded as citations in Chaucer's text. The *Canterbury Tales* may not have circulated as a whole work (remember, it is unfinished), but rather as separate tales or as groups of tales in separate booklets or quires; and this is suggested by the different arrangements of the components of the work in all of the early manuscripts. Thus, not unlike the circulation of *peciae* or *peciae* copies of school texts, Chaucer's *Canterbury Tales* were often read and copied as discrete units, and this doubtless suggested to the Ellesmere editor that the work was in fact structured as a *compilatio*. The Ellesmere Manuscript is the earliest extant manuscript to present the *Canterbury Tales* in an ordered *compilatio* but the term '*compilatio*' is also applied in later copies of the work.[121] Each of the four earliest surviving manuscripts of the

Canterbury Tales reflects the attempts of editors and scribes, if not of Chaucer himself, to impose an external organizing principle on the whole, and this *ordinatio* of a *compilatio* we know to have been a literary device (in part to substitute for the previously non-literate memory) that was developed widely in fourteenth-century preaching handbooks. Doyle and Parkes summarize neatly what we have already seen to be the case in the growth of indexed *exempla* collections:

The *compilatio* was developed in academic and legal circles during the thirteenth century to make inherited material excerpted from the writings of established *auctores* accessible in a more systematic and convenient form. In theory, the compiler added no matter of his own by way of exposition but he was free to rearrange: he imposed a new *ordinatio* on the materials he extracted from the works of others.[122]

The value of a *compilatio* depended on the wealth of the *auctoritates* employed, but its utility depended on the way in which the manuscript interprets the *Canterbury Tales* as a *compilatio* in that it emphasizes the role of the tales as repositories of *auctoritates-sententiae*, and aphorisms on different topics which are indicated by the marginal headings. The overall structure of the work is a pilgrimage. By its clear labelling of the tales with running titles and additional headings, and by its illustrations, it emphasizes the importance of the pilgrims as a major factor in the structure of the work – here, as the device by which the *auctoritates* are redeployed in the *compilatio* – and connects the tales with the General Prologue. The tales are thus clearly labelled as discrete but related units. . . . The nature of Chaucer's literary remains – probably a collection of quires or 'booklets' containing individual tales or groups of tales – suggested the structure of a *compilatio* as an ingenious solution to the problem of presentation afforded by such a collection of fragments.[123]

Whether this *ordinatio* of a literary *compilatio* was editorially imposed or was implicit in Chaucer's own mode of composition as a structuring principle cannot be proved. But it is clear that the Ellesmere Manuscript was not alone in perceiving this kind of order: in the Corpus Christi College, Oxford, MS 198 of the *Canterbury Tales*, each of the tales is considered a chapter, and this is found in later manuscripts of the whole work. It has never been suggested that Chaucer composed in the impulsive manner often attributed (wrongly) to Langland. At the same time, several of the tales have been specifically linked with preaching (as has Langland's work), and we have seen that this was, as a method of composition, a highly structured art. The analysis of scribal and editorial procedure suggests that Chaucer, like his contemporaries, was working in a compositional tradition that favoured *ordinatio* of a *compilatio* of *exempla* or tales, necessitated by habits of remembering and understanding a text that were consequent on the growth of widespread literacy.

The extent of Chaucer's debt to contemporary preaching methods and the contents of sermons, if not their handbook sources, has been demonstrated for the Friar's Tale and the Pardoner's Tale. Wenzel has recently investigated to what degree the Pardoner's Tale is patterned on actual sermons of the period;[124] like Pratt,[125] he shows that many of Chaucer's *exempla* have parallels with those used by the Franciscan John of Wales in his preaching *compilatio*, the *Communiloquium*. Wenzel tries to go further and demonstrate how there is an influence of the language of sermons that extends beyond Chaucer's fitting ready-to-hand stories to his own purposes. Let us recall that the Friar's Tale is a shrewdly observed replica of a friar's manner of preaching: it is in the form of a fabliau with moral *exempla*. For the stories, Chaucer seems to have used Friar Herebert's preaching notes,[126] Bromyard's *Summa Praedicantium*, Thomas of Cantimpré's *Bonum universale de apibus* and other anonymous collections of sermons and *exempla*. The contemporary sermon collection of Master Ripon of Durham provides the matter for the Friar's Tale where a bailiff or judge is carried off to hell by the devil as a consequence of a curse. According to Wenzel, not only are Chaucer's plots frequently the same as preachers' material, but his choice of images, his technical terms and his rhetorical devices are those of the contemporary pulpit.[127]

The *ordinatio* of the *Canterbury Tales* as it was perceived by contemporary readers or scribes, and the preaching matter that Chaucer re-formed to produce his *compilatio* of tales, suggest to us the all-pervasive influence of fourteenth-century preaching – its rhetoric, its arrangement on the page, its content. However, to recognize his sources is not to reduce the originality of his achievement but, in fact, to enhance it. It is the way Chaucer moves away from the strict tradition of composition that prevents us from reducing his work to a mosaic of his sources. The strict theory of composing sermons remained for those who could do little else than string together ready-to-hand *exempla* found by consulting indexed handbooks. For minds like Langland's, Chaucer's or the *Pearl* poet's, there was something more to composition, something other than skilled *ordinatio* and *compilatio* at work. And this was recognized by patrons and audience alike, despite the attempts of more traditional minds to fit these works into familiar categories.

Effects of the trade in vernacular books

An increasing number of people commissioned copies of these works and the London 'book' trade flourished. The growth in the volume of business for vernacular manuscripts at the end of the fourteenth century and the beginning of the fifteenth is shown by the amalgamation of the text-writers and illuminators' gilds (1403), and these were separated from the gild of writers of court letter from 1373 when members of the latter were required to put their names to every deed they transcribed, and thus identify themselves as responsible individuals.[128] The stationers during this period were kept busy by an increasing volume of requests for vernacular books newly composed as well as works translated into the vernacular. While there is no evidence that organized scriptoria for vernacular works existed at this time, and the London book trade was, in Pollard's words, a 'bespoke trade', new copies of books were produced to specific orders with stationers relying on an *ad hoc* arrangement of scribes, lymners (binders) and illuminators who were independent members of several gilds.[129] Those who commissioned such works in increasing numbers may have been largely armigerous by the fifteenth century, but as we have seen, this included a generation of socially mobile men and an expanded gentry who to some extent were now considered 'lered'. When we can put a name to an owner of a fifteenth-century copy of Gower's *Confessio Amantis* or Chaucer's *Canterbury Tales*, it is not only men of the distinction and birth of Humfrey Duke of Gloucester who appear as commissioners of such manuscripts. While the Bedfordshire gentleman named in Bodley 902 and the London mercer in Corpus Christi, Oxford, MS 67 may not have been the first owners of these manuscripts but the heirs of the first owners, as Doyle and Parkes have suggested, they may well represent the kinds of persons who were the first owners and commissioners of works produced in the early part of the fifteenth century.[130] Such men had developed habits of reading or listening to a read text that were based on a deployment of their memory largely in relation to the ordered structure of a work. The texts themselves, as compilations or collections of *exempla*, tales and shorter stories, collected together such a vast quantity of literary matter that the reliance on letters external to the mind was becoming one of the primary means by which men otherwise involved full-time in business and administration could become familiar with traditions of the past and attitudes of the present. And with the demise of the minstrel, whose role was virtually obsolete because social and artistic values could be transmitted directly to the reader, came the development of concern for the author, even as distinct from the compiler or organizer of the message.

The morally responsible and individual author, and particularly the (human) author of Scripture, working *sub deo*, became a subject of interest, and it is here that we can perhaps locate the seed of Wyclif's concern for the necessity of confronting the lay reader with the scriptural *auctor*, writing to men as a *causa efficiens per modum invenientis*, with God as the source of his *auctoritas*. By confronting the text directly, the lay reader no longer had need of the exegetical intermediary of the ecclesiastical preacher who rarely offered the scriptural message itself to his flock. And this fits in with what many have seen as Wyclif's primary concern – to reform Christian society – and his contemporary significance as a political theorist rather than as a theological reformer who founded his theory of ecclesiastical reform on the secular and lay government's possession of direct *dominium* by grace from God who was the source of all *auctoritas*.

As Minnis has shown,[131] the increasing interest in authorial responsibility in the fourteenth century was reflected in Holcot's *Wisdom Commentary*, where he discusses Solomon's authorship but Philo's compilation;[132] more important, because of his influence on Wyclif, was Nicholas of Lyra's interest in the issue. In his *Postilla Litteralis*, Solomon is spoken of as the *auctor principalis*, but the *Wisdom Book* was compiled from the *Sententiae Salomonis* by Philo. Minnis has shown that 'throughout his commentaries on the Sapiential Books, Lyra is mainly concerned with the *auctores humani* who work *sub deo*'.[133] All fourteenth-century exegetes saw *Wisdom* as a compilation, an orderly arrangement of materials; while, in addition, Lyra regarded the Psalter, Proverbs and the Book of Twelve Minor Prophets as *collectiones* which did not have this arrangement. The Psalter in particular was the archetypal *collectio* for Lyra, and Esdras was taken to be the archetypal collector. The formal cause of a work was thus seen as twofold: on the one hand there was the matter; on the other, its arrangement or *ordinatio*;[134] and Lyra especially applied this distinction to the works of the four evangelists. The interest in the integrity of the *auctor*, who wrote *sub deo*, allowed men to read of the personal life of their *auctor*, relating his experiences to their own;[135] and when applied to the accounts of the evangelists, one can see how this could develop into Wyclif's doctrine only when there was a large enough literate laity able to confront the *auctor* directly.

Wyclif: Bible reading and the 'lewd(e)'

The whole issue of precisely who was permitted contact with the Bible, either in its standard Latin prose or in a literal prose translation, is somewhat obscured by the polemical outbursts of Wyclif and his followers and the largely political reaction to them. A sermon printed by Ross sets the problem in another light. It does not appear to be Wyclifite, and if written at the end of the fourteenth century (or at least before Arundel's *Constitutions* of 1407, which forbade the reading or possession of the unauthorized Wyclifite translations, but did not explicitly forbid those done earlier or in verse!) it seems to imply that lay reading of the Bible was not forbidden. Precisely which Bible the sermon refers to is not made clear.

The theme of the sermon is taken from Psalm 77 for the nineteenth Sunday after Trinity.[136] Using a not uncommon rhetorical device of a dialogue between preacher and parishioner, the preacher says:

'Sir' þou seiste paraunter [perchance], 'it is forbede by you prestes and prelates of holy-churche anny lewde man to entermette [meddle with] of holy-writte.' Sir, I sey naye: but itt is forbede anny lewde man to mys-use holywritte for God hym-selfe biddeþ is peple to vndirstonde itt. þan and is peple shall vndirstonde itt, þei muste entermette þer-of; and ȝiff God bidde you cunne or vndirstonde it, trewly I darre nott forbede you to entermete þerof. Of þis lawe þou arte bonde to entermett in peyne of everlastynge dampnacion for þou muste cunne þi Pater Noster þat is in þe gospell, þi Ave Maria, and þi Beleue, þe X Commaundementys, þe vii werkes of mercye bodely and spiritually to fulfill by þi will or þi powere, by all þe determynacion of holy-churche.

Translating this theme as 'my people, vndirstonde ȝe my lawe' the preacher says: 'He seiþ farþurmore "Vndirstonde ȝe", he seiþ not "Rede ȝe lawe" *all-only* [my emphasis] but "Vndirstonde itt for þei þat entermetten þer-of withowte techynge and cunnynge vndirstondeþ it amysse.'[137] He goes on to say that if you are unlearned and a labourer – and the implication is that you either cannot read or are uneducated in some basic form of biblical exegesis – then all you need to do is memorize the twelve articles of faith, the ten commandments, the five uses of the senses, the seven works of mercy.[138] Of further knowledge a man may be *excused*, but not, it would seem, forbidden!

Sir ryght as Criste is well payed with euery man þat can is lawe, and þe more þat he can þer-of þe bettur he is apeid, ryght so euery lewde man and laborere is *exscused generally* to beleue as all holychurche doþe with-owte more lernynge þer-of. ȝit he may not exscuse hym but he muste do is diligence to knowe and to cunne hem þe xii articles, as I haue seid hem etc.[139]

This preacher seems to be saying that it is inappropriate for an unlearned man to misuse the Bible, but he who is able to read and to go further in his education should do so for it pleases (or pays) Christ 'þe more he [one] can þer-of'. It is not enough to read Scripture; one must understand its meaning. The implication, it seems, is that the ability merely to read without understanding – without knowing the traditional interpretations of the text, may be a common enough ability but not one that fulfils Christ's injunction that one understand the religious, or even theological, significance of what one reads.[140] This can make sense only in a society of readers who were literate but not because they were clergy.

As Fisher has recently pointed out in his discussion of the development of Chancery English,

writing in English grew up outside of this educational framework (i.e. outside the grammar school where one learned to construe Latin grammar, although by *c.* 1350 reciting it in English). Like other business skills – accounting, the clerical hand, business law – it was a subject learned throughout this period either by apprenticeship in the houses of the masters of chancery or the houses of guild masters or by extra-curricular tutorials imparting these practical skills to academic students hoping to enter the business community.[141]

And if we reinterpret the sermon above in the manner I am suggesting, then Deanesly's interpretation of instructions in the English *Layfolk's Mass Book* and in the *Merita Missae* must also be reinterpreted. She tries to show that at Mass, even at the end of the fourteenth century, people stood for the reading of the gospels in Latin which they did not understand. But all the quotes she uses from the *Layfolk's Mass Book* and the *Merita Missae* do not say that the gospel was read in Latin to the laity at this time nor that when and if the people did not understand the gospel reading it was because they heard it in Latin rather than that, as in the case of our sermon above, the message was too subtle or mystical for them without further authoritative explanation and interpretation. After all, the 'lewed' clergy are told in the *Merita Missae* to worship God's work and 'lere' (learn) this lesson *from hearing the gospel read*.

Now it may be true that uneducated clergy and laity did not understand the language in which the gospel was read, but the above works do not exactly say this. Instead, the author of the *Merita Missae* uses the *exemplum* of the adder, who understands nothing of what you say to it but when enchanted will understand you; this is used as an analogy with the condition of a theologically unsophisticated laity. The *exemplum* teaches you that as with the enchanted adder, so too if God gives you grace you will understand the meaning of the gospel, that is, its significance; the infusion of God's grace does not necessarily mean you will suddenly understand Latin when the gospel is read if you were previously unable to do so.[142] As Deanesly herself has shown, Hilton's *Epistle on the Mixed Life* (*c*. 1370–80)[143] is an English manual written for the pious who wish to live in the world, and it recommends 'almost indirectly' the reading of the gospels to the laity.[144] One presumes this would be in English. Certainly by Wyclif's time the recommendation that the laity read Scripture for themselves was made also by non-Wyclifites and reflects not only their ability to do so, at least in English, but also a wider interest in the theological matters opened up to them because of their literacy.[145] Furthermore, the concern that people not only read but understand what they read is shown in the Wyclifite text, *The Holi Prophete David Seith*,[146] and I think it is clear that here the author is not referring to people who can read Latin words parrot-fashion, without knowing the meaning of the sentences or verse they utter; he refers rather to those who read without the wilful disposition to understand the significance of a text for their own salvation:

> Treuli if not alle men redynge knowyn God, how schal he know that redith not? Thanne men redynge knowe no treuth whanne thei redyn not wyllynge to fynde treuthe. . . . Therfor though he rede euere he schal neuere fynde, as neithir philosophiris founden, wiche sougten for the same cause. Gessist thou that prestis of Saduceis redden not scripturis? but thei mygte not fynde God in hem, for thei wolde not lyue worthili to God . . . sich is scripture to a man not willynge to lyue aftir God as if ony man expounne lernynge of bataile to an <u>erthe teliere</u> not hauynge will for to figte.[147]   earth-tiller

The question of literacy has become subordinated to that of the readers' intention for this author, and much of the literature of the later fourteenth century at least promoted the same principle. As we shall have occasion to see later, the ability to read was coupled with a desire to become increasingly involved, not only in understanding injunctions to the simple Christian life as set out in the gospels, but in understanding certain current theological issues, popular in the schools, which reached the theologically unsophisticated laity in various literary forms. *Piers Plowman* is not the only text that reproves laymen for involving themselves in theological debate. Ross prints a sermon[148] which also warns the unlearned (the author does not necessarily mean illiterate) against arguing over issues like the nature of the sacrament, and this surely is a kind of negative evidence that they did so:

> For-soþe þei be þe argumentes and þe skill þat may be of þe Sacramente, and þat longeþ not to þe, shewynge well Crist, þat he wold lat no man geþur þe releue but is disciples, shewynge to þe þat arte a lewd man þat it is inow3þ to þe to beleuen as holychurche techeþ þe and lat þe clerkes alone with þe argumentes. For þe more

þat þou disputes þer-of, þe farþur shall be þer-
fro.[149]

Hence the very definition of 'lewd' appears to have altered.

Still another sermon in this collection affirms that Mary's
motherhood and virginity cannot be understood by nature; they
are God's mysteries, and it is unfit for man to seek to penetrate
such mysteries. This is particularly so for the laity:

And so it were ryght sittyng þat euery man held
hym content to commun in maters of ys faculte,
polocy and governaunce, so þat kny3tes, and
oþur gentils with hem shuld sett her besines   business.
abowte þe good governaunce in þe temperalltee
in þe tyme of pees and also abowte divers
poyntes of armes in þe tyme of werre, as þe
lawe and þe cronicle techeþ hem; for þer beþ
many sotell questions and conclusions in mater
of werre and armes as þe phylosofre declareþ,
De Re Militari and Gylus *De Regimine, parte
ultima, processum.* Prestes shuld principally
entermet to lern þe lawe of Criste and lawfully
to teche itt. And lower men shuld hold hem
contente wiþ þe questions and þe sotelte of þer
own labour. For Orace seyþe, *De Arte Poetica*,
tractant fabilia fabri et Boicius, *primo
Topicorum*, techeþ *quod cuilibet credendum est
in facultate sua* þan iff euery parte of Cristes
churche wold hold hem content with here own
occupacions and not to entermet farþur þan
reson and lawe rewels hem to, þan þe grace of
almyghty God shuld floresch and þe more
freshly contynue amonge.

This unfinished sermon was preached before the sovereign,
who Ross considers must have been Henry V, and his queen, so
it is quite late (*c.* 1416). It shows a lay concern for the theological issues that traditionally were considered inappropriate to
their estate, and that had persisted from the early days of Wyclif, if not before. In addition, there is a chance reference to the
structure of early fifteenth-century society which suggests a recognition of a third estate that was increasingly mobile, so that to
refer to it as an estate of 'lewd labourers' would have been inaccurate: in the above quote the preacher speaks of 'lower men',

and later he says: 'There be in þis world þre maner of men: clerkes, kynʒthes and *commynalte*.¹⁵⁰ The poor are recognized as existing in great numbers, and they are frequently maltreated by 'the great' and the law, but these poor comprise the commonalty – a word that reflects their heightened political role in 'the commonwealth': perhaps this is merely a figure of speech, but it is an interesting one, for it reminds us that we are now dealing with the politically vocal 'common pepull' and no longer with the inarticulate land-tied serf or labourer.

The social and political significance of Lollardy

The Platonic insight with which this chapter began, that literacy would foster sedition, describes the situation in England when Wyclif's followers broadcast their ideas. They believed that it was necessary for the laity to read and study the Bible – for their salvation and, more indirectly, to evaluate if not actively to seek to change those institutions and customs that did not conform to biblical injunctions concerning political and ecclesiastical justice in the world. As the translator of the second version of the Wyclifite Bible made clear, the inability to read Latin ought not to prevent men from understanding Scripture directly; and, by implication, they should apply this understanding to institutions and attitudes in their own society. Even if, as it is sometimes said, Wyclif meant Scripture to be studied primarily by the knightly class, the better to enable them to reform English society, and even if he had no intention and no hand in providing a translation of the Bible in the first place, and certainly not one intended for the lesser laity, it is clear that by 1401 his followers were seen to have cast pearls before swine by encouraging precisely the lesser laity to read Scripture and discuss it in conventicles. *De Heretico Comburendo*, which brought in the death penalty for Lollard heretics, drew attention to lay literacy as a fundamental aspect of their sedition: 'They make unlawful conventicles and confederacies, they hold and exercise schools, they make and write books, they do wickedly instruct and inform people.'¹⁵¹ It is presumed that their very name, Lollards, was already a familiar expression applied to heretical lay preachers in the Netherlands, and like their continental counterparts, 'they read the gospels and learnt them by heart in the vernacular, and "mumble" the one to the other'.¹⁵² We may recall a similar description used in the thirteenth century of the Waldensians, some of whom were literate, others of whom read and then memorized vernacular Scripture and preached in people's homes. Aston has supposed that many of the Lollards were only semi-literate and learned their Bible in conventicles where it was read aloud.[153] In the early fifteenth century, Lollard trials certainly uncovered both the literate and semi-literate among artisans, weavers, woolwinders, fullers, wiredrawers or simple labourers.[154] Whether many such men and women were themselves literate or relied on the readers among them, it is clear that the first generation of Lollards had a sufficient number of readers and writers among them to have their books preserved and copied, even after they were caught or forced to recant. And laws passed to the contrary, when several Bohemian scholars visited England in the early fifteenth century they were able, despite all the decrees about book-burning, to get access to Wyclif's work at country parishes like Kennerton in Gloucestershire and Braybrooke in Northamptonshire as well as in Oxford. Wyclif's *De Ecclesia*, the *De Dominio Divino* and the *De Veritate Sacre Scripture* were obtained and copied in England and even corrected for them in Oxford (*c.* 1407–8); a sizeable number of Lollard works including Wyclif's originals could still be found in 1410 for a book-burning at Carfax to have taken place.

It has long been thought that the success of early Lollardy depended on the patronage of certain Lollard knights, among them Sir Thomas Latimer at Braybrooke, who seems to have sponsored a scriptorium where Lollard texts were carefully copied and corrected. If Lollard principles spread out from the literate to influence the illiterate, it is none the less clear that a significant number of Lollards were able to study directly from and reproduce texts as early as 1380. And the critical sense that came with the ability to confront a text was feared by ecclesiastical and lay authorities alike.[155] The chronicler Knighton from Leicester and his continuator, writing from one of the main seats of early Lollardy, insisted that Lollards had translated the gospel so that it was now 'more open to laymen and ignorant people including women who know how to read'.[156] This was considered dangerous (as contemporary sermons pointed out) because a significantly large number of the laity were readers of the sort that had no training in orthodox exegesis. When Archbishop Arundel issued his *Constitutions* to control the extension of vernacular biblical translations, he made it necessary to obtain ecclesiastical permission for any translation, but he did not directly forbid translations as such.[157] In a society with widespread literate skills it may have been nearly impossible to do so. Throughout the fifteenth century, ecclesiastical authorities recognized this and became increasingly obsessed with the dangers of vernacular literature when put in the wrong hands. To exercise some means of control they passed a succession of ordinances to check unauthorized preachers as well as vernacular literature in general, which led to the ludicrous situation of works like the *Canterbury Tales* coming under suspicion of heresy (1464). Heresy was understood as being caused by the possession of vernacular books and the ability to read them, so that the very term 'heresy' extended beyond heterodox religious beliefs to encompass the political. This redefinition was in keeping with Wyclif's principles, which were themselves, in origin, almost entirely political.

A further stumbling block in the detection and control of heresy by the authorities was caused by the Lollard practice of interpolating their beliefs into recognized orthodox texts. Aston has interpreted this practice as a valuable disguise, for by slipping heterodox doctrine into already popular and 'safe' texts, the Lollards had discovered 'a means of climbing into the laps of people, including the gentry – who had come to fight shy of heresy'.[158] But the situation was even more ambiguous than this, because Lollard heterodoxy was not at all easily distinguishable from orthodox texts, which offered traditional, and at the same time increasingly realistic, complaints about current social practices and institutions. The literature of satire and complaint, discussed in Chapter 3, was in so many ways merely reiterated, possibly with greater vehemence and perhaps with greater eloquence and ease, by Lollards who substituted and developed English prose for their purposes. Furthermore, the social upheaval caused by the war, rising taxation and repeated outbreaks of the plague, as well as the expansion of the kind of social mobility that was created by functional literacy, were experiences reflected in the vernacular literature *in general*. Lollard interpolations frequently extended what was already expressed in the literature written in and for orthodox circles. If we look at Lollard texts dating from *c.* 1384–1425,[159] it is evident that the wide spectrum of their interests, and the types of tract ranging from the sermon to the satire, from the political to the theological, can be taken as a literary microcosm of the wider literary trends of the period. But the production of the Lollard texts, unlike the individual productions of satirists and complainers who were not allied to the movement, give evidence of having been produced by a well-organized and prosperous centre for the dissemination of sermon cycles, Bible translations and political tracts. As with Middle English religious prose of the period, the didactic purpose of these texts was paramount, but what was taught concerned not only private salvation but public social abuses.

Despite early Lollardy having come from Oxford, the movement rapidly came to be decidedly anti-intellectual and anti-scholastic. This is reflected in the sermons, which follow an older type rather than the new university style of elaborate divisions recommended by Basevorn and fellow theorists. None the less, their use of the school *determinatio*, their recourse to grammatical analysis and their citation of authorities reveal that Lollardy originated in the university and that its first and most influential disseminators were college men. Lollard texts display a vigorous use of the vernacular for theological and political discussion, and it is their development of the vernacular for this purpose that underlines their literary achievement. But they were not the only writers to develop an English vocabulary to deal with current theological and political issues: Langland also tried, with considerable success, to develop in verse a language that would cope with current theological and pastoral problems that had entered the ambit of lay discussion and concern. What literary Lollardy did, then, was to focus the trends already immanent in fourteenth-century lay discussion, and we may see this more clearly by following Wyclif's own career and the development of his ideas.

In 1354 Wyclif came to Oxford. He seems to have successfully completed the standard course of instruction which, particularly in theology, was influenced by theologians of the earlier generation of Bradwardine and Ockham, known to contemporaries as the *moderni*. Wyclif distinguished himself in logic and in theological dispute, stayed on in Oxford to become master of Bailliol and was in residence at Merton and Queen's. Quite early on he became involved in the political issues that were to cause him to formulate his own position regarding the unjustified possession of temporal estates by ecclesiastical authorities. As early as 1371 the Lords and Commons in Parliament joined for the removal of clerical administration and its replacement by laymen more in touch with the country's needs in time of war. Speeches in Parliament were made against the wealthy possessioners in the Church, and demands were made for the wealth of the Church to contribute to a larger extent to the war effort. Wyclif was present, and heard two Austin friars argue that it was justifiable to seize ecclesiastical property for the common good.[160] Furthermore, what pious laymen had given the Church could, *in extremis*, be lawfully taken back by their heirs in the interests of self-preservation, and churchmen were rebuked as being unpatriotic possessioners in times of national emergency when England was doing poorly in the war with France. The king's privileges were reinforced in patronage cases and the clergy was, as in the earlier *Statutes of Provisors* and *Praemunire* (1351–3),[161] reminded of its obedience to the State, to national taxation, and to the right of the king to appoint to vacant benefices.[162]

Now Wyclif had been called on to represent the crown in negotiations with the papacy in the 1370s, and to argue for the restoration of royal freedom of patronage and election to ecclesiastical posts, to prevent appeals going to the papacy that interfered with royal prerogatives and, particularly in time of war, to prevent citations of Englishmen to Avignon. Perhaps most important, he was to make clear that, in time of war, the English clergy could not afford papal taxes and the pope should relax taxation until peace was secured (1373). Wyclif seems to have been employed in this capacity by John of Gaunt and the widow of the Black Prince, and during this period he composed tracts of a highly political if theoretical nature, making the case for the government's rights to despoil the wealthy clergy. In the 1370s he composed arguments to refute the clerical argument of long-standing that the Church's spiritual authority, being higher than the authority of the State, granted her immunity from any secular interference in her property.

Wyclif was not alone in rejecting such traditional views. The influential Archbishop of Armagh, Richard FitzRalph, had already composed a tract against the mendicants in which he argued that *dominium*, particularly in secular but also in spiritual matters, depended on grace, and that mendicant abuses of their privileges caused them to forfeit their privileges. For FitzRalph, God himself was the chief lord of all possessions; from him every man held so far as any true property rights were concerned, and it was to him that service was due. The man who failed in his service by falling into mortal sin, forfeited his rights. Wyclif admired FitzRalph and, as McFarlane pointed out, took a similar line, but saw the government and laity as the instruments of reform, depriving undeserving possessioners of their secular power and wealth.[163] Neither pope nor emperor was the fount of secular authority; God is the *dominus capitalis* who had delegated his powers to the king or prince. In so far as the prince is above human laws and derives his just power from the grace of God, it is secular lordship that alone is justified in the world.

Wyclif developed his ideas on *dominium* in instalments, and his full thesis appeared in 1378. The papacy lost little time in condemning his political views. In 1377 Gregory XI sent Bulls to London, listing nineteen of Wyclif's errors. Attempts in 1378 to condemn him in England were unsuccessful, probably because the patronage of John of Gaunt was too strong, and proceedings ground to a halt when the papal schism broke. In a flurry of literary production, Wyclif produced his full-blown theories during 1378–9: *De Veritate Sacre Scripture, De Ecclesia, De Officio Regis, De Potestate Papae* and finally the *De Eucharistia*. It was the last work, and its theological unorthodoxy, rather than his earlier political stance, that would constitute his downfall. In 1380 an Oxford commission was called to consider his eucharistic views. He defended his condemned opinions and, despite Gaunt's journey to Oxford to convince him of the wisdom of recanting, he refused to do so and, it is thought, lost Gaunt's support.[164] In 1381 the 'peasants' revolted and Wyclif retired to Lutterworth, his name linked with the rebellion, although without real justification.

There is little doubt that Wyclif's importance lies in his university career from 1356 to 1381 and his subsequent influence on Oxford clerks, who would then disseminate in popularized versions, some of his views on Church and State, theology and politics. His first followers flourished for some time in the hinterland. Nicholas Hereford, John Aston, Laurence Steven, Robert Alington, John Ashwardby, Philip Repyngdon and John

Purvey moved out from Oxford to preach Wyclif's doctrines, particularly in the region around Leicester and in the West Country. But with Courtenay elevated to the archbishopric of Canterbury, these itinerant preachers were no longer immune. At the Blackfriars' council in 1382 Courtenay was able to get Oxford opponents to attempt to try Wyclif and his followers: nine bishops along with Courtenay, thirty-six theologians and canon and civil lawyers were present, a vast preponderance of whom were also friars whom Wyclif had denounced as unlawful beggars, and whom the Oxford Lollards wanted to prevent from taking university degrees. This council, known as the Earthquake Council because something akin to an earthquake broke up the proceedings, concluded that ten Wyclifite propositions were heretical and fourteen, erroneous. Fearing the response of Wyclif's university supporters, the council had been held in London, but the university prepared its defence and the chancellor chose Hereford to preach in English and incite the people to come to Wyclif's defence. This was to little avail, and it is interesting to see how Courtenay's perseverance succeeded in making Lollardy a movement that centred on the laity outside the university, sometimes led on by his university followers but more often by a second string of lesser clergy and pious laity.

After 1382 the remnants of his followers were able to set themselves up in cloth-weaving towns and prosperous villages in the Bristol area. Nicholas Hereford, after returning from Rome, where he made an unsuccessful appeal which sought the reversal of Courtenay's decree of heresy, also settled in the West Country. Such men seemed to have powerful local support and they survived and preached; but they were pursued by various West Country bishops, and decrees went out to prevent them from disseminating Wyclifite doctrine in these dioceses. Hereford himself recanted eventually, and ended his career in the sanctity of orthodoxy as the chancellor of Hereford Cathedral (1394)! Others recanted and pursued heretics as vehemently as they had formerly denounced the mendicants and the ecclesiastical hierarchy.

After Courtenay's triumph in 1382 Wyclif wrote his *Trialogus*, a summary of his views, and further edicts were passed against his writings and followers. There appears to have been a rapid switch from viewing his ideas as attractively radical to regarding them as dangerously unorthodox, and as a result of the efficient attempts to eradicate his writings by the authorities, beginning in 1382, we are forced to confront later Lollard texts instead of Wyclif's own, and thus some of his career remains obscure to us. The order and dates of his writings cannot be fully determined, and most if not all of the English works, although based on Wyclif's Latin tracts, are thought to be compositions of followers.

Quite early in his Oxford career, Wyclif composed twelve works on theology and ecclesiastical polity which dealt with law, divine and civil, scrutinizing the structure of Christian society as an ideal and in practice. He, like numerous contemporaries, was concerned with Church abuses. The largely political character of his expositions was recognized by Gregory XI, whose Bulls of 1377 attacked Wyclif's teaching on lordship, dominion and grace, and rejected his views on the validity of papal and episcopal jurisdiction. Archbishop Sudbury and Bishop Courtenay were to examine Wyclif's writings and try to convince Prince Richard and the nobility that this doctrine was detrimental to *all* government. Papal policy was anxious to stamp out Wyclif's theories, and he was ordered to be put in prison in chains or cited to the papal court itself.

But Wilks has argued convincingly that Wyclif's was, above all, a political movement, the significance of which would not be determined by the Church but by the political policies pursued by English political leaders and by the interaction of political circumstances.[165] Thus, despite papal decrees, Wyclif was never dealt with in the manner suggested. In effect, the English ecclesiastical hierarchy waited for Wyclif to hang himself by his own theological views, particularly on the Eucharist. But what was really obnoxious to the English Church was the political character of his theology, his notion of ecclesiastical reform by the laity, and his policy of church disendowment. As Wyclif moved from political to theological matters in his writings, he merely altered the balance but not the content of his early arguments. He first wrote the political works, *De Officio Regis* and the *De Potestate Papae*, and this order of composition meant that he was primarily concerned with the need for a great renewal and reform of Christian life which would only come about through a restructuring of Christian society. Doctrinal reform would come second and only after the political reformation.[166] He conceived of a new age in which tyrant priests would be dispossessed and forcibly returned to a recreated apostolic church, a vision that informed the apocalyptic writings of the radical Franciscans from the later thirteenth century and throughout the fourteenth as well. It is clear that Wyclif was not against property ownership as such, but that a possessionate clergy was a misinterpretation of its spiritual function; theirs was a perversion of the very nature of dominion. True dominion in temporal matters belonged to the king and through him to his knights. In one sense, Archbishop Courtenay himself recognized the overriding royal power in matters of heresy, for after the condemnation of Wyclif's doctrines in 1382, Courtenay petitioned the King in Parliament for additional powers to deal with heretics, and, as Richardson pointed out, the price the Church paid for the lay power granting speedy process was that the king and council had the deciding voice in such matters.[167] Likewise, in Wyclif's terms, the king was to head the commonwealth of the righteous, the *communitas iustorum*, the true state:

In order to achieve his true self, his public identity – in order to identify himself with the respublica of the just – every individual had to become a king's man, owing allegiance to the king, in the first instance Christ, the heavenly king, and in practice his vicar, the lay ruler.[168]

Wyclif, therefore, saw an end to the separation of Church and State, and the Church was no longer to be taken as a separate, possessionate corporation.

In 1388 the role of lay government was expanded further in matters of heresy, for after the Merciless Parliament,[169] the Lords and Commons petitioned the king to provide further remedies against the spread of heretical opinions. English books were to be examined and inquisitions were appointed in every county to search for heretical tracts, for the possessors and supporters. On the other hand, early Lollards themselves looked to Parliament and the king to hear their cases. William Swinderby appealed to Parliament, suggesting that his case be heard by Gaunt.[170] The 1388 commission to ensure the seizure of heretical writings was established under the *king's council* rather than under the clergy.

Thus Wyclif and his followers, as well as their enemies, recognized the overriding role of royal government, and had the secular arm been interested in adopting Wyclf's theory in practice, what happened with success in Bohemia would have occurred in England. But the lay lords who were the key to Wyclif's theory of reform were immersed in bureaucratic factions, and were more interested in which faction controlled the machinery of government than in asking what government was supposed to be doing.[171] Thus from the standpoint of both the Lollards and their opponents, it was clear that in England the assent of the king and council, i.e. *political* assent, was necessary before a decision could be made about the success or failure of Lollardy. The Church was powerless to enforce the death penalty and, therefore, bring England in line with continental practices regarding heretics, and the Church required the co-operation of the king to repress heterodoxy effectively if at all. The supremacy of king in Parliament was thereby recognized by ecclesiastical authorities as well as by Lollard teaching.[172] In 1389 Lollards themselves produced a manifesto that said that they would submit to the law of the king and his chivalry, clergy and commons. The king's law was the final arbiter, and Wyclif fitted this into his theory of dominion early on.

A corollary of his notions of civil dominion was Wyclif's preference for scriptural authority over the collected wisdom of the Church. In his *De Veritate*, c. 11 (1378) he argued for the defence of a literal interpretation of Scripture against those who argued, as we saw in the *Merita Missae* and vernacular sermons printed by Ross, that scriptural mysteries were in need of official interpretations. The real heretics, according to Wyclif, were those who found inconsistencies and obscurities in the Word of God. McFarlane noted that Wyclif did not seem to think that any form of scriptural exegesis was necessary and, thus, Scripture could be safely placed in the hands of the laity.[173] Wyclif argued that all Christians, and especially lay lords, ought to know holy writ and defend it, for the Church was not only the prelates and priests, but members of the whole congregation of the faithful who were imbued with grace and, therefore, predestined. The king as vicar of God, however unjust, was above all human laws, and if necessary had to act on his duty to reform the Church. Consequently he was to correct the worldly pursuit of ecclesiastics for honours and offices, punish simony and remove ecclesiastics from positions of temporal lordship. Instead, the clergy would live, in an apostolic manner, surviving on tithes and the alms offerings of the faithful,[174] and tithes could be withheld from non-residents. This kind of writing was aimed at a powerful lay audience capable of reading his arguments in Latin. He argued much the same in his Latin sermons.

Of the sermons Wyclif actually preached, only a few survive, although it appears that he also wrote a sermon anthology which Anne Hudson calls 'a literary production' for the use of other preachers. His early interest in the Bible, shown by his early commentary (1371), which is the only complete biblical commentary to survive from the second half of the fourteenth century, and by his last work, the *Opus Evangelicum* – another biblical commentary which is highly controversial – helped to set the tone of his followers' attempts to translate the Scriptures for the laity.

Wyclif was not a scholar with many original ideas; Gregory XI saw him as an heir of the political theorists Marsilius of Padua and Jean of Jandun. But what is of crucial importance is the unity of his thinking. He combined theological, political and popular radicalism in a single programme of reform that was not only intellectually unified, but also appealed beyond university circles. The unity of his theological and political stance is indicative of a more general trend in fourteenth-century thought, when orthodox poetry and prose was also expressing religious, social and literary complaints simultaneously. Langland and Gower uttered very similar complaints against the contemporary *ordo* of Church and State, and Lollards merely expanded on the more scholarly presentation of complaint found in Wyclif's works to publicize them in a more manageable form to a literate laity.

What emerges from a reading of Lollard writings is a definite continuity with Wyclif's thought, but one also sees that an alteration takes place in their analysis of contemporary ills which goes far beyond Wyclif's own programme. Among their more radical beliefs, they argued that the ministers of the Church are only intermediaries, and when they err or go against God's judgement their acts are invalid and blasphemous. Furthermore, excommunication by pope or bishop is valid only if they themselves are in a state of righteousness, and God alone has absolute knowledge of man's mind and intentions. The Church is itself made up of the congregation of the faithful on the one hand, and in a wider sense is composed of the predestined to salvation and the foreknown to damnation. There is a strict separation of the Church as the spiritual power from the State with its wholly temporal jurisdiction, and it follows that there can be no just temporal power or possession for the Church. Because the Bible alone is the true source of authority in the Church, it should be better known among the laity, and thus translated into their language.

Lollards also took a radical stance against all killing: 'it is not lawful to slay any man neither in judgement nor out of judgement, neither Saracens nor pagans by battle as knights do when they assail the Holy Land, for it is said in the gospel that thou shalt not slay'. This last point is of considerable interest, stated as it was during a period in which knightly feats were lauded by those of Richard's courtiers who were convinced by Philippe de Mézières's proposals for a new Order of the Passion to win back the Holy Land. Lollards went further, and rejected not only crusades and crusading orders, but also orders of celibates; they advocated instead marriage for widows and nuns, to prevent women from getting into trouble and taking drugs to induce abortions! They went considerably beyond Wyclif's teaching when they argued against paying for the services of chantry priests to sing masses for the departed, and more generally, they were against the payment for the priestly administration of the sacraments. They rejected fasting on holy days, taking oaths, and abjured the execution of criminals. But where they go beyond Wyclif they none the less owe him the greatest debt – both in thought and phraseology. And Wyclif himself helped to inspire such offshoots from his own theories by supporting if not initiating wandering 'poor priests' to educate the laity in the nature of the proposed new reform of society. It is not altogether clear if he had a hand in popularizing his own Latin works, but Wyclif's ideas were not bounded by the schoolroom, and his early university-educated followers soon gave rise to those who had never been beyond the local grammar school.

That his followers were numerous for more than a thirty-year period, and that his or similar ideas were preached abroad or written and disseminated, raises a question that has troubled many who have studied the rise and dissemination of heresy on the Continent and its comparative non-existence, particularly before Wyclif, in England. Lollard texts disclose the widespread nature and support of heresy in late fourteenth- and early fifteenth-century England, but all but a few of the episcopal registers are largely silent on the trials of heretics. It seems likely, as is demonstrated by a series of investigations into Lollards in Norwich, that records of such proceedings were kept elsewhere, in separate, private and perishable books. The reason for this is not clear. But the evidence exists. Take, for example, the memorandum book of John Lydford, which has a section that appears to be nothing other than a private file kept by a clerk attached to Bishop William Wykeham's court.[175] Lydford was a successful member of the ecclesiastical establishment, a canon lawyer and an advocate of the court of Canterbury. He had acted as assessor in the 1382 Blackfriars' council when Wyclif was condemned, and maintained connections with Exeter, his native diocese, where he was a residentiary late in life, in 1393. He was a contemporary of Courtenay, another Devon man, and was part of his Oxford circle; he also spent time in Avignon, probably as Courtenay's proctor when Courtenay was at Hereford. Lydford seems to have been consulted about the affair at Queen's College, Oxford (1376) when the appointment of a new provost caused an uproar and men like Trevisa and others left the college taking with them manuscripts that would have been useful in the eventual production of a vernacular Bible. He was, therefore, well placed to know of the series of condemnations of Wyclif and his followers; and, after being an assessor at Blackfriars, he kept up with events at Oxford when the chancellor refused to silence Wyclif, Hereford and Repyngdon's preaching and instead attended their sermons. Appeals to Rome were made and Lydford included in his book Hereford's appeal and the refutation found in a slightly different form in the *Fasciculi Zizaniorum*.

Did Lydford have some expertise in heresy cases?[176] At least he retained enough interest in the various trials to insert records of their proceedings, including the articles prepared against William Thorp the heretical preacher (1395) and Thorp's reply. Owen notes that his preoccupation with heresy was entirely a legal one; he was a lawyer before he became an administrator;[177] but it is still puzzling that such private records were maintained when we cannot find much similar material in public accounts. Lydford's memorandum contains the following:

No. 206   Articles drawn up by Baldwin Shillingford for Robert Braybrooke Bishop of London against William Thorp chaplain of York diocese, accusing him of heretical preaching at St Martin Orgar and elsewhere in London [1395].[178]

No. 209   Reply of William Thorp to Bishop Braybrooke's accusations. A note of his condemnation and mandate of excommunication.[179]

No. 210   Appeal to the Roman court by Nicholas Hereford and Philip Repingdon against proceedings taken against them for heresy by the Archbishop of Canterbury, Courtenay [1382].[180]

Whatever Lydford's reasons were for documenting the steps in the condemnation of Wyclif's followers, Courtenay's action in 1382 proved to be the beginning of the end of the Lollard movement for the next generation. With the loss of Gaunt's support, Wyclif's revolutionary scheme for a *reformatio* of English society was destroyed, for it was wholly dependent on the support and imposition of his theory from the top. Wyclif never assumed that the people would take the reform into their own hands. He spoke against the 'peasants' revolt', but in a way that also expressed sympathy for the abuses they suffered and which led to their rising. Heavy taxation was the fault of the clergy. But revolt was, according to Wyclif, the wrong method. It was better to preach than to get involved in bloodshed.[181] The people should not have moved against the clergy without parliamentary authority, that is, without the consent of the lay lords and the king who made up his *communitas regni*.[182]

Lollardy, like the 'peasants' revolt', had moved along the chief highways of England, spreading from one town to the next. Both were urban movements in the sense that villages along main routes were the centres of preaching for the poor preachers. Similarly, as Wilks has pointed out, because the revolt was an urban event, it was often ecclesiastical centres like St Albans and Bury St Edmunds that bore the brunt of the violence. It is also important to realize that the first targets of the rebellious populace had been the clergy, and Courtenay had recognized this. Their initial target was Canterbury and not London. The change in target that moved them towards London still led them in an amazingly co-ordinated way from London to Canterbury and back, and Wilks has described their long march as 'a sort of political Canterbury pilgrimage, a travelling classroom for the purpose of teaching the masses on the way the purpose, aims and methods of revolt'.[183]

Although the Lollards and Wyclif in particular were not, so far as we can tell, responsible for the revolt, it is understandable how their opponents were able to suggest their culpability.

Likewise, even after the revolt, Lollardy persisted among what McFarlane called 'the new industrial groups both in town and village . . . [it was] particularly noticeable in the number who were concerned with the processing of cloth, were fullers, dyers, weavers, tailors. . . . It is clear that in those crafts where literacy was usual or necessary the tendency towards heresy was strongest'.[184] To them, works like the *Complaint of the Ploughman*, *Jack Upland* and *Pierce the Ploughman's Crede* would express the moment. For the more learned followers in the 1380s, the Latin poem printed by Wright with the English 'O and I' refrain chronicled the events of the Earthquake Council of 1382.[185] The treatise *On the Seven Works of Mercy* (bodily and 'ghostly') dated *c*. 1382 also has, this time in English, fourteen pages referring to the Earthquake Council. Numerous anti-mendicant complaints produced by Lollard sympathizers circulated, and the controversial *De Blasphemia Contra Fratres* not only attacked the eucharist doctrine of the mendicants, their begging and their letters of fraternity, but referred incidentally to the right way to answer inquisitorial questions! During the 1390s political pamphlets like (Purvey's?) *Ecclesiae Regimen* continued to argue against the temporal possessions and power of the clergy, suggesting that these should be revoked by the government and the people, particularly when necessary for the survival of the commonwealth. And around 1395 a Latin and English version of *Twelve Conclusions of the Lollards* was nailed to the doors of Westminster Hall and St Paul's; whether they were ever presented to Parliament directly is questioned, but here we see the popularized principles of Lollardy expressed succinctly. All are written to chronicle events and more generally to propose ways 'for amending the realm'. An examination of E. W. Talbert and S. H. Thomson's chapter in the *Manual of the Writings in Middle English*,[186] and Anne Hudson's series of recent articles,[187] gives us a good picture of Lollard political, literary and theological interests. The list of such literature is long, and much of it is undistinguished as literature. But the prose text *Of Servants and Lords* (*c*. 1382) presents in a moving way important material reflecting Lollard attitudes to men's stations and duties in the modified feudalism of the later fourteenth century, where no feudal tie was more binding than that between lay lord and God. Indirectly, and by denying the pope's 'usurped' power, Wyclif and his followers were giving laymen a new freedom with increased individual responsibility. While Wyclif, in particular, wrote about his plans to establish and enforce voluntary poverty in the Church, his concern was with church disendowment and not with private property, and this is clarified in the Lollard text *Of Servants and Lords*; 'of servauntis and lordis hou eche schal kepe his degree'.[188]

Servants should truly and gladly serve worldly lords and masters in an uncomplaining and loyal manner, and 'holde hem paied of þe staat of servauntis, in which god haþ ordeyned hem for here beste to holde hem in mekeness aʒenst pride, and besi traveile aʒenst ydelnesse and slouþe'. Drawing on St Paul, the author emphasizes that such meek service is not meant primarily to please men but that servants are to consider themselves

servauntis of crist, doynge þe wille of god of herte, wiþ goode wille servynge as to þe lord of alle lordis and not to men, wittynge þat eche man what euere good þing he do schal resceyue þat of þe lord, be he servaunt or bonde or free man. ... What þing euere ʒe don <u>worche</u> ʒe of   perform
herte, þat is wisdom and wille, as to þe lord and not to men, witynge þat of þe lord ʒe schulle take retribucion, þat is mede or reward, of heritage in heuene ... þat is o man schal not be sparid in goddis dom for his richessis or lordschipis or heiʒ blood and a pore man be ponyschid for a litel trespas, as men don in þis wickid world, but eche man schal be ponyschid after his owene gilte and eche man rewardid after his owene goode lif. But here þe fend moveþ summe men to seie þat cristene men schullen not be servauntis or þralis to heþene lordis, <u>siþ</u> þei ben false to god and lasse worþy   since
þan cristene men; neiþer to cristene lordis, for þei ben breþeren in kynde, and ihu crist bouʒte cristene men on þe crois and made hem fre. ...[189]

But Paul preaches that we are to honour or worship all lordship, be it heathen or Christian. Furthermore, Peter teaches that Christians should have such a good conscience and a good life that all enemies of the faith who speak against Christianity shall be confounded.

and also þei þat falsly chalengen oure goode lif in crist be stoppid. and petir spekiþ more plenly of þis matir and comaundiþ cristene men to haue goode lyuynge amonge heþene men . . . þat þei beholden and see us of oure goode werkis and glorifie god in þe tyme of visitacion.[190]

The author then moves on to a defence of poor priests, denying that they incite servants and tenants to withhold rents and service from wicked lords:

and þei maken þis false lesyngis vpon pore prestis to make lordis to hate hem and not to meyntene treuþe of goddis lawe þat þei techen opynly for worschipe of god and profit of þe reume and stablynge of þe kyngis pouer and distroynge of synne.

The poor priests, on the contrary, charge servants to be subject to lords 'þouȝ lordis be tirauntis':

for as seynt poul seiþ, eche man owiþ to be suget to heiȝere potestatis, þat is to men of heiȝe power, for þer is no power but of god; and so he þat aȝenstondiþ power, stondiþ aȝenst þe ordynaunce of god . . . and þerfore poul biddiþ þat we be suget to princes bi nede, and not only for wraþþe but also for conscience, and þerfore we laien tributis to princis for þei ben mynystris of god.

Thus, servants should truly and wilfully serve lords and their masters, living in peace and charity, stirring lords, even though they be heathen, to follow the Christian faith and a holy life by their example of patience and open, true and meek life.

There is an interesting ambiguity here where the poor priests point out the evil of some lords' lives and yet advise obedience to them. The clerks of antichrist are those who say that it is just that servants and tenants withdraw their service and rents from their lords who live a 'cursed lif'. The preacher wants on the one hand to chastise evil-living lords but at the same time to appear to be maintaining the traditional social values, and thus inspire the majority of the knightly class to support the Lollard cause:

And þis is a feyned word of anticristis clerkis þat, ȝif sugetis may leffully wiþdrawe tiþes and offryngis fro curatis þat openly lyuen in lecheries or grete oþere synnes and don not here office, þan seruantis and tenauntis may wiþdrawe here seruyce and rentis from here lordis þat lyuen opynly a cursed lif. For to þe first sugetis had þe auctorite of godis lawe and mannus lawe also, but not to wiþdrawe seruyce and rentis fro wickid lordis; but ben chargid of god bi petir and poul to be þus suget to wickid lordis.

But we do not read, says the author, that any apostle paid tithes to wicked high priests, and thus he affirms that payment and service to ill-living clergy are not forthcoming. The Church, as an institution, ought to be disendowed.

Also lordis han power of mennus bodies and
catel in resonable maner and temperale swerd
and worldly power bi goddis lawe to compelle
men to do here seruyce and paie rentis, but bi
þe gospel and cristis lif and his apostlis, prestis
han not siche power to constreyne men to paie
hem dymes and principaly whanne þei don not   taxes, tithes
here gostly office, but harmes here sugestis in   spiritual
fals techynge and evyl ensaumple of lif.[191]

Even if the clergy lived well and performed their office appropriately, if men still refused to pay them, they should suffer this meekly as Christ did.

   The author goes on to discuss how lords should live and emphasizes that they should know God's law and study it. By knowing and studying it they should then practise it by destroying wrong and supporting the poor 'in here riȝt to lyue in reste, pees and charite', preventing their own men from extorting, beating and harming the poor. He instructs them in how the lords can help the poor, the ill, the widowed. Because the office of kingship and lordship is concerned with protecting and avenging the sins of men, and at the same time with rewarding those who do well, lords are warned that those who forget their duty and maintain sinful men, may rightly fear that their kingdom and lordship will be transferred to others, and he quotes Ecclesiasticus 10:8:

A kyngdom is translated from o peple into anoþer for vnriȝtwisnesse and iniuries and wrongis and contekis or debatis and for dyverse giles or disceitis.[192]

And from here he passes on to the traditional complaint that nowadays men are more concerned to lose worldly friendship and perform deeds in order to please earthly men rather than to obey God's law. They love worldly goods more than heavenly bliss. The poor are harmed in many ways, not least by prelates, who do not teach them God's law 'neiþer in word ne ensaumple of holy lif, and ȝit þei cursen faste for here dymes of offryngis of pore men whanne þei schulden raþere ȝeve hem worldly goodis þan take of hem'. The poor who are maintained in poverty and wretchedness see their treasure wasted by prelates who feast in pride and gluttony. Such men are unwilling to perform the sacraments, hallow churches, altars or churchyards unless they are paid for it. And the clergy are not alone in maltreating the poor: the author now attacks lords who act unjustly and lists specific and timely grievances against them:

Lordis many tymes don wronges to pore men bi	
extorcions and unresonable <u>mercymentis</u> and	payments
unresonable taxis and taken pore mennus	
goodis and paien not þerfore but white sticks	
and dispisen hem and <u>manassen</u> hem and sum-	menace
tyme beten hem whanne þei <u>axen</u> here peye.	ask for
And þus lordis devouren pore mennus goodis in	
glotonye and waste and pride and þei perischen	
for myschief and hunger and þrist and colde	
and þere children also. And ȝif here rente be	
not redily paied here bestis ben <u>stressid</u> and þei	taken in custody
pursued wiþouten mercy þouȝ þei be neuere so	
pore and nedi and overcharged wiþ many chil-	
dren. And ȝit lordis wolen not mekely here a	
pore mannus cause and helpe hym in his riȝte,	
but suffre <u>sisouris of contre</u> to distroie hem, but	jurymen of the
raþere <u>wyþholden</u> pore men here hire for	countryside
whiche þei han spendid here fleisch and here	
blood.[193]	

This is most powerful prose, and it demonstrates the Lollard development of English as a polemical and realistic language of complaint, analytical and moving. Even when the author denounces the specific evils visited on the poor by powerful men, and their alliance with lawyers, the description is a realistic chronicle of deeds, which has left behind the *topoi* of handbook complaints found in contemporary sermons and undistinguished complaint verse.

And ȝit men of lawe þat schulden distroie siche	
falsenesse bi here offices and don eche man riȝt	
and reson, meyntene wrong for money and fees	
and robis and forbaren pore men fro here riȝt	
þat it is betre to hem to pursue not for here riȝt	
be it neuere so opyn, þan to pursue and lese	
more catel for disceities of delaies and <u>cavella-</u>	
<u>cions</u> and evele wilis, þat þei usen. . . .	objections

Also stryues, contekis and debatis ben used
in oure lond for lordis stryuen wiþ here tenauntis
to brynge hem in þraldom, more þan þei schulden bi reson and charite. . . .[194]

From here, the author moves into the traditional complaints
of how lords are fooled by hypocritical clergy and false mendicants who unite to persecute the poor priests. The catalogue of
false confessors, lawyers, servants and merchants is brought out,
but even such standard complaint is punctuated with a realistic
understanding of the nature of contemporary worldly law and
custom:

And lordis schullen don non extorsions to here
pore servauntis bi ne worldly lawe ne customes,
for alle þes lawes and customes ben noþing worþ
but ȝif þei ben reutid bi charite and good conscience.

The lord who permits his officers to do wrong in his name,

forsakiþ þe riȝt feiþ and [he] is worse þan an
heþene man; for he doþ more harm to a cristene man and distroieþ more cristene religion
and makiþ hate and grucchynge and discension
bitwixt pore and riche and <u>anemtis god</u>. . . .[195]   alienates

Lords should warn their officers that if they badly treat tenants
they will be dismissed from office and lose the friendship and
lordship of the lord.[196] Thus the presence of the rightful lord
should be able to destroy such wrongs, far more effectively

þan many letteris sent to evyl officeris for þei
charge not to do riȝt after þe letteris for þer is
no more pursuet don after þe deed lettre.[197]

Lords should destroy the worldly and covetous life of the
clergy for it is the duty of secular lords to keep the Church in
order. Otherwise 'myȝtten Kyngdomes ben conquerid for necligence of coveitouse prelatis, as it was in þe lond of israel'. Nor
should the clergy be exempt from secular law and its punish-
ments because it is they who incite men 'to disturblynge of
rewmes'. The clergy have no place in secular offices, as auditors
of powerful men, as stewards of secular courts, as almoners,
counsellors and 'reuleris of here worldly pees, arraies and worldly

deeds *as þou3 no man coude worldly office but þei!'*

Thus the author affirms not only the abuses of the age but also the widespread literacy that would enable secular men to take up posts in the courts of the great, replacing a clergy that no longer possessed the skills of an elite. He closes with a phrase that warns us that we are dealing with a society where social mobility consequent on literacy, and moneyed as opposed to landed wealth, was not unique. He speaks with disdain of 'many ietteris of contre þat wolen make hem self gentell men and han litel or nou3t to lyue onne'. They are the ones who misuse the wealth of the kingdom, especially of the poor, because they flatter worldly prelates who invite them to great feasts paid for by the sweat and blood of the poor common people.

It is clear from this text that Wyclif's theology was of interest to the broader lay following that he amassed only when it was integrated into his social ethic; and, as was pointed out, his whole system was a work of unparalleled unity founded on a political theory that was perceived as strikingly relevant to the times. It is not often that we confront a political theory in the Middle Ages which so directly illustrates and provides a solution to the traditional and cliché abuses in the current society. It is this that brought Wyclif's doctrine out of the schools with such ease. He came to believe that human freedom of action had to go hand in hand with divine necessity,[198] rejecting his earlier position, argued hotly in the schools, that things were necessary because and only if God had so willed them.

One of the topics which many study from their boyhood is the subject of divine necessity. I used to hold the view that things were necessary only if God willed that they should be so and for no other reason.[199]

This we recognize, of course, as the same issue that is debated in Chaucer's Nun's Priest's Tale. If everything depended on God's absolute will, there would be no place left for rationality and free will. Wyclif, therefore, changed his mind. The trouble with the realists and nominalists in the schools who argued over the relation of man's deeds to God's will, he said, was that they insisted on dealing with divine things in isolation.[200] Wyclif wanted to integrate secular, rationally based political theory into 'things divine', and it is important that we take him at his word at the beginning of his *De Dominio Divino*, where he says that he began writing with the Bible open at one hand and Averroës's commentary on Aristotle at the other.[201]

That his ideas, not only concerning the solution to clerical abuses but also on the validity of placing Scripture in the hands of the laity, were taken seriously not only by lay preachers and their semi-literate followers in rural backwaters and villages but also by Oxford scholars of later fourteenth- and early fifteenth-century England, is shown by the continuing debate over the social issues that Wyclif and his followers had raised. In the early fifteenth-century debate in Oxford over Bible translation, Ann Hudson has suggested that Archbishop Arundel's fierceness may well have resulted from a realization that Wyclif's views were still not regarded with outright hostility and that university members, like many Lollards in rural areas, were still not unimpeachably orthodox.[202] And by employing a traditional method of argument with lists of authorities – biblical, patristic, canonistic and historical – the Lollard viewpoint was presented within a frame that had traditionally brought attacks on contemporary polemical targets to the notice of the literate. Theirs was no fly-by-night operation, for the publicity attained by Lollard writings was ensured, as with the Wyclifite Bible, by a considerable amount of money that was made available for the production of their tracts and sermons. Theirs was a strong organization, and the manuscripts were neither cheaply produced nor carelessly copied.[203] Most of these Lollard works, drawing on Wyclif's more formal Latin treatises, were concerned with the relation of pastoral theology, political theory and social criticism. And these issues came up on parliamentary agenda: in 1395–7 Parliament debated the legality of vernacular Bibles. The ability of laymen to read them was unquestioned, and this is corroborated by Wyclif's own statement in the *Expositio Matt.* XXIV, 8, that by 1383 lay lords could read the Bible for themselves. It was available and readily assimilated. Wyclif may not have desired more than that priests should read the biblical texts to the laity and gloss them accurately. Trevisa in his *Dialogue Between Clerk and Knight* may well have described the method of the poor priests when he equated preaching in English with 'translation', saying: 'such Englysshe prechyng is very translacon and such Englyssh prechyng is good and nedefull, thene Englyssh translacon is good and nedefull'.[204] But if even the poor priests were to summarize and translate for themselves and their parishioners relevant biblical passages, it seems appropriate to assume that even these lesser clergy were not as illiterate in Latin and English as hostile sources make out.

We can bring this long discussion of literacy and its consequences for memory and social mobility to a close by letting the reflections of a Wyclifite compiler of a New Testament concordance speak for us. This north-east Bedfordshire man, writing in the early fifteenth century, summarizes what happens when men lose their memories but retain their wisdom through their literacy. What he was doing, in providing an organized and easily consulted table of contents to substitute for memory, was what had been done across the board for those expanding numbers of the laity who had recently acquired the skill of confronting their traditions on the page.

Mannes mynde, þat is ofte robbid of þe tresour of kunnyng bi þe enemye of science, þat is forȝetyng, is greetly releeved bi tablis maad bi lettre aftir þe orde of þe ABC. Ensaumple, if a man haue mynde oonly of oo word or two or sum long text of the Newe Lawe and haþ forȝetyn al þe remenaunt, or ellis if he haþ forȝeten in what stede it is writen, þis concordaunce wole lede him bi þi fewe wordis þat be cofrid in his mynde unto þe ful text, and shew him in what book and in what chapitre he shal fynde þe textis whiche him list to have. . . .[205]

5 Theology, non-scholastic literature and poetry

The unity of Wyclif's political and theological *theory* was a particularly successful attempt at marrying politics and theology, two subjects that were, in any case, viewed as inseparable in the Middle Ages. It has been argued that his social and political ideas were more influential, however, than his theological conclusions. This was not because theology was only a specialist interest. There was also great interest in the topics of scholastic theological dispute outside university circles, and it is to poetry like *Piers Plowman* that one turns to see the specialized concerns of school debates rendered in the vernacular for a reading, non-clerical public. Such a public need not have been present in Oxford or Cambridge in order to become familiar with the topics of current debates, because theology in the fourteenth century was opened up by grammatical, logical and natural science studies. Much of what would have been expressed in the thirteenth century as straightforward issues of salvation and predestination, and thus reserved for professional debate in theological circles, got expressed in the language of logic, speculative grammar and Aristotelian physics. This language was learned, in the first instance, in the arts faculties of the universities and cathedral schools and in mendicant *studia*, but it passed thereafter into a literature that may be called non-scholastic. It filtered down further into vernacular texts, and *Piers Plowman* gives evidence of the opening up of theological issues to important men – who were not clerics, but who, none the less, discussed doctrinal matters at table. The following is an extract from the B text (X, ll. 104–33), dated *c.* 1377+:

Dame Study:

I haue yherd hei3e men etynge at þe table

Carpen as þei clerkes were of crist and of hise my3tes,   Dispute

And leyden fautes vpon þe fader þat formede vs alle,

And carpen ayein clergie crabbede wordes:

'Why wolde our Saueour suffre swich a worm in his blisse
That biwiled þe womman and þe wye after,
Thoruӡ which werk and wil þei wente to helle,
And al hir seed for hir synne þe same deeþ suffrede?
Here lyeþ youre lore' þise lordes <u>gynneþ</u> dispute,   begin
'Of þat ye clerkes vs kenneþ of crist by þe gospel:
Filius non portabit iniquitatem patris &c.'
Why shoulde we þat now ben for þe werkes of Adam
Roten and <u>torende</u>? Reson woulde it neuere!   be destroyed
Vnusquisque portabit onus suum &c.'
Swiche motyves þei <u>meue</u>, þis maistres in hir glorie,   argue
And maken men in mys bileue þat muse on hire wordes.
Ymaginatif herafterward shall answere to youre purpos.
<u>Austyn</u> to swiche argueres he telleþ þis teme: Augustine
Non plus sapere quam oportet.
<u>Wilneþ</u> neuere to wite why þat god wolde   Do not desire
Suffre Sathan his seed to bigile,
Ac bileueþ <u>lelly</u> in þe loore of holy chirche,   loyally
And preie <u>hym</u> of pardon and penaunce in þi lyue,
And for his muche mercy to amende vs here.
For all þat wilneþ to wite þe whyes of god almiyӡty,
I wolde his eiӡe were in his ers and his hele after,
That euere eft wilneþ to wite why þat god wolde
Suffre Sathan his seed to bigile,
Or Iudas þe Iew bitraye.
Al was as he wolde – lord, yworshiped be þow,
And al worþ as þow wolt whatso we dispute.

Compare the A text (XI, ll. 56–76), dated *c.* 1360:

Clerkis and <u>kete</u> men carpen of god faste,   keen-witted
And han hym muchel in here mouþ, ac mene men in herte.
Freris and faitours han founden vp suche questions
To pleise wiþ proude men, siþen þe pestilence tyme,
þat defouliþ oure feiþ at festis þer þei sitten.
For now is iche boy bold, and he be riche,
To tellen of þe trinite to be holden a sire,
And fyndiþ forþ fantasies oure feiþ to apeire,
And þe defame þe fadir þat vs alle made,
And carpen aӡens clergie crabbide wordis:
'Why wolde oure sauiour suffre such a worm in his blisse
þat he <u>gilide</u> þe womman and þe wy aftir,   beguiled
þoruӡ whiche a werk and wille þei wenten to helle,
And alle here seed for here synne þe same wo suffrid?'
Suche motifs þei meuen, þise maistris in here glorie,

And make men to mysbeleue þat musen on here wordis.
Ac austyn þe olde for alle such <u>prechide</u>,   preached
And for suche tale telleris suche a <u>teme</u> shewide:
Non plus sapere quam oportet.
Wilneþ neuere to wyte why that god wolde
Suffre sathan his sed to bigile, . . .

And compare further B X, ll. 52–8:

Ac if þei carpen of crist, þise clerkes and þise lewed,
At mete in hir murþe whan Mynstrals beþ stille,
Than telleþ þei of þe Trinite how two slowe þe þridde,
And bryngen forþ a balled reson, taken Bernard to witnesse,
And puten forþ presumpcion to preue þe <u>soþe</u>.   truth
Thus þei dryuele at hir deys þe deitee to <u>knowe</u>,
And gnawen god in þe gorge whanne hir guttes fullen.

The clergy and the 'lewed' evidently discussed the meaning of
original sin and its consequences, debating about the reasons
that God may have had to allow evil into the world and to cause
some men to reject their own salvation.

The question of predestination, which deals with God's foreknowledge of the saved and those who will be damned, and the
relation of man's deeds to God's foreknowledge of their actions
was current enough for Chaucer to speak of these issues as well.
From the Nun's Priest's Tale (ll. 3234–51):

But what that God <u>forwoot</u> <u>moot</u> nedes bee,   foreknows; must
After the opinioun <u>of</u> certein clerkes.
Witnesse on hym that any <u>parfit</u> clerk is,   perfect
That in scole is greet altercacioun
In this mateere, and greet disputasoun,
And hath been of an hundred thousande men.
But I ne kan nat <u>bulte</u> it to the <u>bren</u>   sift it to [collect] the bran
As kan the hooly doctour Augustyn,
Or Boece, or the Bisshop Bradwardyn,
Wheither that Goddes worthy forwityng
<u>Streuneth me nedely for to doon a thyng</u> –   Forces me necessarily
                                                                  to do a thing
'Nedely' <u>clepe</u> I symple necessitee;   call, refer to as
Or elles, <u>if</u> free choys be graunted me
To do that same thyng, or do it noght,
Though God forwoot it er that it was wroght;
Or if his wityng streyneth never a deel
But by necessitee condicioneel.
I wol nat han to do of swich mateere;

It may be true that a literate laity came to discuss pastoral theology more frequently because they were concerned with issues as central as those raised by the creed, the seven works of mercy, vernacular tracts on devotional piety and so forth. Thus pastoral theological issues as discussed by laymen may well have filtered *upwards* and influenced school theology, inspiring a re-evaluation of the ethics of Christian living at a sophisticated level. But what we know of the very particular issues that grew out of the specialized and difficult theology of Franciscans like William of Ockham and his followers also filtered downwards to a startling degree. It is to this issue, the nature of contemporary theological concerns, that we must now turn, and then to the non-scholastic literature that served as a halfway house for the eventual vernacularization of current theology, if we are to broaden our picture of the range of interest of English literature at the end of the fourteenth century, and our understanding of *Piers Plowman* in particular.

Contemporary theology

Fourteenth-century theology naturally grew out of the thirteenth-century scholastic synthesis provided by Thomas Aquinas, whose use of Aristotle and the Arabic commentaries on Aristotle's works altered the scope of what theology as a scientific study was seen as capable of achieving. Oxford in particular became the setting for a development of theology as a science, where the use of mathematics and geometry played a greater role than previously. Duns Scotus (*c*. 1265–1308), the Franciscan theologian who divided his time between Paris and Oxford, understood 'theology' as the science of God, and by science he meant that discipline which seeks to demonstrate the properties of a thing to be known, as a geometer would demonstrate the properties of a geometrical figure.[1] But in dealing with the subject of theological science – God – theologians came to feel their inadequacy as scientists when it came to knowing and demonstrating properties of the divine essence, for they knew this only as a general idea and not as a distinct object of knowledge. Their discomfort resulted from an extremely important event that occurred in Paris in 1277. Two hundred and nineteen propositions attributed to a group of Arts Faculty philosophers in Paris were condemned because they treated theological issues entirely from the standpoint of philosophy and rationalism.[2] Theologians who sought the cloak of orthodoxy, therefore, were forced into elaborating a science of theology that was not only rationalistic, but also took into consideration revelation. Theology as a science had to justify itself. Where philosophers had shown that everything that happens, happens necessarily, and thus implied that God was not free, theologians had to counter this by proving that God was free. Consequently, theologians came to rely on a distinction, already found in Aquinas, between two powers by which God could be said to act: the *potentia absoluta* and the *potentia ordinata*.[3] The difference between the absolute and the ordained power of God came to be one of the major distinguishing characteristics of the theology of the *moderni*, a group of contemporary fourteenth-century theologians.

The *potentia absoluta* ensured God's freedom in all things, no matter what He may have promised to man in the Old and New Testament covenants. The *potentia ordinata* was that relative power God had Himself limited by entering into a covenant with man whereby salvation was promised to those who fulfilled their part of the covenant. Furthermore, only *a priori* principles concerning God that could be shown to be logically or experientially demonstrable in the *ordinata* were taken to comprise the legitimate science of theology. Theologians like William of Ockham, the Franciscan who was in Oxford during the 1320s, was particularly concerned with the role that language played to demonstrate the truth or falseness of principles, and he developed the analysis of logical and physical demonstration in relation to his understanding of how the mind develops concepts and has contact with the extra-mental world. But his analysis of the relation of cause and effect in nature stopped short of God. For Ockham and his followers, the primacy and unity of God, like the Trinity, were indemonstrable; the realms of experience and faith were consequently divided as they had not been for thirteenth-century thinkers. Logical analysis was henceforth applied more to what was said to be the operation of God in the world, the *ordinata*, than to God's own nature. Predestination, foreknowledge, justification and salvation were to be analysed from our end of things, as it were; and a greater attempt was made to understand man's duties and role in the order that God had set up out of His own choice and liberality, this order being a contingent rather than a necessary one.[4] One of the more central issues with distinct pastoral applications came to be the relationship of man's obligation and God's reward. And the covenant theology of theologians like Ockham, who helped to establish what was called the *via moderna*, meant that man was no longer to be seen primarily as a second cause moved by God the prime mover and first cause. Instead, man was given personal responsibility as an appointed representative of God, responsible for his own life, society and world, within the limits of the *pactum* or covenant that was stipulated by God.[5] Man's partnership with God replaced the older notion of subordination with co-ordination.

Thus four general characteristics of fourteenth-century philosophy and theology can be outlined to indicate the new trends that were being set in school discussions. (1) There was, as a result of the 1277 condemnation, a more cautious and critical attitude towards the purely rationalistic and deterministic interpretation of Aristotle at Paris and Oxford. (2) There was an increasing interest in problems that concerned the contingent and the possible. (3) There was also a more rigorous establishment of the criteria for demonstration and a related concern for the degrees of probability. (4) And with a greater emphasis on formal logic and the logic of language, the individual – be it word, proposition or person – was a point of focus in all areas of thought. Ockham said in his early work, the *Summa Logiae*,[6] that he had written it to teach theologians the precision of logic because they were falling into error through their ignorance of strict modes of thinking. Basevorn, we recall, had also said that logic as a *forma* was the foundation of philosophy, just as the rules for preaching were the basis of the *ars praedicandi*. The issue at hand for theologians was how, in a contingent world, a world that was not eternal or necessary, logic could aid men to understand the order in which they lived. God alone was infinite, eternal and a necessary Being, but contingency rules the whole order of nature and even the order of grace.[7] If the world is so utterly contingent, how is it possible to teach necessary truths about it, and, more practically, how was it possible to establish a true and fixed ethical or moral order to guide men's lives? Are not all truths about what actually exists contingent, and therefore may they not be otherwise? Such questions led to the framing of assertions about the world in the language of possibility, stressing that what was possible was, therefore, not contradictory. Maurer has recently summarized the position by saying that the possible was seen as offering the mind a necessary object of contemplation, and necessary propositions could be formed about this object. Duns Scotus, for example, based his proof of God's existence on the *notion* of the *possibility* of an infinite being which contained no contradiction, and he then demonstrated that an infinite being actually exists as the only reason for its possibility.[8] In the schools, therefore, propositions were made in the hypothetical mode: 'If . . . then', and philosophy's concern was with essences as *possible* bearers of existence.[9] Logic was, therefore, fundamental to any philosophical inquiry. For William of Ockham, philosophy could not be the study of the actually existing world; it was the science of universal statements *about* the world expressed in hypothetical propositions so that philosophy itself concerned the verbal and mental language we construct to enable us to deal with the world that is made up of discrete individuals. If, as Ockham and his followers asserted, no one discrete individual thing can be known through another, then we are left with the process of analogy or allegory rather than with a doctrine of identity whenever we group things together. Because we can never strictly prove or demonstrate that one thing is the direct and efficient cause of another, we can be assured of the relations between discrete individuals only through our own capacity to experience the world by what Ockham called *evident intuition*.[10] This emphasis on the reality of the discrete individual can be seen to have had a direct influence on the later notion of responsibility in the social and literary realms. 'If nothing is real save the individual, there can be no social or communal reality; a society is nothing but the sum of individuals of which it is composed.'[11]

In a less abstract manner, the Franciscan John of Rodington asked whether we could ever have certain knowledge of *any* truth purely on the basis of natural principles and he answered 'no', if by knowledge we meant that any rational truth could be known so clearly as not to be doubted. 'The intellect cannot naturally know something without being able to doubt that it knows it.'[12] This natural scepticism can be taken to be reflected in the starting point for the discussion of the limits of 'kynde knowing' in *Piers Plowman*, where Will wants to know truth naturally and certainly, and asks Holy Church to help him in this quest.

Thanne I courbed on my knees . and cryed hir [Holy Church] of grace,
And preyed hir pitousely . prey for my synnes,
And also kenne me kyndeli . on criste to bileue,
That I miȝte worchen his wille. that wrouȝte me to man;
'Teche me to no tresore . but telle me this ilke,
How I may saue my soule . that seynt art yholden?'

Piers Plowman, B I, ll. 79–84

'ȝet haue I no <u>kynde knowing</u>,' quod I. 'ȝet mote ȝe kenne me better,
natural knowledge
By what craft in my corps . it comseth and where.'

B I, ll. 136–7

As in *Piers*, so too for Rodington and the other 'modern'
theologians: philosophizing without faith could not bring one to
the certainty of truth, for natural reason alone can yield only
probable truths. In *Piers Plowman*, the Pardon cannot be taken
to be a certain guarantee of salvation for Piers or anyone else; it
is only a probable truth, beyond which unaided reason cannot
go, and therefore Piers tears it out of frustration.

Treuthe herde telle her-of . and to Peres he sent,
To taken his teme . and tylyen the erthe,
And purchaced hym a pardoun . *a pena et a culpa*
For hym, and for his heires . for euermore after.
And bad hym holde hym at home . and <u>eryen his leyes</u>,   plough his
fields

And alle that halpe hym to erie . to sette or to sowe,
Or any other <u>myster</u> . that myȝte Pieres auaille,   craft
Pardoun with <u>Pieres</u> plowman . treuthe hath ygraunted.

B VIII, ll. 1–8

For wite ȝe neuere who is worthi . ac god wote who hath nede;

B VIII, l. 78

'Pieres,' quod a prest tho . 'thi pardoun most I rede,
For I wil construe eche clause . and kenne it the on Engliche.'
. . . *Et qui bona egerunt, ibunt in vitam eternam*;
   Qui vero mala, in ignem eternum.
'Peter!' quod the prest tho . 'I can no pardoun fynde,
But "Dowel, and haue wel . and god shal haue thi sowle. . . ." '
And Pieres for pure <u>tene</u> . pulled it atweyne,   anger
And seyde, *si ambulauero in medio umbre mortis, non timebo mala;*
   quoniam tu mecum es.

'I shal cessen of my sowyng,' quod Pieres . 'and <u>swynk</u> nouȝt so harde,
                                                                       work
Ne about my <u>bely-ioye</u> . so bisi be namore!   appetite
Of preyers and of penaunce . my plow shal ben herafter,
And wepen whan I shulde slepe . though whete-bred me faille.
. . . We shulde nouȝt be to bisy . aboute the worldes blisse;
[At the day of judgement] How thow laddest thi lyf here . and his
    lawes keptest. . . .
    . but if Dowel ȝow helpe,
I sette ȝowre patentes and ȝoure pardounz . at one <u>pies hele</u>!   pie-
                                                                      crust
For-thi I conseille alle Cristene . to crye god mercy . . .
That god gyue vs grace here . ar we gone hennes
Suche werkes to werche.

                                          B VIII, ll. 106–98

Development of logic

The development of logic in the university arts course owed much to those who brought the increasingly sophisticated thirteenth-century material in the grammatico-logical hand-books, like Peter of Spain's *Summulae Logicales*,[13] to bear on theological issues. Their detractors saw them as excessively concerned with the logic of language when they analysed Christian doctrine and Scripture, and they were denounced for pressing the methodology of speculative grammarians and logicians of the arts course on to issues of dogma. Instead of grammar, logic and theology remaining separate but interrelated disciplines in the university, antagonists of this new methodology saw everything being subsumed under the conceptual rubric of logic. Theology was being 'dragged down' by the logicians. All knowledge was being resolved into propositions, and rational dialectic as it was taught in the schools did nothing but emphasize dispute techniques on the basis of the soundly argued sophism, whose grammatical structure was analysed into the parts of speech. When applied to Scripture or doctrine this was taken to have disastrous consequences for faith. If it was true that all knowledge, thought, language could be broken down into the terms of propositions, then any mere grammarian could have free access to the Word of God!

But the new logical methodology of the schools was not the only threat to traditional orthodoxy. Many fourteenth-century

theologians were not only scientists of language but also propo-
nents of a moral theology that inspired the Mertonian and
future Archbishop of Canterbury Thomas Bradwardine to
equate them with the new Pelagians.[14] Because of their concept of
God's *potentia absoluta*, it was said that nothing was impossible
to God barring self-contradiction. According to Bradwardine,
these theologians had developed a doctrine of probability and
indeterminacy with regard to the certainty of things in this world
and this life, which meant that God could go back on anything
He had previously ordained or decreed or created. But while
God's *absolute* freedom was assured, theologians like Ockham
and the Dominican Robert Holcot also exalted man's private
and individual responsibility in the realm of nature, or the
ordinata. Such theologians could be interpreted as having taught
that the covenant assured man that he could work for and
achieve his own salvation purely through the exercise of his free
will. This doctrine, that man could effect his own salvation, was
what Pelagius had taught in the late fourth/ early fifth century
and against which Augustine had successfully argued. While
Bradwardine's characterization of the *moderni*, the contemporary theologians, was extreme, and largely overlooked the variations in their teaching, he was able to simplify the positions of
the two opposing camps: the necessitarian and determinist
Augustinians on the one hand (of which he was one), and on
the other, the contingent probabilists. His work, the *De Causa
Dei*, which he wrote for some of his colleagues at Merton College, was circulated and epitomized in learned extra-mural circles. It is to his views that Chaucer is referring in the quotation
above (page 234) from the Nun's Priest's Tale. And as we shall
see later, Bradwardine was able to put forward his side of the
debate in an English sermon delivered to King Edward III and
his men returning from victory at Crécy.

If we go beyond the methodology of many of the modern
fourteenth-century theologians, we find that one of the interesting characteristics of their theology in general was its tendency
to treat moral issues at the expense of dogmatic theology. This
tendency was peculiar to England.[15] The focus of their discussions was the active and passive role of the Christian pilgrim or
viator as he persevered through life as a member of civil society
and of God's Christian society, the Church. 'What', it was
asked, 'was required of man to conform to God's reward of jus-

tification and acceptance?' One of the most widely read
theologians and preachers, the Dominican Robert Holcot, concluded that 'to those who did their very best naturally, in this
life (*ex puris naturalibus*), God would not withhold grace.
Facientibus quod in se est Deus non denegat gratiam.'[16] As a
result of this statement, Holcot was classified by antagonistic
contemporaries as a semi-pelagian, because he appeared to
believe that an individual could earn salvation simply by doing
well naturally and without the help from the grace of God
added to his efforts. Holcot's intention, however, was to
emphasize the freedom of God's will, which could dispense with
the covenanted rules of conduct that obtained in the *ordinata*.
God could (note the possibility), accept, justify and therefore
save anyone under any circumstances, should He so will it.
Surely He could accept purely natural acts without making them
worthy of acceptance, that is, without informing these acts with
His supernatural grace. At the same time, God was not man's
debtor. According to His will He need not reward even the
worthy man. Although the righteous man, according to God's
potentia ordinata, could probably count on being saved, *de
potentia absoluta* God was not forced by necessity and covenan-
tal promises to save him. Clearly this raised a dilemma for pastoral theology, because the nature of the meaning of righteousness was at stake. Like Ockham, Holcot understood man to be
able to do something good naturally; doing well was in his
natural power, and this could be rewarded by eternal salvation
should God so will it. The relationship between doing well,
doing better and doing best in *Piers Plowman* can be seen as the
vernacular expression of a hierarchy of deeds beginning with the
purely natural ability to follow the teaching of the creed and the
works of mercy and thence proceeding to those acts gradually
informed with charity or divine grace, ending with the reception
and aid of the grace that saves. The emphasis on doing well
naturally, by 'kynde knowing', in the Visio and Dowel sections
of the first part of the Vita (*passus* I–VIII; IX–XIV) in *Piers
Plowman* parallels Holcot's emphasis on the good deed performed *ex puris naturalibus*. But unlike Ockham, who placed
great importance on the active exercise of man's free will in the
performance of a worthy act, Holcot defined the worthy act as
the one that simply conformed with God's will. This, of course,
could mean that a sinner or an unbeliever could attain salvation,

for Holcot recognized no power in man's freedom of will; man merits if God so judges.

The centrality of the concept of man's obligation, and the idea of merit and reward in theological discussions, focused school interest on what was in fact a practical pastoral issue – that of the act worthy of the reward of salvation. They asked, therefore, 'What must one do to be worthy of receiving the reward of eternal life?' Is it sufficient to labour 'as the world asks', or is there a more direct and certain road which can help the man who does his best naturally to persevere onwards towards being numbered among the elect? What precisely does each man owe, and how does he merit reward? What must he do *necessarily* to ensure salvation? Can we even speak of the *natural* act that is *necessary* to salvation apart from that act which is performed with the help of supernatural grace towards the same end?[17] Such issues quite easily found their way into non-scholarly discussions which concerned the appropriate *via salvationis* for the average layman. Not only is this subject matter easily opened to pastoral discussion, but it was frequently couched in a language that was not exclusively theological, but rather logical, and eventually was discussed in sermons and verse.

Despite the tradition of calling thirteenth-century theology 'synthetic', more than any preceding medieval century the fourteenth has a right to this designation in the special sense that academic practitioners of different and separate school disciplines used techniques and raised issues taken up by faculties other than their own. The fourteenth-century Merton College *Commentaries* on Aristotle's *Physics*, for instance, in which a geometrical means of describing and measuring velocities and accelerations of moving bodies was developed, served to show theologians how they too could 'measure' qualities like *caritas* or grace.[18] Because the medieval arts course consisted of a hierarchy of subjects, largely following the *Organon* of Aristotle and then branching out to include all aspects of the liberal arts, trivium and quadrivium, by the time a student reached the lofty pinnacle of theological studies, he was already a grammarian and a logician and something of a philosopher. Likewise, the thinker who engaged in political theorizing was often first a theologian or a canon and civil lawyer. From recent reconstructions of the Oxford arts course, a fourteenth-century university education appears to have been a formidable and expensive undertaking.[19] But it attracted increasing numbers of students, many of whom stayed only for the arts course or a part thereof. To some extent many of them would have become familiar with the most heatedly debated issues, and this is certainly true of the scandals surrounding Wyclif. The trends of school debates can be followed not only in Wyclifite circles outside Oxford, but also, and with regard to other current theological issues, in intellectual circles like episcopal households. Richard de Bury's circle in Durham was known for post-prandial debates on current theological topics. Cathedral chapters, such as Exeter under the patronage of Bishop Grandisson or his protégés, heard the *questiones in scolis* of Thomas Buckingham which dealt with a series of 'modern' theological subjects.[20] With a greater place given to the question of personal responsibility and morality in treatments of the issue of salvation, the theoretical material of the school debates, quite naturally, became the material for practical exposition in sermons to cathedral chapters; the more political and ecclesiastical ramifications of modern theology could be heard in sermons delivered at Paul's Cross.

Thus a very large proportion of fourteenth-century thinkers working at different levels of theological sophistication were busy with the issues of man's free will, meritorious works and the relationship of chance to fate and fate to providence. In considering the role of chance, fate and providence, there was a renewed interest in Boethius's *Consolation of Philosophy*, and Chaucer himself prepared a translation. Furthermore, with the distinction made between God's operation in the *ordinata* and his *potentia absoluta*, arose the problem concerning the nature of justice in each order. If an individual adhered to the precepts of the Bible and to the dictates of reason, could he be assured of receiving justice in the heavenly court in return, and thereby be saved, just as, if he obeyed customary and positive law of civil society, he could expect to receive just treatment in a civil court of law?

An understanding of law and justice in the *ordinata* was further complicated by a tension that existed between justice according to the Old Testament law and that of the New Testament: the strict and the merciful. Through faith, the Christian is taught to believe in God's promise to reward with mercy the man who does his best in following the precepts of 'the law'. He must believe that it is possible for God to give the reward of salvation freely and mercifully, as a gift that is in excess of what is earned by deeds done. The reward of salvation is not given out of strict justice, because enough could never be done by man as equivalent compensation. One can never be owed beatitude. This is the problem for the reluctant Dreamer in *Pearl*, who cannot understand the evident salvation of his child. One can only hope for salvation and persevere in adhering to the covenant through which God promised to reward the person who did his best. Adherence to the covenant meant that it was sufficient to use one's reason to guide one's will in taking steps towards salvation. According to Ockham this meant that one was preparing one's soul for the reception of grace as one prepares the soil, making it fertile for seeds to grow. But this situation was an ambiguous one, because even with this preparation the man who does his best may not receive the reward of glory. He may receive a helping grace but not necessarily salvation. This is because rationality may be the key to the *ordinata*, but beyond this contrived state God was not man's debtor.[21] *De potentia absoluta*, His freedom was not limited by covenants and contracts. The problem that wanted solution in theological discussions, therefore, centred on the need to reconcile man's idea of just reward, which is rational and proportional to deeds performed, with God's notion of just reward, which is suprarational, possibly merciful and possibly brutal, and neither just nor merciful as man understands these terms. A reconciliation of the two *iustitiae* would establish a comprehensible ethical system for a Christian society, and it is the central problem in the Visio and Dowel sections of *Piers Plowman*, particularly in the episodes with Lady Mede.

What must be answered is the question concerning man's obligation to work with his natural powers and merit one kind of reward, and then to work with the help of grace added to his natural capacity and so merit salvation. Ockham believed that man can receive God's aid only after he has acted on his free will naturally, *ex puris naturalibus*, and man can understand that initial obligation because the *ordinata* has been set up in accordance with a rational plan. Right reason is the infallible guide to the laws of the *ordinata*.

Right Reason plays an important part in Ockham's theology,[22] and it is also a primary character in *Piers Plowman*. The former can illuminate Langland's meaning. Ockham believed that both the dictates of natural law and the infallibility of reason, while manifestations of the *ordinata*, are nothing more than the inscrutable workings of the divine omnipotence. This is tantamount to saying that God's will, ultimately, is the rule of all justice, man's and God's. But this must not be construed to mean that to God is ascribed an arbitrary code of lawless behaviour. It merely indicates that in all God's actions *ad extra*, where He does not willingly limit Himself to the laws of the covenant, He does not necessarily act either in accord with our preconceived ideas of the nature of strict justice, or in accord with the ordained *lex christi* that operates in the world now, but with His own concept of justice. For man, however, the only link between the *ordinata* and the *absoluta* is made by natural law and his use of right reason.

Ockham explains this when he distinguishes three ways of speaking of natural law in his *Dialogus*.[23] The first kind of natural law conforms with unfailing natural reason. The second kind of natural law conforms with a natural equity that all men share but that has not yet been promulgated into positive law. The third conforms with common law or customs and is available to 'evident reason' or common sense. Unfailing natural reason he explains as a kind of prudence or practical knowledge that is obtained through experience, which enables human nature to behave in a morally correct way. Traditionally, the scholastic analysis of *recta ratio*, right reason, included more than prudence; it also included *conscientia*, which was a knowledge of personal duties and obligations. But Ockham separated the faculties of conscience and reason, and defined the latter, both as practical knowledge already acquired and preserved in the intellect *and* as an objective guiding principle to enable the will to make morally correct choices concerning its obligations. The reason is, therefore, the guiding principle of the will, and reason works in conjunction with conscience. Conscience is not an aspect of reason but a separate faculty which accepts guidance from *recta ratio*. This is like the situation in *Piers Plowman*, where Conscience and Reason are two distinct characters with separate functions, and Reason guides Conscience.

Likewise, Ockham's understanding of the function of the will was central to his ethics, and there is a parallel relationship with the role of the main character Will in *Piers Plowman*. Ockham and his followers are often characterized as voluntarists, and by this is meant that they took acts of the will to be the only acts that legitimately could be judged intrinsically virtuous or vicious.[24] A man's wilful intentions rather than his overt acts determine his ethical status. The exterior act serves only as a possibly truthful sign of one's internal disposition to do the good. It has been said that Ockham 'found it conceivable that God could have created a world in which acts of understanding were intrinsically virtuous or vicious rather than acts of the will, but he did not believe he had done so'.[25] Hence, according to Ockham, a man deserves reward or punishment for his acts of will rather than for his acts of reason. The latter were purely responses of the natural, rational capacities of the mind. They were not specifically chosen. Natural reason guides human nature towards the good, but the will takes the crucial step of choosing and accepting and intending, towards what it has been shown to be a rationally correct choice. So too Langland's Dreamer Will must be guided and educated. In the end it is Will who shall be judged as having chosen, accepted and intended. The proper education of the will, to enable it to engage in activities leading to salvation, is the propelling theme of *Piers Plowman*.

By emphasizing the importance of the will, Ockham and his followers developed a spiritual ethics above and beyond the political ethics of positive law in society. In this way they could show that perfection, and therefore salvation of the individual lay in the inclination of the individual's will rather than in legally enforced external behaviour.[26] Formal, structured government was seen as necessary, however, because of human nature's proclivity towards evil as a consequence of the Fall. Government and kings are set up according to the natural law, which is in agreement with right reason. Particular laws of the general common law are, in Ockham's theory, agreed on or rejected by those who are governed by these laws. But once a positive legal order is instituted with the consent of the governed, man's duty is to adhere to this common law for the common good. Not only does the survival of the ethical system of society depend on such obedience to the common law; man's duty to adhere to it, a duty that is dictated by his right reason, is an obligation of natural law. Similarly, Langland also includes the adherence to society's laws as part of Will's more general education concerning his obligations prior to salvation. Will, guided by Reason and Conscience, is the one whose intentions shall be judged worthy or not as he steps forward along the *passus* to salvation. At first he labours for reward on the basis of his natural knowledge, adhering to the precepts of the law. But he cannot be absolutely certain that this will be rewarded with life everlasting. Why some are saved and not others can be explained only in part through natural reason. The nature of justice and the difference between divine and human justice is essential to Will's understanding of worthiness, as is shown in the Mede episode where Theology tries to explain the difference between mede as bribery and mede as merciful divine reward.

Theology argues that Mede is good because she was engendered by Amends, her mother.

Thanne tened hym Theologye . whenne he thys tale herde,
And seyde to syre Symonye . [Cyvile, in B] 'now <u>sorwe</u> mote thow
    haue,   sorrow
Such a weddyng to worche . that wrathe myghte Treuthe.
And er this weddyng be wroughte . wo to al ȝoure consail!
For Mede is <u>moillere</u> . Amendes was here dame;   good woman,
                                              wife

Thouh Fals were hure fader . and Fykel-tonge hure syre,
Amendes was hure moder . by trewe mennes lokyng.
With-oute hure moder Amendes . Mede may noght be wedded,
For Truth plyghte hure treuthe . to wedde on of hure douhteres,
And god grauntede it were so . so that no gyle were,
And thow hast ygeue hure as Gyle taughte . god ȝyue the sorwe!'

                              C III, ll. 116f. [A II, ll. 79f; B II, ll. 115f.]

Reward is promised to post-lapsarian man when he labours to make amends for the original sin of Adam and Eve. In Christian society, after Christ's crucifixion made amends for mankind, and after baptism formally brought the individual under the *lex christi*, the *viator* could hope for the reward of eternal life if he did his best. Holy Church, on the other hand, had wished to understand Mede as excessive temporal reward alone, by which in reality the Church was plagued (B II, ll. 20–8, 40–3; and C III, ll. 19–24, 41–2). Consequently, Holy Church shows how Mede will be married only to False. Theology, however, insists that true Mede will be given only to those who are truthful; the truthful or godly receive the mede or reward of *caritas*. The labourer deserves his hire: *dignus est operarius* (B II, l. 123).

Whoever does what is truly in him deserves his reward. Theology believes that a perverse interpretation of Mede has come about only through a false understanding of justice. The corruptions of the law of the land have caused reward to be given to the deceitful and the avaricious. But Theology knows the scriptural texts. True justice means that only the truly deserving shall be rewarded, and he takes as an example Lawrence the Levite.[27] Lawrence asked God for grace and for entry into heaven because he 'deserved' this reward, having lived according to the Old Testament understanding of Truth. Having fulfilled his part of the covenant he asked for the recompense of salvation, but he lived only in the *hope* of reward rather than in the certainty of it.

Ich Theologie the tixt knowe . and trewe dome wytnesseth
That Laurens the Leuite . lyggynge on the gredire lying on the
                  gridiron
Loked vp to oure lorde . and a-loud seide,
'God, of thy grace . heucne gates opene,
For ich, man, of thy mercy . mede haue deserued!'
And syththe man may an hey . mede of God deserue, in heaven
Hit semeth ful sothly . ryght so on erthe,
That Mede may be wedded . to no man bote to Treuthe;

                 C III, ll. 129–36

This kind of merciful mede is what contemporary theologians meant when they spoke of being judged worthy of reward by God's merciful judgement.

The salvation of the righteous heathen

A particular instance of the difficulty in understanding the two orders of justice and reward was highlighted further both by Ockham and his followers and by Langland, and this is the problem of the salvation for the righteous but non-Christian man. If a man had not been taught the Christian faith but did his best according to his right reason, could he be saved? Was membership in the Church and a knowledge of Christ necessary to salvation? There were various opinions on this matter in the schools but, in general, those theologians who recognized the absolute power of God's free will said that he could save whomever he willed, and this might include not only the heathen who did his best but also the evil man like the thief on the cross crucified next to Christ. In FitzRalph's *Summa de Quaestionibus Armenorum* (1340–4), he treated this question in relation to Armenian Christians, whom he wished to convince of their errors and bring into the communion of European Christendom.[28] FitzRalph concluded that salvation, for Armenians and for Moslems, can be won only within the Church. The Benedictine Uthred of Boldon was directly opposed to such views, and although thirty of his articles were censured by a monastic committee in 1367–8, his opinions were well known and were later developed by Wyclif, who somewhat altered their meaning.[29] Uthred believed that all men could enjoy a clear vision of God at the moment immediately preceding death, at which point the soul chose or rejected God and by that choice determined its own fate in eternity. All human beings, whether Christians, Jews, Saracens, pagans, adults, children or still-born infants, were to have this ill-defined *clara visio* and the subsequent choice. This vision was not the beatific vision, so the infidel along with the Christian might yet exclude his own soul from salvation. But article three explicitly says that an infidel might pass through life without giving the assent of faith and still may choose God in the clear vision and be saved. Uthred seems to have neglected the importance of a moral life of doing one's best, and instead made salvation hinge on that single decision of the soul just prior to death.

For Wyclif, in the *De Fide Catholica*, Islam is considered a heresy, a 'sect' to be brought back to the fold of Christendom.[30] 'Man can be saved from any "sect" ', he says, 'even from among the Saracens if he places no obstacle in the way of salvation.' Taking Uthred's position further, he says that 'from Islam and from other sects those who at the moment of death believe in the Lord Jesus Christ will be judged to be faithful Christians'. For Wyclif, then, salvation is not for heathen who remain outside Christendom; but he is willing to recognize God's hidden workings when predestination is involved, and affirms that there are individual Christians outside Christendom who possess the grace of the predestined.[31]

A summary of scholastic attitudes to the question of the salvation of righteous heathen can be found in Thomas Buckingham's Exeter *Questiones*.[32] He alters the standard format somewhat by treating 'whether all adults and children who died before Christ in mortal sin and without the present justification, through Christ, and remission of sins and satisfaction of grace, were bound perpetually to do without the divine vision'. He answers with what he calls the 'common opinion'. The philosophers and poets of antiquity who had lived virtuously before Christ's coming could indeed be recipients of grace. Nor would they be denied the 'clear vision' of God. However, they are detained in Limbo, not because of sin, but because of insufficient worthiness which could be had only once Christ was sacrificed. They too, of course, with God's antecedent grace, could merit salvation, and now they await the second coming to dwell in paradise. In the thirteenth century Thomas Aquinas had denied adult heathens even this Limbo. But Dante placed the pagan emperor Trajan and Ripheus in Paradise, for he said they died 'pagans in body but Christian in faith'.[33]

Langland speculated on this issue and presented the range of differing views in the B and C versions of his poem.[34] He focused on the case of the emperor Trajan. In B X and XI he argues for the salvation of heathens through their conversion although he recognizes that baptism may not be an absolute surety for salvation. Langland then tells the story of Trajan, the 'true knight', who broke out of hell, was an unbaptized heathen and was none .the less awarded salvation. Trajan lived justly according to principles acknowledged by Christians and pagans alike, but was not, as Langland tells the story, converted, and his salvation implies that membership in the Church is not, after all, a necessity. He lived according to *caritas* and *leaute* and was saved. 'Love and my own deeds saved me, Sarrasyn, soul and body both' (B XI, ll. 140–59 and C XIII, ll. 86–7). The later C text is even more explicit in showing that adherence to the natural law saved Trajan. In both redactions the Trajan *exemplum* teaches that God can and does respond to him who does his best naturally and that he may reward such a man with salvation. Further resolution of the problem of salvation for the righteous heathen comes later in B XII (C XV)[35] and achieves a final solution in B XV (C XVIII)[36] by Free Will. In the end Langland came to believe, like Wyclif, that the heathen may be saved but only if he eventually believes in the Church. The C text places greater emphasis throughout on the role of divine mercy and the gratuity of reward. The *combination* of divine grace and natural merit enables man to live justly so that all that is good in his deeds comes from God. To receive the final reward for a just life ultimately depends on God's 'courtesy', that is, on gratuity rather than on the covenant. But in addition, C XVIII resolves the problem by preaching conversion of the misguided heathen for whom only the 'right' faith suffices for salvation.

In fact, what we see in the C version is a movement away from the more radical ethic of Ockham and Holcot, which emphasizes salvation through good works performed naturally, to an emphasis similar to Wyclif's, on the activity of God's will in granting the grace that saves. It is significant that in the earlier *passus* Langland had the more intellectual faculties propose the more radical 'modern' position: the salvation of the righteous heathen through works and adherence to natural law alone. But at last, Liberum Arbitrium, Free Will, indicates the necessity of deeds and divine grace working in concord, and this concord can be achieved only within the Christian faith. Langland's view in C complies with that of both FitzRalph and Wyclif. Langland has provided the vernacular equivalent of the scholastic presentation of the issue of the righteous heathen's salvation.

The idea of 'just reward'

The difficulty in understanding the meaning of 'just reward' is illustrated in yet another way by Langland which also demonstrates his intimate familiarity with the issue as it was discussed in theological circles and elsewhere. In the B text, *passus* II and III, it is made clear that the only kind of mede that ought to be desired is not of this world; the socially motivated desire for worldly reward is, according to Conscience, an evil. There are three kinds of mede, or reward, discussed in B: heavenly reward, measurable hire and illicit worldly mede or bribery. But the C text expands on this in an additional ninety-one lines by explaining the concept of reward in grammatical and logical terms, and this gives us some insight into what Langland's audience was expected to understand. To explain a theological subtlety by means of grammatical analogy indicates that his audience would have been prepared to use the language of the arts faculty or even of the grammar school to have explained to them a theological point that was of interest.

Conscience distinguishes between mede and mercede: both

are rewards offered on earth by men to men and are thought to be deserved payment for deeds performed. Here mede is explained not in terms of heavenly reward for good deeds performed, as it was in the B text; instead, mede is understood as bribery, where it is often given before any works are performed or before it is deserved, and this contradicts reason and natural law. He who is paid *pre manibus*, a term Wyclif also used to mean simoniacal payment,[37] before the deed is performed, is 'nouht trewe' and like 'harlotes and hores . . . their asken hure hyre er they hit haue deserued'. But he who receives payment for a task performed receives mercede, 'a manere dewe dette for the doynge' and 'both the lord and the laborer ben leeliche [loyally] yserued' (C IV, ll. 292–312). Like B, C says that payment in return for merchandise is not mede but 'a permutacioun a-pertelich [plainly] o pene-worth for another' (C IV, l. 316). When a king or a pope offers land or lordship to those who are loyal, they are giving gifts out of love, from generosity, to those who in turn have loved them and served them loyally. As soon as such men neglect their duties the king or pope can take back their gifts. A parallel is drawn with the Old Testament, where God gave Solomon the gift of grace on earth along with riches and the power to use his reason. But when Solomon did not follow the will of God, these gifts were withdrawn. Langland, therefore, presents a discernible parallel of the two kinds of justice that operate in the *ordinata*, God's and man's. In the civil order, if the king's men desert him and act treacherously, the king can disavow any oaths and any promise of patronage and choose others to receive of his bounty. Those who go against the established law, whether against the social contract or against the biblical covenant, may be disinherited and any claims to reward made null and void. An abrogation of the social contract or of the covenant with God results in disinheritance and reprobation. We are told that God never gives anything where sin will not cause the gift to be revoked. The withdrawal of patronage and social dignities are the civil corollaries of God's reprobation (C IV, ll. 317–34).

Thus mede and mercede are two kinds of relations. If we can understand how mercede is a direct relation with God as well as an equitable payment for deeds, then the following grammatical analogy will exemplify how man may best fulfil the laws of the covenant. Just as an adjective is directly related to the noun of a sentence in number, gender and case, and thereby appropriately follows the rules of grammar, so too man is in a direct relation with God when he receives mercede for deeds performed in accordance with the laws of the covenant.

Thus ys mede and mercede . as two manere relacions,
Rect and indyrect . rennynge bothe   running
On a sad and a syker . semblable to hym-selue –   sober; sure
                                                                                            (direction)
As adiectif and substantyf . vnite asken,
Accordaunce in kynde . in case and in numbre,
And ayther ys otheres help – . of hem cometh retribucion,
That ys the ʒifte that god ʒyueth . to alle leelle lyuynge,   loyal
Grace of good ende . and gret ioye after;
Retribuere dignare, domine deus, omnibus nobis, et cetera.

Piers Plowman, C IV, ll. 335–42

Conscience explains this further to the king who does not re-cognize these terms as English, 'for Englisch was it neuere'. Con-science begins by describing direct and indirect relation in ethi-cal terms. Direct relation is a record of truth, a truth that was recorded prior to the deed performed; in other words it was fore-ordained. Consequently, the man who is in a direct relation with God's antecedent fore-ordaining power is related to God's antecedent will the way an adjective is related to its antecedent noun in gender, number and case. Man acts according to God's law just as an adjective and noun follow grammatical laws. A man who is in direct relation with God performs deeds according to the law that was pre-established in eternity, and by this law his deeds are directly related to the reward they shall receive in heaven. God has anticipated these acts and recorded them; man's duty is to seek out what these pre-recorded obligations are and subsequently perform them, *quia antelate rei est recor-dativum.* Once the individual understands something about God's *potentia* (strength) and the fundamental laws of a Christian life, he then firmly holds to them in a way that is similar to the adherence of noun and adjective. The individual firmly follows the laws of the covenant – the *lex christi* – remaining one in nature, number and purpose with Christ. The rules of grammar are accepted on faith and are unquestioned; an adjective fulfils its function and agrees with the noun. Likewise, a labourer ful-fils his function by performing his task, believing in the rule of

Christ's justice that payment shall be forthcoming. Even if he fails in the performance of his duties, he has confidence in the hope that his master will reward him for his efforts.

Thus ys mede and mercede . as two manere relacions,
Rect and indyrect . rennynge bothe
On a sad and a syker . semblable to hym-selue –
As adiectif and substantyf . vnite asken,
Accordaunce in kynde . in case and in numbre,
And ayther ys otheres help – . of hem cometh retribucion,
That ys the ȝifte that god ȝyueth . to alle leelle lyuynge,
Grace of good ende . and gret ioye after;
Retribuere dignare, domine deus, omnibus nobis, et cetera.
Quath the kynge to Conscience . 'knowen ich wolde
What is relacion rect . and indyrect after,
And thanne adiectyf, and substantif . for Englisch was it neuere.'
'Relacion rect', quath Conscience . 'ys a record of treuthe,
Quia antelate rei est recordativum,
Folwyng and fyndyng out . the foundcment of strenthe,
And <u>styuelyche</u> stonde forth . to strengthe of the foundement,
                                                              strongly
In kynde and in case . and in cours of noumbre;
As a leel laborer . that by-leuyth with hus maistre
In hus paye and in hys <u>pyte</u> . and in hus pure treuthe,   pity (mercy)
To paye hym yf he performeth . and haue pyte yf he faylleth,
And take hym for hus trauaile . al that treuthe wolde.
So of hol herte cometh hope . and hardy relacion,
Seketh and <u>suweth</u> . hus substantif sauacion,   pursue
That ys god, the grounde of al . a graciouse antecedent,
And man ys relatif rect . yf he be ryht trewe;
He a-cordeth with Crist in kynde . *verbum caro factum est*;
In case, *credere in ecclesia* . in holy kirke to byleue;
In numbre, <u>rotie</u> and <u>aryse</u> . and remyssion to haue,   perish; arise
Of oure sory synnes . asoiled and clansed,
And lyue, as oure crede ous kenneth . with Crist withouten ende.
Thus in relacion rect . ryht as adiectif and substantif
A-cordeth in alle kyndes . with his antecedent.'

Piers Plowman, C IV, ll. 335–64

This difficult passage, thus far, has established that the substantive noun, the subject of the sentence and of the pilgrim's quest, is salvation. There is a kind of reward, salvation, that is set in direct relation with the deeds man performs. It is directly earned by doing well, but it can only be hoped for as recompense for the good deed. All good deeds that are judged worthy require God as the 'gracious antecedent'. Consequently, salvation requires God's antecedent decision in eternity, first to establish the covenant with man, then to accept Christ as justifying man, and lastly to accept man's intentions and deeds, all of which are foreknown, as adequate fulfilment of the contract that shall earn him salvation. This grammatical passage is, therefore, explaining the complex issue of predestination.

Just as the reward is set in direct relation with the deed, so too man can be in a direct relationship with the laws of the *ordinata* 'yf he be ryht trewe'. Langland presses the grammatical analogy still further. If man accords with Christ in the sense that Christ is recognized as an ideal and the pilgrim lives an *imitatio christi* so far as he is able, then his sins shall be absolved. Living according to Christ's rule, the *lex christi*, consists in being of one nature or gender (kynde) with Christ; having a unified purpose or goal (case), that is, salvation, while believing in the Church, and lastly, recognizing that man has his origins and his sustinence from a single source from which he shall receive remission of his sins: God.

The agreement of gender, case and number is also used in the reverse analogy: here Christ took on man's nature, died for the purpose of man's salvation, and became one with men. Grammatically speaking, then, 'man' and 'mankind' are the substantive nouns requiring the adjective 'trinitas unus deus' to modify the relation between man and God and thereby to make it a direct or just and right one. Thus the man who lives according to the law is in a direct or right relation with God and can hope for reward (mercede) in return for deeds he performs when conforming with the law. Ockham and Holcot's theology also stressed that man could only hope that God would not go back on His promise to adhere to the workings of the *ordinata* and thus reward the man who did his best naturally. Man hoped for the generous response of God offered to the labourer who did his best naturally to fulfil the law, even if he failed. It is clear that Langland is explaining elements in the process of salvation in the only language he was likely to know: that of his contemporaries who were familiar both with current theology and the grammar of the schools.

As adiectif and substantyf . ys as ich er tolde,
That ys, vnyte, acordaunce . in case, gendre and numbre;

And ys to mene in oure mouth . more ne <u>mynne</u>,   less
Bote that alle manere men . wommen and children,
Sholde conformye to on kynde . on holy kirke to by-leyue,
And coueite the case . when thci couthe vunderstonde,
To sike for hure synnes . and suffre harde penaunce,
For that ilke lordes loue . that for oure loue deyde,
And coueited oure kynde . and be cald in oure name, *Deus homo*,
And <u>nymen</u> hym into oure numbre . now and euere more;   receive
Qui in caritate manet in deo manet, et deus in eo.
Thus is man and mankynde . in manere of a substantif,
As *hic et hec homo* askyng an adiectif
Of thre trewe termysons . *trinitas unus deus*;
    Nominativo, pater et filius et spiritus sanctus.

                Piers Plowman, C IV, ll. 397–409

Langland has already explained mede as indirect relation.

Indirect thyng ys . as ho so coueited
All <u>kynne kynde</u> . to knowe and to folwe,   kinds of natures
With-oute case to <u>cacche</u> to . and come to bothe numbres;   seize
                                              upon
In which beth good and nat good . and graunte here nothers wil.
That is no3t reisonable ne rect . to refusy my syres sorname,
Sitth y, his sone and seruaunt . suwe for his ryghte.
For who so wol haue to wyue . my worldliche daughter,
Ich wol feffe hym with hure fayre . and with hure foule taylende.
    [I will endow him both with fare and foul tallying.]
So indirect thyng ys . inliche to coueyte
To a-corde in alle kyndes . and in alle kynne numbre,
With-oute cost and care . in all kynne trauaile,
With-oute resoun to rewarde . nau3t recching of the peple.

                Piers Plowman, C IV, ll. 365–76

An indirect relation with God consists in moral neutrality. Without the singular, unifying goal of salvation, 'with-oute case to cacche to' certain men wish to maintain their right to shift their loyalties and obligations as they see fit at the time. By over-emphasizing man's free will and his ability to choose both good and evil, such men are ready to accept whatever reward is available in this life. The uncertainty of most of mankind's final end leads some who are without hope and faith in the covenant to be morally indecisive. They consider themselves in no direct way morally bound to exercise their free will and choose only the good. Conscience argues that this position is neither reason-

able nor just. According to civil law, you cannot reject the sur-
name of your father if you thereafter expect to inherit his rights
and privileges. Similarly, if you reject the expectations of the
covenant and do not fulfil the contract of the *lex christi*, how
can you then expect eternal reward? Here we see the linking of
the two laws of the *ordinata*: the civil or common law with the
divine, as we saw it in Ockham's *Dialogus*. If a man desires
earthly reward alone, then not only shall he receive it, but he
shall also be held responsible for simony and accepting graft.
The indirect relation between man and God, between reward
and deed, therefore, consists at the very best in moral neutrality,
and at its worst, in man's choosing evil without caring about the
spiritual cost.

Conscience applies the analogy of direct relation to the common law, where customary law, 'rytful custome', is 'relacion
rect'. He says that an example of direct relation in customary
law is the king's claim that the Commons follow his will and
also provide him with counsel. The Commons in turn require
certain things of the king: law, love and loyalty. In fulfilment of
their part of the social contract, the Commons are to follow the
king's will and love him unconditionally, not as a consequence
of his patronage. The king is antecedently lord; he has the right
and power to rule before he proceeds actively to govern by
means of the law of the land.[38] As king, he is antecedent to all
contracts made between Crown and community, and 'haldyng
with no partie' he stands as does Christ – as a standard of justice, legislating strict justice and mercy. Theoretically, at least, it
is in this way that the king mediates between men and divinity
so that the two *iustitiae* of the *ordinata* are brought together in
his person.

Ac relacion rect . is a ryhtful custome,
As, a kyng to cleyme . the comune at his wille
To folwe hym, to fynde hym . and fecche at hem hus consail,
That here loue thus to him . thorw al the londe a-corde.
So comune cleymeth of a kyng . thre kynne thynges,
Lawe, loue and leaute . and hym lord antecedent,
Bothe here hefd and here kyng . haldyng with no partie,   head,
                                                             chief
Bote stande as a stake . that styketh in a muyre
By-twyne two londes . for a trewe marke.
Ac the moste partie of the puple . pure indirect semeth,

For thei wilnen and wolde . as best were for hem-selue,
Thauh the kyng and the comune . al the cost hadde.
Al reson reproueth . such imparfit puple,
And halt hem vnstedefast . for hem lacketh case.

Piers Plowman, C IV, ll. 377–90

Customary law, 'ryhtful custome', is a direct relation for Langland, and like Ockham, it is clear that Langland also believed Reason to be sufficient in guiding men away from an indirect relation with reward and with God.

Al reson reproueth . such imparfit puple,
And halt hem vnstedefast . for hem lacketh case.

C IV, ll. 389–90

Reason can indicate man's obligations in the *ordinata*. The will, guided by natural reason, is sufficient to bring the individual into a direct relation with God. With an affirmation that Reason shall rule in the perfect kingdom, Conscience concludes his discourse on the two manners of mede with an apocalyptic prophecy. In better times than the present, worldly reward shall be superseded and natural love shall join with conscience to make 'the law into a labourer' rather than as a source of personal gain. Every man shall labour honestly for the love of God and shall thereby be worthy of the reward of *caritas*. Men shall do their natural best and thereby be judged. Truth will judge either mercy or no mercy. Civil law and common law courts shall merge with the divine court and there shall be one justice. The *ordinata* shall be fulfilled and justice shall be rendered, so that the justice operative in this world shall no longer be distinguished from that of the *absoluta*.

It is beyond doubt that the *modern* theological understanding of worthiness, reward and justice in the *ordinata* underlies the entire scheme of worthiness, reward and justice in these *passus* on Mede.

All that has been said so far about the parallels in *Piers Plowman* with selected current theological subjects of dispute and the similar methodology of argument gives us only some vague idea of the overall pattern and structure of the poem. Indeed, it says little of the significance of what is evidently a mosaic of style, structure and message. In its three versions, *Piers Plowman* can be seen as a distinctive personal journey through the thicket of current theological disputes, the poet himself opting for different conclusions to current religious issues in the different versions of the poem. Furthermore, I think we must accept his amassing of examples and viewpoints on, for instance, the status of the righteous heathen, as an encyclopedic, vernacular verse attempt to explain contemporary positions and somewhat unsuccessfully to arrange these views as a progression to a conclusion. In his own day, orthodoxy had the same difficulty in presenting a single unifying conclusion to the same issues.

But can we go further, and see *Piers Plowman* in its successive versions as a verse treatment of current social and religious themes, having been composed with the aid of the preachers' and confessors' handbooks and having run wild? The compositional methods of *amplificatio* and ornamentation, real and verbal concordance, are used by Langland to such an extent as to obliterate any apparent form and structure of his poem. He alternates the didacticism of the sermon – extensively amplified by jumping from one concording biblical text to another – with dramatic allegory. Langland moves from the relatively simple situation of a wandering Dreamer seeking Truth in the world between a tower – Jerusalem – and a dungeon – Babylon – to a confrontation with the teachings of Holy Church, a discourse on the natures of heavenly and earthly just and illicit reward, a sermon followed by confessions of the seven deadly sins, to the momentary appearance of the simple ploughman Piers, who works his field and receives a pardon and a promise of life eternal. The pardon is explained as not necessarily being a guarantee of salvation, and Piers tears it in anger. In summarizing the Visio, or first part of the poem in this way, we lose the most characteristic feature of the work: its fantastic crowding of *exempla*, concording texts, allegory and personification of institutional and theological abstractions, which could only have been achieved by a poet trained in the alliterative tradition but who seems to have rejected the ordering principles of the art of memory in favour of the encyclopedic, concording handbook.

In the next section of the poem, named Dowel, the Dreamer debates with various abstract personifications: Wit, Thought, Dame Study, Ymaginatyf and Conscience – each in the temporary role of Will's instructor. None provides the solution to Will's quest after the proper means to salvation. If the quest ends as it begins, with Will seeking Conscience who has become a pilgrim in search of Piers, it may well be considered by us a most ambiguous quest with no satisfactory and certain ending. But it reflects in an astonishing manner the very lack of certainty concerning the proper *via salvationis* and the discomfort felt concerning only a *probable* salvation for the apparently just man who does well, better and best, that was consequent on the contemporary school discussions of such issues. If this is what we mean when we speak of this period as an age of both crisis and disintegration,[39] in style and message, then *Piers Plowman* is a record of some similar kind of breakdown.

My picture of the 'three Langlands', working on this mammoth poem throughout a lifetime spent otherwise by singing in chantries in memory of some benefactor's soul, is of a man familiar with the confusing varieties of theological interpretations and social and political critique, thumbing continuously through the handbooks on his desk to help him find an orderly, vernacular path through the thicket of theological and social opinion on the vexed question of Christian salvation and 'rendering what one owes' for it.

Non-scholastic literature

In the Register of Bishop Wakefield of Worcester (1375–95)[40] there is a reference to an exchange of a chantry outside London for one within the city – a not uncommon event: in 1374 the vicar of Ampney Crucis, Gloucestershire, exchanged his living with a cantarist in the church of St Michael, Cornhill, London.

In his analysis of the careers of fourteenth-century schoolmasters in the West Country, Orme discovered that such men were usually of local origin and sometimes were Oxford graduates. Many served as grammar school masters for only a few years and then moved on to more lucrative posts, several ending their lives as rectors or vicars.[41]

In the C text, *passus* VI, Langland speaks of living in London, in Cornhill, and how, when he was young, his father and friends supported his schooling where he learned what holy writ meant, and what is best for body and soul. Now he lives by saying the *pater noster*, teaching from a primer, and reciting the *placebo*, *dirige* and the psalms of the psalter, singing for other men's souls. It is only reasonable that a man thus trained, he says, should either sing masses or sit and read and write.[42] Dialect studies of the manuscripts and references in the text itself tell us that Langland originated from the Malvern Hills not far from Gloucester. His analysis of mede and mercede tells us that he knew his grammar as well as the topics of current disputes in Oxford and Cathedral schools concerning salvation, just reward and predestination. And he says himself that he earned his living in London chantries, while residing in Cornhill.

Now, what if Langland's career followed the above pattern but did not lead him to Oxford or Cambridge? Would he still have been able to write a vernacular exposition of current school theological themes, and where would he have learned the intricacies of the arguments he presents? Of course, he could have been educated at a Cathedral school and attended the theological lectures given by the chancellor. The work of Alford already showed how Langland composed using the kind of alphabetically arranged preachers' handbooks like Bromyard. To acquaint himself with current theology he would have need of a corpus of writings that made school issues more widely available to those not favoured with a long stay in Oxford. Just as the *summae confessorum* were meant for those with cures of souls, to enable them to keep up with the views of the ecclesiastical elite on current pastoral issues, but who did not have access to original tracts on the subjects, so too a body of non-scholastic writings disseminated the topics of debate in the university theology faculty.

But these works do not constitute a unified genre. Instead, they were written for those familiar with Latin and who read, as Chaucer did, for reasons other than that such men were connected with the schools. Tracts like Boethius's *Consolation of Philosophy* received numerous commentaries, and Chaucer did a translation into English; Holcot's *Commentaries* on the *Wisdom Books* of the Bible were exploited for, among other things, their lore on the significance of dreams, and Chaucer used them as the basis for his exposition in the Nun's Priest's Tale; Bradwardine's *De Causa Dei*, epitomized and circulated, informed Chaucer of the current controversy over free will and necessity; Bradwardine's *Sermo Epinicius* made available his ideas in English; Trevisa translated FitzRalph's argument with the friars on mendicancy, as well as standard tracts on political theory.

The non-scholastic literature available to the literate, in Latin and with increasing frequency in English, served to broadcast political and theological themes that one century before would have been the preserve of a university and clerical elite. And when, as we have seen, theology treats with greater frequency ethical issues instead of doctrinal issues, then the problem of the correct *ordo*, proper justice – in fact the problem of the social structure appropriate to the later fourteenth century – becomes a topic of concern for lay administrators. What was once the ideology of a literate, clerical elite gets analysed, discussed and re-evaluated by an expanded group of responsible governors whose expanding economic freedom and power marks them out as a new patron class, conscious of their social responsibilities and of their private responsibility regarding their own salvation. If, as we have seen, school theology became increasingly concerned with the active role of the individual in confronting his fate and creating his future, privately and publicly, then we ought not to be surprised when, even in the 1330s, Ockham could complain that laymen and old women bothered Oxford lecturers about the question of free will: if God's foreknowledge of the future necessitated their actions, how was the will free?[43] If an individual was to work towards his own salvation, how was it possible to consider him actively and responsibly choosing right from wrong if his salvation was pre-established in eternity? The threefold problem of a fixed future, contingency and necessity, all in relation to man's understanding of his free will, affected the individual Christian pilgrim, be he school-man, *literatus* or illiterate in Latin but a reader of English.

Holcot's Wisdom *commentary*

The Dominican Robert Holcot wrote a series of commentaries on the *Wisdom* books, the theological complexity of which does not seem to have hindered their popularity. It was a 'best seller', attested to by the number of surviving manuscripts and its numerous citations in contemporary literature. He probably read them as a series of lectures at the Dominican friary at Cambridge; he also taught at Northampton, an important education centre for Dominicans. There he would have been training specialists to be general educators who, as preachers, would be most effective if they could supplement their theological expositions by citing moral *exempla*. Beryl Smalley noted that Holcot's students 'might also teach in priory schools or in bishops' schools for clergy who did not get as far as the university'.[44] While Holcot speaks to current school issues he provides more practical examples by moralizing extensively and supplementing his *moralitates* by presenting questions on some point. A glance at the table of contents illustrates the kind of topics he discusses:[45]

Can man, assisted by grace, earn eternal life by his own merit?
Lectio 36

Can original justice be considered a supernatural gift?   Lectio 14

Is the gift of the Holy Spirit given necessarily to the man who prepares himself for the reception of this grace?   Lectio 46

Is everything subjected to divine ordination?   Lectio 105

Are we permitted to observe signs in order to know future events?
Lectio 160

Are mercy and justice both conjoined in every work of God?   Lectio 52B

Holcot's concern is primarily a moral one: to define man's state in the world, his realm of operation and the contingents that impinge on the freedom of his self-determining will. He deals with the question of how man is to conduct his life piously, given both his limitations and his natural capacities in conjunction with God's mercy. He concludes that 'nature does not lack what is necessary to salvation', and thus he relies on man's intellect as the guiding principle of wisdom, for to him, wisdom is knowing how to do all that is necessary to salvation.[46] The moral life cannot be had without the work of the intellect, which he equates with right reason.[47] Man's reason is finite, but according to Holcot so is the knowledge that is necessary for one's salvation when this knowledge is gratuitously bestowed. He sees the necessity for recognizing the workings of divine *prudentia* or providence in conjunction with the principle that 'to him who does his natural best God will not withhold the grace that saves'. Prudence or providence derives from God, but is achieved and realized by man through the application of right reason. Without right reason there is no moral virtue, and Holcot quotes Solomon who says 'lead me in my works to be sober and to measure all things by right reason'. Although the incalculable element in life may fill each pilgrim with uncertainty about whether or not he has chosen well, it is nevertheless certain that none may attain heaven without labour. Prudent labour, choosing well, is the *sine qua non* of salvation.

Sicut autem peregrinus veniens ad concursus viarum eligere potest pro quam velit ambulare, nullam tamen ivit sine labore. Ita homo positus in hac vita multas vias vivendi invenit in divitiis et paupertate, et honore et servitute, in delitiis et miseriis, sed nullam accipiet in qua magnum laborem non invenit [Ecclesiastes 31]. Generaliter et quasi naturaliter nascimur ad laborem dicit Job.

Lectio 120A

Holcot was not alone in drawing on the biblical *Wisdom* literature as a source for his analysis of moral action. The *Wisdom* literature had already come into vogue as the source for homilies and sermons in the later thirteenth century, and the fourteenth-century preacher Thomas Brinton, an Oxford Benedictine who became Bishop of Rochester, made extensive use of *exempla* from *Wisdom* in his sermons. Beryl Smalley justly called *Wisdom* the biblical counterpart of Giles of Rome's *Regimine Principum* for an age that was developing a concern for political theory, since *Wisdom* addresses rulers and kings on good government.[48] In addition, the *Wisdom* books comprised one of the main sources of the deepening of the doctrine of providence, pointing to God's perfect knowledge of each person and his present and future acts. *Wisdom* described each individual's necessary sense of moral responsibility as operating within the larger divine scheme of reward and retribution. Most of the modern theologians supported their arguments for a *ratio* of justice in this world with *Wisdom* texts, for although man could not understand the workings of God's justice and mercy, he was advised to trust in divine providence and in the covenant. That certain occurrences seemed irrational to man pointed to the limitations of reason in interpreting what could be described as God's works *ad extra*, that is, *de potentia absoluta*. But a faith in the workings of the *ordinata*, and in God's promise to adhere to the covenant, glorified the role of right reason as an accurate guide to understanding events in the created order. The use of right reason affected one's future by allowing one to choose well with relative certainty. Without diminishing nature, Holcot was able to supersede it by emphasizing the role of reason in man's self-government.[49]

Bradwardine's Sermo Epinicius

But the *Wisdom* literature also served as supporting sources for those, like Bradwardine, who were antagonistic to the modern theological emphasis on self-determination. In his preface to the *De Causa Dei*,[50] Bradwardine attacked the *moderni* for neglecting God's prevenient providence and grace and for their consequent over-emphasis of the significance of man's free will in labouring for eternal reward. He complained that 'nowadays, one never hears of grace from the philosophers'. Bradwardine wanted to demonstrate God's sovereignty in all realms – *ordinata* and *absoluta* – and he publicized his views in English when he delivered a sermon to the victorious Edward III and his nobility, returned from Crécy, and then again near Durham, after the successful battle at Neville's Cross.[51] Like other sermons that were delivered in the vernacular, this *Sermo Epinicius* was transcribed in Latin, prepared by the papal legate, Anibaldus, Bishop of Tusculum. Likewise the series of more than eighty sermons of Richard FitzRalph, dating from the 1340s to 1350s, delivered *in vulgari anglico ad populum*, have been preserved in Latin.[52]

Bradwardine's theme is from 2 Corinthians 2: 14: 'God who always leads us in triumph grants victory to those whom he wills and he wills to grant victory to the virtuous.' Citing repeatedly from the *Wisdom* literature, he wants to clarify the conditions of victory in the *ordinata*. Victory in war, he shows, is had neither by man's prowess nor by the configuration of the stars, but by decision in heaven. In arguing against those who say that the English victory over the French at Crécy resulted from prudent human counsel, Bradwardine points out that wisdom, counsel and prudence derive from God. And God thereby grants victory to whom he wills.[53] He places wise counsel in the humble and simple, 'saves the poor from the sword' and 'takes the wise in their own craftiness'. In opposing the semi-pelagianism of thinkers like Holcot, Bradwardine cites the Psalms to show that virtue in a king or in anyone else is not, by itself, salvific. All rests in God's will. Divine sovereignty comes first.

Bradwardine defines seven erroneous views held on providence and men's fate, dividing his theme in order to move towards the central consideration of Fortune as the *causa latens* in all events. Because men are ignorant of the cause of many

contingent effects around them, they attribute them all to Fortune. But constant reference must be had to the divine will to
which any *causa latens* and *causa agens sive accio* must be
reduced.[54] Victory should not be attributed to *fatum*, that is to
the classical poets' three sisters Clotho, Lachesis and Atropos,
but to God's wisdom and providence. He ordained the universe
for all time, and by his ordination, all obey him and his laws. He
established it in eternity and unfolds this order through the precepts and laws of the ages. No deed is, therefore, unordained
for all proceeds from divine providence.

Gracie Dei non fecit vel illud: gracia fecit vincere et de adversariis
triumphare ... non stelle, non tempus, non fortuna non casus, non
fatum non omen, ymmo nec ego, set gracia Dei mecum.[55]

What we have in this *sermo epinicius* is a more popular attempt
to interpret providence in accord with God's determining will
and a reliance on the *Wisdom* literature as it interprets the good
rulership that derives from this will. It shows Bradwardine's
concern to counteract the modern theologians who seemed to
him to deny the universal causality of the divine will by giving
too great a place to man's free will operating without grace.

This sermon, like other writings meant for a non-university
milieu which none the less offered to its listeners the issues at
the heart of current theological debates, makes plain one of the
channels by which the laity gained a familiarity with the vernacular expression of fourteenth-century theology. Here was the
problem of human liberty, of chance and fate as these affected
one's personal future. Here was also the concern for an appropriate understanding of the meaning of 'just reward' for deeds or
intentions that were freely performed. From such expositions,
these concerns passed into the repertory of discussion beyond
the schools to emerge, as we have seen, at the dinner tables of
the laity.

Theology in English

At the beginning of this chapter I argued that Wyclif's influence
derived more from his social and political views than from his
theology. In fact, Lollards grew antagonistic to university men
and they argued that Christ's apostles did not have academic
degrees. In many ways Lollard theology was extremely simple in

contrast to the increasingly complicated theology of the schools, and one could argue that Lollard theology was developed to some extent in order to counteract current scholasticism. Apart from the evident social import of Lollard teachings, it was their aim, and here they were successful, to write an uncomplicated theology in English. But we have seen that Langland, and to some extent the *Pearl* poet also, attempted to expound doctrine in verse. It was the efforts of the Lollards in prose, however, that recalled to later fifteenth-century minds that a serious attempt had been made, and an unorthodox one at that, to write theology in English. Thus it was a brave step that Reynold Pecock, Bishop of Chichester, took when in the 1450s he wrote a series of theological works in English, precisely to combat Lollard teaching.[56] It has been argued that after 1415, when Sir John Oldcastle led a Lollard revolt which was decisively quashed, Lollardy was not a serious socio-political movement; but it is also clear that at least aspects of their theology and their teaching in conventicles survived underground throughout the fifteenth century. Pecock warned his readers among the laity that he had no intention of vulgarizing theology, making it simple when it was not, and he deliberately broke into Latin when he found no vernacular terminology to deal with 'high theology'. But Pecock's theology was none the less suspected, and he was prosecuted and forced to recant – in English. He had not been afraid to write in the plain style, as Wyclif's followers had done, and like both the Lollards and the theologically learned Langland, he had to develop a philosophical and theological vocabulary in English; his was in the dialect of the East Midlands, to account for 'the seid language ben not stabili & foundamentali written'.[57] What Pecock seems to have done in his *Book of Faith*, *Repressor of over much blaming of the clergy*, *The Folewer of Donet* and *The Donet* was to counteract the Lollard theological simplicities with a revival of many of the theological subtleties of the fourteenth-century *moderni*; and it is in this light that we can trace the posterity of what I have called non-scholastic literature into the fifteenth century.

Like many of the 'modern' theologians, Pecock was criticized for having assigned too great a place in his system to reason at the expense of scriptural authority. He argued that the Lollard overemphasis on faith in Scriptures must be countered with a definition of faith that could accommodate the intellectual, rational element. In order to believe we are called upon (by God) to determine the *probability* of the evidence. Faith is a kind of 'kunning' (knowing), and must involve an exercise of reason. Surely this harks back to the teachings of 'moderns' like William of Ockham. Pecock goes on to distinguish, in his *Book of Faith*, I c. 3 – just as Ockham had distinguished them – faith based on opinion and faith based on science, and he asked the peculiarly fourteenth-century 'modern' question of whether God is demonstrable. We may recall that Duns Scotus and Ockham discussed the demonstrable nature of true science and concluded that theological truth, not being demonstrable, is not a true science.

Pecock was forced to confront two opposing trends in fifteenth-century theology, and he was defeated. The school theologians went considerably further than Ockham in the direction of logical scepticism: all experience may be illusory. But on the other hand, and here the Lollards won an indirect and unacknowledged victory, there were churchmen who wished to emphasize the devotional life, the ardour of faith, at the expense of the encroachment of reason. The production of numerous copies of devotional works like the *Cloud of Unknowing* and the *Book of Privy Counselling* indicates how exceedingly popular they were in the fifteenth century; and, like Lollardy itself, the boom in the literature of affective piety may be seen as reactions against the complicated logical methods of school theology and the dense issues that the schools tried to elucidate. The didactic poetry of a Langland, while reflecting the contemporary controversies in the schools, was in the fifteenth century overwhelmed by a simpler, devotional attitude and its literature of pious certainty and comfort. As E. F. Jacob showed, early printers like Caxton and Wynkyn de Worde published vast numbers of works of devotional piety.

Pecock's intentions may have been good, but they were archaic. He had, as Jacob said, little of the mystic or devotionally pious about him. 'It was his purpose to show that scholasticism could be adapted to the understanding of lay people and could provide the rational basis required for the moral liberty of the individual.'[58] And this leads us to conclude, as we have already done on the basis of evidence for fourteenth-century shifting patterns of mobility and literacy, that the non-scholastic literature of the preceding century was also a sign of a society in transition. Theological confusion and the mixture of traditional literary genres were hallmarks of a period in which the 'middle class' was seeking to be heard. By the second decade of the fifteenth century their language was English and their concerns were increasingly practical, pious and private; they revived the romance and purchased the literature of devotion, written to be read alone in one's chamber. The non-scholastic literature of the previous century may have aired the debates in the schools and in scholarly circles for an increasingly literate laity, but it was such men and women who in the fifteenth century saw themselves as the new governors; it was they who patronized the literature that expressed security, order and uncomplicated entertainment and piety. The fifteenth century as an era of prosperity and enterprise had probably had enough of the social, theological and literary disruptions of the later fourteenth century and sought a literature that soothed, entertained and comforted, rather than one that disrupted and questioned.

This is perhaps best expressed in the words of one of the Vernon lyrics (Brown no. 106), which provides us with a key to what would become one of the dominant trends of much fifteenth-century literature, particularly in its rejection of the debates of the non-scholastic literature and the endless quests in the didactic poetry of the preceding transitional epoch:

. . . Wharto wilne we forte knowe
Þe poyntes of Godes privete?   secrets
More þen Him lustes forte schowe
We schulde not knowe in no degre,
And idel bostis forte blowe
A Mayster in Divinite.
Þenk we lyue in eorþe her lowe,
And God an heiʒ in mageste.
Of material mortualite
Medle we & of no more maistrie.
Þe more we trace þe Trinite,
Þe more we falle in fantasye.
. . . Whon al vr bokes ben forþ brouht,
And al vr craft of clergye
And al vr wittes ben þorw-out souʒt,
ʒit we fareþ as a fantasye.
. . . For þis world is but fantasye.

6 Conclusion

In this century we have had several generations of impressive, even inspired, contributions to our understanding of fourteenth-century English literature and its literary context. Somewhat less successful have been the attempts, until quite recently, to place literary history back into its non-literary environment, that daily life of both audience and poets in which warfare, political wrangling, religious piety, plague and illness, legal proceedings and economic complaint constituted the immediate experience of English men and women. But from this daily experience emerged a literature of instruction, complaint and entertainment that provided food for thought after the long day's dealings with the exigencies of living in an age of transition. The poets and patrons of this literature, which was written to be read, aloud or silently, were more numerous than they had ever previously been. And it was the acquisition of literate skills, particularly in English but also in Latin, that helped to create what we have come to recognize as that great literature of the later fourteenth century: alliterative, Ricardian and Chaucerian.

It is often said that the medievalist has far fewer facts to help him construct the currents of contemporary feeling and values, the transformations in contemporary ways of seeing, than the historian of more modern times, whose documents can bury him beneath their claims to relevance. But medieval history is no longer merely a recitation of kings and battles; it has long since passed into a more sophisticated analysis of intentions, values and sensibilities as expressed in the documents that do survive, and historians have taken a new interest in the 'common man' and in the documents that express the values of relatively inarticulate groups. None the less, it has been unclear to many not only that fourteenth-century literature requires a knowledge of non-literary history to understand it, but that the literature is itself superb data for a reconstruction of the history of the late medieval aesthetic and moral temperament. Setting the poetry into its own times can help us to evaluate the literature of an age more accurately in terms of how contemporary writers, readers and listeners reacted to it and thereby helped to create it as an expression of something peculiarly of its own time. But we have been hindered from attempting to bridge the poetry of the fourteenth century with the non-literary history of the period because of our own too-ready acceptance of an attitude to literature that has sought to raise the text above its times and, in the words of Charles Muscatine, to grant the literary text a 'special ontological status'.

Our problem is that the age of literary analysis – the New Criticism – seems to have reached a dead end. Conceived in reaction to a simplistic 'positivistic' kind of history, it turned our attention to the text in and for itself and taught us to read poetry with the minute intensity that is now part of our standard equipment. The New Criticism taught us that the archaeological parts of scholarship – editing texts, tracing sources, were ancillary to the great act of reading and elucidating the text in and for itself; that the text's meaning was somehow hedged against historical relativism; that the literary work enjoyed a special *is*ness, a special ontological status. The new-critical position, despite all it has taught us, can no longer be defended as an end in itself; it has led us quite naturally into a concern with literary texts so narrow as to merit the label 'aestheticism'. Turning us away from a bad kind of history, it has tended to turn us away from history itself. . . . A certain territorial concern . . . was greatly promoted by the New Criticism. To purge literary studies of the irrelevant, the unliterary, was to fence them in against biography, psychology, sociology, philosophy. This territoriality fit into . . . a certain aping of the hardness and specialisation of more scientific disciplines on the campus. . . . We would, in fact, be in an excellent position to contribute to cultural history if we knew more history and if we were more expert in finding the terms and categories in which literature and history connect.[1]

What does it mean to find terms and categories that connect literature with history? Does it mean that a knowledge of English social and political history of the fourteenth century and a familiarity with contemporary literary texts must lead us to develop a third, metalanguage which enables us to understand poets like Langland, Chaucer and the *Gawain/Pearl* poet as literary men of their time and place? Is the answer to the question, 'how do their works fit into a full and complex sense of their time?'[2] dependent on our forging a *new* language of critical theory? Must the study of style necessarily start from the one text under discussion and, thereafter, *choose* whether or not it will branch out to examine if this work of art confirms dominant tendencies in the culture? What unquestioned principles of literary criticism can legitimately be invoked to permit us to make this *choice* as to whether or not we relate the hypostasized text to its culture? If, as is claimed by some, a study of literary style must be conscious of the variant as well as the conventional, then is it not incumbent on the reader to try to uncover the dialectic that operates between a literary work, the cultural reason it exists, its contemporary message and its possible capacity to transcend the context in which it was written, in order to offer general observations of contemporary values which the author has illuminated through his invoking of the particular? It is now becoming attractive to view literature as an aspect of the cultural history of a period, but is it necessary to create a new and separate language to describe this relationship? If we are able to perceive in a literary work 'intimations of meaning unbeknownst to or repressed by the artists themselves',[3] must we speak of these in a language that itself is given a special ontological status? Can we not be satisfied with an ordinary language which speaks of historical events and literary style and content, without demanding a third, higher, critical diction, a professional jargon?

These kinds of questions, I hope, will have been at the back of the reader's mind as he read this book. I have discussed various aspects of fourteenth-century English life: its very transitional nature as evidenced in the growth in schools and literacy, the social mobility of the second and third estates, the opening up of certain theological issues to the laity, and the reflection of these experiences in the verse and prose. My interest is primarily in the content, the message and the purpose of the verse and prose discussed, but I have also tried to say something about form. It is impossible to divorce form from content when speaking about a literature that consciously used its form and style to signal to its audience that the author was writing in a tradition or consciously breaking with it. This book has tried to show how much of the poetry and prose written during the fourteenth century in Anglo-Norman, Latin and Middle English grew out of a wider social, political and religious context, and it argued that a knowledge of this context gives us, as readers, the heightened ability to recognize when literary craftsmen transcended the ordinary, traditional and routine that marked the structure and content of the works of less talented contemporaries. Literature, like all art forms, has a social function, and in the fourteenth century it was a consciously wrought medium used either to support a contemporary ethic or incite to change. Relatively few late fourteenth-century works are 'mere' entertainment and escapist. It seems to me that the tone of most of the recognized great works, as well as that of the undistinguished verse and prose, is increasingly 'realistic'; and its restlessness, questing, questioning and criticism (of ethical values and social abuses) find parallels with the naturalism in the pictorial arts of the time. Where much of the poetry is didactic, the authors of *Piers Plowman* and *Pearl* have read back into their frequently spiritual themes the worldly and realistic context of their times; they have put flesh on the dry and prosaic bones of their theological exegesis. They have combined current events with current interpretations of the past, present and future, mixing the present and momentary with the eternal and enduring. In general, authors 'historicized' their characters, placed them in the present, selected and mixed discrete, traditional genres; and even where we think them to be purveyors of traditional theological fare, a closer examination shows them to have been threading their way cautiously amidst what was no longer a single and fixed theological orthodoxy.

So far as we are able to tell, the great poets of the later fourteenth century were not poets by vocation. Chaucer, for instance, was in his own day a well-known master of realism, satire and entertainment, a poet above all whose works were widely copied for contemporary patrons. But the vast collection of official records of his life makes not a single reference to his having been a poet. He is mentioned, instead, as a courtier and public servant, a man whose political and presumably economic fortunes rose and fell with the fortunes of those to whom he was politically and economically allied. As a literary artist his works reveal him as having chosen among stylistic alternatives to instruct and entertain his readers: he uses satirical irony, courtly idealism and a kind of pathos that links some aspects of his work with religious writings that emphasize the pathetic side of

Christ's life and suffering. Whatever his alternatives, and of course his art lies in his deployment of each of these traditions, they are stylistic traditions which ought not to be considered divorced from their context. Such traditions were developed and altered by self-conscious artists often with civil service or minor ecclesiastical posts, to serve a public and private purpose: providing a literary dimension to a non-literary perception of reality.

Characteristic of much fourteenth-century literature is its subjective observation of the present, while using a modified but traditional form, mixing the allegorical dream vision, the dialogue or debate, the complaint, the satire, the methods of the pulpit, all in one work. *Piers Plowman* is perhaps the most extreme example of this eclecticism. But Chaucer and Gower also mixed traditions: Gower said he wanted to write a book 'in the middel weie' possessing 'somewhat of lust, somewhat of lore' (Prologue, *Confessio Amantis*, Book 1, l. 17). Chaucer also consciously sought to balance 'sentence' and 'solas' (delight). Both men read widely in French and Latin, presumably after hours, for both were civil servants devoting themselves to the common weal. In *The Book of the Duchess*, *The Parlement of Fowles* and *The House of Fame* Chaucer called attention to a characteristic that was becoming more widespread among the gentry and urban 'middle classes': he, like them, read alone, in the evening and for pleasure or instruction. The solitary character of the reader, the development of the practice of writing private letters, the increasingly frequent emphasis on the private nature of spiritual devotion and piety, and the individual responsibility of the Christian – in society and for salvation – combine to present a picture of fourteenth-century society as dominated by its 'middle class'. This bourgeoisie was not a unified, self-conscious 'class' in the minds of contemporaries; in fact, its distinguishing characteristic is precisely its emphasis on individualism and personal responsibility. Paradoxically, if there is anything that unites the bourgeoisie as a distinct group it is satire against it focusing on the political and economic ambitions of its members. The very lack of unity among this bourgeoisie permitted it to be ridiculed, and it is not surprising to find among Chaucer's most fully detailed 'characters' members of this group.

As I have tried to show, the fourteenth century in England is

characterized by the rise to dominance of the literate, professional groups, merchants and gentry, in politics, economic affairs,
and in literature, as authors and patrons. It is precisely the *lack
of unity* of the 'middle class', the antagonism between a patriciate and the *petit bourgeoisie*, the fluidity of social status in this
group, that is mirrored in much of the poetry and prose; for so
much of the really distinguished literature of the period is based
on tensions between social groups. Bronson accurately noted
how Chaucer's pilgrimage proceeded entirely by a group of
strangers motivated by latent and explicit social and psychological antagonisms.[4] And it is satire that develops by means of the
powerful tool of 'realistic' reportage, particularly in the complaint verse of this period. As an incitement to action and to
social change, satire was the literary equivalent of political
revenge, reversing social inequalities and, therefore, contrasting
social and political realities with ideals.

Perhaps a word needs to be said once again about my use of
the term 'realism' in discussing not only poems like *Piers Plowman*, but the far less inspired complaint verse which contributed
to the traditional Abuses of the Age genre. A good deal of the
undistinguished poetry is, in the modern sense of the word,
realistic, a kind of biased journalism that has little subtlety and
intends to point a finger at those who were involved in social
and religious misdemeanours and too often went unpunished.
There is, in fact, a considerable amount of information, fact and
value, in complaint verse, for instance, that at least can be supported if not duplicated in so-called non-fictional sources. But
Elizabeth Salter and Derek Pearsall have argued that the structure of the thought behind *Piers Plowman*, in particular, cannot
be understood exclusively either in terms of allegory or social
realism, and I would agree. Instead, they prefer to use the word
'figural', because it is the typological and figural that draws on
the real *and* the spiritual and co-ordinates these. Whatever
social realism there is in *Piers Plowman*, it is always interpreted
sub specie aeternitatis. This is an illuminating way to read all
three versions of Langland's poem, and their introduction to
their selections from the C text, MS HM 143 (X), where they
discuss the varieties of allegory, the structure of the poem and
its use of pulpit devices is the best, short discussion of the many
difficulties encountered when reading Langland that I know of.[5]
But I have emphasized the realistic reportage to be found in

much of the poetry, including Langland's, because the references to political, social and religious events in this literature are
not mere occasional milestones used to highlight a fictional or
purely spiritual pilgrimage. There is a view held by some literary
critics that, because literature is not life, art is, and must be
completely governed by its own form and substance.[6] This, I
think, goes considerably beyond the view that literature ought
not to be measured against the yardstick of historical accuracy.
And it misconceives a poetry whose very *raison d'être* is social,
political and religious satire with an intent to chastise and force
reality to conform to accepted ideals. The poetic voice was also
an ethical and political voice in the fourteenth century, and to
refer to *Piers Plowman* or even Chaucer's *Canterbury Tales* as
nothing more than 'a great fiction' is seriously to misunderstand,
because of contextual ignorance, the social function of the poetic enterprise in the fourteenth century.

The book ended with a discussion of some of the most important themes in fourteenth-century theology, the theology of the
moderni, which found their way into literature that was meant
not for a clerical elite but for an educated laity; its logical and
theological subtlety created a great deal of confusion among the
learned and unlearned alike, and this is reflected in some of the
contemporary didactic poetry in Middle English, particularly
Piers Plowman. I have spent virtually no time at all on the other
dominant strain of religious poetry – that of affective piety –
because it has been so thoughtfully treated by others, especially
by Douglas Gray.[7] The religious lyric is concerned with the life
of Christ and his redemptive act for mankind. The more
speculative, logical and theological matter of the didactic poetry
reflects the subject matter of the school debate and leaves
Christ's significance largely to one side, focusing instead on
man's deeds, moral attitudes and the acts appropriate to the salvation of the *viator*, the Christian pilgrim. While the Middle
English lyric has been described as supplicatory, a meditation,
prayer and petition, the expression of adoration, thanksgiving, a
celebration of Christ's life and God's mercy, the didactic poetry
tells the story of the quest for that mercy. The didactic strain of
religious poetry is a reflection on how man ought to live in
order to receive of God's bounty, and therefore is more
interested in the workings of man's own natural gifts and their
relation to the promised reward. It may be appropriate to clas-

sify the didactic poetry as concerned with the active or at least the mixed life, whereas the lyric emerges from the contemplative, meditative state of static reflection and praise. The simple language of the devotional lyric emphasizes the simple creatures who reflect and praise Christ's life. This is contrasted with the poetry of pilgrimage, quest, uncertainty and insecurity concerning whom God rewards and why. As Gray points out, it is what Auerbach called *sermo humilis* that is found at work in the devotional lyric. The more theological poetry, however, is not content to set forth, as Gray puts it, the paradoxes of a God who is man, a virgin who is yet a mother, that the dead may yet live, and leave it here.[8] The didactic poetry is characterized by the attempt it makes to resolve the paradoxes the lyric takes for granted: 'Beleeue, and leave to wonder', does not satisfy the Dreamer, either in *Pearl* or in *Piers Plowman*.

In a fifteenth-century lyric (Index 2342) there is a stanza that goes:

Sithen it is wele, wele we do,   Since
For there is none but one of two,
Heuen to gete or heuen forgo;
Oder mene none there is.
I counsaill you, sin it is so,
That ye wele do to win you bliss.

Now this is the religious lyric commonplace. What appears in the didactic poetry like *Piers Plowman* and *Pearl* is the questioning of the meaning of the commonplace: what does 'do well' mean? and is doing well sufficient 'to win you bliss'? There is, then, a tension between the two strands of fourteenth-century religious poetry, and it is the didactic poetry that offers us a view of what lay beneath the assumed smooth surface of an age of simple faith. We know enough about the fourteenth century to affirm that it was not an unperturbed age of faith, and we possess a literature that expressed the doubts and insecurities in the language of a pious but questioning laity. Just as social and political ideals and realities were in transition, so too were religious ideals and realities. The Lollards and their literature show us something of the turmoil of the period epitomized.

A transitional epoch should be set between periods of *relative* conservation, stability and order. The transitional late fourteenth and early fifteenth centuries witnessed decisive shifts in the social structure and tenurial relationships. During the fifteenth century the population declined further and then stagnated, but there was also a prolonged era of high living, prosperity and enterprise, to such an extent that the early fifteenth century saw a buoyant demand for land, a spectacular growth in the woollen textile industry and its exports, and a dramatic decrease in the numbers of the labouring poor. The period from 1430 to 1460 for the agricultural worker, the builder, the third estate in general, was one in which a real rise in living standards occurred; food was cheaper. In fact, it has been seen by an increasing number of historians as the golden age of the English labourer.[9] It was also a period in which burgesses consolidated their economic, and by extension political, power. The pious religious commonplace of the devotional lyric, with its soothing, uncomplicated, comforting message and its emphasis on individual meditation, proved to be exceedingly popular. The romance in its pious English form came back into fashion.

Only one factor, ever prevalent in the pictorial art of the period, hints that all was not well. The high living standards of the fifteenth century were not due to advances in agricultural techniques or the efficiency of the economic structure but to the simple fact that fewer people were sharing the resources of the nation. Living standards were maintained and even improved by the persistence of a very high death rate, which simply stopped the English population from recovering from the demographic havoc wreaked on England and the Continent by the Black Death of 1349 and its recurrences. It was indeed the golden age of the English labourer, simply because there were not very many of them left. Depictions of the dance of death and the persistent reminder of man's mortality in numerous meditations served as a counterpoint to the literature of stability and prosperity that was written for the gentry and urban bourgeoisie of the fifteenth century. The fifteenth century was the great age of the fourteenth-century romance, copied and, in effect, rewritten for urban burgess and rural gentry households, at first still in verse but increasingly in prose for the private reader.[10] The period of theological and social transition and upheaval, of 'peasants' revolts' and Lollard disruptions and trials, seemed not only ended, but scarcely recalled. No one wanted to hear school theology explained in English, and when the Bishop of Chichester attempted to combat the remnants of Lollardy with an explanation of the role of reason in faith, he was himself suspected of heresy and forced to recant. His efforts were untypical of his times, but they were exceedingly common in the transitional later fourteenth century.[11]

There have already been attempts, successful I believe, at delineating a distinctive literary tradition developed during the reign of Richard II, and we may call it Ricardian with its characteristic lengthy narrative.[12] What I have tried to illustrate, further, is the genesis of a didactic, socially and religiously critical verse and prose with a mixed pedigree, emerging from an earlier verse tradition with another social function – appropriate to a different kind of society. The literature appearing during the reign of Richard II for a varied public was, like the society that it reflected and that patronized it, experiencing transition. The reader cannot help but be disorientated by the unstable genres and the shifting narrative focus of many of the long and didactic poems. But the themes are remarkably constant when we know the non-literary context and something about the probable methods of composition: the diffuse, the amplified, the cross-referenced, tell us about the role of memory in a period that increasingly confronted its standards frozen on the page. But perhaps most important is the recurrence of the questing theme, be it religious or social; and it is the active, reforming character of a socially mobile and increasingly literate fourteenth-century English society that saw itself mirrored in the literature of its own time.

Notes and references

Chapter 1: Introduction

1 Jean Froissart, *Chroniques*, ed. S. Luce (Paris 1869–88), vol. 1, pt
2, from the Rome MS (3ième rédaction, *c*. 1400), pp. 214–15:

> Englès sont de mervilleuses conditions, chaut et boullant, tos
> esmeu en ire, tart apaisié ne amodé en doucour; et se delittent et
> confortent en batailles et en ocisions. Convoiteus et envieus sont
> trop grandement sus le bien d'autrui, et ne se pueent conjoindre
> parfaitement ne naturelment en l'amour ne aliance de nation
> estragne, et sont couvert et orguilleus. Et par especial desous le
> solel n'a nul plus perilleus peuple, tant que de *hommes mestis*,
> comme il sont en Engleterre. Et trop fort se diffèrent en
> Engleterre les natures et conditions des nobles aux *hommes mes-
> tis** et vilains, car li gentilhomme sont de noble et loiale condition,
> et li communs peuples est de fèle, perilleuse, orguilleuse et
> desloiale condition. Et là où li peuples vodroit moustrer sa felon-
> nie et poissance, li noble n'aueroient point de durée à euls. Or sont
> il et ont esté un lonch temps moult bien d'acort ensamble, car li
> noble ne demande au peuple que toute raison. Aussi on ne li souf-
> ferroit point que il presist, sans paiier, un oef ne une poulle. Li
> homme de mestier et li laboureur parmi Engleterre vivent de ce
> que il sèvent faire, et li gentilhomme, de lors rentes et revenues;
> et si li rois les ensonnie, il sont paiict, non que li rois puist taillier
> son peuple, non, ne li peuples ne le vodroit ne poroit souffrir. Il i a
> certainnes ordenances et pactions assisses sus le staple des lainnes,
> et de ce est li rois aidiés au desus de ses rentes et revenues; et
> quant ils fait gerre, celle paction on li double. Engleterre est la
> terre dou monde le mieulz gardée. Aultrement il ne poroient ne
> saueroient vivre, et couvient bien que uns rois qui est lors sires, se
> ordonne apriès euls et s'encline à moult de lors volentés; et se il
> fait le contraire et mauls en viengne, mal l'en prendera ensi que il

Homme mestis is translated in the *Dictionnaire Historique de
l'ancien langage français* (vol. 7, Paris 1880, p. 364) as 'de classe
moyenne; ambigu, croisé'; in other words, 'mixed breed'.

fist à ce roi Edouwart, dont je parloie maintenant, liquels fu fils au bon roi Edouwart qui tant fu de proèce plains que il desconfi par pluisseurs fois en bataille les Escocois. . . .

2   Froissart, *c.* 1388, cited in Peter E. Thompson (trans.), *Contemporary Chronicles of the Hundred Years War* (London 1966), p. 14.

Chapter 2: Vernacular literacy and lay education

1   M. V. Clarke, 'Forfeitures and treason in 1388', *Fourteenth Century Studies* (Oxford 1937). See also the will of Master Geoffrey Le Scrope, canon of Lincoln, 1382, in C. W. Foster (ed.), *Lincoln Wills*, vol. 1: *1271–1526* (Lincoln Record Society, no. 5), p. 17: he belonged to the famous Yorkshire family, being the fifth son of Sir Geoffrey Le Scrope, chief Justice of the King's Bench (d. 1340). 'Bequeathed to Thomas his chamberlain my Norfolk Bed [worked] with birds, with carpets, and with a cillour, curtains, and one pair of sheets, blankets . . . and other daily necessities lying in the chamber.' Geoffrey was a lawyer and ecclesiastic with, it is thought, an Oxford Ll.B. The will of Henry Le Scrope of Masham is full of bequests of books; he was a Knight of the Garter and ex-Treasurer of the Exchequer.

2   Clarke, p. 121. Also V. H. Scattergood in *The Library*, vol. 23 (1968), pp. 236–9.

3   Henry J. Todd, *Illustrations of Chaucer and Gower* (London 1810), pp. 161–2; Madeleine Blaess, 'L'Abbaye de Bordesley et les livres de Guy de Beauchamp', *Romania*, vol. 78 (1957), pp. 511–18.

4   Lambeth Library, *Register Arundel*, vol. l, fos. 163v–164v; cited by K. B. McFarlane, *The Nobility of Later Medieval England: the Ford Lectures for 1953 and Related Studies* (Oxford 1973), pp. 236f. In general, see ch. 6, 'The education of the nobility in later medieval England', pp. 228–47.

5   Viscount Dillon and W. H. St John Hope, 'Inventory of the goods and chattels belonging to Thomas, Duke of Gloucester', *Archaeological Journal*, vol. 54 (1897), pp. 275–308. See also J. Nichols (ed.), *Royal Wills* . . . (London 1780), pp. 181–3, and Clarke, p. 121.

6   *Rolls of Parliament* (*RP*), vol. 3, p. 378. The debate over Gloucester's Bible translation was still open in 1401–2: see Anne Hudson in *English Historical Review* (*EHR*), vol. 90 (1975), pp. 1–18.

7   The will of Sir John Cavendish, the chief justice who was hanged by the mob on 1 April in the 1381 revolt, says that he begins in Latin but because he is better able to communicate understandably in

French, he will continue 'in linguam Gallicam scribere': Norwich District Probate Registry, *Register Heydon*, fo. 190r; cited in McFarlane, p. 241.

8   Kenneth Fowler, *The King's Lieutenant: Henry of Grosmont, First Duke of Lancaster, 1310–1361* (London 1969); *Le Livre de Seyntz Medicines*, ed. E. J. F. Arnould (Oxford 1940). A decline of French in aristocratic circles in the fourteenth century is referred to in *Arthour and Merlin* (ll. 23–6):

Freynsche use þis gentilman,
Ac everich Inglische Inglische can;
Mani noble ich have yzeiȝe,   seen
þat no Freynsche couþe seye: could

9   Fowler, pp. 26, 193–6; *Le Livre de Seyntz Medicines*, p. 239.

10 Fowler, p. 195. 'In what other century', said McFarlane, 'has the peerage been so active in literature?' (p. 242). In the autumn of 1395 a list of books used for the private education of Henry Bolingbroke's children was drawn up: seven books of Latin grammar in one volume for the future Henry V, then eight years old. In 1397: two books of ABC for children (Latin), meant for Blanche who was five years old and her sister Philippa, aged seven and a half. See McFarlane, p. 244. The nobility were no strangers to Latin.

11 Cited in Margaret Aston, *Thomas Arundel* (Oxford 1967), p. 327. She suggests the possibility that Anne's Bible was, in fact, the 'illegal' Lollard Bible with glosses by a Wyclifite, possibly John Purvey.

12 F. J. Furvinall (ed.), *The Earliest English Wills*, Early English Text Society (London 1882), p. 5.

13 In the household of his mother, Joan of Kent, Richard had had contact with Sir Lewis Clifford, a friend of the French poet Eustace Deschamps, and with Sir John Clanvowe. Later, at his own court, one of his intimates was Sir John Montague, later Earl of Salisbury, friend and adviser to Christine of Pisan, the French poet, and he was himself the author of poems in French which Christine admired. Already in his youth, Richard was familiar with a literary aristocracy that composed in French and English. See the 'Introduction' in G. W. Coopland (ed.), Philippe de Mézières's *Letter to King Richard II* (Liverpool 1975), p. xvii. Coopland notes that Richard 'must have been almost bilingual, like many of his contemporaries, in French and English, and perhaps, had some knowledge of Latin' (p. xvii). A fundamental discussion of the use of vernacular languages, at court and elsewhere, and the circulation and publication of texts, is still H. J. Chaytor, *From Script to*

Print: an Introduction to Medieval Vernacular Literature (London 1945).

14   J. Froissart, *Oeuvres*, ed. K. de Lettenhove (Brussels 1863), vol. 2, p. 419.

15   Gervase Mathew, *The Court of Richard II* (London 1968), p. 58.

16   Derek Pearsall, *John Lydgate* (London 1970).

17   Mathew, pp. 68–72.

18   M. D. Legge, in *Anglo-Norman Literature and its Background* (Oxford 1963), says Gower continued the Anglo-Norman tradition and is its true heir. Chaucer alone turned the literary tide to English. 'John Gower shows what French poetry in England might have become if Chaucer had not flung his cap over the windmill and plunged into the English language' (p. 357). 'It so happens that Gower's is the last name on the roll of Anglo-Norman writers. Chaucer's could have stood beside it, but it was he who sounded the death-knell of Anglo-Norman literature, and cast off the tradition which Gower was content to foster' (pp. 360–1). But J. H. Fisher, *John Gower, Moral Philosopher and Friend to Chaucer* (London 1965), has noted how Chaucer was a translator of French, not Anglo-Norman, works, and whereas Chaucer was indebted to French court poets, Gower's debt is to earlier troubadours and the English tradition of French (Anglo-Norman) composition (p. 77).

19   Suggested by Mathew, p. 79.

20   Sr Carmeline Sullivan, *Latin Insertions and the Macaronic Verse in Piers Plowman* (Washington DC 1932). John Alford, 'The role of quotations in *Piers Plowman*', *Speculum*, vol. 52 (1977), pp. 80–99.

21   There is a similar use of grammatical analogy in the English writings of the Lollards. See, for example, the explanation of 'falsehood' in the late fourteenth/early fifteenth-century text of *Sixteen Lollard Beliefs*, printed in Anne Hudson (ed.), *Selections from English Wycliffite Writings* (Cambridge 1978), no. 2, p. 20: 'Know well this that when a copulative is made, though there be many truths, if it affirms a falsehood, it shall be denied all together.'

22   See E. W. Tristram, *English Medieval Wall Painting: The Fourteenth Century* (London 1955); E. W. Tristram, 'Piers Plowman in English medieval wall painting', *Burlington Magazine*, vol. 31, (1917); Mathew, p. 95; W. H. Bird, *The Ancient Mural Paintings of Gloucestershire* (London 1927), p. 11.

23   Bodleian Library, MS Selden, *supra* 38, fo. 27.

24   Merton College, Oxford, MS 248. See Carleton Brown and G. V. Smithers (eds.), *Religious Lyrics of the Fourteenth Century* (Oxford 1956), nos. 35–41.

25 See Edward Wilson, *A Descriptive Index of the English Lyrics in John of Grimestone's Preaching Book*, Medium Aevum Monographs (Oxford 1973). Grimestone's alphabetical sermon manual (1372) is discussed below, ch. 3. The manuscript is Advocates' Library, 18.7.21, National Library of Scotland.

26 Ed. C. Horstmann (Heilbron 1881). For a good general discussion of these handbooks and the growth in lay devotional reading in the vernacular, see Derek Pearsall, *Old English and Middle English Poetry* (London 1977), pp. 133–40.

27 McFarlane, pp. 238f. M. T. Clanchy, *From Memory to Written Record: England 1066–1307* (London 1979), deals with the question of literacy up to the early fourteenth century. See also Franz Bäuml, 'Varieties and consequences of medieval literacy and illiteracy', *Speculum*, vol. 55 (1980), pp. 237–65.

28 Thorlac Turville-Petre, 'Humphrey de Bohun and *William of Palerne*', *Neuphilologische Mitteilungen*, vol. 75 (1974), pp. 250–2. Also see Thorlac Turville-Petre, *The Alliterative Revival* (Cambridge 1977), p. 41.

29 These categories are discussed by M. B. Parkes, 'The literacy of the laity', in D. Daiches and A. Thorlby (eds.), *Literature and Western Civilization*, vol. 2: *The Medieval World* (London 1973).

30 Sylvia Thrupp, *The Merchant Class of Medieval London* (London 1948), pp. 162, 248–9.

31 Francis Steer (ed.), *Scriveners' Company Common Paper 1357–1628* (London 1968).

32 Parkes, p. 565.

33 For a thorough survey of schools, schoolmasters and curricula in the fourteenth century, see the study by Nicholas Orme, *Education in the West of England, 1066–1548: Cornwall, Devon, Dorset, Gloucestershire, Somerset, Wiltshire* (Exeter 1976). For full and current information, see Nicholas Orme, *English Schools in the Middle Ages* (London 1973).

34 H. Keil (ed.), *Grammatici Latini* (8 vols., Leipzig 1855–9), for the standard texts. *Register of W. Wykeham, Winchester*, ed. T. F. Kirby (Hants. Record Society, no. 13, 1899), vol. 2, p. 287.

35 Orme, *English Schools*, p. 183.

36 Orme, *Education in the West of England*, pp. 48–50, 165, 211.

37 ibid., p. 193.

38 ibid., p. 192.

39 Students remained until the age of 18 and were then sent to the sister college at Oxford where seventy scholars were supported to read arts and then enter the ecclesiastical administration: Orme, *English Schools*, p. 187.

40 See J. N. T. Miner, 'Schools and literacy in late medieval Eng-

land', *British Journal of Educational Studies*, vol. 11 (1962–3), pp. 16–27. *Register G. Welton*, fo. 52.

41   See E. A. Savage, *Old English Libraries* (London 1911), p. 272.

42   Orme, *English Schools*, pp. 65ff.; Kathleen Edwards, *Victoria County History: Wiltshire*, vol. 3 (London 1956), pp. 369–85; Kathleen Edwards, *The English Secular Cathedrals in the Middle Ages*, 2nd ed. (Manchester 1967), pp. 185–92.

43   Orme, *Education in the West of England*, p. 23: the chancellor must lecture in theology, a customary duty made statutory by 1348 by papal decree. W. A. Pantin, *The English Church in the Fourteenth Century* (Cambridge 1955), p. 16, noted that most divinity lectures now extant for the fourteenth century are those delivered at the cathedrals. Other theologians, like William de Forneste STP, vicar of Mildenhale, in the diocese of Norwich, received an indult of non-residence for two years, while lecturing in theology in the church of Salisbury, to which office he was elected by Simon de Sudbiria, then Chancellor of Salisbury: *Calendar of Papal Letters*, vol. 3, 6 Innoc. VI, 1358, p. 596.

44   Also see the discussion of Summae for Confessors below, ch. 4, and Thomas Tentler, 'The summa for confessors as an instrument of social control', in H. Oberman and C. Trinkaus (eds.), *The Pursuit of Holiness in Late Medieval and Renaissance Religion* (Leiden 1974), pp. 103–25.

45   Alan Cobban, *The King's Hall within the University of Cambridge in the Later Middle Ages* (Cambridge 1969), p. 50. R. W. Hunt, 'Oxford grammar masters of the later Middle Ages', in *Oxford Studies presented to Daniel Callus* (Oxford 1964), pp. 163–93.

46   H. G. Richardson, 'An Oxford teacher of the fifteenth century', *Bulletin of the John Rylands Library*, vol. 23 (1939), pp. 436–57.

47   Trevisa's translation of R. Higden's *Polychronicon* tells us of grammar masters teaching in English. As J. H. Fisher has noted, 'the innovation credited to John of Cornwall and Richard Pencrich (*c.* 1350) who "chaunged þe lore in gramer schole and construccioun of Frensche into Englische" was merely that *recitation*, what up until that time had been in French, was changed to English. The grammar being construed was still Latin.' Discussed in 'Chancery and the emergence of standard written English in the fifteenth century', *Speculum*, vol. 52 (1977), p. 893. See *Polychronicon Ranulphi Higden*, ed. C. Babington, vol. 2 (London 1896), pp. 158–61.

48   See R. E. Kaske, 'Ex vi transicionis and its passage in *Piers Plowman*', *Journal of English and Germanic Philology*, vol. 62 (1963), pp. 32–60.

49   See below, ch. 5. M. B. Hackett, *The Original Statutes of Cam-*

bridge University (Cambridge 1970), pp. 130–1, 265–6, for a discussion of the degree course in grammar, established by statute in 1385.

50 Alford, 'The role of the quotations in *Piers Plowman*', and below, ch. 4.

51 Cobban, *The King's Hall*. See also Pearl Kibre, *Scholarly Privileges in the Middle Ages* (London 1961).

52 T. F. Tout, *Chapters in the Administrative History of Medieval England* (Manchester 1920–3), vol. 3, p. 281. 'Hence the first lay chancellor Robert Bourchier is found in 1360 and at the same time a feeling becomes evident that Englishmen, and lay Englishmen at that, should manage their own affairs': N. Denholm-Young, *The Country Gentry in the Fourteenth Century, with Special Reference to the Heraldic Rolls of Arms* (Oxford 1969), p. 12.

53 There is a couplet in an *exemplum* (from a preaching text?) of an English bishop of low birth who recalls his origins when he views a wall-painting depicting a farmer's boy leading the oxen pulling a dung cart:

Undyrstonde what thow were and art,
ffor sumtyme thow dreve thy fadyr cart.

Cited by S. Wenzel, 'Unrecorded Middle English verses', *Anglia*, vol. 92 (1974), p. 74; from MSS Lambeth Palace 78, fo. 225v and Caius College, Cambridge 351, fo. 97r. Also Cobban, *The King's Hall, passim*.

54 Cobban, pp. 13–14.

55 W. A. Pantin, *The English Church in the Fourteenth Century* (Cambridge 1955), is still a classic work on this subject. Also see K. Edwards, 'Political importance of English bishops during the reign of Edward II', *English Historical Review*, vol. 59 (1944) pp. 311–47.

56 John Hody, who was to become the chancellor of Wells Cathedral, had the following background, according to an unusual biographical fragment from the late fifteenth centrury – written, it is believed, by a hostile source who wished to discredit the Hodys: 'Adam Hody was a bondeman to my Lorde of Awdeley and heywarde of Woolavington, and he had ii sonnys, John and Thomas. Thys John went to schole with a chawntery prest in Wolavyngton and fro that to Oxford, and so he hadde lycens of the Lorde of Awdely and was i-made a prest and after that be fortune he was a chanon yn Wellys and chawnceler yn Wellys.' The account continues, describing how John Hody, b. *c*. 1375 (Chancellor of Wells and Archdeacon of Dorset), found his nephews to school, secured their manumission and when he died left goods

with his younger nephew, Sir Alexander Hody, to purchase lands for chantry priests of Woolavington 'for the love that he had to it, for there he began his first learning'. Cited by Orme, *Education in the West of England*, pp. 108–9 and H. C. Maxwell-Lyte, 'The Hody family', *Somerset and Dorset Notes and Queries*, vol. 18 (1925), pp. 127–9.

57   Pantin, *The English Church*, pp. 10–14; Cobban, *The King's Hall*, pp. 293–6.

58   See below, ch. 5.

59   Joseph Dahmus, *The Metropolitan Visitations of William Courteney, Archbishop of Canterbury 1381–96* (Illinois 1950), p. 103, from *Register Courtenay*, fo. 100.

60   For information on Richard de Bury see N. Denholm-Young, 'Richard de Bury (1287–1345)', *Collected Papers on Medieval Subjects* (Oxford 1946), pp. 1–26. Reference to his circle and post-prandial discussions in Savile's introduction to Thomas Bradwardine's *De Causa Dei* (London 1618), p. vi.

61   Alexander Murray, *Reason and Society in the Middle Ages* (Oxford 1978), pp. 302–13.

62   ibid., p. 302.

63   See Guy Fitch Lytle, 'Patronage patterns and Oxford colleges *c*. 1350–*c*. 1530', in Lawrence Stone (ed.), *The University in Society* (Princeton–London 1974), vol. I, pp. 111–49.

64   Murray, pp. 307–8.

65   On the rationalization of churches see Colin Platt, *The English Medieval Town* (London 1976), pp. 168–70; and Rosalind Hill, 'A chaunterie for soules: London chantries in the reign of Richard II', in F. Du Boulay and C. Barron (eds.), citing *Register Braybrooke* (London 1382–1404).

66   Richard de Bury, *Philobiblon* (*c*. 1345), ed. and trans. E. C. Thomas (London 1888).

67   ibid., p. 219 (trans. p. 102).

68   ibid.

69   Information on Trevisa may be found in A. J. Perry's introduction to the edition of the *Dialogus inter Militem et Clericum, FitzRalph's Sermon Defensio Curatorum*, etc. translated by Trevisa, EETS o.s. 167 (1925), and supplemented by David C. Fowler, 'John Trevisa and the English Bible', *Modern Philology*, vol. 58 (1960), 81–98; 'New light on John Trevisa', *Traditio*, vol. 18 (1962), pp. 289–317; 'John Trevisa: scholar and translator', *Transactions of the Bristol and Gloucester Archaeological Society*, vol. 89 (1970), pp. 99–108; 'More about John Trevisa', *Modern Language Quarterly*, vol. 32 (1971), pp. 253–4; and, most recently, *The Bible in Early English Literature* (London 1977),

especially pp. 156–7. On Trevisa's role in translating the Bible see M. Wilks, 'Misleading manuscripts: Wyclif and the non-Wyclifite Bible', *Studies in Church History*, vol. 11 (1975), pp. 147–61.

70 Pearsall, *Old English and Middle English Poetry*, p. 143. His discussion of English romance is illuminating, pp. 143–8.

71 See Laura Hibbard Loomis, 'The Auchinleck MS and a possible London bookshop of 1330–1340', *Publications of the Modern Language Association (PMLA)*, vol. 57 (1942), pp. 595–627.

72 For an excellent study of Middle English romances see Dieter Mehl, *The Middle English Romances of the Thirteenth and Fourteenth Centuries* (London 1968).

73 Pearl Kibre, 'Intellectual interests reflected in libraries of the fourteenth and fifteenth centuries', *Journal of the History of Ideas*, vol. 7 (1946), pp. 257–97.

74 ibid., p. 273.

75 See Turville-Petre, *Alliterative Revival*, pp. 35f.

76 See below, ch. 4.

77 For a discussion of the growth of incorporated boroughs and town independence see Colin Platt, *The English Medieval Town* (London 1976), pp. 140–6.

78 *Mum and the Sothsegger*, ed. M. Day and R. Steele, EETS o.s. 199 (London 1936).

79 ibid., Introduction, pp. xxvi–xxix.

80 See D. Embrée, '*Richard the Redeless* and *Mum and the Sothsegger*: a case of mistaken identity', *Notes and Queries*, vol. 120 (1975), pp. 4–12. Also Turville-Petre says *Mum and the Sothsegger* and *Richard the Redeless* are two poems, possibly by the same author, but both incomplete and now extant in two different manuscripts, although a sixteenth-century reference suggests both were once included in the same codex' (*Alliterative Revival*, p. 32).

81 The later poem, *Mum* (*c*. 1402), is an attack on the household of Henry IV, members of which remain 'mum' about the bad state of affairs in the kingdom. Only a wise beekeeper is eventually found who will speak the truth: the sothsegger.

82 George Holmes, *The Good Parliament* (Oxford 1975), pp. 100–3, citing the report in the contemporary *Anonimale Chronicle*, ed. V. Galbraith (Manchester 1927, reprinted with minor corrections 1970), pp. 80–2.

83 Cited in Holmes, p. 136 from *Chronicon Angliae*, p. 73.

84 Holmes, p. 139.

85 Rodney Hilton, *The English Peasantry in the Later Middle Ages, the Ford Lectures for 1973 and Related Studies* (Oxford 1975). Also see John Hatcher, *Plague, Population and the English Economy 1348–1530* (London 1977). On the consequences of

English society having passed from memory to written record, see Clanchy, *From Memory to Written Record.*

86 See D. W. Robertson, 'Historical criticism', in Alan S. Downer (ed.), *English Institute Essays, 1950* (New York 1951).

87 As well illustrated by Jill Mann, *Chaucer and Medieval Estates Satire, the Literature of Social Classes and the General Prologue of the Canterbury Tales* (Cambridge 1973).

88 Denholm-Young, *Country Gentry in the Fourteenth Century.* Also see the conclusions drawn from the research of Richard Smith in Alan MacFarlane, *The Origins of English Individualism: The Family, Property and Social Transition* (Oxford 1978).

89 *The Ploughman's Complaint*, printed in T. Wright (ed.), *Political Poems and Songs* (London 1859–61), vol. 1, p. 335.

90 See Helen Cam, *Liberties and Communities in Medieval England* (Cambridge 1944), pp. 54–5; and V. Galbraith, 'Thoughts about the peasants' revolt', in F. R. H. DuBoulay and C. Barron (eds.), *The Reign of Richard II, Essays in Honour of May McKisack* (London 1971), p. 55.

91 Rodney Hilton, *The English Peasantry in the Later Middle Ages* (Oxford 1975), p. 24. Along the lines of functional and economic classification of society and its poetic representation in *Piers Plowman*, first in the Prologue (B), where the Dreamer sees a field full of folk 'working as the world asks', and then in the description of the Dreamer himself 'robed in russet', the following passage from the *Statutes of the Realm* I, 378, 37 Edward III (1368), and *RP*, vol. 2, p. 278 is of interest:

And that carters, ploughmen, drivers, oxherds, cowherds, shepherds, swineherds, dairywomen, and other keepers of beasts, threshers of corn, and all manner of men engaged in husbandry, and other people who have not goods and chattel worth 40s, shall wear no cloth save blanket and russet, 12d the yard.

92 Parliaments for November and January 1380: a graduated poll tax was levied for the war, the richer aiding the poorer. 'All artificers, labourers, servants and other lay persons over the age of fifteen, and not beggars, shall be assessed according to the rate of his (or her) condition.' *Rolls of Parliament (RP)*, vol. 3, p. 88.

93 A petition, 1363 *RP*, vol. 2, p. 279, notes that, as a result of the pestilences and winds of late, many manors, lands and tenements, held of the king and others, are so ruined, and because tenants in villeinage can no longer be found as before – the lords are forced, in order to have some profit from their lands, to lease them, in whole or part, for life tenancies.

94 Hilton, p. 27.

95 For an excellent discussion of later fourteenth-century sources see 'Introduction' to the *Anonimale Chronicle*, ed. V. Galbraith (Manchester 1927, reprinted with corrections 1970).

96 *Anonimale Chronicle*, and discussion of authorship in Galbraith, 'Thoughts about the peasants' revolt'.

97 Denholm-Young, *Country Gentry in the Fourteenth Century*, p. 39.

98 For a fascinating discussion of the multilingual skills of monks see the Introduction to Galbraith's edition of *Anonimale Chronicle*, p. xvi.

99 See the letter from the clerk Michael de Northburgh inserted in Robert of Avesbury's *Chronicle* (1346), in French; also a letter from Sir Bartholomew Burghersh in Adam Murimuth's *Chronicle* (1346), to the Archbishop of Canterbury, John Stratford, also in French, on the progress of the war in France. See also the letter of the Prince of Wales to the mayor, aldermen and community of the City of London, concerning the Battle of Poitiers (1356), in French; all in the *Letter Books of the City of London*. For a discussion of the significance of letters see Galbraith's Introduction to *Anonimale Chronicle*, p. xxxv.

100 *Margery Kempe's Book*, ed. S. B. Meech and H. E. Allen for EETS no. 212 (London 1914) gives a good idea of current speech from the King's Lynn region.

101 From the *Stonor Letters and Papers 1290–1483*, ed. C. L. Kingsford (London 1919). There is an interesting letter from brother Edmund de Stonor to Edmund de Stonor about the latter's son: his illness, and his progress in preparatory school. He is learning his Donatus 'lente et modeste' in a school run by a married schoolmaster. Dated *c*. 1380, it is in Latin. Many of the fourteenth-century Stonor letters deal with litigation and property. The Stonors were great landowners in several counties, typical of the gentry. Most early letters of the Stonors are for or from Edmund de Stonor, sheriff of Oxfordshire and Berkshire, 1377–8, Knight of the Shire for Oxfordshire in 1380, January, Parliament. In 1380 he was on commission to inquire into lands of St Frideswide's Priory, Oxford. He was a commissioner of peace for Oxfordshire and in 1380–1 was a commissioner against (Lollard?) unlawful assemblies (see ch. 5 below). He suffered from the 'peasants' revolt', 1381, when rebels burned his charters and muniments. 'His career was simply that of a country gentleman living on his estates and discharging such public duties as fell to his lot' (p. xvii) (C. L. Kingsford). The Stonors were raised to public prominence by chief justice of the King's Bench John de Stonor (d. 1354), but thereafter none had a public career of any importance. They maintained their wealth through land and good marriages. They served as sheriffs

and parliamentary representatives (pp. xxxviii–xxxix), and they wrote numerous letters in French and Latin, mostly formal, but a few of a private nature that was to become increasingly common in the fifteenth century.

102 For a general discussion of the approach of current anthropologists see Jack Goody and Ian Watt (eds.), *Literacy in Traditional Societies*, and in particular the chapter, 'The consequences of literacy' (Cambridge 1968). See below, ch. 4.

103 French seems to have maintained its hold in the law courts despite this parliamentary agreement. See M. D. Legge, 'Anglo-Norman and the historian', *History*, vol. 26 (1941–2), on the ineffectiveness of the act. The reason given in the *Statutes of the Realm*, I, 375 (1362) for English to be used for pleading in the courts is that 'according to reason the said laws and customs would the sooner be learned and known and better understood in the native tongue, so that everyone could the better conduct himself without breaking the law and the better safeguard his inheritance and possessions. The said pleas will be enrolled in Latin.'

104 Many of the above examples are given by Holmes, p. 64.

105 Cited by John Barnie, *War in Medieval English Society: Social Values and the Hundred Years War 1337–99* (London 1974); *RP*, vol. 2, pp. 147, 158. It is thought that the growth of the English language and patriotic sentiment became generally associated with one another. Even among the aristocracy at the royal court, French as spoken in France was in decline in the last decade of the century, as is made clear by the linguistic problems over the peace treaty negotiations in 1393. Froissart tells of the close scrutiny of the French proposals by the English embassy, led by the Dukes of Gloucester and Lancaster, who said that 'the French they learnt at home during their childhood was not of the same nature as that of France and which legists used in their agreements and conferences'. Froissart, *Oeuvres*, vol. 15, pp. 114f., as cited by Barnie, p. 100.

106 George Unwin, *The Gilds and Companies of London*, 2nd ed. (London 1925); Sylvia Thrupp, *The Merchant Class of Medieval London* (London 1948); E. Carus-Wilson, *Medieval Merchant-Venturers* (London 1967); Elspeth Veale, 'Craftsmen and the economy of London in the fourteenth century', in A. Hollaender and W. Kellaway (eds.), *Studies in London History* (London 1969); A. R. Myers, *London in the Age of Chaucer* (London 1972); Colin Platt, *The English Medieval Town* (London 1976).

107 R. R. Sharpe (ed.), *Calendar of Letter Books of London, H 1375–99* (London 1899–1907).

108 *Piers Plowman*, B III, ll. 76–86 (C IV, ll. 76–118):

Meires and maceres . that menes ben bitwene   mayors, mace
                                                          bearers
The Kynge and the comune . to kepe the lawes.
To punyschen on pillories . and pynynge stoles   punishment stools
Brewesteres and bakesteres . bocheres and cokes;
For thise aren men on this molde . that moste harme worcheth
To the pore peple . that parcel-mele buggen.   buy piecemeal
   For thei poysoun the peple . priveliche and oft,
Thei rychen thorw regraterye . and rentes hem buggen   charging
                                                     interest; collect
With that the pore people . shulde put in here wombe;   stomach
For toke thei on trewly . thei tymbred nouȝt so heiȝe,
Ne bouȝte non burgages . be ȝe ful certeyne.
   [For if they were honest they would not build such large timbered
houses; Nor would they buy property.]

109 A. R. Myers, 'The wealth of Richard Lyons', in T. A. Sandquist
     and M. Powicke (eds.), *Essays in Medieval History Presented to
     Bertie Wilkinson* (Toronto 1969), pp. 301–29. Ruth Bird, *The
     Turbulent London of Richard II* (London 1949).
110 Cited by Unwin, p. 194.
111 On the Feste du Pui see the *Liber Custumarum*, vol. 1, pp. 216–28
     in *Munimenta Gildhallae Londoniensis*, vol. 2, pt 1, *Rerum Britan-
     nicarum Medii Aevi Scriptores* (London 1859).
112 Francis Steer, *Scriveners' Company Common Paper 1357–1428*
     (London 1968) p. x.
113 One Thomas Pantier, a foreigner, who set up in business although
     he was not qualified – he was a hireling with a scrivener for two
     years but never apprenticed – was sent to the pillory during the
     mayoralty of Adam Bamme (1390–1). Steer, pp. x and 3.
114 ibid., pp. x, 4–5.
115 *Wynnere and Wastoure*, ed. I. Gollancz (London 1920).

Chapter 3: The literature of social unrest

  1 N. Denholm-Young, *The Country Gentry in the Fourteenth Cen-
     tury* (Oxford 1969), p. 2. Beaumont was not on good terms with
     Archbishop Melton of York, whom he tried to prevent carrying
     out a lawful visitation with the use of violence, hiring an army of
     excommunicated robbers and thieves: *Register Melton*, fo. 489v;
     cited by R. M. T. Hill, 'Uncovenanted blessings of ecclesiastical
     records', *Studies in Church History*, vol. 11 (1975), pp. 142–3.
     Could this slander about his illiteracy reflect the troubled rela-
     tions between Beaumont and the Church? Kathleen Edwards

showed that he was maligned, in 'Bishops and learning in the reign of Edward II', *Church Quarterly Review*, vol. 38 (1944), pp. 62–4.

2　K. B. McFarlane, *The Nobility of Later Medieval England* (Oxford 1973), p. 273.

3　The use of the lesser earls, barons and country gentry in local administration was supported early by Edward III. Adam Murimuth's *Chronicle* notes how Edward III, having abandoned the siege of Tournai for lack of finance, returned to England in 1340 to inquire into the management of tax collection for the war effort. In each county he appointed a chief justice, 'with whom he associated others of middle condition'. He took counsel of younger men and revised local government. This is mentioned in an interesting Latin poem which refers to Edward's time as a golden age, when the king was religious, good to the monks, victorious in war; he revised the laws in favour of the people and laboured to remove bandits and all transgressors of the law. See T. Wright, *Political Poems and Songs* (London 1859–61), vol. 1, pp. 222–3.

4　From Walsingham's *Chronicon Angliae*: 'When the peasants and common people grew in number so that they feared resistance from none, they began to punish all and sundry learned in the law, both apprentices and justices, and all jurors of the countryside whom they could lay hands on ... declaring that the realm could not enjoy its natural liberty until such men were slain.'

5　For information on Chaucer's life see Martin Crow and Clair Olson, *Chaucer Life-Records* (Oxford 1966).

6　Denholm-Young, p. 27.

7　K. B. McFarlane, 'Parliament and "bastard feudalism" ', *Transactions of the Royal Historical Society*, 4th series, vol. 26 (1944), pp. 53–79; see especially pp. 64–70, and p. 68.

8　ibid., p. 69.

9　ibid., *passim*.

10　See E. L. G. Stone, 'The Folevilles of Ashby Foleville, Leicestershire, and their associates in crime, 1326–1347', *Transactions of the Royal Historical Society*, vol. 7 (1957), pp. 117–36.

11　In general see Ralph Pugh, *Imprisonment in Medieval England* (Cambridge 1968). J. R. Maddicott, 'The birth and setting of the ballads of Robin Hood', *English Historical Review*, vol. 93 (1978), pp. 276–99, suggests the *Gest* of Robin Hood is historically based rather than being based on earlier literature or myth. The wicked abbot was probably Thomas le Multon, Abbot of St Mary's, York (1332–59); Geoffrey Le Scrope, the abbot's retainer. The action takes place in Barnsdale, Yorkshire.

12 See Elizabeth Salter, *'Piers Plowman and The Simonie'*, *Archiv fur das Studium der neuern Sprachen und Literaturen*, vol. 203 (1967), pp. 241–54. Remarks along these lines were also made in the Cambridge University English faculty 'circus' on *Piers Plowman*, 1977. Also see Charles Muscatine, *Poetry and Crisis in the Age of Chaucer* (London 1972): 'The great artistic schemes that Langland attempts and abandons had all been adapted before him to expressing the security of the medieval Christian vision. His failure with them, his failure to organise and "see" by means of them, suggests that for a man of his sensitivity, responding to the culture around him, those schemes had lost their meaning. For him, the road to the New Jerusalem has become newly devious, the structure of the moral world newly problematical. . . . [The poem] carries the instability of the epoch in its very structure and style as well as in its argument' (p. 107). I myself am not so certain that the structure and style is as shaky and disordered as Muscatine believes, although I think it is clear that Langland's subject matter is centred on man's spiritual disorientation amidst social crisis.

13 See R. H. Robbins, 'Poems dealing with contemporary conditions', in Albert Hartung (ed.), *Manual of the Writings in Middle English 1050–1500* (Connecticut 1975), vol. 5, p. 1387. This is the continuation of Wells's *Manual*.

14 ibid., p. 1386.

15 For an account of the trials and tribulations of Walter Brut see K. B. McFarlane, *John Wycliffe and the Beginnings of English Nonconformity* (London 1952), pp. 134–5.

16 Brut was tried by the Bishop of Hereford, 1391–3.

17 Noted by C. T. Allmand, 'The war and the non-combatant' in K. Fowler (ed.), *The Hundred Years War, Problems in Focus Series* (London 1971), p. 176, citing *The Register of John Trefnant, Bishop of Hereford* (1389–1404), ed. W. W. Capes (Hereford 1914).

18 Noted by Sylvia Thrupp, who draws the parallel with late medieval society: 'Hierarchy, illusion and social mobility', *Comparative Studies in Society and History*, vol. 2 (1959–60) pp. 126–8.

19 Denholm-Young, pp. 6–7.

20 See the argument in Alan MacFarlane, *The Origins of English Individualism: The Family, Property and Social Transition* (Oxford 1978).

21 H. Pirenne, *Medieval Cities* (Princeton 1925, 1956); see the chapter on the middle class, pp. 93–5f.

22   Rodney Hilton, *The English Peasantry in the Later Middle Ages* (Oxford 1975), p. 85. Also see the collection of essays edited by Hilton: *The Transition from Feudalism to Capitalism* (London 1976).

23   V. J. Scattergood, *Politics and Poetry in the Fifteenth Century* (London 1971), ch. 10, pp. 350–78.

24   ibid.

25   See Anne Hudson's remarks in the Introduction to her *Selections from English Wycliffite Writings* (Cambridge 1978), p. 12. But Norman Blake has argued that because there is little formal distinction between alliterative poetry and prose, the two must be considered simultaneously; see N. F. Blake, 'Middle English alliterative revivals', *Review*, no. 1 (1979), pp. 205–14.

26   On this point see Derek Pearsall, *John Lydgate* (London 1970), p. 10.

27   See Anne Middleton, 'The idea of public poetry in the reign of Richard II', *Speculum*, vol. 53 (1978), pp. 94–114, who notes that 'the complex experiments of Langland and Gower were not derived from earlier Latin satire or pulpit oratory, to which they are sometimes compared' (p. 107).

28   See n. 13 above.

29   Robbins, p. 1401.

30   See below, ch. 4.

31   See M. Wilks, 'Reformatio regni: Wyclif and Hus as leaders of religious protest movements', *Studies in Church History*, vol. 9 (1972), pp. 109–30.

32   Hudson, *Selections*, p. 13.

33   Dorothy Owen, 'Ecclesiastical jurisdiction in England 1300–1500: the records and their interpretation', *Studies in Church History*, vol. 11 (1975), pp. 199–221.

34   Friar's Tale, *Canterbury Tales*, ll. 1301–10.

35   B. L. Woodcock, *Medieval Ecclesiastical Courts in the Diocese of Canterbury* (Oxford 1952); this is the best general account of medieval church courts.

36   Dieter Mehl, *The Middle English Romances of the Thirteenth and Fourteenth Centuries* (London 1968).

37   ibid., pp. 17–18.

38   Suggested by R. M. Wilson, *The Lost Literature of Medieval England* (London 1952), pp. 114f.

39   Carleton Brown and Rossell Hope Robbins (Brown–Robbins), *The Index of Middle English Verse* (New York 1943), no. 3428.

40   Mehl, p. 19.

41   Text in Latin, 15 March 1346, in Rymer, *Foedera*, III. Barbara Harvey has also noted how the Benedictine chapter required

their preachers to be trained in the vernacular as well as in Latin, so that by the fourteenth century even the provincial chapter occasionally heard chosen preachers in English, and the public was admitted to these religious and socially conscious sermons. Barbara Harvey, 'The monks of Westminster and the University of Oxford', in F. DuBoulay and C. Barron (eds.), *The Reign of Richard II: Essays in honour of May McKisack* (London 1971), pp. 118–19; citing W. Pantin, *Documents Illustrating the Activities of the General and Provincial Chapters of the English Black Monks* (Camden third ser.), vol. 2, p. 15.

42 National hostility to the French was expressed early. See MS Harley 2253, *On the Flemish Insurrection*, printed in T. Wright, *The Political Songs of England* (London 1839), pp. 187–95. The battle is dated 1302 and the poem must have been written soon after.

43 T. Wright, *Political Poems and Songs*, vol. 1, p. xxviii.

44 See below, Gower's *Vox Clamantis*, from *The Major Latin Works of John Gower* (Seattle 1962), annotated translation into English by Eric W. Stockton. Citations in English are from this work.

45 T. Wright, *Political Poems and Songs*, vol. 1, p. xxvi.

46 ibid., p. 79.

47 ibid., p. 67.

48 ibid., p. 70.

49 ibid., p. 70.

50 ibid., p. 79.

51 ibid., p. 80.

52 ibid., p. 80.

53 ibid., p. 81.

54 ibid., p. 82.

55 ibid., p. 83.

56 ibid., p. 90.

57 John Barnie, *War in Medieval English Society: Social Values and the Hundred Years War 1337–1399* (London 1974), p. 72. Compare Walsingham, *Historia Anglicana* for 1348: 'Edward III had secured peace for England and there was an abundance of goods. There was no woman of account who did not possess something of the spoils of Calais, Caen, and other French cities: garments, furs, pillows, household utensils, tablecloths, necklaces, gold and silver cups, linen sheets, were in all the great houses throughout England. The English ladies prided themselves on their French clothes.' This pride in luxurious clothes was shared by the Commons, and in the 1360s sumptuary laws were passed with minute regulations drawn up for the apparel of all ranks.

58 Barnie, p. 82.

59   ibid. p. 119.
60   Froissart, *Oeuvres*, vol. 15, ed. K. de Lettenhove (Brussels 1863), p. 155.
61   Philippe de Mézières, *Le Songe du Vieil Pèlerin*, ed. G. W. Coopland (2 vols., Cambridge 1969), vol. 1, pp. 395–403.
62   Sir John Clanvowe, *The Two Ways*, in *The Works of Sir John Clanvowe*, ed. V. J. Scattergood (Cambridge 1975). ll. 484–90, where he condemns war and slaughter.
63   Bodleian, Vernon MS fo. 410v. See K. Sajavaara, 'The relationship of the Vernon and Simeon MSS', *Neuphilologische Mitteilungen*, vol. 68 (1967), pp. 428–39; also N. S. Baugh, *A Worcester Miscellany*, compiled by John Northwood *c.* 1400, edited from BM MS Add. 37787 (Philadelphia 1956).
64   R. H. Robbins (ed.), *Historical Poems of the Fourteenth and Fifteenth Centuries* (New York 1959), no. 39.
65   Elizabeth Salter, 'Piers Plowman and The Simonie', *Archiv für das Studium der neuern Sprachen und Literaturen*, vol. 203 (1967), pp. 241–54.
66   Wright, *Political Poems and Songs*, suggested the Benedictine of Leominster. But for a discussion see I. Aspin (ed.), *Anglo-Norman Political Songs from Harley 2253* (Oxford 1953); here are examples of English/French and French/Latin macaronic verse up to the mid fourteenth century (pp. 24–5 and 105–7). M. D. Legge, *Anglo-Norman Literature* (Oxford 1963), p. 353, notes how 'there exists so much macaronic verse and so much bilingual too, that it is possible that two versions of (for instance) Langtoft's English and French songs existed'.
67   See Aspin, pp. 108–11.
68   The argument in verse is not unlike many of the points made by the knight Peter de la Mare at the October 1377 Parliament (*RP*, vol. 3, p. 5). He suggests that a committee of eight sufficient persons be established to be in continual attendance at the king's council, so that mischief is not done, 'In such a way that the commons may be clearly certified of the names of these councillors, who shall have the spending and ordaining of what they will grant for the wars, and so the commons may have more confidence in that which they are charged to do. . . . And that what shall be granted for the maintenance of the war be expended on the war, and not otherwise, in aid and discharge of this said commons.' Also, in the proceedings of the Gloucester Parliament, 1378, the Commons were pressed for yet another war subsidy, but they pleaded poverty. They asked that the king show them how, and in what manner the previously granted great sums of money were spent (*RP*, vol. 3, p. 33). 'The king agreed to show

the commons the receipts and expenses, not as their right or by
compulsion, but from his own will to show these things.'

69 Compare the early *Song of the Husbandman*, also from Harley
2253: 'that er werede robes, nou wereth ragges'.

70 Aspin, p. 107. Translations of the following extracts are from
Aspin.

71 See R. Higden, *Polychronicon*; ed. J. R. Lumby and C. Babington (London 1883), p. 334 under 1339: 'such plenty of
goods and scarcity of money that one quarter of wheat was fetch-
ing at London [only] two shillings and a fat ox [only] half a
mark'. Also Adam Murimuth, *Continuatio Chronicarum*, ed. E.
M. Thompson (London 1889), p. 89, speaks of low prices and
abundance of corn but lack of money.

72 Aspin, pp. 107–8. See also E. B. Fryde, 'Parliament and the
French War 1336–40', *Essays . . . B. Wilkinson*, ed. T. A. Sandquist and M. Powicke (Toronto 1969), pp. 250–69, for a discussion of the resistance to war subsidies and taxes in the Commons.
The resentment at the heavy war taxes combined with demands
for the redress of grievances (*RP*, vol. 2, pp. 104–5) was expressed by knights and burgesses possibly for the first time in so
determined a manner, and collectors of the fifteenths and tenths
in 1339–40 experienced great difficulties. Fryde asks if, apart
from discussions of subsidies, the magnates and Commons were
allowed to debate seriously the issues of peace and war (pp.
253f.). There was a parliamentary agreement for setting up an
English wool company which promised to finance the war (Stam-
ford 1337) and later the agreement was confirmed by a more
representative assembly of English businessmen, thus indicating
that England's foreign policy was dependent on its trading middle
class, as the poetry affirmed. Fryde notes that 'it was natural for
an English king in the first half of the fourteenth century to base
his hopes for the financing of a continental coalition on the
exploitation of the wool trade' (p. 257). A large part of the
poorer population was ruined financially by the practice of pur-
veyance (the royal right to buy supplies on credit for the king's
household and armies) during 1336–9, and the Commons
petitioned against such practices. The Commons petition
(undated, *c*. 1337) asserted 'no free man ought to be assessed or
taxed without the common consent of parliament'. See H. G.
Richardson and G. Sayles (eds.), *Rotuli Parliamentorum Anglie
hactenus inediti (1279–1373)*, (London 1935), p. 268.

73 See the mid fourteenth-century Gough Map: Bodleian, Gough
Gen. Top. 16, which is a contemporary record of all the well-
established carting routes radiating from London. F. M. Stenton,

'The road system of medieval England', *Economic History Review*, vol. 7 (1936), p. 21. W. G. Hoskins, *Provincial England* (London 1963), pp. 61–3.

74 J. J. N. Palmer, *England, France and Christendom 1377–99* (London 1972), p. 2.

75 The extent of the problem of the unemployed soldier and the lawless is reflected in Summae for confessors. Angelus de Clavasio, *Summa*: on restitution for murder, following the early fourteenth-century theologian Duns Scotus, who teaches that the murderers are to labour for the rest of their lives against heretics or infidels, or else spend it in prayer, almsgiving, etc. These penances are to be imposed by the confessor. Cited by T. Tentler, 'The summa for confessors', in H. Oberman and C. Trinkaus (eds.), *The Pursuit of Holiness in the Later Middle Ages* (Leiden, 1974), p. 121.

76 Scattergood suggests it was more likely a pilgrimage than a crusade for Clanvowe: *The Works of John Clanvowe*, ed. V. J. Scattergood (Cambridge 1975), p. 27.

77 Philippe de Mézières, *Letter to King Richard II (Epistre au roi Richard), a plea made in 1395 for peace between England and France*, ed. and introduction and trans. G. W. Coopland (Liverpool 1975).

78 ibid., fo. 15v, and p. 14 translation.

79 ibid., fo. 31r, p. 27 translation and p. 100 text.

80 ibid., fo. 59r, p. 51 translation.

81 ibid., fos. 61r–61v, pp. 52–3 translation.

82 Palmer, p. 188.

83 In Wright, *Political Poems and Songs*, vol. 2, p. 10.

84 In Wright, *Political Poems and Songs*, vol. 1, pp. 356–63: *De lucis scrutinio*.

85 Gower, Prologue, *Confessio Amantis*, ll. 22–3.

86 *Confessio Amantis*, IV, ll. 1615f.

87 See J. A. Burrow, *Ricardian Poetry: Chaucer, Gower, Langland and the Gawain Poet* (Oxford 1971), p. 50.

88 *Confessio Amantis*, III, ll. 2251f; and Burrow, p. 56. Also, *Confessio Amantis*, III, ll. 2490–6:

Sone myn,
To preche and soffre for the feith,
That have I herd the Gospell seith;
But forto slee, that hiere I noght.

In *Confessio Amantis* IV, ll. 1608ff., the lover has no interest other than his lady, and argues against the holy war; given Gower's support of the crusade elsewhere, this should be taken as irony or as written to order for a patron whose views were against all warfare.

That <u>me were levere</u> hir love winne	I would prefer

Than kaire and al that is thereinne;
And forto slen the hethen alle,
I not what good ther mihte falle,
So muchel blod thogh ther be schad.
This finde I writen, hou Crist bad
That noman other scholde sle.
What scholde I winne over the se
If I mi ladi loste at hom? . . .
A Sarazin if I sle schal,
I sle the soule forth withal,
And that was nevere Cristes lore.

This very much echoes the opinions of the Lollards.

89 Burrow, p. 57.
90 The complaint against the worthiness of contemporary knights is, in the views of many, a *topos* from St Bernard in the twelfth century onwards. Larry Benson, in his chapter, 'Fifteenth-century chivalry' in Malory's *Morte D'Arthur* (Cambridge, Mass. 1976), argues that chivalry as a way of life was always more a literary convention than a realistic guide to historical behaviour of any period in which the ideal operated. There is, however, something more significant about these fourteenth-century complaints about 'the lost light of chivalry', as I try to show.
91 See Mehl, p. 4.
92 P. Gradon has pointed out that Gower's satirical mode in the complaint prologue to his *Confessio Amantis* is akin to the romance mode in that it involves posings and exemplifications of a standard against which actuality is to be measured. Likewise, anticurial satire is essentially of the same kind, contrasting courtly life with the honest and simple life. Pamela Gradon, *Form and Style in Early English Literature* (London 1971), p. 319.
93 Matthieu de Vendôme, *Ars Versificatoria*, ed. E. Faral (Paris 1924), p. 154.
94 J. Kail (ed.), *Twenty-Six Political and Other Poems (Digby 102)*, EETS o.s. 124 (London 1904). This poem is no. 2 in this collection, pp. 6–9.
95 Mehl, pp. 6 and 264, n. 15.
96 In fact, in the presumably late fourteenth-century Northern *Sir Degrevant* (Thornton MS Lincoln Cathedral Lib. A.5.2 and Cambridge University Lib. Ff I.6) we have a picture of the ideal Christian knight who is religious, fights in the Holy Land before

he courts Melidor, and returns there to die a martyr after her death. It is less surprising to find this in a romance written in the North, where a more strictly feudal form of society with chivalric ideals survived longer than in the South, but Sir Degrevant's piety is characteristic of the English romance, even though there is no discussion of war as anything other than ennobling. Compare the 'travaylyng man's' attitude to the tenth conclusion from 'The Twelve Conclusions of the Lollards' (printed in Hudson, pp. 24f.):

The tenth conclusion is that manslaughter by battle or pretense [?] law of righteousness for temporal cause or spiritual without special revelation is express contrarious to the New Testament, the which is a law of grace and full of mercy. [This is taught by Christ's earthly preaching], the which most taught for to love and to have mercy on his enemies, and not for to slay them. The reason is of this that for the more party where men fight, after the first stroke, charity is broken. . . . It is an holy robbing of the poor people when lords purchase indulgences *a pena et a culpa* to them that help to his host and gather to slay the Christian men in far lands for temporal goods, as we have seen. And knights that run to heathen [lands] to get themselves a name in slaying of men get much less of the king of peace, for by meakness and suffrance our belief was multiplied and fighters and manslayers Jesu Christ hates and threatens. [p. 28]

97   Compare Gower, *Vox Clamantis*, VI, ch. 5: 'O you [judge] who are greedy for everything, why do you abandon yourself? You own everything that is on earth but you do not possess yourself. O you who know others but not yourself, you, known to one and all, you do not know that your knowledge is worth nothing to you. Therefore, know yourself first and me second. . . .' (from E. W. Stockton translation; cf. n. 44 above).
98   Digby 102, fo. 101v, no. 4 in Kail.
99   Compare Gower, *Vox Clamantis* VI, ch. 10: 'Let noble and peasant bear an equal burden, and let nothing violate a secret at your hands.'
100   Digby 102, fo. 103v. no. 5 in Kail.
101   Robbins, *Historical Poems of the Fourteenth and Fifteenth Centuries*, no. 13.
102   Digby 102, fo. 100, no. 3 in Kail.
103   Compare Gower, *Vox Clamantis*, V, ch. 16: 'As long as the talkative fellow, Talebearer, dwells in the city, he utters many slanders in abuse of people.'
104   Digby 102; in Kail, p. ix. 'This makes us understand his rather

detailed knowledge of the proceedings in parliament and his lively interest in the cause of the commons.'

105   R. H. Robbins, 'Middle English Poems of Protest', *Anglia*, vol. 78 (1960), pp. 193–203; p. 198. But note, the Commons were not peasants but the gentry, knights and burgesses.

106   In Wright, *Political Poems and Songs*, vol. 1, pp. 270f.

107   Compare the well-known episode in *Piers Plowman* of the belling the cat fable.

108   See *RP*, III, p. 230.

109   J. A. Tuck, 'Richard II's system of patronage', in DuBoulay and Barron, *The Reign of Richard II*.

110   As cited by G. Mathew, *The Court of Richard II* (London 1968), p. 17.

111   ibid., p. 95.

112   Colin Platt, *The English Medieval Town* (London 1976), p. 15, speaks on the one hand of the increase in urban wealth and related political power of cities, and on the other of the surprising (to Italian visitors) small scale of English urbanization until 1500. The rising importance of the 'middle class' by the end of the fourteenth century was as much a rural as an urban phenomenon, with widespread literary significance in both places.

113   *Mum and the Sothsegger*, ed. M. Day and R. Steele, EETS o.s. 199 (1936), and see A. Blamires, 'Mum and the Sothsegger and Langlandian idiom', *Neuphilologische Mitteilungen*, vol. 76 (1975), pp. 583–604, here p. 593.

114   Blamires, p. 593 with reference to *Mum*, ll. 330–49.

115   Blamires, p. 598 and *Mum*, ll. 978f.

116   *Mum*, l. 1065.

117   *Mum*, ll. 1122–3.

118   *Mum*, ll. 1191f.

119   *Mum*, l. 1224.

120   *Mum*, l. 1281.

121   *Mum*, ll. 1457f.

122   In Wright, *Political Songs of England*, pp. 323f.

123   Elizabeth Salter, 'Piers Plowman and the Simonie', *Archiv fur das Studium der neuern Sprachen u. Literaturen*, vol. 23 (1967), pp. 241–54.

124   ibid., pp. 248–9.

125   Compare Gower, *Vox Clamantis*, VI, ch. 7: 'The clergy now blame the people and the people blame the clergy, but both persevere in their guiltiness. Envious of one another, each man blames the other and no group mends its own course.'

126   Printed in Robbins, *Historical Poems of the Fourteenth and Fifteenth Centuries*.

127 Printed in Wright, *Political Poems and Songs*, vol. 1, p. 137.

128 W. W. Skeat (ed.), *Richard the Redeless* printed with his edition of *Piers the Plowman* (Oxford 1886; 1965), pp. 603–28.

129 Compare Gower, *Vox Clamantis*, VI, ch. 10: 'Let an elderly man render justice to the people and let respect be demanded, where there is maturity well versed in just laws. And yet – even though the man himself be young, he whose wisdom confirms his mature intelligence is old enough. I do not approve of either old-fashioned, hidebound intellects or of fatuous youth; maturity does not confer her privileges thus. Very often a dotard has a juvenile character while a young fellow exhibits the behaviour of an elderly man. You should, therefore, examine both ages quite circumspectly, good king.'

130 See Millard Meiss, *Painting in Florence and Siena after the Black Death* (Princeton 1951).

131 A. C. Spearing, *Medieval Dream-Poetry* (Cambridge 1976), p. 5.

132 Elizabeth Kirk, *The Dream Thought of Piers Plowman* (New Haven 1972), p. 17.

133 In his *Secular Lyrics of the Fourteenth and Fifteenth Centuries*, 2nd ed. (London 1955), Robbins says the secular lyrics had some small circulation; for instance, Friars' miscellanies contained such lyrics, but after the Black Death Harley 2253 was forgotten. 'There is not a single later lyric that shows any influence of this or any other 'friar' anthology. Harley 2253 is only one part of Middle English poetry and not the most enduring one. When the secular lyric threads are picked up again they go elsewhere – they do not lead back to Harley 2253' (p. lii.). We must remember that Harley 2253 comprises not secular love lyrics alone but political complaint poetry in English and French, and has much in common with later fourteenth-century complaint verse and with fifteenth-century secular poetry, of which Lydgate was the prime and most popular example. See especially Lydgate's *Regement*.

134 The standard work on Gower is John H. Fisher, *John Gower, Moral Philosopher and Friend of Chaucer* (London 1965); see also J. H. Fisher, 'A calendar of documents relating to the life of John Gower, the poet', *Journal of English and Germanic Philology*, vol. 58 (1959), pp. 1–23.

135 Many of these thirteenth-century ideals were to be found in fourteenth-century handbooks and compilations, often gathered together for and by preachers. See below, ch. 4.

136 *Vox Clamantis*, VII, 1469f.

137 John H. Fisher, 'Chancery and the emergence of standard written English in the fifteenth century', *Speculum*, vol. 52 (1977), pp. 870–99, has a brief discussion of the chancery clerks and their

linguistic abilities.

138 Maria Wickert, *Studien zu John Gower* (Cologne 1953).
139 See Fisher, *John Gower*; Fisher also reminds us that Gower's use of the imagery of light and illumination in *De Lucis Scrutinio* (n. 84 above) is even more striking when we realize it was written when he was losing his own sight; cf. p. 130.
140 Fisher, *John Gower*, Preface, p.v.
141 ibid., p. 36.
142 ibid., pp. 80–1.
143 *Vox Clamantis*, I, ch. 14.
144 John Gower, *Mirour de l'Omme (Speculum Meditantis) on current abuses (1376–79)*, ed. G. C. Macaulay (Oxford 1901).
145 Fisher, *John Gower*, p. 97.
146 *Vox Clamantis*, IV, ch. 19.
147 *Cronica Tripertita*, is translated after the *Vox* in Eric Stockton's *The Major Latin Works of John Gower* (Seattle 1962).
148 Fisher, *John Gower*, p. 106.
149 Referred to by Fisher, *John Gower*, p. 111.
150 ibid., p. 136.
151 ibid., p. 144.
152 ibid.
153 ibid., p. 183.
154 ibid., p. 189.
155 ibid., p. 178.
156 *The Major Latin Works of John Gower, Vox Clamantis and Tripartita Chronicle*, trans. Eric W. Stockton (Seattle 1962).
157 See below, ch. 5.
158 This work was translated into English by Trevisa in the 1370s.
159 See John Hatcher, *Plague, Population and the English Economy 1348–1530* (London 1977).
160 See McFarlane, *Nobility of Later Medieval England* and G. A. Holmes, *The Estates of the Higher Nobility in Fourteenth Century England* (Cambridge 1957). Also, K. B. McFarlane, *Lancastrian Kings and Lollard Knights* (Oxford 1972) and Denholm-Young, *Country Gentry in the Fourteenth Century*.
161 For an account of the Appellants and their policy see Anthony Goodman, *The Loyal Conspiracy 1355–97, the Lords Appellant under Richard II* (London 1971), also J. A. Tuck, *Richard II and the English Nobility* (London 1973).
162 See Mathew, *Court of Richard II*, where he notes that Richard modelled his reign and personal image on the imperial ceremonial of the Luxemburg house, namely his wife, Anne of Bohemia's family. Richard's model was her father Charles IV (p. 17). Anthony Tuck, in the *Listener* (30 January 1977, p. 850),

noted the friendship between Richard and Charles VI of France. The absolutist ideas and the sense of sacred majesty of kingship were more ingrained in the French court than in the English, and Richard's 'absolutist' political ideas seem to have developed in the 1390s. It was then that Charles VI of France and Richard planned their joint crusade to recover the Holy Land from the Turks. See the discussion above, concerning Philippe de Mézières's letter to Richard and his crusading Order of the Passion. Tuck notes that it was the French court influence that created the milieu out of which the Wilton diptych emerged.

Chapter 4: Memory, preaching and the literature of a society in transition

1 Plato's *Phaedrus*, in *Plato* (Loeb ed.), trans. H. N. Fowler (London 1921–9), vol. 1, 274C–275B: '. . . for they will read many things without instruction and will therefore seem to know many things when they are for the most part ignorant. . . .'

2 Karl Popper, *Objective Knowledge: An Evolutionary Approach* (Oxford 1972; rev. ed. 1979).

3 S. Scribner and M. Cole, 'Literacy without schooling: testing for intellectual effects', Vai Literacy Project Working Paper no. 2 (Rockefeller University, New York 1978).

4 Jack Goody notes that anthropologists have more recently shied away from using these two strict, antithetical categories, mythical and logico-empirical, but he argues that they still have some use. 'The consequences of literacy', in J. Goody and I. Watt (eds.), *Literacy in Traditional Societies* (Cambridge 1968). For an interesting discussion of the role of literacy in ancient Greece, see this study.

5 Bracton, *De Legibus et Consuetudinibus Angliae*, ed. G. E. Woodbine; reissued with English translation by Samuel Thorn (Cambridge, Mass. 1968–77).

6 See M. T. Clanchy, *From Memory to Written Record, England 1066–1307* (London 1979), p. 27.

7 See below, ch. 5.

8 Goody and Watt, p. 48.

9 Preface to his translation of Higden's *Polychronicon*, ed. E. Babington and J. Lumby (London 1883).

10 R. W. Chambers, *On the Continuity of English Prose from Alfred to More and his School*, EETS (1932); extract from Introduction to *Nicholas Harpsfield's Life of Sir Thomas More*, ed. E. V. Hitchcock and R. W. Chambers, p. cxvi.

11 Margaret Aston, *Thomas Arundel* (Oxford 1967), p. 326; Cham-

bers, *On the Continuity of English Prose*, p. cxvi.

12 The confession of Thomas of Woodstock, Duke of Gloucester, as an Appellant, in English, *Rolls of Parliament* (*RP*), vol. 3, p. 378. In a brief, mutilated and tampered form this was read to Parliament in 1397. Gloucester died (was murdered?) at Calais after his confession. In general on the significance of English prose see N. F. Blake, *The English Language in Medieval Literature* (London 1977), and N. F. Blake, 'Middle English alliterative revivals', *Review*, vol. 1 (1979), pp. 205–14.

13 The formal renunciation of allegiance addressed to Richard in the Tower by Sir W. Thyrning was in *RP*, vol. 3, p. 424. Parliament 1399 (August): the estates and people accepted Richard's resignation and Henry of Lancaster got up and claimed the kingdom 'in the mother tongue'; *RP*, vol. 3, p. 416.

14 J. H. Fisher, 'Chancery and the emergence of standard written English in the fifteenth century', *Speculum*, vol. 52 (1977), pp. 870–99.

15 Anne Hudson, 'A Lollard sermon cycle and its implications', *Medium Aevum*, vol. 40 (1971), pp. 142–56. See also Margaret Aston, 'Lollardy and literacy', *History*, vol. 62 (1977), pp. 347–71.

16 David C. Fowler, *The Bible in Early English Literature* (London 1977).

17 Anne Hudson, 'Some aspects of Lollard book production', *Studies in Church History*, vol. 9 (Oxford 1972), pp. 149–56.

18 Thorlac Turville-Petre, *The Alliterative Revival* (Cambridge 1977), pp. 20–2.

19 ibid., p. 22.

20 *Wynnere and Wastoure*, ed. I. Gollancz (London 1920), ll. 20–30:

Whylome were lordes in londe þat loued in thaire hertis   once
To here makers of myrthes, þat matirs couthe fynde,
Wyse wordes with-inn, þat wr[iten] were neuer
Ne redde in no romance þat ever renke herde.
Bot now a childe appon <u>chere</u>, with-owtten chyn-wedys
                                       (high) chair
þat neuer wroghte thurgh witt th[ree] wordes to-gedire,
Fro he can jangle als a jaye, and japes [can] telle,
He schall be levede and louede and lett of a while
Wele more þan þe man that ma[kes] hym-selven.
Bot neuer þe lattere at the laste, when ledys bene knawen,
Werke witnesse will bere who <u>wirche kane</u> beste.   can work

21 Turville-Petre, p. 31.

22   ibid., pp. 35f.
23   Ruth Finnegan, *Oral Poetry, Its Nature, Significance and Social Context* (Cambridge 1977). F. Magoun in L. E. Nicholson (ed.), *An Anthology of Beowulf Criticism* (Notre Dame 1971), p. 190.
24   Larry Benson, 'The literary character of Anglo-Saxon formulaic poetry', *Publications of the Modern Language Association (PMLA)*, no. 81 (1966).
25   Goody and Watt, pp. 48–9.
26   See Marie Boroff, *Sir Gawain and the Green Knight: A Stylistic and Metrical Study* (New Haven 1962). Ruth Finnegan is sceptical about a stable enough notion of 'formula' to enable any meaningful calculation to be performed. See above, n. 23.
27   For a summary and application of Parry's work (1930) see A. Lord, *The Singer of Tales* (Cambridge, Mass. 1960).
28   V. H. Galbraith, *Studies in the Public Records* (London 1948), p. 26: 'Early society is ordered and governed by oral tradition. . . . Then there is a long twilight of transition, during which the written record encroaches more and more upon the sphere of custom. In this way the volume of written evidence available steadily increases until we reach a time – not I think earlier than the thirteenth century – when most of the society's major activities find some sort of written record. . . .' Cited by Clanchy, p. 4. Galbraith wants to show that with the beginnings of official archives (Latin) in the thirteenth century we pass from the traditional, oral society to the age of the record. For the consequences of this literacy to filter down to the laity – not only in terms of Latin documents recording land tenure, for instance, but to be incorporated in vernacular literature by and for the laity – we need to wait until the fourteenth century.
29   Turville-Petre, p. 35.
30   Finnegan, p. 237.
31   A. J. Spearing, *Medieval Dream-Poetry* (Cambridge 1976). He wants to link this new consciousness of the increasing role of didactic literature as a mirror of the contrast between the social 'is' and the 'ought' of 'moral sentence' with the appearance of dream poetry. He does not want to classify this consciousness as 'a completely distinct literary kind', but rather sees it as a consciousness of writers working within a distinct literary tradition of dreams and visions: p. 3.
32   Finnegan, p. 160 (my emphasis).
33   Spearing, p. 44.
34   ibid., pp. 119f.
35   As cited by Finnegan, p. 237.
36   ibid., p. 253.

37　See E. A. Havelock, *Preface to Plato* (Oxford 1963).

38　Elizabeth Salter, 'Medieval poetry and the figural view of reality', *Proceedings of the British Academy*, vol. 54 (1968), pp. 73–92; p. 85.

39　For an amusing summary of the variety of interpretations of *Sir Gawain*, see the essay by G. Kane in *Essays and Studies*, n.s., vol. 29 (1976).

40　R. Scholes and R. Kellogg, *The Nature of Narrative* (New York 1966), p. 13.

41　ibid., p. 112.

42　See, for example, the differing attitudes to the salvation of the righteous heathen in the B and C texts, discussed below, ch. 5.

43　The violence of the Rohan master and the explicit sufferings of Christ in German and Spanish later fourteenth- and fifteenth-century art is paralleled with late medieval (fifteenth-century?) meditation and prayer manuscripts for devout readers. See John Hirsch, 'Prayer and meditation in late medieval England: Ms Bodley 789', *Medium Aevum*, vol. 48 (1979), pp. 55–66.

44　It is interesting that when Peter Waldo, the rich heretic of Lyons, had two priests work on a translation of the Bible in the thirteenth century, Waldo then memorized the translations and preached to the poor from memory; in turn, he taught village people the gospel by heart even though they were simple, illiterate men and women, and they then went out and preached in houses and open places. *Anecdotes Historiques . . . Etienne de Bourbon*, ed. A. Lecoy de la Marche for La Société de l'Histoire de France (1877), p. 291; cited in Margaret Deanesly, *The Lollard Bible and Other Medieval Biblical Versions* (Cambridge 1920; reprinted 1966), p. 26. The emphasis on memory skills among the illiterate was described by Etienne de Bourbon:

For I myself have seen a young cowherd who for the space of only a year stayed in the house of a certain Waldensian heretic, who learned by heart and retained forty of the Sunday gospels (without counting the feast days) and he had learnt all these in his own tongue word for word, apart from other words of sermons and prayers. For I have seen some lay people who were so imbued with their teaching that they could repeat by heart much of the evangelists, as for instance, Matthew or Luke . . . so that they would hardly miss a word there, but repeat them in order. [*Anecdotes Historiques . . .*, pp. 307–9; cited in Deanesly, pp. 38–9]

Waldensian 'preaching' appears mainly to have been Bible 'reading' in translation, and it seems that quite a number of the laity *could* read from 'a certain [vernacular] book'.

45   See R. H. Rouse and A. A. Goddu, 'Gerald of Wales and the *Florilegium Angelicum*', *Speculum*, vol. 52 (1977), pp. 488–521.

46   R. H. Rouse and M. A. Rouse, 'The *Florilegium Angelicum*: its origins, content and influence', in *Medieval Learning and Literature: Essays Presented to Richard William Hunt*, ed. J. J. G. Alexander and M. T. Gibson (Oxford 1976).

47   Dated *c.* 1280.

48   They copied the work from *peciae* hired out in instalments from stationers. See Graham Pollard, 'The *pecia* system in the medieval universities', in *Medieval Scribes, Manuscripts and Libraries: Essays presented to N. R. Ker*, ed. M. B. Parkes and Andrew G. Watson (London 1978), pp. 145–62; p. 159.

49   See N. Denholm-Young's edition of Richard de Bury's *Liber Epistolaris* (Roxburghe Club, Oxford 1950).

50   See the discussion by Michael Richter, 'A socio-linguistic approach to the Latin Middle Ages', in *Studies in Church History*, vol. 11 (Oxford 1975), pp. 69–82.

51   Jocelin de Brakelond, *Cronica*, ed. J. G. Rokewode, Camden Society o.s. 13 (London 1840), p. 30; cited by Chambers, p. xciv.

52   *The Exempla or Illustrative Stories from the Sermones Vulgares of Jacques de Vitry*, ed. Thomas F. Crane. Publications of the Folklore Society, vol. 26 (London 1890).

53   An Anglo-Norman rhymed sermon for Ash Wednesday by an anonymous mid thirteenth-century preacher also shows how the clergy were listening to sermons in a mode thought to have been more common for the laity. See Robin F. Jones, 'An Anglo-Norman rhymed sermon for Ash Wednesday', *Speculum*, vol. 54 (1979), pp. 71–84. This sermon is on the 'dust to dust, ashes to ashes' theme. Jones says little on the verse used other than that it reflects how the lower clergy were not literate in Latin, which I believe is not a necessary conclusion to be drawn from this type of sermon circulating in a clerical milieu. Maurice de Sully, *c.* 1170, also preached in the vernacular – see C. A. Robson, *Maurice de Sully* (Oxford 1952).

54   G. R. Owst, *Preaching in Medieval England* (Cambridge 1926), p. 251.

55   From BM MS Royal 17 C viii, fo. 3; also Add. 22283 and Add. 22558.

56   Barbara Harvey, 'The monks of Westminster and the University of Oxford', in F. DuBoulay and C. Barron (eds.), *The Reign of Richard II* (London 1971).

57   ibid., pp. 118–19. Also see W. Pantin, *Documents Illustrating the Activities of the . . . English Black Monks, 1215–1540* (London

1931–3), vol. 2, pp. 15, 60–1; pp. 76, 155.

58 Harvey, p. 119.

59 Richard Excestre, Benedictine, d. 1397, possessed a Bromyard *Summa Praedicantium*, a *Scholastica Historia*, *Excerpta de Viciis et Virtutibus*.

60 *Vita edita a fratre Jordana*, sect. 45 in J. Quétif and J. Echard (eds.), *Scriptores Ordinis Praedicatorum* (Paris 1719–21), vol. 1, p. 23.

61 Jean-Claude Schmitt, 'Receuils Franciscains d'exempla et perfectionnement des techniques intellectuelles du XIIᵉ au XIVᵉ siècle', *Bibliothèque de l'Ecole des Chartes*, vol. 135 (1977), pp. 5–23; p. 9.

62 Owst, *Preaching*, p. 239.

63 ibid., p. 229.

64 Crane, *The Exempla of Jacques de Vitry*, p. lxxii.

65 See the study by Beryl Smalley, *English Friars and Antiquity in the Early Fourteenth Century* (Oxford 1960).

66 Robert A. Pratt, 'Some Latin sources of the Nonnes Preest on dreams', *Speculum*, vol. 52 (1977), pp. 538–70.

67 *Paradiso*, Canto XXIX, ll. 103–20.

68 The *Corpus Hermeticum* has been edited by A. D. Nock and A. J. Festugière (4 vols., Paris 1945–54). Many of the scholars in de Bury's circle mention in their works the name of Hermes Trismegistus, one of the main characters of the hermetic corpus, usually cited as an authority in matters of God's providence and the foreknown future. Selected texts like the *Asclepius* dialogue were known and used in the fourteenth century along with pseudo-hermetic writings to support arguments for divine foreknowledge. For the significance of this issue, see below, ch. 5. The oldest documents in the *Corpus Hermeticum* are astrological treatises of the second century BC; later accretions included a monotheistic cosmology and a Genesis story in the form of a collection of dialogues with the Son of God (Pimander, in *Corp. Herm.*). The *Asclepius* dialogue, known as 'the perfect discourse', was included in its Latin translation from the Greek. See Nock and Festugière, vol. 1, p. iv; also A. J. Festugière, *La Révélation d'Hermes Trismegiste* (Paris 1950–4). Lactantius knew the works in Greek in the third century AD, and Augustine knew something about the corpus and Hermes (probably only in Latin) in the fifth century. Augustine believed Hermes to have been an authentic philosophical personage, and cited from the *Asclepius*; see *City of God*, Book VIII, ch. 29. It is not known when the various dialogues were collected together as a corpus, but by the eleventh century the Greek scholar Michael Psellus knew them as such.

See also P. Kristeller (ed.), *Catalogus translationum et commentariorum* (Washington, DC 1960), vol. 1; the article by K. H. Dannenfeld, 'Hermetica Philosophica', p. 144. Hermes was taken to be a prophet of Christianity by several of the Latin church fathers. De Bury's group seems to have known: *Asclepius* and the *De Verbo Aeterno* (*De VI Rerum Principiis*). The latter has been edited by Theodore Silverstein, 'the liber hermitis de VI rerum principiis', in *Archives d'Histoire Doctrinale et Littéraire du Moyen Age* (1955), vol. 22, pp. 217–302. This work was a twelfth-century pseudo-hermetic text having no contact with the original Greek texts. See H. Oberman, 'Facientibus quod in se est. . . .', *Harvard Theological Review*, no. 55 (1962) for a brief discussion of the use made by Holcot and Bradwardine of the *Corpus Hermeticum* and the reasons de Bury's group did so.

69 Leonard Boyle, 'The date of the *Summa Praedicantium* of John Bromyard', *Speculum*, vol. 48 (1973), pp. 533–7.

70 Thomas N. Tentler, 'The Summa for Confessors as an instrument of social control', in H. Oberman and C. Trinkaus (eds.), *The Pursuit of Holiness in Late Medieval and Renaissance Religion* (Leiden 1974), pp. 103–25; p. 106.

71 ibid., p. 108.

72 See Boyle's commentary on Tentler's argument in Oberman and Trinkaus, p. 128.

73 Owst, p. 228.

74 See Crane edition, p. cxxix, using Bibliothèque Nationale, Paris, MS. Lat. 17, 509 of de Vitry's *Sermones Vulgari*, fo. 100r. See p. 206, n. 142 for another use made of this exemplum.

75 Edinburgh MS Advocates' Library 18.7.21. See partial edition by Edward Wilson, *A Descriptive Index of the English Lyrics in John of Grimestone's Preaching Book*, Medium Aevum monographs (Oxford 1973).

76 Wilson, p. 13.

77 ibid., p. 15.

78 ibid., p. 17; attributed to St Anselm in the MS.

79 ibid., p. 20.

80 ibid., p. 21.

81 ibid., p. 22.

82 ibid., p. 26.

83 Deanesly, p. 192.

84 Wilson, p. 42; also printed from BM MS Harley 3954 in Furnivall, EETS o.s. 15 (1903).

85 Carleton Brown and G. V. Smithers (eds.), *Religious Lyrics of the XIVth Century* (Oxford 1956).

86 W. O. Ross, *Middle English Sermons, edited from BM MS Royal*

18 B xxiii, EETS o.s. 209 (London 1950), sermon no. 38, p. 218.

87 From the early fourteenth century; J. Small (ed.), *English Metrical Homilies from MSS of the Fourteenth Century* (Edinburgh 1862).

88 David C. Fowler, *The Bible in Early English Literature* (London 1977).

89 See *The Pepysian Gospel Harmony, MS Pepys 2498*, ed. M. Goates for EETS o.s. 157 (London 1922). This is believed to be South-East Midlands. Explanation is either by defining or, more often, by replacing biblical words and phrases with homely equivalents. St John the Baptist did not eat 'locusts and wild honey' (Matt. 3: 4) but 'garlic and bryony' (ramesones and wilde-nepes). The Gospel Harmony of Clement of Llanthony was extremely popular and was translated by the Lollards. Like compilations of *exempla* for preachers, this Harmony was also provided with a summary and alphabetical table of contents for easy reference by one of Archbishop Arundel's chaplains and dedicated to him. See Deanesly, p. 175.

90 Anna Paues (ed.), *A Fourteenth Century English Biblical Version* (Cambridge 1902).

91 This question was put by Margaret Deanesly, *The Lollard Bible*. She noted (pp. 19–20) that around 1355 French Dominicans prepared a translation of most of the Old Testament for King John the Good, and Raoul de Presles revised for Charles V the old thirteenth-century French Bible prepared by booksellers of the University of Paris around 1380. Most of the translations on the continent were of parts of the Bible, and even when the husband in *Le Ménagier de Paris* (1394) advised his wife to read the Bible in French along with the *Vitae Patrum* in French, it is not clear if the complete text was available in prose translation. In the thirteenth century the collector of *exempla* Etienne de Bourbon OP tells how Peter Waldo of Lyons contacted two priests, one to be a scribe to the other, who would translate many (not all) the books of the Bible. The Dutch Maerlant translated Peter Comestor's *Historia Scholastica* into Dutch verse in the thirteenth century, and Comestor's work is a reworking of Old and New Testament history. Maerlant also translated the French *Bible Historiaulx* into Dutch; the French work was a free translation made by Guyart Desmoulins (1271), a canon from Artois. See Deanesly, p. 19, n. 2. It seems that what is meant when one speaks of Bible translations existing in France are the *Bibles Historiales* (Deanesley, p. 289). The translation of Desmoulins was later combined with a French translation of some of the biblical books. For John of Gaunt's allegation that 'other nations have God's law in their

mother tongue, we will [now] have ours in English no matter who complains of it', see the Lollard tract on translation, below, n. 204.

92   But see below, ch. 5 for discussion of vernacular literature that does reflect a higher degree of theological and philosophical sophistication.

93   See above, ch. 3.

94   See ch. 5.

95   Robert of Basevorn, *Forma Praedicandi*, text in Th.-M. Charland, *Artes Praedicandi* (Paris 1936), pp. 233–323. A translation by L. Krul OSB, is in J. J. Murphy, *Three Medieval Rhetorical Arts* (Berkeley 1971), pp. 114–215.

96   See the introductory essay by H. Oberman in Oberman and Trinkaus, *Pursuit of Holiness*.

97   Basevorn in Murphy, p. 115.

98   It is of interest that the relatively recent and innovative use of a table of contents is employed by Basevorn.

99   Basevorn in Murphy, p. 114.

100   ibid., pp. 127f, ch. vii.

101   ibid., ch. iv.

102   ibid., ch. iv, p. 124.

103   ibid., p. 135.

104   ibid., ch. xxxi.

105   ibid., p. 180.

106   Ross, pp. 2f.

107   See Ross, introduction, for a discussion of the parts of the modern sermon and the use of real and verbal concords.

108   Basevorn in Murphy, p. 183.

109   John Alford, 'The role of the quotations in *Piers Plowman*', *Speculum*, vol. 52 (1977), pp. 80–99. Also see his 'Biblical imitatio in the writings of Richard Rolle' *ELH*, vol. 40 (1973), and 'Haukyn's coat: some observations on *Piers Plowman* B XIV: 22–27', *Medium Aevum*, vol. 43 (1974), pp. 133–8.

110   Alford, 'The role of the quotations', p. 82.

111   Bonaventure's *Breviloquium* is translated by José de Vinck (Paterson, New Jersey 1963), pp. 18–19.

112   See BM MS Royal 18 xxiii in Ross, p. 72.

113   Alford, 'The role of the quotations', p. 86.

114   ibid.

115   Basevorn in Murphy, p. 204, ch. xlix.

116   Graham Pollard, 'The *pecia* system in the medieval universities' in M. B. Parkes and A. G. Watson (eds.), *Medieval Scribes, Manuscripts and Libraries* (London 1978), p. 150; W. A. Pantin, 'The halls and schools of medieval Oxford: an attempt at recon-

struction' in *Oxford Studies Presented to Daniel Callus* (Oxford 1964), pp. 31–100.

117 Pollard, p. 156.

118 A. I. Doyle and M. B. Parkes, 'The production of copies of the *Canterbury Tales* and the *Confessio Amantis* in the early fifteenth century', in Parkes and Watson, *Medieval Scribes, Manuscripts and Libraries*, p. 186.

119 Frances Yates, *The Art of Memory* (London 1966), p. 107.

120 See Doyle and Parkes, p. 190.

121 ibid., n. 61, p. 191.

122 M. B. Parkes, 'The influence of the concepts of *ordinatio* and *compilatio* on the development of the book', in *Medieval Learning and Literature: Essays Presented to R. W. Hunt* (Oxford 1976), pp. 115–41.

123 Doyle and Parkes, pp. 190–1.

124 Siegfried Wenzel, 'Chaucer and the language of contemporary preaching', *Studies in Philology*, vol. 73 (1976), pp. 138–61.

125 Robert Pratt, 'Chaucer and the hand that fed him', *Speculum*, vol. 41 (1966), pp. 619–42.

126 See Carleton Brown in *Sources and Analogues of Chaucer's Canterbury Tales*, ed. W. F. Bryan and G. Dempster (New York 1941; reprinted 1958), pp. 447–85.

127 Wenzel, p. 151.

128 Graham Pollard, 'The company of stationers before 1557', *The Library*, 4th series, vol. 18 (1937), pp. 1–37; p. 7.

129 Doyle and Parkes, p. 197; and Pollard, 'The company of stationers', p. 15.

130 See their appendix, p. 209.

131 A. J. Minnis, 'Discussions of "authorial role" and "literary form" in late medieval scriptural exegesis', *Beiträge zur Geschichte der deutschen Sprache und Literatur*, vol. 99 (1977), pp. 37–65.

132 Lectio 2, ch. 1.

133 Minnis, p. 46.

134 ibid., p. 59.

135 ibid., p. 51.

136 Sermon no. 3.

137 Ross, p. 13.

138 Compare the Prologue to *The Abbey of the Holy Ghost* (c. 1370): those with a cure of souls taught their parishioners in English six things by which God is known: '(1) fourteen points that fallen to truth (Creed); (2) the ten commandments; (3) seven sacraments; (4) seven works of mercy unto our evenchristians; (5) seven virtues that each man shall use; (6) seven deadly sins that each man shall refuse'. Parishioners were to hear

and learn the above by frequent rehearsal. See Deanesly, p. 199.

139   Ross, p. 15.

140   Compare the statement in the non-Wyclifite prose translation of the thirteenth-century *Mirror* of Robert of Greatham, which comprises selections from the gospels and homilies. The translator says he writes the gospels in English, 'for me and for all men, for all ne have nought *all* holy writ. [My emphasis] Such hear the gospel and read it that ne understandeth nought it, what is saith'. That this work is a translation not only of Scripture but also of homiletic explanations may allow us to interpret this statement as saying that without such exegetical aid those who read or hear Scripture – in English or Latin – 'ne understandeth nought it'. It may, of course, mean that those who learned to read Latin for the church service could not understand what they read. This is the more traditional interpretation. See Deanesly, p. 316.

141   Fisher, 'Chancery and the emergence of standard written English', pp. 870–99; p. 893.

142   Deanesly, pp. 213–14. This is the *exemplum* found in Bromyard, from Jacques de Vitry. See p. 312, n. 74 and p. 180 where it is 'misused'. There the grace of God is to get the man *out* of church rather than enabling him to understand the sermon.

143   EETS o.s. 20.

144   Deanesly, p. 218.

145   Contemporary with the Wyclifite translations of the Bible were the non-Wyclifite North Midlands translation of Matthew, Mark and Luke plus a gloss mainly drawn from Peter Lombard; also the North Midlands version of the Pauline Epistles, where the Latin is given in single sentences followed by the literal translation and a short gloss; around 1400 there is a North Midlands unglossed version of Acts and part of Matthew combined with a southern version of the Epistles. There is also a prose translation of the Sunday gospels with English homilies of the last quarter of the fourteenth century. See Deanesly, pp. 314–15. As she has said: 'The last quarter of the fourteenth century would almost certainly have seen the production of some biblical translations in English, even if Wycliffe had not turned the attention of his followers to the popularisation of the biblical text' (p. 298).

146   This is printed in an Appendix in Deanesly.

147   Deanesly, p. 450.

148   Sermon no. 22.

149   Ross, p. 128.

150   ibid., p. 237.

151   *Statutes of the Realm*, vol. 2, pp. 126–7; cited by M. Aston, 'Lol-

lardy and literacy', *History*, 62 (1977), pp. 347–72; pp. 354–5.

152 Henry Crump, the Cistercian, in 1382 preached against the Lollards from St Mary's, Oxford, thus describing them. See *Anecdotes Historiques . . . d'Etienne de Bourbon*, ed. Lecoy de la Marche, p. 307. Crump was himself tried for heresy in 1385 and 1392. *Fasciculi Zizaniorum*, ed. W. W. Shirley (London 1858), pp. 343–59.

153 Aston, 'Lollardy and literacy', p. 354.

154 ibid., p. 356.

155 ibid., p. 360: 'those who wrote against Lollards, those who acted against them and those who devised new procedures to deal with them, all similarly concentrated upon the heretics' use and dissemination of vernacular texts – particularly the Bible'.

156 Henry Knighton, *Chronicon*, ed. J. R. Lumby (London 1889–95), vol. 2, pp. 151–2.

157 Text in Wilkins, *Concilia*, vol. 3, p. 317, dated 1407.

158 Aston, 'Lollardy and literacy', p. 365.

159 A collection of such texts is in Anne Hudson (ed.), *English Wycliffite Writings* (Cambridge 1978).

160 See K. B. McFarlane, *John Wycliffe and the Beginnings of English Nonconformity* (London 1952), for an account of Wyclif's life; here, pp. 45–6.

161 Bertie Wilkinson, *Constitutional History of Medieval England (1216–1399)* (London 1958), vol. 3, p. 29 and document VII, p. 398.

162 'Prelates and the like with advowsons of benefices from the king or other lay lords are to hold services and keep collations freely in the manner enfeoffed by their donors. For those reserved by Rome, when vacant, the *king and his heirs* have collations to archbishoperics and other elective dignities.' *Statutes of the Realm*, vol. 1, pp. 316–18. *Praemunire*, 1353: 'Lords and commons are not to go outside the realm to papal courts with pleas that may be treated by the king's courts'. *Statutes of the Realm*, vol. 1, p. 329.

163 McFarlane, *Wycliffe and the Beginnings of English Nonconformity*, pp. 59f.

164 ibid., pp. 97–9.

165 M. J. Wilks, 'Reformatio Regni: Wyclif and Hus as leaders of religious protest movements', in *Studies in Church History*, vol. 9 (1972), pp. 109–30; p. 111.

166 ibid., p. 116.

167 H. G. Richardson, 'Heresy and lay power under Richard II', *English Historical Review*, vol. 51 (1936), pp. 1–28; p. 9.

168 Wilks, 'Reformatio Regni', p. 119.

169 Knighton, vol. 2, pp. 260f.

170 Richardson, p. 11.

171 Wilks, 'Reformatio Regni', p. 121.
172 'The idea that Parliament is the final arbiter, not only in deciding the fate of any particular person but in determining general issues which involved the question of heresy, runs through Lollard literature of the early period.' Richardson, p. 23.
173 McFarlane, *Wycliffe and the Beginnings of English Nonconformity*, p. 91.
174 See *On the Office of King*, 1379.
175 Dorothy M. Owen (ed.), *John Lydford's Book*, Devon and Cornwall Record Society, new series, vol. 20 (London 1974).
176 ibid., introduction, pp. 10–11.
177 ibid., pp. 16 and 18.
178 ibid., p. 108.
179 ibid., pp. 110–12.
180 ibid., pp. 112–17, including summaries of what one can find at greater length in the *Fasciculi Zizaniorum*, where the precise list of heretical beliefs is responded to and the list of heretical documents is conceded as heretical or erroneous. See *Fasciculi Zizaniorum Magistri Johannis Wyclif cum Tritico*, ascribed to Thomas Netter of Walden (Carmelite), ed. W. W. Shirley in *Rerum Britannicarum Medii Aevi Scriptores* (London 1858).
181 Wyclif's *De Blasphemia*, Book V, p. 76.
182 Wilks, 'Reformatio Regni', p. 127.
183 ibid., p. 126.
184 McFarlane, *Wycliffe and the Beginnings of English Nonconformity*, p. 180.
185 Wright, *Political Poems and Songs*, Rolls series, vol. 14 (London 1859–61), vol. 1, p. 261.
186 *A Manual of the Writings in Middle English*, ed. J. B. Severs, vol. 2: *Wyclif and his followers* (Connecticut 1970), pp. 518–21.
187 Anne Hudson, 'A Lollard sermon cycle and its implications', *Medium Aevum*, vol. 40 (1971), pp. 142–56; 'Contributions to a bibliography of Wycliffite writings', *Notes and Queries* (December 1973), pp. 443–53; 'The examination of Lollards', *Bulletin of the Institute of Historical Research*, vol. 46 (1973); 'The debate on Bible translation, Oxford, 1401', *English Historical Review*, vol. 90 (1975); 'Some aspects of Lollard book production' in *Studies in Church History*, vol. 9 (Oxford 1972); 'A Lollard compilation and the dissemination of Wycliffite thought', *Journal of Theological Studies* n.s., vol. 23, pt 1 (1972), and other studies.
188 F. D. Matthew (ed.), *The English Works of Wyclif hitherto unprinted*, EETS o.s. 74 (London 1880), pp. 226–43.
189 ibid., p. 227.
190 ibid., p. 228.

191   ibid., pp. 228–30.
192   ibid., p. 232.
193   ibid., p. 234.
194   ibid., p. 234.
195   ibid., p. 239.
196   ibid., p. 240.
197   ibid.
198   *Responsio ad Strode*, p. 177.
199   Cited by M. J. Wilks, 'The early Oxford Wyclif: papalist or nominalist?', *Studies in Church History*, vol. 5 (Leiden 1969), pp. 69–98; p. 74. From the *De Statu Innocentiae*, 9, 518.
200   ibid., p. 81.
201   ibid., p. 95.
202   Hudson, 'The debate on Bible translation, Oxford, 1401', p. 11.
203   Hudson, 'A Lollard sermon cycle', p. 150.
204   See M. J. Wilks, 'Misleading manuscripts: Wyclif and the non-Wyclifite Bible', in *Studies in Church History*, vol. 11 (1975), pp. 147–61; p. 158, n. 48. For a lucidly argued defence of English translation of the Bible, see the text printed by Curt Buhler, 'A Lollard tract: on translating the Bible into English', *Medium Aevum*, vol. 7 (1938), pp. 167–83. Buhler proposes *c.* 1407 as the date of the tract. I have provided excerpts below because of its great interest:

Aȝens hem þat scyn þat Hooli Wryt schulde not or may not be drawen into Engliche, we maken þes resouns. ffirst seiþ Bois [Boethius] in his boke de disciplina scolarium, þat children shulde be tauȝt in þe bokis of Senek [Seneca] and Bede expowneþ þis, seying: children schulden be tauȝt in vertues ffor þe bokis of Senek ben morals, and for þei ben not tauȝt þus in her ȝoungþe, þei conseyuen yuel maners & ben vnabel to conseyue þe sotil sci- ense of trewþe; ... and Algasel [al-Ghazali] in his logik seiþ.... O siþen heþen philosofris wolden þe puple to profeten in natural science, how myche more schulden Cristen men willen þe puple to profiten in science of vertues, for so wolde God; ffor wane þe lawe was ȝouen to Moises in þe mounte of Synay, God ȝaf it in Ebrew for þat al þe pupel schuld vnderstonde it & bad Moises to rede it vnto hem to þe tyme þei vnderstodyn it. And he rede it as is pleyn in Detronomie 31 c. And Esdras also redde it ... apertly in þe stret and þe eeres of þe puple weren enten[t]ly ȝouen þerto and þei vnderstoden it; and þis þei miȝt not haue done but if it hadde ben redde in þer moder tounge, so þat þe pupel hering felle in-to grete wepinge. [Since the Jews understood and were com- manded in Hebrew] ... If God wole, he loueþ not lesse vs Cristen

men in þes daies þan he dide þe pupel in þe olde testament but
better, as he haþ scheued be þe mene of Cristis passioun & be þe
newe perfite lawe ȝouen to vs. . .& þis is myche better þan al-onli
to have devocioun in wordes and not in vnderstanding. & þis
proveþ þe texte after þat seiþ: how schal he sie amen upon þis
blessing þat wot not wat þou seiste. And on þis seiþ þe doctor Lire
[Nicholas Lyra]: if þe puple vnderstood þe preyour of þe prest, it
schal þe better be lade in-to God & þe more deuouteli answere
amen. . . . Also seuenti doctoris withouten mo by-fore þe Incar-
nacioun translatiden þe Bible in-to Greek ouȝt of Ebrew, and
after þe Ascension many translatiden al þe Byble, summe in-to
Greek & summe in-to Latyne. But Seint Ierom translatide it out
of Ebrew in-to Latine wos translacioun we vsen most; [and thereafter there were translations into Spanish, French, German
etc.]. . . . It was herde of a worþi man of Almaine þat summe tyme
a Flemynge, his name was James Merland, translatid al þe Bibel
in-to Flemyche, for wiche dede he was somoned be-fore þe Pope
of grete enmyte & þe boke was taken to examynacion & truely
aproued; it was delivered to hym aȝene in conf[u]cioun to his
enmyes. [Bede also translated a great part of the Bible into Eng-
lish]. . . . Also a man of Lonndon, his name was Wyring, hadde a
Bible in Englische of norþen speche, wiche was seen of many men
and it semed too houndred ȝeer olde . . . and on-þis argueth a
clerk & seiþ; if is leuefful to preche þe naked text to þe pupel, it
is also lefful to write it to hem & consequentliche, be proces of
tyme, so al þe Bibil. Also a nobil holy man Richerde E[re]myte
drewe oon Englice þe Sauter with a glose of longe proces & les-
souns of dirige & many oþer tretis, by wiche many Englische men
han ben gretli edified. . . . Also Sire Wiliam Thorisby, Erchebi-
schop of Ȝork, did do to drawe a tretys in Englisce be a worschip-
ful clerk wos name was Gaytrik in þe wiche weren conteyned þe
articulis of þe feiþ, seuene dedli synnes, þe werkes of mercy & þe
ten comandementes, and sente hem in smale pagynes to þe comyn
puple to lerne þis & to knowe þis, of wiche ben ȝit manye a com-
ponye in Englond. But þer ben summe þat seien if þe Gospel were
on Engliche men myȝten liȝtly erre þer-inne. But wel couchiþ þis
holi man Richard Hampol suche men, expownynge þis tixte: Ne
anferas de ore meo verbum veritatis vsquequaque; þer he seiþ
þus: þer ben not fewe but many þat wolen sustene a worde of
falseness for God, not willing to beleue to kenynge and better þan
þei ben; þei ben liche to þe frendes of Jobe, þat wiles þei enforsiden
hem to defende God, þei offendeden greuosly in hym, & þouȝ suche
ben slayne & done myracles þei neverþeles ben stynkyng martirs.
And to hem þat seien þat þe Gospel on Engliche wolde make men to

erre, wyte wele þat we fynden in Latyne mo heretikes þan of all oþer langagis, ffor þe decres rehersiþ sixti Latyn eretikes. Also þe hooli Euaungelistis writen þe Gospelle in diverse langages, as Matheu in Indee. Marke in Ytalie, Luck in þe partyes of Achaie and John in Asie, after he hadde written þe Apocalips in the yle of Pathomos; & al þes writen in þe langage of þe same cuntre; as seiþ Ardmakan, [FitzRalph, of Armagh]. Also Ardmakan, in þe bock of questiouns [*Questiones on the Armenians*], seiþ þat þe Sacrament mai wel be made in iche comoun langage, for so as he seiþ diden þe Apostilis. But we coueteyten [sic] not þat but prey anticrist þat we moten haue oure bileue in Englische. Also we þat han moche comyned wiþ þe Jewis knowen wel þat al myȝty men of hem in what londe þei born ȝit þei han in Ebrew þe Bible & þei ben more actif [in] þe olde lawe þane any Latyn man comonli; ȝhe! as wel þe lewde men of þe\Jewes as prestis. . . And þe Grekis, wiche ben nobel men, han al þis in þer owne langage, but ȝit aduersaries of trewiþ seien, wane men rehersen þat Grekis and Latyns han al in þer owne langage, þe clerkis of hem speiken gramaticalliche & þe pupel vnderstodiþ it not; witte þei þat þouȝ a clerke or anoþer man þus lerned can sette his wordis on Engliche better þan a rewde man, it foloweþ not her-of þat oure langage schuld be destried. It were al on to sei þis & to kitte oute þe tunges of hem þat can not speke þus curiosly; but þei schulde vnderstande þat gramaticaliche is not ellis but [þe] abite of riȝt spekyng and riȝt pronounsyng & riȝt writynge. [Then he speaks of the enemies of St Jerome made for translating the Bible]. . . . Also it is knowen to many men þat in þe tyme of Kyng Richerd, whos soule God asoile, in-to a parliment was put a bille, be assent of two erchebischopis & of þe clergie, to anulle þe Bibel þat tyme translatid in-to Engliche, and also oþer bokis of þe Gospel translatid in-to Engliche, wiche wanne it was seyn of lordis and comouns, þe good duke of Lancastre Jon [of Gaunt], wos soule God asoile for his mercy, answered þer-to scharpely seying þis sentence: we wel not be þe refuse of alle men, for siþen oþer naciouns han Goddis lawe, whiche is lawe of oure byleue in þer owne modir langage, we wolone haue oure in Engliche wo þat euere it bigrucche; and þis he affermede with a grete oþe. Also þe bischope of Caunturbiri, Thomas Arundel, þat nowe is, seide a sermon in Westminster þer as weren many hundred puple at þe biriying of quene Anne, of wos soule God haue mercy, & in his comendynges of hir, he seide: it was more joie of hir þan of any woman þat euere he knewe ffor not-wiþstanding þat sche was an alien borne, sche hadde on Engliche al þe foure Gospeleris wiþ þe doctoris vpon hem. And he seide þei weren goode and trewe, and comended hir in þat sche was so grete a lady & also an alien, & wolde so lowliche studiee in so vertuous bokis. And he blamed in þat sermoun scharpeli þe necligence of prelatis and of oþer men, in so miche þat summe seiden he wolde on þe morowe leue up his office of chaunceler and for-sake þe worlde & þan it hadde be þe best sermoun þat euere þei herde.

205 From BM MS Royal 17.B. 1, as cited by Angus McIntosh, 'Some linguistic reflections of a Wycliffite', in *Franciplegius: Medieval and Linguistic Studies in Honor of F. P. Magoun*, ed. J. B. Bessinger and R. P. Creed (New York 1965), pp. 290–3. He has, thus, rejected the Platonic equation of literacy with false wisdom and sedition.

Chapter 5: Theology, non-scholastic literature and poetry

1 For an excellent general survey see Paul Vignaux, *Philosophy in the Middle Ages* (New York 1959) and his *Nominalisme au XIVe siecle* (Paris 1948).

2 F. Van Steenberghen, *Aristotle in the West, The Origins of Latin Aristotelianism*, 2nd ed. (Louvain 1970).

3 On the two *potentiae* see Heiko Oberman, *The Harvest of Medieval Theology* (Michigan 1967).

4 Gordon Leff, *William of Ockham, The Metamorphosis of Scholastic Discourse* (Manchester 1975).

5 Heiko Oberman, 'The shape of late medieval thought', in H. Oberman and C. Trinkaus (eds.), *The Pursuit of Holiness in the Later Middle Ages* (Leiden 1974), p. 15.

6 Ockham's *Summa Logiae*, ed. P. Boehner (St Bonaventure, New York 1974), p. 6, ll. 21–8.

7 Armand A. Maurer, 'Some aspects of fourteenth-century philosophy', *Medievalia et Humanistica*, n.s. vol. 7, ed. P. M. Clogan (Cambridge 1976), p. 179.

8 ibid., p. 177 citing Duns Scotus, *Ordinatio* I d. 2, p. 1 qq. 1–2 in the edition by Balic, vol. 2 (Vatican 1950), pp. 125–221.

9 Maurer, p. 180.

10 A lucid analysis of this difficult subject may be found in Leff's excellent book on *William of Ockham*.

11 As noted by Maurer, p. 184.

12 See Bruno Nardi for the text of Rodington in *Sogetto e Oggetto del Conoscere nella Filosofia Antica e Medievale* (Rome 1952), pp. 74–92; p. 80.

13 Peter of Spain, *The Summulae Logicales*, ed. and trans. J. P. Mullally, 2nd ed. (Notre Dame, Indiana 1960).

14 See Gordon Leff, *Bradwardine and the Pelagians* (Cambridge 1957).

15 See Damasus Trapp, 'Augustinian theology of the fourteenth cen-

tury', *Augustiniana*, vol. 5 (1956) (American series) *1256–1956*, pp. 146–274; p. 149.

16 Heiko Oberman, 'Facientibus quod in se est . . .: Robert Holcot OP and the beginnings of Luther's theology', *Harvard Theological Review*, vol. 55 (1962), pp. 317–42.

17 For an up-to-date discussion of the *via moderna* see William Courtenay, 'Nominalism and late medieval religion' in Oberman and Trinkaus, pp. 26–59. This is probably the best summary to date.

18 See Janet Coleman, 'Jean de Ripa and the Oxford calculators', *Mediaeval Studies*, vol. 37 (1975), and John Murdoch, 'Mathesis in Philosophiam scholasticam introducta, the rise and development of the application of mathematics in fourteenth-century philosophy and theology', in *Arts Libéraux et Philosophie au Moyen Age, Actes du Quatrième Congrès International de Philosophie Médiévale* (Montréal, Paris 1969), pp. 215–54.

19 J. A. Weisheipl, 'Developments in the Arts curriculum at Oxford in the early fourteenth century', *Mediaeval Studies*, vol. 28 (1966), pp. 151–75, and 'Curriculum of the Faculty of Arts at Oxford', *Mediaeval Studies*, vol. 26 (1964), pp. 143–85.

20 See J. A. Robson, *Wyclif and the Oxford Schools* (Oxford 1961), and M. D. Chenu, 'Les Questiones de Thomas Buckingham', in *Studia Medievalia in Honorem . . . R. J. Martin* (Bruges 1949), pp. 229–41.

21 Texts supporting these views in Holcot and Ockham are numerous, but a selection is given below: Holcot, I *Sent.* Q. 4 a. [H]: '. . . non includit contraditionem quod deus hominem sine charitate beatificet.' Ultimately neither grace nor any supernatural *habitus* is a *necessary* step en route to salvation since God's will, operating among all possibles, can dispense with it as with everything. Also I *Sent.* Q.1 a. 4D: 'Deus potest acceptare actus naturales . . . dicendo quod actus naturales sit meritorius si deo placet, et hoc quia eque libere posset illum acceptare ad vitam aeternam.' Also I *Sent.* Q.1 a.4: 'Dico tunc istam conclusionem quam deus potest acceptare ad vitam aeternam omnes actus naturales alicuius hominis et facere omnes actus liberos atque indifferentes aut non meritorios.' Similarly in his Wisdom Commentaries, *Sap.* Lect. 28 B. Likewise for Ockham, Oxoniensis, I *Sent.* d. 17, q.3 n.29: 'Dico quod Deus de potentia absoluta bene potuisset acceptare naturalem beatificabilem acceptatione spirituali praedicta existentem in puris naturalibus.' III *Sent.* d. 19 q.u, F: 'Meritum quia acceptum non autem e converso.' However, Ockham, III *Sent.* Q.5 and I *Sent.* d. 17 q.3 F and d. 17 q.2 C: 'Nihil est meritorium nisi quia voluntarium. . . .' *Quodlibet* VI

q.1: 'Nihil est meritorium nisi quod est in potestate nostra.' For a simplified Lollard version of the inscrutability of God's decision to save or damn some and not others, see *Jack Upland*, ed. P. L. Heyworth (Oxford 1968), ll. 335–40. Arguing against the mendicant friars, Jack says:

Frere, whi ben ʒe so foole hardi to graunte to eche man þat wole paie ʒou þerfore, bi lettris of fraternyte, part & meryt of alle ʒoure massis & oþere good dedis? & ʒe witen not where ʒoure dedis displesen God for ʒoure synnes, and also wheþer þat man be worþi to resceyue merit for his owne lyuynge. For if he schal be dampned, hise owne dedis ne ʒouris schulen neuer availe hym to blisse.

22 A very useful discussion is David Clark, 'William of Ockham on right reason', *Speculum*, vol. 48 (1973), pp. 13–36.

23 III *Dialogus* II, 3, vi, ed. J. Trechsel in Ockham's *Opera Plurima* I (Lyons 1494). On the relation of natural law and right reason for Ockham see Arthur McGrade, *The Political Thought of William of Ockham* (Cambridge 1974), especially pp. 177–85. For selected translation of the *Dialogus* see R. Lerner and M. Mahdi (eds.), *Medieval Political Philosophy: A Source Book* (New York 1963), pp. 492–506. Another illuminating study is Francis Oakley, 'Medieval theories of natural law: William of Ockham and the significance of the voluntarist tradition', *Natural Law Forum* (Notre Dame, Indiana), vol. 6, (1961), pp. 65–83.

24 Ockham, III *Sent*. q. 12 G: 'Nullus actus alius ab actu voluntatis est intrinsece virtuosus vel vitiosus.'

25 McGrade, p. 186. *Quodlibeta*, VII, iv, 6 and III *Sent*. q. 12 XX: 'Tale (formaliter et intrinsece bonum) nihil potest ex natura sua nisi solus actus voluntatis'.

26 Ockham cites the definition of virtue from Aristotle's *Nicomachean Ethics*: 'Virtue is an elective habit consisting in the mean, determined by reason.... Ethical good is thus what is willable according to right reason.' III *Sent*. q.12 EEE. See Clark, p. 23.

27 We can compare Wyclif's Latin sermon XXXIV, delivered in Oxford *c.* 1381–3 on the same *exemplum*.

28 See Gordon Leff, *Richard FitzRalph, Commentator of the Sentences, A Study in Theological Orthodoxy* (Manchester 1963).

29 M. D. Knowles, 'The censured opinions of Uthred of Boldon', *Proceedings of the British Academy*, vol. 37 (1951), pp. 305–42. W. A. Pantin, 'Two treatises of Uthred of Boldon on the monastic life', in *Studies in Medieval History Presented to F. M. Powicke*

(Oxford 1948), pp. 363–85.

30 *De Fide Catholica*, Wyclif, *Opera Minora*, ed. J. Loserth (London 1913), p. 112. Also see the discussion in R. Southern, *Western Views of Islam in the Middle Ages* (Cambridge, Mass. 1962), pp. 78–82.

31 'Aliqua ergo racio abscondita et a Deo singulariter ordinata facit quod sint membra sancti matris ecclesie ... predestinacionis gratia.' *Opera Minora*, p. 109.

32 From MS New College, Oxford, 134 fo. 395v, partially represented in Chenu, pp. 229–41. Also see Robson, *Wyclif and the Oxford Schools*, for a discussion and correction of Chenu's edition.

33 *Paradiso*, Canto XX, ll. 121–4.

34 See R. W. Chambers, 'Long Will, Dante and the Righteous Heathen', in *Essays and Studies ... English Association*, vol. IX (1924), pp. 50–69; G. H. Russell, 'The salvation of the heathen: the exploration of a theme in *Piers Plowman*', *Journal of the Warburg and Courtauld Institutes*, vol. 29 (1966), pp. 101–16. Neither of these studies takes into account the range of current theological opinion on this matter.

35 'Alle thise clerkes', quod I tho . that on Cryst leuen,
Seggen in hir sarmones . that noyther Sarasens ne Iewes,
Ne no creature of Cristes lyknesse . with-outen Crystendom
   worth saued.'
'*Contra*' quod Ymagynatyf tho . and comsed to loure,
And seyde, *saluabitur vix iustus in die iudicij*;
Ergo saluabitur', quod he . and seyde namore Latyne.
'Troianus was a trewe kny3te . and toke neuere Cristendom,
And he is sauf, so seith the boke . and his soule in heuene.
For there is fullyng of fonte . and fullyng in blode-shedynge,
And thorugh fuire is fullyng . and that is ferme bileue;
Aduenit ignis diuinus, non comburens, sed illuminans, etc.
Ac trewth that trespassed neuere . ne trauersed a3eines his lawe,
But lyueth as his lawe techeth . and leueth there be no bettere,
And if there were, he wolde amende . and in suche wille deyeth,
Ne wolde neuere trewe god . but treuth were allowed;
And where it worth or worth nou3t . the bileue is grete of treuth,
And an hope hangyng therinne . to haue a mede for his treuth.
For, *Deus dicitur quasi dans vitam eternam suis, hoc est, fidelibus*;
   et alibi, si ambulauero in medio umbre mortis, etc.
The glose graunteth vpon that vers . a gret mede to treuthe,
And witt and wisdome', quod that wye . 'was somme tyme tres-
   ore

To kepe with a commune . no katel was holde bettre,
And moche murth and manhod:' – and ri3t with that he van-
  esched.

Piers Plowman, B XII, ll. 275–93

'And that is loue and large huyre . yf the lord be trewe,
And cortesie more than couenant was . what so clerkes carpe
For al worth as god wole' – . and ther-with he vanshede.

Piers Plowman, C XV, ll. 215–17

36 And sith that thise Sarasenes . Scribes, and Iuwes
Han a lippe of owre byleue . the li3tloker, me thynketh,
Thei shulde torne, who so trauaille wolde . to teche hem of the
  trinite,
Querite et inuenietis, etc.

Piers Plowman, B XV, ll. 492–4

Ac Pharasewes and Sarasenes . Scribes and Grekis
Aren folke of on faith . the fader god thei honouren;
And sitthen that the Sarasenes . and also the Iewes
Konnethe firste clause of owre bileue . *Credo in deum patrem
  omnipotentem,*
Prelates of Crystene prouynces . shulde preue, if thei my3te,
Lere hem litlum and lytlum . *et in Iesum Christum filium,*
Tyl thei couthe speke and spelle . *et in spiritum sanctum,*
And rendren it and recorden it . with *remissionem peccatorum,*
Carnis resurreccionem, et vitam eternam. Amen.

Piers Plowman, B XV, ll. 594–601

'Ac yf preestes do her deuer wel . we shullen do the bettere.
For Saresyns mowe be saued so . yf thei so by-leyuede,
In the lengthynge of here lyf . to leyue on holychurche.'

Piers Plowman, C XVIII, ll. 122–4

Ac meny manere men ther beoth . as Sarrasyns and Iewes,
Louyeth nat that lorde a-ryght . as by the Legende *Sanctorum,*
And lyuen oute of leel by-leyue . for thei leyue in a mene.
A man that hihte Makamede . for Messye thei hym heolde
And after hus lerynge thei lyuen . and by lawe of kynde.
And when kynde hath hus cours . and no contrarye fyndeth,
Thenne is lawe lost . and lewete vnknowen.

Piers Plowman, C XVIII, ll. 156–62

37 See Wyclif's *De Simonia*, Introduction, p. xxi.
38 Compare this with the similar views of Wyclif discussed in ch. 4.
39 This is not quite the meaning of Charles Muscatine, *Poetry and*

Crisis in the Age of Chaucer (Notre Dame, Indiana 1972).

40 *A Calendar of the Register of Henry Wakefield, Bishop of Worcester 1375–95* (Worcester 1972), ed. W. P. Marrett, fo. 6.

41 Nicholas Orme, *Education in the West of England 1066–1548* (Exeter 1976), pp. 50–1.

42 *Piers Plowman*, C VI, ll. 1–29.

43 Ockham, *Tractatus contra Benedictum*, III, ch. 3 in *Opera Politica*, ed. H. S. Offler, vol. 3, p. 231.

44 Beryl Smalley, 'Robert Holcot, OP' *Archivum Fratres Praedicatorum*, vol. 26 (1956), pp. 7–28; pp. 28–9.

45 *Sapientiae, Lectiones*, from the Cologne 1479 edition.

46 *Sap. Lect.* 121 from 1511 edition: 'conclusionibus sapientia scit idest scire facit omni et omnia necessaria ad salutem.'

47 *Sap. Lect.* 121: 'Unde ad prudentem pertinet bene consiliari circa totam vitam hominis et bene eligere, quia sine prudentia nullus potest habere virtutem moralem; [sicut Salom.] – De ducet me inquit in operibus meis sobrie idest mensurate recte rationis.' fo. clxxxiiii va.

48 Smalley, p. 11. In *Sap. Lect.* 120 Holcot asks the political question: 'utrum melius reges eligere quam succedant?' Is it better for kings to be elected or acquire the throne by hereditary succession? In the tradition of Aristotle he asks whether it is man's appropriate end to live and be governed in a civil community? and how should such a city be governed? *Lect.* 2. (1689 edition).

49 *Sap. Lect.* 28 B: 'quia natura non deficit in necessariis . . . ergo per rationem naturalem potest homo acquirere omnem noticiam necessarium ad salutatem . . . Natura supponit pro deo'.

50 Thomas Bradwardine, *De Causa Dei*, ed. H. Savile (London 1618).

51 *Sermo Epinicius* by Bradwardine is found in Merton College, Oxford, MS H.I.II (Coxe 180), and has been edited by H. Oberman and J. A. Weisheipl in *Archives d'Histoire Doctrinale et Littéraire du Moyen Age*, vol. 33 (1958).

52 See Aubrey Gwynn in *Proceedings of the Royal Irish Academy*, vol. 44 (1937) for a discussion of FitzRalph's sermons from MSS St John's College, Oxford, 64 and Lansdowne 393.

53 Compare *Piers Plowman*, B XIX, ll. 28–33.

To be called a kniȝte is faire . for men shal knele to hym;
To be called a kynge is fairer . for he may knyȝtes make;
Ac to be conquerour called . that cometh of special grace,
And of hardynesse of herte . and of hendenesse, bothe,
To make lordes of laddes . of londe that he wynneth,
And fre men foule thralles . that folweth nouȝt his lawes.

54   *Sermo Epinicius*, p. 312.
55   ibid., p. 315.
56   E. F. Jacob, 'Reynold Pecock, Bishop of Chichester', in *Essays in Later Medieval History* (Manchester 1968).
57   ibid., p. 22.
58   ibid., p. 34. See *The Donet* (summary of Pecock's *Reule of Crysten Religioun)*, ed. E. V. Hitchcock, EETS o.s. 156 (London 1921), and *The Folewer of Donet*, ed. E. V. Hitchcock, EETS o.s. 164 (London 1924), *Repressor of Over Much Blaming of the Clergy*, ed. C. Babington (London 1860).

Chapter 6: Conclusion

1   Charles Muscatine, *Poetry and Crisis in the Age of Chaucer* (Notre Dame, Indiana 1972), pp. 4–5.
2   ibid., p. 25.
3   ibid., p. 8.
4   Bertrand H. Bronson, *In Search of Chaucer* (The Alexander Lectures) (Toronto 1960), p. 62.
5   *Piers Plowman*, ed. Elizabeth Salter and Derek Pearsall, York Medieval Texts (London 1967), Introduction, pp. 1–58.
6   Martin Stevens, 'Chaucer and modernism: an essay in criticism', in R. H. Robbins (ed.), *Chaucer at Albany, Middle English Texts and Contexts*, 2nd ed. (New York 1975), pp. 193–216.
7   Douglas Gray, *Themes and Images in the Medieval English Religious Lyric* (London 1972).
8   ibid., p. 64.
9   John Hatcher, *Plague, Population and the English Economy 1348–1530* (London 1977), pp. 11–16.
10   Derek Pearsall, 'The English romance in the fifteenth century', *Essays and Studies*, vol. 29 (1976), ed. E. Talbot Donaldson, pp. 56–83.
11   Lollardy did persist throughout the fifteenth century, but in what appears to have been an intellectually discredited form. See the works of Anne Hudson cited above, and J. A. F. Thomson, *The Later Lollards 1414–1520* (Oxford 1965; 2nd ed. 1967); M. Aston, 'Lollardy and the Reformation: survival or revival?', *History*, vol. 49 (1964), pp. 149–70.
12   John Burrow, *Ricardian Poetry; Chaucer, Gower, Langland and the 'Gawain Poet'* (London 1971).

Index